KW-221-927

Shakespeare's Imagined Persons

The Psychology of Role-Playing and Acting

Peter B. Murray

Barnes & Noble
Books

First published in Great Britain 1996 by
MACMILLAN PRESS LTD
Houndmills, Basingstoke, Hampshire RG21 6XS
and London
Companies and representatives
throughout the world

A catalogue record for this book is available
from the British Library.

ISBN 0–333–63448–9 hardcover
ISBN 0–333–64836–6 paperback

First published in the United States of America 1996 by
BARNES & NOBLE BOOKS
4720 Boston Way
Lanham, MD 20706

ISBN 0–389–21015–3 hardcover
ISBN 0–389–21016–1 paperback

Library of Congress Cataloging-in-Publication Data applied for

© Peter B. Murray 1996

All rights reserved. No reproduction, copy or transmission of
this publication may be made without written permission.

No paragraph of this publication may be reproduced, copied or
transmitted save with written permission or in accordance with
the provisions of the Copyright, Designs and Patents Act 1988,
or under the terms of any licence permitting limited copying
issued by the Copyright Licensing Agency, 90 Tottenham Court
Road, London W1P 9HE.

Any person who does any unauthorised act in relation to this
publication may be liable to criminal prosecution and civil
claims for damages.

10   9   8   7   6   5   4   3   2   1
05   04   03   02   01   00   99   98   97   96

Printed and bound in Great Britain by
Antony Rowe Ltd, Chippenham, Wiltshire

KING ALFRED'S COLLEGE
WINCHESTER

822.33 MUR | 01609904

SHAKESPEARE'S IMAGINED PERSONS

JF
ER

KA 0160990 4

Also by Peter B. Murray

A STUDY OF CYRIL TOURNEUR
A STUDY OF JOHN WEBSTER
THOMAS KYD

Contents

For Karen

Acknowledgements

I want to express my gratitude to a number of people who have contributed to the development and completion of this book. These include several of my faculty colleagues at Macalester College who have read and advised me regarding the material on psychology. Henry R. West, a colleague in philosophy, read my discussions of Aristotle's writings on the psychology of behavior; Sears Eldredge, a colleague in dramatic arts, read the chapter on the psychology of role-playing and acting; and Walter D. Mink, a colleague in psychology, read the chapters on behaviorism and the psychology of role-playing and acting. Irwin Rinder, a sociologist and the psychologists Roxane H. Gudeman, Lynda LaBounty, and Charles C. Torrey have each read the chapters on psychology and have also team-taught courses with me that included much of the material on psychology. Charles Torrey and Lynda LaBounty have, in addition, advised me extensively during the writing of the book, Charles especially on the psychology of role-playing and acting, and Lynda especially in my efforts to understand B. F. Skinner's radical behaviorism. In this connection, I am also indebted to the late Kenneth MacCorquodale, a close associate of Skinner, for his generous praise of my interpretation of Skinner's work.

In the field of English I want to thank Richard Wertime for encouraging me after reading an early version of my ideas about the psychology of role-playing and acting in Shakespeare. And I want to thank Thomas D'Evelyn for his careful reading and his suggestions for revisions of the manuscript. Giles Gamble, my colleague in Shakespeare studies at Macalester, has read and re-read every part of the book, and I am very thankful to him for the great help and encouragement he has given me over the years.

I am grateful to Macalester College for a special leave for research that was supported through money from a grant provided to the College by the Mellon Fund. I am thankful to the staff of the Macalester College and University of Minnesota libraries, especially James Summerfield at Macalester, for their assistance in obtaining materials for my research.

I also want to thank Charmian Hearne, the editor at Macmillan who took an interest in my work and has shepherded it through the process of publication.

I owe a debt of gratitude as well to the people who have helped me by doing the word-processing for the manuscript, Marit Enerson, Diana

Lundin, and more recently Rhonda Isaacs, who has seen me through a series of revisions.

Finally, I want to thank my wife, Karen Olson Murray, for her unflagging interest and support as a scholar in helping me to think through the ideas the book presents and as a writer in helping me to edit the manuscript.

The author and publishers wish to thank the following for permission to reproduce copyright-material:

Benziger Publishing Company, for the extracts from St Thomas Aquinas, *Summa Theologica*, trans. Fathers of the English Dominican Province, 3 vols (1947–8).

Everyman's Library, David Campbell Publishers Ltd, for the extracts from *The Essayes of Michael Lord of Montaigne*, trans. John Florio, 3 vols.

The publishers and the Loeb Classical Library, for the extracts from Quintilian, *Institutio Oratoria*, trans. H. E. Butler, 4 vols (Cambridge, Mass.: Harvard University Press, 1921–2).

Macmillan, for the extracts from Aristotle, *The Nicomachean Ethics*, trans. Martin Ostwald (1962).

Oxford University Press, for the extracts from *The Dialogues of Plato*, trans. B. Jowett, 2 vols (1937).

Routledge, Chapman, and Hall, for the extracts from William Shakespeare, *As You Like It*, ed. Agnes Latham; *The First Part of King Henry IV*, ed. A. R. Humphreys; *Hamlet*, ed. Harold Jenkins; *King Henry V*, ed. J. H. Walter; *The Second Part of King Henry IV*, ed. Andrew S. Cairncross; and *The Winter's Tale*, ed. J. H. P. Pafford.

In quotations, all texts using Early Modern English spelling have been modernized in spelling and typography.

1

Not just art

Introduction

According to the conventional wisdom of literary theory, it is not appropriate to respond to characters in literature as if they were real people. Today, in the context of post-structuralist theory, some critics question whether art does or can create stable representations of the world, whether language as a medium is used or even can be used to create characters that seem to behave in ways that accord with human psychology.[1] I think the conventional wisdom and the post-structuralist views turn us away from important modes of response to Shakespearean drama that depend on construing characters much as if they were real people.[2] In this study I will argue that Shakespeare's plays invite us to construct his characters as imagined persons, and I will explain how the psychology of his time and ours can be used to support this thesis.

I want to make clear what my thesis does and does not entail. I will not argue that Shakespeare's characters are psychologically realistic in every way. In addition, my view is not that Shakespeare designed his characters to be subjected to psychological analysis, but that the intelligibility of their psychology was implicitly important to him as part of the basis for the audience's responses to his plays. My analysis is thus intended to help us respond to the plays, not to make psychology appear to be the subject of the plays for its own sake. In creating a character, Shakespeare drew on his dramatic, literary, and historical sources, and also, no doubt, on his observations of other people and himself. In addition, it is likely that some characters were partly shaped by unconscious projections from his own psyche. Thus as he shaped characters he may not have thought analytically about psychology at all. Some of Shakespeare's characters can be construed as approaching an illusionistic realism at times, and most can be construed as psychologically coherent, but for some there are episodes when there is little or no psychological coherence or realistic motivation. Also, characters sometimes say things that seem more appropriate as utterances of the actor or dramatist. Finally, the use of such conventions as the actors speaking verse precludes any notion that Shakespeare's theater depended on inducing the audience to believe that what they beheld in the playhouse was actual rather than fictional behavior.

It has been argued that many elements of Shakespeare's dramaturgy lead the audience away from responding to his characters as we would to

(where)

1

actual persons. We are frequently reminded that we are watching a play – not people behaving but actors performing. We should not, however, construct an absolute opposition between representational and non-representational elements, for the non-representational can provide perspectives on representation that do not conflict with and may even "help the audience to perceive and accept the fiction of the play" (Styan, "In Search" 190). Our involvement with Hamlet may be increased by our excitement over the brilliance of an actor's performance, for example, and metatheatrical perspectives may deepen our understanding of the representation.[3]

But I want especially to invoke the principle that our interpretive procedures should start with an examination of the ideas current at the time of a work's composition. We should ask what notions were circulating in Shakespeare's time about the purpose of plays, the effect of dramatic poetry, the function of actors, the audience's response, and the relation of actors and audience to dramatic characters. On each of these points the Elizabethan discourse is based on the view that plays provide representations of imagined persons, and from Aristotle to Sir Philip Sidney and Thomas Heywood – even including the Puritan critics of the theater – it was generally understood that these representations move the audience in some way.[4] I believe that the texts of Shakespeare's plays, as part of this discourse, generally imply that the audience should be ready to be moved by the performance of actors as imagined persons.

According to the discourse that supported the theater, including statements in Shakespeare's plays, the audience for a tragedy should especially feel pity and other empathic emotions. The audience's experiencing these emotions depends on an understanding of the motives and the feelings of the tragic figure.[5] Moreover, the audience will only be moved if the actors are moved so they will express the emotions of the characters with authenticity. This idea was derived from the traditional theory of oratory, in which the actor's work is regarded as having most of the same effects as the orator's.[6] The principles of oratory taught an actor that by vividly imagining the events which move the character and responding fully to the script's language, he could "force his soul so to his own conceit" that he would be carried into the thoughts and emotions of the character.[7] Indeed, actors were commonly praised for appearing to *be* the characters they played and for moving the audience.[8] Since the theory held that this depended on the actor's feeling the character's emotion, the praise frequently suggests that such an assimilation of the actor to the character occurred.

This notion of assimilation is explicit in Richard Flecknoe's 1664 description of Richard Burbage as having been "a delightful Proteus, so wholly transforming himself into his part, and putting off himself with his clothes, as he never (not so much as in the tiring-house) assumed himself again until the play was done" (95). Whether in fact actors often felt they became their characters in this sense,[9] the view that they should do so evidently caused them at least to try to appear to do so, since this appearance is what won praise. In any case we can say of this whole set of notions that it was assumed that dramatic characters can seem real insofar as a real person is supposed to be able to feel what a character feels. Scholars have debated whether Elizabethan acting was what we would regard as natural or stylized, but the crucial point is that Elizabethans praised as natural or "to the life" an acting style that used heightened poetic language to make the expression of emotion seem authentic and thereby moved the audience.

Here I want to explain this important aspect of the Elizabethan psychology of acting and of audience response more fully. Quintilian, whose *Institutio Oratoria* was studied in schools in the Renaissance, wrote that orators' words should re-create scenes they wish to convey with such *enargeia* or forceful vividness that they seem "not so much to narrate as to exhibit the actual scene . . ." (bk 6, ch. 2, sec. 32). Writing in the same tradition in *The Defense of Poesy*, Sidney says the "high-flying liberty of conceit proper to the poet" seems "to have some divine force in it" (8). The poet "yields to the powers of the mind an image" that has the capacity to "strike, pierce," and "possess the sight of the soul" (17).[10]

Although the roles of author and performer are combined in oratory and separate in the theater, what Quintilian says about the orator and the actor implies that playwrights, too, should imagine themselves to be the characters they create. This implication is clear in a passage from Quintilian that Hamlet echoes in describing the player who forced his soul so to his own conceit that he not only shed tears but even turned pale – an effect difficult to counterfeit.[11] Quintilian has just quoted the poetry of Virgil to illustrate the sort of emotionally expressive language he thinks is required to move the speaker and the audience, and he continues:

Again, when we desire to awaken pity, we must actually believe that the ills of which we complain have befallen our own selves, and must persuade our minds that this is really the case. We must identify ourselves with the persons of whom we complain that they have suffered grievous, unmerited and bitter misfortune, and must plead their case and for a brief space feel their suffering as though it were our own, while our words must be such as we should use if we stood in their shoes. I have often seen actors, both in tragedy and comedy, leave the theatre still drowned in tears after concluding the performance of some moving role. But if the mere delivery of words written by another has the power to set our souls on fire with fictitious emotions, what will the orator do whose duty it is to picture to himself the facts and who has it in his power to feel the same emotion as his client whose interests are at stake? Even in the schools it is desirable that the student should be moved by his theme, and should imagine it to be true; indeed, it is all the more desirable then, since, as a rule in scholastic declamations, the speaker more often appears as the actual litigant than as his advocate. Suppose we are impersonating an orphan, a shipwrecked man, or one in grave peril. What profit is there in assuming such a role unless we also assume the emotions which it involves? I have thought it necessary not to conceal these considerations from my reader, since they have contributed to the acquisition of such reputation for talent as I possess or once possessed. I have frequently been so much moved while speaking, that I have not merely been wrought upon to tears, but have turned pale and shown all the symptoms of genuine grief.

(Bk 6, ch. 2, sec. 34–6)

The psychological assimilation of author, actor, and character in this passage may well have suggested to dramatists that as they imagined characters they should seek ways to facilitate the actors' assimilation to the characters they would play.

Shakespeare brought actor and character together in one way through the social and psychological notion that "All the world's a stage, / And all the men and women merely players" (*AYL* 2.7.139–40). In recent years many critics have explored the implications of these lines.[12] Among the most interesting of these studies are seminal essays by Peter Ure and Maynard Mack suggesting that Shakespeare's mode of characterization especially focuses on a character's style and degree of engagement with a role, including a sense of self or personal identity as a role (Ure "Character" and Mack "Engagement and Detachment").

Intrigued by such ideas, I began some twenty years ago to search for an explanation of how the way we play a role affects and is affected by our thoughts and feelings. I first read much of Freud and Jung and their interpreters and then a wide range of other psychologists, from cognitive to humanistic and existentialist, but did not find anything that seemed to fit the phenomena I saw in such characters as Hamlet, Prince Hal, and Rosalind. Finally I read B. F. Skinner. Even more than in studying other psychologists I had to learn to read past statements that seemed to make the ideas irrelevant to my purposes. In Skinner's case, these were especially statements that we do not need to take intentions into account in explaining behavior: I was particularly interested in explaining how conduct and intentions relate to each other. To use Jerome Bruner's terms in *Actual Minds, Possible Worlds*, I wanted to be able to understand "the drama of human intentions and their vicissitudes" (88). In much recent discourse

Skinner has been dismissed because, as Bruner puts it, he attributes causality to the environment and denies "the role of intention in the realm of human events" (88). This is certainly the impression that Skinner himself often seemed to foster, evidently to counteract the influence of mentalistic psychology and persuade us to change social conditions, not minds, if we are to improve the human lot ("Humanism and Behaviorism," esp. 51).

In Skinner's view, however, by changing social conditions we will also change minds, and his "radical behaviorism" provides a powerful analysis of the relations among circumstances, conduct, and cognition that I think critics should test and explore.[13] (See Chapter 2 for an explanation of radical behaviorism that especially brings out the functions of cognitions.) Skinner's work enables us to offer an unusually fine-grained analysis of the way a person – or an imagined person – responds to a situation, to others, and to his or her own words, thoughts, feelings, and actions in the moment-to-moment dynamics of behavior. Regarding the vicissitudes of intentions, we can, for example, see how intentions relate to motives a person may not be aware of, how intentions along with other motivational factors affect behavior, how intentions relate to rationalizations, and how rationalizations may become full-fledged intentions.

My new understanding of Skinner led me to take a fresh look at Elizabethan psychology to see whether the basic ideas there about the relations among circumstances, cognition, and conduct are compatible with radical behaviorism. I found that they are to such an extent that I think it is reasonable to call the tradition of the psychology of human conduct from Plato and Aristotle to Montaigne "proto-behaviorism" because one of its basic concepts is that habituation is central in forming character and determining how a person thinks (on the similarity of Aristotle and Skinner, see Robinson's history of psychology, 84–93). This tradition, despite its central place in Western psychology up to the modern era, has been little discussed in works on the history of psychology, on Elizabethan psychology, or on Shakespeare.[14]

In order to see how this tradition is important, let us consider more questions raised in the current debate about Shakespeare's characters. The notion that the actor was to assimilate himself to the character as an imagined person does not in itself tell us enough about the conception of a person that was implied or assumed. In the current debate about Shakespeare's representation of character several specific questions about psychology are at issue, and these questions are discussed in relation to the discourses of his culture and his place within those discourses. To what extent were concepts of human nature essentialist? When did the idea develop that the human being as a subject – as a locus of subjectivity – is shaped by social processes so that a person's ways of thinking and feeling are produced by culture, by historical social conditions? When do

we first find the corollary that the subject "Because informed by contradictory social and ideological processes, . . . is never an indivisible unity,
never an autonomous, self-determining centre of consciousness"? (Jonathon
Dollimore 269. These questions, raised by materialist critics, are based on
the kind of ideas we find also in radical behaviorism.) The final set of
questions about Elizabethan psychology is whether people were thought
to have a psychobiological core of being that provides a sense of personal
continuity through all the vicissitudes of psychological transformation
during life, or to have some sort of selfhood or inner psyche as an aspect
of identity.[15]

The central issue about essentialism is whether, for example, humans
have the potential to become compassionate, or whether it is normal
"human nature" to feel compassion for others. Dollimore explains that
"the materialist conception of subjectivity, . . . in so far as it retains the
concept of essence, construes it not as that which is eternally fixed but as
social potential materialising within limiting historical conditions. Conditions will themselves change – in part under the pressure of actualised
potential – thus enabling new potentialities to unfold" (251). Dollimore
recognizes that humans are generally born with the potential to feel compassion and other emotions, to see and think, and to desire food, drink,
and sexual contact. Further, the actualization of social potential of course
assumes the capacity to learn.

In these terms it seems to me that the most important ideas about human
nature from the Greeks to Shakespeare's time were not essentialist. The
thinking tended toward essentialism in writers who held that we are born
with a natural goodness disposing us to virtue or that at least God created
the first humans with such a disposition. The second of these views is a
commonplace in the Reformation, but it is balanced if not canceled by the
accompanying idea that the Fall deprived us of this natural goodness so
that we need grace to acquire virtue and may or may not actually do so.
Moreover, although the soul's essence as intellectual principle (or potential)
is immortal, the immortality of the soul does not give it an essence determining whether it will become blessed or damnable. Still, the question
about essentialism especially focusses on the idea of the soul, and more
must be said about it here.

The capacities attributed to the soul include reason and will; the senses,
imagination, and memory; and the appetites and passions. Of these, reason
is the one we today may see as the most fully created through a person's
experience, not given by nature, and the Elizabethans saw it this way, too.
The ideas about functional relations among these capacities, such as the
belief that there is often a conflict between appetites and reason, figured
in the understanding of how a person acquires a certain character and
subjectivity, not as essential attributes, since it was emphasized that the

outcome for individuals depends on whether they become virtuous and learn to use reason rightly. A cultural materialist's account of the shaping of subjectivity will need to include some sort of functional relations to explain, for example, how persons come to be biased toward their own and their group's interests in the processes that lead to the formation of their subjectivity.

Judging by what is said in Shakespeare's plays, "soul" was often used *Soul* informally in the vernacular to refer to a person's inner psyche or self. "Spirit," "mind," and sometimes "self," especially in compounds such as "myself," could be used in much the same sense. Occasionally we even find "soul" and "mind" used interchangeably in a single passage. The impression conveyed is that the speakers are not so much thinking of the soul as immortal or an essence but as their deepest, truest, most personal and individual source of thought, feeling, and action. This usage can be illustrated beginning in Shakespeare's earliest works merely by reproducing the sort of fragmentary quotations we are given in concordances:

> Say as you think, and speak it from your souls. . . .
> (*2H6* 3.1.247)

> Dive, thoughts, down to my soul: here Clarence comes.
> (*R3* 1.1.41)

> Think you in your soul the Count Claudio hath wronged Hero?
> (*Ado* 4.1.327–8)

> Thou . . . / That knew'st the very bottom of my soul . . .
> (*H5* 2.2.96–7)

> I have unclasp'd / To thee the book even of my secret soul.
> (*TN* 1.4.13–14)

Hamlet illustrates the full range of the use of "soul," from the religious, seen especially in speeches concerned with the sinful state of Claudius and Gertrude, to the more secular sense I have just illustrated. Here are a few examples of borderline uses and of the more secular sense of the word as a term for the psyche in *Hamlet*: "Taint not thy mind nor let thy soul contrive / Against thy mother aught" (1.5.85–6), "There's something in his soul / O'er which his melancholy sits on brood . . ." (3.1.166–7), "O, it offends me to the soul to hear a robustious periwig-pated fellow . . ." (3.2.8–9), "Since my dear soul was mistress of her choice . . ." (3.2.63), and climactically:

> Soft, now to my mother.
> O heart, lose not thy nature. Let not ever
> The soul of Nero enter this firm bosom;
> Let me be cruel, not unnatural.
> I will speak daggers to her, but use none.
> My tongue and soul in this be hypocrites:
> How in my words somever she be shent,
> To give them seals never my soul consent.
>   (3.2.383–90)

Hamlet assumes it would be an act contrary to human nature to kill his mother, but it is clear that what is deemed natural is not an essence but a norm, for the passage expresses Hamlet's concern that he might actually kill his mother, and the example of Nero reminds him that people have acted unnaturally.

Another matter to consider in relation to essentialism is the notion emphasized by some Renaissance writers that the four bodily fluids known as "humors" determine temperament. Thus a person may tend to be choleric or sanguine or phlegmatic or melancholy, or to have a more balanced temperament. The humors are not essences, however, because their permutations and combinations can be so various. Moreover, the humors were usually thought to function interdependently with other causes.[16] Timothy Bright, probably the most important Elizabethan interpreter of the humors psychology, writes that the humors are subject to dietary and environmental conditions and especially to the activities which habituate a person to have one or another of the humoral dispositions.[17]

In view of Bright's ideas, to attribute causal force to the humors is like saying a person's honest behavior is caused by the trait of honesty. This is not invalid, but it does not explain how a person comes to have the trait, and as I have indicated, the Elizabethans did not generally believe that virtues such as honesty or compassion are essential features of human nature. For the explanation of how people were chiefly understood to acquire honesty, compassion, and other traits of character, we must turn to the psychology of habituation I introduced earlier. This psychology is also central to Elizabethan discourse on humans as subjects and – not incidentally, as we shall see – to ideas about the psychology of acting I have not yet discussed.

In the Induction of John Marston's *Antonio and Mellida* two actors are talking of their parts (lines 68–79).[18] One is worried because in the role of a prince he will have to put on the "feigned presence of an Amazon." The second actor points out that if the first "cannot bear two subtle fronts under one hood," he will have to leave "this world's stage." The first actor's reply suggests it is not the falseness the role demands that troubles him, but the truth it may create: "Ay, but when use hath taught me action to hit the right point of a lady's part, I shall grow ignorant, when I must turn young prince again, how but to truss my hose." Although this actor is jesting, the psychology employed in this passage is as old as Plato's *Republic*, where it is familiar to us as one of the main objections to the representation of human vice, weakness, or emotionality in the theater. First, speaking of the poet, Socrates explains what he means by imitation or mimesis: ". . . when the poet speaks in the person of another, may we not say that he assimilates his style to that of the person . . . ? . . . And this assimilation of himself to another, either by the use of voice or gesture, is the imitation of the person whose character he assumes?" (bk 3, sec. 393). A little later he is discussing whether the future guardians of the republic should be allowed to act in plays:

> if they imitate at all, they should imitate from youth upward only those characters which are suitable to their profession – the courageous, temperate, holy, free, and the like; but they should not depict or be skilful at imitating any kind of illiberality or baseness, lest from imitation they should come to be what they imitate. Did you never observe how imitations, beginning in early youth and continuing far into life, at length grow into habits and become a second nature, affecting body, voice, and mind? (Bk 3, sec. 395)

Plato's warning is repeated by Quintilian: "repeated imitation passes into habit" (bk 1, ch. 11, sec. 3). The idea became a part of the basic lore of European psychology before Descartes.

Shakespeare provides descriptions of the way imitated or "assumed" behavior can change a person through habit (also referred to as "custom" or "use" in the sense of becoming accustomed or used to an activity). Hamlet instructs his mother in how to overcome her sexual vice:

> Good night. But go not to my uncle's bed.
> Assume a virtue if you have it not.
> That monster, custom, who all sense doth eat
> Of habits evil, is angel yet in this,
> That to the use of actions fair and good
> He likewise gives a frock or livery
> That aptly is put on. Refrain tonight,
> And that shall lend a kind of easiness
> To the next abstinence, the next more easy;
> For use almost can change the stamp of nature . . .
> (*Ham.* 3.4.161–70)

Another example is Coriolanus's reply to his mother's attempt to instruct him in how to "perform a part" he has not played before, to beg the plebeians for their votes so he may become consul:

> Well, I must do't.
> Away my disposition, and possess me
> Some harlot's spirit! My throat of war be turn'd,
> Which choired with my drum, into a pipe
> Small as an eunuch, or the virgin voice
> That babies lull asleep! The smiles of knaves
> Tent in my cheeks, and schoolboys' tears take up
> The glasses of my sight! A beggar's tongue
> Make motion through my lips, and my arm'd knees
> Who bow'd but in my stirrup, bend like his
> That hath receiv'd an alms! I will not do't,
> Lest I surcease to honour mine own truth,
> And by my body's action teach my mind
> A most inherent baseness.
>
> (*Cor.* 3.2.110–23)

In these passages the speakers assume that when we assimilate ourselves to a mode of conduct we habituate ourselves to the conduct, with the result that our character becomes what this conduct indicates it to be. A remarkable aspect of the psychology here is that behavior tends to produce the character and way of thinking and feeling that support it even when a person regards the behavior and the new character with abhorrence.

In the traditional discourse surrounding these ideas, the answer to our question about the human as subject is clear. Plato repeatedly states that social practices shape subjectivity and that within the context of a culture's practices, people's own actions shape their character and determine how they think. He says reason is in the immortal soul and therefore has an existence and a capacity independent of the body, but while it is in the body, reason's rule depends on proper education. Summarizing Plato's view, Raphael Demos puts it very bluntly: "owing to the force of habit, the whole character of man is determined in infancy." For Plato, Demos adds in terms analogous to Skinner's, the central process in moral education is to habituate the child "to take pleasure in the good and be pained by evil. Virtuous habits will be formed with the aid of praise and blame and punishment, until what is administered from without gradually becomes a law within the soul" (354–5). Plato writes:

> Pleasure and pain I maintain to be the first perceptions of children, and I say that they are the forms under which virtue and vice are originally

present to them. As to wisdom and true and fixed opinions, happy is the man who acquires them, even when declining in years; and we may say that he who possesses them, and the blessings which are contained in them, is a perfect man. Now I mean by education that training which is given by suitable habits to the first instincts of virtue in children; – when pleasure, and friendship, and pain, and hatred, are rightly implanted in souls not yet capable of understanding the nature of them, and who find them, after they have attained reason, to be in harmony with her. This harmony of the soul, taken as a whole, is virtue; but the particular training in respect of pleasure and pain, which leads you always to hate what you ought to hate, and love what you ought to love from the beginning of life to the end, may be separated off; and, in my view, will be rightly called education. (*Laws* 653)

Thus pleasure and pain can be used to condition children to behave virtuously before they have the capacity to understand virtue and vice. Later, when they come to understand virtue and vice and are able to reason about them, reason joins with habituated virtuous behavior to form true virtue. This accords well with Skinner's view that we can be conditioned to behave in a certain way without having to understand what is happening, but we can learn to use cognitions to control behavior we have been conditioned to engage in.

Plato says infants should suffer as little fear, sorrow, and pain as possible, but should not be habituated to pleasures, for that would spoil them rather than habituate them to virtue (*Laws* 791–2). Children should learn to take pleasure in virtue through play, through training in situations requiring virtue, and through imitation. Plato emphasizes the importance of play in children's earliest education:

the teacher should endeavour to direct the children's inclinations and pleasures, by the help of amusements, to their final aim in life. The most important part of education is right training in the nursery. The soul of the child in his play should be guided to the love of that sort of excellence in which when he grows up to manhood he will have to be perfected. (*Laws* 643)

These terms are easily translated into Skinner's main idea about education, that we learn best when our efforts are positively reinforced, when we have success and pleasure in learning.

Following childhood in Plato's scheme, youths are to acquire the "habit of courage," for example, by being repeatedly exposed to perils under circumstances in which social esteem and self-esteem are at stake (*Laws*

647–9). In the same way the virtue of temperance is acquired by exposure to "shameless pleasures." Plato here stresses the fear of shame as
strengthening a person's self-control, but in general he also implies that
the person is being trained to take pride in being "perfectly temperate"
(*Laws* 647). In Skinner's terms, if we are shamed until we behave coura-
geously or temperately, our behaving in the desired manner is negatively
reinforced by the cessation of the shaming, positively reinforced by praise.

The use of what Skinner calls operant conditioning, depending on positive reinforcement, is clear in Plato's ideas about teaching the love of
virtue through imitation. The "music" of the choristers – their conjoined
movement, words, and melody in imitating good souls in hymns and songs
– is most important for Plato as a force "charming the souls of youth, and
inviting them to follow and attain virtue by the way of imitation" (*Laws*
812). In the *Laws* he repeatedly endorses the use of literature which makes
virtuous characters attractive so that a child will want to imitate them.
Very early in a child's life, when "the character is being formed and the
desired impression is more readily taken," mothers and nurses should
"fashion the mind" with tales of virtue "even more fondly than they
mould the body with their hands" (*Rep.* 377). Similarly, youths should
memorize poems which teach and exemplify virtue, such as the dialogue
in the *Laws* itself, which Plato regards as a poem (*Laws* 811–12).

Thus through play and music the child should acquire "the habit of
good order" which is the basis for further development (*Rep.* 425). Plato
says of the youth educated in the Muses that he will rejoice over the good
and "blame and hate the bad . . . even before he is able to know the reason
why; and when reason comes he will recognise and salute the friend with
whom his education has made him long familiar" (*Rep.* 402). In sum, the
works of the Muses affect us in a way that does not depend on reason and
that Plato sometimes says is by habituation. The presentation of virtuous
figures as beautiful and praiseworthy reinforces loving thoughts of virtue
and a wish to be virtuous. Imitation of these attractive models actively
confirms the virtuous disposition through habituation: as I have said, in
Skinner's terms all this can be analyzed as operant conditioning.

The control of what gives pleasure is crucial in Plato's theory of habituation to virtue through imitation. Indeed, pleasure – a factor in much
though not all positive reinforcement – figures as a most potent force in
Plato's ideas about human nature and behavior. Thus, what we regard as
the highest good to pursue is determined by what we love (*Rep.* 581–7).
This view implies that habit controls thought, for we have seen that what
we love is determined by habituation to pleasures or to virtue. We always
seek what we see as the good, but self-love tends to make us think and
choose in self-serving ways (*Laws* 731–2). The source of evil, then, is an
ignorance of the good caused fundamentally by self-love making the

immediate pleasures of the flesh and passions the most satisfying, with the result that habits of virtue cannot take hold or be maintained strongly enough against them. This ignorance is a state of self-deception in which a person's powers of persuasion are in the service of the pleasures he or she loves. Hence the arts of persuasion with their appeals to emotion and not pure reason are to be regarded as chiefly useful in defending bad causes (*Gorgias* 479–81). Even philosophical dialectic is not to be entrusted to the men being trained as rulers until they are mature, for logical disputation can be used to prove anything, with the possible result that they would lose the belief in virtues they were brought up to have and turn to the life which gives them immediate pleasure (*Rep.* 537–9). Reason itself can easily become an instrument of rationalization (Demos 319–21).

It appears in all of this that Plato believes, as does Skinner, that we act *and think* according to our conditioning. The habit of virtue is needed to *cause* reason to guide a person toward virtuous action. Nevertheless, reason is all-important in the pursuit of the good. Beyond the moral virtues shaped through habituation, a person needs philosophy (*Rep.* 504, 619; *Phaedo* 81). But as Plato describes the role of reason in learning virtue and philosophy, it is generally clear that the main function of moral philosophy is to teach the use of thinking for making behavior "rule-governed," in Skinner's phrase. We should learn to use thought to rehearse outcomes of possible actions in order to choose the best way to achieve the good our habituation has caused us to seek. Thus in the *Protagoras* Plato writes that to learn virtue we must learn to use reason in comparing greater and lesser pleasures and in calculating whether to suffer a present pain for the sake of a future pleasure, and so on. Such cognitions Skinner calls "covert operations" – his term for all cognitive activity, intended to emphasize that thinking is a form of behavior.

It may appear that a behaviorist interpretation is refuted when Glaucon and Adeimantus point out that since the person who can seem just while acting unjustly will have the greatest rewards, praise and rewards for justice may only teach a person to *appear* just (*Rep.* 357–67). But a behaviorist would agree that merely rewarding acts of virtue may only teach a person to act virtuously for the sake of reward, that Plato's way of making a person want to be virtuous – by making it rewarding to *love* justice because models of justice have been made attractive in stories, plays, and songs – is a good way to shape a virtuous character. Still, it may seem that Plato transcends all behaviorist thinking when he says that beyond all the moral virtues a person needs to know the essential Good (*Rep.* 504–5). Yet even in this case the learning that goes beyond the moral virtues, that is, beyond what habit can shape, is to be built on the foundation of these habituated virtues. To go beyond habituated virtue, the person needs to progress from the love of particular virtues to the love of the Good, and of course much of Plato's eloquence is devoted to making the Good attractive so that its acceptance will be pleasurable, that is, reinforced.

Further, in the allegory of the cave the psychological process of coming to know the truth of Being is described as habituation (Demos 330–1). Plato says that the *capacity* to "learn by degrees to endure the sight of being" is not, like the moral virtues, created by "habit and exercise" (*Rep.* 518). But learning to see in the light or the dark is described as habituation (*Rep.* 516, 520). Francis Cornford comments that this is "the moral – the need of habituation by mathematical study before discussing moral ideas and ascending through them to the Form of the Good" (229n).

Because the mass of men live only in the cave, the ruler must rely mostly on habit in its social form as custom to maintain social order. The ruler can determine for the people the belief which "will be of the greatest public advantage, and then use all his efforts to make the whole community utter one and the same word in their songs and tales and discourses all their life long" (*Laws* 663–4). Once people have become habituated to a set of customs through such means, there should be no changes in these social laws if order is to be maintained. Hence, too, there should be no innovation in music, because such novelty "imperceptibly penetrates into manners and customs" and causes lawlessness, as opposed to the "habit of good order" created by use of music in a stricter system (*Rep.* 424–5). The forms and rules of children's play and games should also be kept unchanged, for these, too, shape "the habits of our minds," and "children who make innovations in their games, when they grow up to be men, will be different from the last generation of children, and, being different, will desire a different sort of life, and under the influence of this desire will want other institutions and laws" (*Laws* 797–8). We could hardly have stronger statements of the view that individual subjectivity is shaped by social processes.

Now of course there are many passages in which Plato does not specify the processes of learning and does not imply that he is thinking of habit or imitation. And there are many passages which it would be absurd to describe as specifically behaviorist. But even these passages are consistent with behaviorist psychology in the sense that behaviorism offers a causal explanation of all thinking. Thus Plato's ideas about the movement of thought toward the apprehension and contemplation of transcendent abstractions are generally comprehensible within the terms of Skinner's "covert operations."

Aristotle's major work on the psychology of behavior, in the *Nicomachean Ethics*, is also based on the concept of habituation, and I will not repeat the ideas that are virtually the same as Plato's.[19] Aristotle explains more fully than Plato does, however, the relation between habituation and thinking in causing and guiding behavior. Because Aristotle sometimes says thinking *controls* behavior, it is most important to determine whether he means our thoughts autonomously *cause* our actions. In the Appendix, I analyze key passages in the *Nicomachean Ethics* and *On the Soul* to show that his ideas are congruent with Skinner's view that thoughts do not cause but can *guide* behavior caused by our conditioning. Here it must suffice to summarize my reading of Aristotle and compare Skinner's ideas about the relation between cognitions and actions.

The basic question is about the causes of behavior, and Aristotle's view, like Plato's, is that our habituation determines our choice of ends to pursue (*Nicomachean* 1103a–b, 1113a15–1114b). If we are habituated to virtue we can learn to use right reason to *guide* our actions to the end our virtuous disposition *aims* us toward, but if we lose our virtuous habit, we will also lose our proper ideas about how to act (1140b, 1143b–5a; cf. Anscombe 62, Shute 75–8, Hardie 37). If we are devoted to vice, our thinking will justify the vice and direct us in seeking the pleasures of vice (1146b–7b, 1150a–1a).[20] Persuasions employing right reason only persuade a person habituated to virtue (1179b). Thought and desire work together to produce action, but in the final analysis it is the desirable object and one's desire for it, which is based on habituation, that cause one to move toward the desired object (*On the Soul* 433a).[21] Skinner's view is that in the presence of an object we desire, we may articulate to ourselves some form of an intention that guides our behavior in reaching toward the object, but the intention does not cause the behavior because the intention is part of a chain of behavior culminating in overt action. An intention arises as a result of the same conditioning that causes the overt behavior that follows. This understanding is consistent with Aristotle's view in the key passages on this issue that I have cited.

Following Plato and Aristotle, proto-behaviorist ideas about character and behavior continued to be important in the later Greek and Roman periods and in the Middle Ages, the Renaissance, and the Reformation (see the Appendix). In the theology of St Thomas Aquinas, who draws especially on Aristotle for moral psychology, the process of habituation can create moral virtues, but we need grace to avoid all sin and for the infusion of the theological virtues of faith, hope, and charity. St Thomas's explanation of vice is basically the same as Aristotle's. Even the Florentine Platonists and such Christian humanists as Erasmus and Richard Hooker regard reason only as a potential or capacity, saying that *if* we use reason as it should be used we can approach truth and live virtuously. And they assert or imply that the ability to use "right reason" depends on learning to do so through a process which includes habituation to virtue.

Although Protestant thinkers such as Luther and Calvin hold that all virtuous thoughts and deeds are caused directly by God's grace, they still allow habits a function in moral psychology to explain vice – which in their view, especially, includes much of what we do. Moreover, Lutheran education emphasized habituation, and the important English Calvinist William Perkins wrote of the need "to exercise and increase our faith and repentance, both which be much strengthened and confirmed, by the practice of good works."[22] We are saved by faith and not good works, and we require grace to have faith, but the proto-behaviorist understanding of character and behavior continues to have a place in this way of thinking.

In saying that proto-behaviorist thinking is found in many writers in the Western tradition I do not mean to say that this understanding was the only one available and it therefore must explain Shakespeare's characters. Nor in arguing that Plato and Aristotle's ideas about the causes of behavior are consistent with Skinner's do I mean that these or later writers would necessarily accept Skinner's conceptualizations or all of his conclusions. And there are also important differences between Aquinas or Erasmus and Calvin or Luther. My contention is that for the study of Shakespeare we need to understand what I call proto-behaviorist thinking because in the context of the discourses of his time Shakespeare's own thinking about behavior is close to that of Aristotle – and closer still to that of Montaigne in a sense I will shortly explain. My central thesis is that Shakespeare's understanding is close enough to behaviorism that an analysis employing radical behaviorism can illuminate his characters, showing how they are imagined persons. Of course if Shakespeare's characters are in any terms psychologically valid and Skinner's system is valid, a Skinnerian analysis will illuminate the characters, and this may be seen as one way to state my thesis, but I also think Shakespeare's texts bear the distinctive marks of a behaviorist way of thinking, as already shown in the quotations from *Hamlet* and *Coriolanus*.

Continuing with our questions about persons as subjects, we find that the traditional psychology also explains how most people's subjectivity will be not unified but divided. There are, Aristotle writes, four types of moral character, each formed by the processes of habituation. The *sophron* or self-controlled person and the thoroughly vicious person are so strongly habituated to virtue and to vice, respectively, that their thinking does not deviate from their habituation. But between these extremes are morally strong persons, who take pleasure in the appetites but whose habituation to virtue is strong enough that they do not yield to temptation, and morally weak persons, who have been habituated to love the noble and believe they should do good, but in whom the passions and appetites have not been sufficiently habituated to virtuous conduct to prevent lapses into vice (*Nicomachean* 1146a–52a). Of course most people are in the two middle groups, and hence subjectivity is usually divided between the moral values inculcated by the culture and opposed personal wishes and desires arising from appetites and passions. This understanding of human character implies that the inculcation of the potentially conflicting values of family, class, nation, and religious group can also create divisions in subjects.

If subjectivity was thus understood to be divided in most persons, was an individual believed to have a coherent character, a psychologically coherent inwardness? Catherine Belsey argues, as does Jonathan Dollimore, that liberal humanist critics project the Enlightenment notion of the subject as autonomous and unified onto the dramatic figures in Renaissance plays. Belsey's position as a post-structuralist critic is that "The quest for the truth of the self, our own and others', endlessly fascinating, is precisely endless, since the subject of liberal humanism is a chimera, an effect of language, not its origin" (*The Subject* 54). That is, "In so far as signifying practice always precedes the individual, is always learned, the subject is a subjected being, an effect of the meanings it seems to possess. Subjectivity is discursively produced and is constrained by the range of subject-positions defined by the discourses in which the concrete individual participates" (5). And because these discourses contain contradictions, the subject lacks unity as well as autonomy.

One can agree with the basic thrust of this view and still not agree with what it leads Belsey to say about a character such as Hamlet. It is true that Hamlet's subjectivity is divided, that in Acts 1–4 he is "Alternately mad, rational, vengeful, inert, determined," and that "It is as if the hero is traversed by the voices of a succession of morality fragments, wrath and reason, patience and resolution," and therefore that he is not an autonomous agent or a unified subject in whom we could locate "the true, the essential Hamlet." But I do not think it follows that Hamlet is a "discontinuous" character or that the play has tried and failed "to define an interiority as the origin of meaning and action, a human subject as agent" in the sense Belsey attributes to liberal humanism, "an analysis which in 1601 does not yet fully exist" (41–2). Instead, Hamlet has the sort of interiority, the limited self-knowledge and self-control of a divided, conflicted subjectivity that characterized a person according to the traditional psychology still important in 1601. There is no denying the importance of interiority in the discourses of the various viewpoints within the Western tradition, whether we look to the essays and plays of Seneca, to the introspections of St Augustine and Marcus Aurelius, to the tradition of "know thyself," to Petrarch and later sonnet writers, to the Calvinist emphasis on self-examination, to the courtesy literature, or to the introspections of Montaigne which so greatly influenced Shakespeare.[23] In all these we find the sense of an inward life and being and the understanding that a person may conceal this inwardness from others. In terms of these discourses, most of them based at least indirectly or in part on the traditions stemming from Plato and Aristotle or from Augustine, Hamlet is a psychologically coherent character, as his internal conflicts and his variability are all motivated in his interaction with his changing situation.

The traditional psychology, especially as it was developed by Plutarch and Montaigne, can explain change in a person's basic character and subjectivity as well as situational variability. Plutarch describes a process that is in effect an early form of "behavior modification" through which habituation can re-shape us in the course of the seven parts we play on the stage of life ("Busybody," "Compliancy," and "Talkativeness"). As my allusion to the seven ages speech reminds us, this psychology accommodates our modern view that a person experiences a developmental process, and this process was understood to have a biological basis in the notion that the passions and appetites themselves become habituated. Persons could thus experience themselves as having a psychobiological core which, along with their sense of a personal "self," "spirit," "mind," or "soul" could give them a sense of a continuous identity despite changes due to maturation and aging as well as to habituation within each developmental "act" or age.

Michel de Montaigne's psychological insights are the most significant in the later development of the proto-behaviorist tradition before Shakespeare.[24] Montaigne echoes the traditional ideas about the importance of habituation in forming character, and he especially emphasizes how habituation to social practices governs subjectivity because he sees that we think virtually any practice to be right and natural if it is customary in our social group.[25]

Montaigne also writes of the way habits of vice cause our thoughts to support our conduct, but for the most part in discussing human frailty and error he emphasizes how much our thinking is controlled by self-love and the self-deceiving passions, vanities, and fantasies it generates.[26] In a behaviorist view, it is correct to focus on self-love, self-interest, and received practices and beliefs more than on habits *per se* as the sources of bias in human thinking, since these factors indicate crucial sources of reinforcement for behavior. Habit is merely behavior that is probable because it has been reinforced, and a person's self-interested conduct and the thinking that goes with it are shaped and maintained in strength by positive reinforcement related to what the proto-behaviorist tradition calls self-love.

Although Montaigne emphasizes that habit creates a second nature which has great power (e.g. "How One Ought" 3:261), he also emphasizes that we are so inconsistent that "there is as much difference found between us and ourselves, as there is between ourselves and other" ("Of the Inconstancie" 2:14; cf. Ellrodt 43–4). Human behavior is so variable that it is "difficult to combine our actions one unto another" or to say of a person "what kind of man" he is ("Of Experience" 3:336). Those with a strong habit of virtue may be constant in character ("Of the Inconstancie" 2:12). Yet "custom and use" can "inure and fashion us, not only to what form they please . . . but also to change and variation . . ." and the best thing habit and practice can do for us is to make us flexible. He himself has certain inclinations, Montaigne continues, which are more customary for him than others, but it is not hard to make himself behave according to the opposite habit ("Of Experience" 3:344). A little earlier he says that habit governs, but that his habits have varied with changes in circumstances (3:340).

Now, this very important insight was not much developed by earlier writers, that indeed our habits vary with circumstances. This is because habits are actually produced by operant conditioning, which shapes behavior that varies with changes in circumstances. In a number of essays concerned with human inconstancy, Montaigne discusses how human character is affected by changes in environment and how our interests and activities are subject not only to our emotions but also to what we are currently thinking and imagining and to chance circumstances of many kinds.[27]

Montaigne also describes how we are changed by our own behavior, and here there are especially keen insights into the way pretense creates reality and action shapes being. He states the principle that imitation passes into habit ("How a Man" 2:415), and his specific descriptions and analyses take us well beyond this general notion. Repeatedly Montaigne writes of his own strong imagination, and in telling of his ability as an actor when he was a schoolboy he mentions "dexterity in conforming myself to the parts I undertook" ("Of the Institution" 1:189). Writing of himself later in life, he says "I am of an apish and imitating condition. . . . Whom I behold with attention, doth easily convey and imprint something of his in me. What I heedily consider, the same I usurp: a foolish countenance, a crabbed look, a ridiculous manner of speech." But evidently he does not mean that he deliberately imitates these behaviors, for he refers to his condition as one of being very "apt at unawares to entertain these superficial impressions" ("Upon Some Verses" 3:103–4).

Regarding the psychology of acting, Montaigne asserts the traditional view that the emotions expressed in poetry move actors so that they move the audience ("Of Cato the Younger" 1:246). We gain more specific insights when Montaigne comments on the way he and others have been affected by their own speech. "I cannot well contain myself in mine own possession and disposition, chance hath more interest in it than myself; occasion, company, yea the change of my voice, draws more from my mind than I can find therein, when by myself I . . . endeavor to employ the same" ("Of Readie" 1:51). Particularly interesting here is the effect his own voice has on him. In explaining how he has come to believe opinions he undertook to defend only in sport, he suggests that earnestness of speech is the source of the emotion that leads a person to believe his own statements ("Apologie" 2:281). In another essay he says that although he has always made a point of being truthful, nevertheless "being earnested, either by the resistance of another, or by the earnestness of my narration; I swell and amplify my subject by my voice, motions, vigor and force of words: as also by extension and amplification, not without some prejudice to the naked truth" ("Of the Lame" 3:280).

But, Montaigne continues, he is quickly able to yield to the truth and to contrary opinion, and for the most part he is particularly pleased with himself for being flexible and self-detached, not obstinate of opinion but open to all opinions. In discussing the value of detachment Montaigne writes of the importance of not allowing oneself to become totally absorbed in social and official roles ("How One Ought" 3:262–3). Yet he is aware of his own strong tendency to total absorption in his customary inclinations and activities (see, e.g. "Of Three Commerces" 3:38). It is partly the tension between his self-detachment and his self-absorption that makes his essays such fascinating reading.

All these concerns of Montaigne are found together in the essay "Of Diverting and Diversions." He writes of the danger of becoming intensely absorbed in mourning, revenge, or love and says he overcomes his own strong tendency to become absorbed by diverting himself with a change of "place, exercise, and company." He uses his common human "inconstancy" to displace "that first apprehension, how forcible soever it be" (3:57). He cites the example of women who, to divert gossip about their love affairs, "did by counterfeit and dissembled affections, over-shadow and cloak true affections. Amongst which I have noted some, who in dissembling and counterfeiting have suffered themselves to be intrapped wittingly and in good earnest; quitting their true and original humor for the feigned. . . ." The explanation of how we can be changed so easily and even become what we pretend is simple: "A little thing doth divert and turn us; for a small thing holds us. We do not much respect subjects in gross and alone: they are circumstances, or small and superficial images that move and touch us . . ." (3:58).

Thus we are moved to grief by remembering a particular moment with a deceased loved one and by "The very sound of names, which jingleth in our ears, as, *Oh my poor master*; or, *Alas my dear friend*; *Oh my good father*; or, *Alas, my sweet daughter*. When such like repetitions pinch me, and that I look more nearly to them, I find them but grammatical laments," but "the word and the tune wound me" nevertheless. "Grief by these provocations / Puts itself in more passions," as Lucan wrote (3:58). A little later Montaigne sums up much of this psychology by repeating the traditional idea that orators are moved by their "feigned agitations" to feel "a lively and essential sorrow." He continues that those who are hired "to aid the ceremony of mourning" at funerals, "although they strive to act it in a borrowed form, yet by habituating and ordering their countenance, it is certain they are often wholly transported into it, and entertain the impression of a true and unfeigned melancholy." Montaigne concludes here with Quintilian's remarks, quoted earlier, about actors who are moved by their parts and about how he has been moved by his oratory (3:59–60).

Montaigne's general point in all this is not so much that we become what we pretend but, as I noted above, that we are very changeable, easily diverted by many stimuli – including those generated by our own behavior – from one thought and feeling to another. Here is another telling example from the essay "Of Diverting and Diversions":

> If one demand that fellow, what interest he hath in such a siege; *The interest of example (will he say) and common obedience of the Prince*; I nor look, nor pretend any benefit thereby; and of glory I know how small a portion cometh to the share of a private man, such as I am. I have neither passion nor quarrel in the matter; yet the next day shall you see him all changed, and chafing, boiling and blushing with rage, in his rank of battle, ready for the assault. It is the glaring reflecting of so much steel, the flashing thundering of the cannon, the clang of trumpets, and the rattling of drums, that have infused this new fury, and rancor in his swelling veins. A frivolous cause, will you say. How a cause? There needeth none to excite our mind. A doting humor without body, without substance overswayeth and tosseth it up and down. Let me think of building castles in Spain, my imagination will forge me commodities and afford me means and delights wherewith my mind is really tickled and essentially gladded. How often do we pester our spirits with anger or sadness by such shadows, and entangle ourselves into fantastical passions which alter both our mind and body?
>
> (3:60–1)

To sum up, Montaigne develops proto-behaviorism beyond the traditional idea that repeated action results in a habit which, though changeable through further action, is a characteristic difficult to change. In modern behaviorist terms, this traditional view attaches too little importance to the effect of a changing environment and of the many stimuli, including thoughts and emotions, which contribute to the shaping of behavior. Montaigne gives us the full human complexity, the paradox of an individual's thought and action coming to have certain characteristics and yet also being quite variable. Thus he is close to modern behaviorism, as he also is very close to some of the most important features of Shakespeare's representation of character, including a keen interest in the psychology of role-playing.

The next chapter presents an explanation of B. F. Skinner's radical behaviorism that especially brings out his ideas about the way thoughts as well as emotions affect and are affected by our behavior. Chapter 3 presents a behaviorist analysis of how the processes that develop a person's character and cognition are basically the same as those that affect a person living a social role or an actor trying to enter into the psychological experiences the script creates for a character as an imagined person. The chapter explains the processes that lead to absorption and belief in a self or a role on the stage or in social life, and also the causes of detachment or self-alienation. I hope to make a contribution of the sort Liam Hudson and Clifford Geertz have suggested scholars in the humanities should attempt in the theory and social psychology related to sociological applications of the all the world's a stage metaphor. The chapter draws on a broader range of work in research-based cognitive, developmental, and social psychology than is usual in literary study. In thinking about psychology and literature we still have much to learn from ideas generated through experimental and observational studies. Although my analyses of psychology in this chapter are behaviorist, they can easily be translated by cognitive and other psychologists into their own theoretical terms.

Chapters 4–7 give readings of Shakespeare by the light of radical behaviorism and ideas from social psychology, with references to ideas from the proto-behaviorist tradition as well. Chapter 4 is a study of Hamlet – I discuss him first because in *Hamlet* Shakespeare draws the most explicitly on proto-behaviorist psychology, and I discuss him in detail to show that his variability reflects psychological complexity rather than incoherence. Chapter 5 traces the character of Prince Hal through his evolution into King Henry V. Chapter 6, on *As You Like It*, focusses especially on how Rosalind's style of self-enactment leads her to playful self-realizations. Chapter 7 is a brief study of Perdita's enactment of Flora, in which she manifests the royal power to "crown" her every action.

2

The Behaviorism of
B. F. Skinner

In Chapter 1 I have claimed that B. F. Skinner's radical behaviorism is an especially appropriate psychology to use in explicating Shakespeare's dramatic characters as imagined persons. This chapter presents a fresh account of radical behaviorism that brings out the important functions of cognitions and emotions. Skinner's view of the human being as subject will become clear as I explain his ideas about the way the conditions of life control behavior and the way thoughts, feelings, and actions affect each other.[1] (My examples are drawn from middle-class Western culture, but the psychological principles are held to be universals.) Skinner's ideas will be faithfully explained, but whereas he emphasizes that we are not "initiating agents" as causes of our behavior, I want to clarify the precise sense in which he means this. Some of his statements are easy to read as meaning we are compelled to behave in certain ways by the environment. Thus it is not generally understood that Skinner explains how knowledge of the causes of human behavior can be used to learn modes of self-control and of agency for social change. As subjected subjects we can have a kind of agency that is "beyond freedom," in Skinner's phrase, but none-theless powerful.

Let us begin with a central issue concerning the subject and the causes of human behavior. Skinner says our thoughts and feelings do not cause our behavior because they are themselves caused by the causes of our behavior: thoughts and feelings are dependent variables. For example, the weather is an independent variable, and a practical intention to carry an umbrella depends on the weather. Yet in advancing this view Skinner acknowledges and, better, explains the role of intentions in the control of behavior, and he also explains how an emotional state influences thought and action. I will elaborate on this in what follows, first taking up inten-tions and their relation to independent variables in producing behavior.

The independent variables, which cause behavior, are in the environ-ment, in a person's genetic endowment as a human being and as an individual, and in a person's "learning history" – acquired tendencies to behave in certain ways because of past experience. For example, if we buy a lawnmower it is because our old one is worn out, because we have learned to use a lawnmower, because there is grass to mow, and because we have experienced rewards of some sort for mowing the lawn. These and factors such as the availability of money are independent variables, and the intention to buy a lawnmower is a dependent variable: the lack of a usable lawnmower causes the intention to buy one *and* the act of buying it in a person whose learning history includes the use of a lawnmower.

Skinner thus sees the intention and the act of buying to be parts of the same complex action. That is, he denies mind–body dualism and says that to formulate an intention is to *do* something. Deciding, intending, and planning to buy are the first steps on the way to the store, activities as much caused by the independent variables as the buying itself is. But the deciding and planning, as intentions, do specify the further steps to be taken – they *guide and control* the action. Thus we *direct* our behavior, and this is a common sense notion of causality. We would think it odd, however, if we found ourselves buying a lawnmower without causes external to ourselves – and in this we would acknowledge the behaviorist concept of causality.

That a thought does not directly cause an act should be obvious on close inspection: I can intend my arm to rise and it will not rise unless I also actually move it: the things I do to move my arm are separate from what I do when I formulate an intention to move my arm. My intention to do something I cannot do will not enable me to do it. I can intend to mail a letter and not do it because habit carries me along a street with no mailbox. If I notice the letter in my hand, I may change my course toward a street with a mailbox: an intention must be kept in conscious thinking in order to guide action effectively. If I think of something I should do before I mail the letter, my intention changes: changed conditions cause changes in intentions. More importantly, sometimes we have "good intentions" we do not act on, and sometimes strong intentions to stop overeating or smoking yield to temptation or habit. Furthermore, a sincerely stated intention may be a rationalization and not the true cause of our conduct.[2]

There is another notion of intentions as causes to consider, the concept of intention as characteristic commitment, as implicit in an action and not necessarily articulated but inferable when we think about our motives. Analysis of this idea leads directly to Skinner's view. For example, people who have a characteristic commitment to the values of a social class and act for those values do not think they are caused to act by their intention to do so but that they should act because of conditions or events. The causality here has two sets of independent variables: (1) the facts of the situation and (2) the learning history of these people, the way their past has shaped their interpretation of the situation, their commitment to the values of their class, and their tendencies to act as they do. Thus character, as the embodiment of a person's learning history, is a cause of his or her actions, along with all the factors in the environment.

In denying mind–body dualism, Skinner uses "behavior" as a neutral term for both "mental" and "physical" activity to avoid the traditional dualistic connotations of words such as "thought" and "act." For the same reason, he uses "covert operations" as a neutral term for thinking and imagining and other "mental" activities. In what follows, however, I will use "thinking" and "imagining," being careful that my sense is consistent with Skinner's view of these as "operations" which do something, "private events" but nonetheless events having an impact. Applying the term "behavior" to thinking does not *reduce* it but begins to account for it. The issues are whether it is true that to think is to do something and how thinking is related to other behavior.

To explore these issues Skinner invokes the process he calls "operant conditioning." He describes this process as an extension of the principle of "selection by consequences" in evolution, through which mutant forms that are well adapted to the environment are best able to survive (see "Selection"). At some point in evolution, the changing environment gave an advantage for survival to biological changes enabling creatures to be conditioned so they could acquire new behavior in response to new situations without having to undergo a further anatomical mutation. Skinner explains how this kind of conditioning is controlled through selection by consequences. A creature responds to a novel situation a certain way, and if the behavior has successful consequences, the probability is increased that in the future the creature will respond to similar conditions with the same type of behavior. Skinner calls any particular type of behavior an "operant": the creature responds to its situation by "operating" in some way. "Conditioning" is the process that alters the probability of the creature's behavior: each time it behaves a certain way and is successful, it is changed physiologically and neurologically so that this behavior becomes more likely under similar circumstances. What I have described as a "successful" outcome Skinner would regard as "reinforcement." I will explain what kinds of things are reinforcers a little later.

As Skinner says, some day the biological sciences will explain the organic changes operant conditioning produces. However, a great deal of experimental data suggests that the process of operant conditioning does not enable an animal to "perceive" the connection between its behavior and the success so it can have a cognition that it should behave this way again. Needless to say, humans have evolved the capacity to make many cognitive connections, and the cause of this cognitive behavior is also operant conditioning. The evolution of the ability to speak made it possible to describe the connections between acts and their consequences, so that adaptive behavior could be learned more readily. As cultures evolved, again according to the principle of selection by consequences, rules were constructed to teach and guide culturally normative as well as adaptive behavior. Formulating a rule is operant behavior that is acquired, as other behavior is, when it has a reinforcing outcome for an individual or a group.

Although we are thus able to articulate knowledge of many connections between cause and effect in behavior, often we do not need to articulate such knowledge, and we can be operantly conditioned without having to think about why our behavior is changing. In learning to walk, we do not have cognitions about how our movements respond to gravity or about what our body structure requires us to do. And once we have learned to walk, thinking about how we do it would interfere with normal walking. Behavior we learn mostly by "doing," by responding to conditions as we perform the activity, Skinner calls "contingency-shaped," "intuitive," in contrast to behavior learned and consciously guided by the application of rules. Behavior we at first use rules to guide but learn so well that we need not think about how we do it is also performed intuitively. In behaving intuitively we respond to features of our situation that we do not analyze but have learned to respond to in other situations. Intuition sometimes provides solutions to problems that resist systematic thinking. In Skinner's view it is an error to think of behavior performed intuitively as rule-governed just because it *can* be analyzed or guided by the conscious application of rules. Even speech is mostly intuitive. We usually do not think about each phrase before we utter it, but launch ourselves into sentence patterns we have learned to use, combining and revising these intuitively.

In connection with operant conditioning we must consider the concept of the stimulus. Although Skinner's theory is widely believed to be a "stimulus–response" psychology, the notion that he conceives of behavior as stimulus-bound is quite mistaken. Any phenomenon, whether it is a thing, a person, an action, a thought, a feeling, or a single aspect of any of these, can be a stimulus. Many responses to a stimulus are possible, and what causes a response to be linked with a stimulus is its being reinforced. When we come to behave a certain way in response to a stimulus, this stimulus is called a "discriminative stimulus" for the behavior. That is, the presence of this stimulus or one similar to it discriminates the behavior that is most probable. Skinner applies the phrase "contingencies of reinforcement" to the relations among a stimulus situation, the response to the situation, and the resulting reinforcement. Awareness of these contingencies enables us to guide our behavior more effectively.

In general, then, a particular stimulus can evoke many responses, and which of these occurs depends on other stimuli and on the person's history and present condition. Thus a toothbrush is a discriminative stimulus chiefly for thinking about brushing teeth and for brushing them, but depending on circumstances it may evoke instead the response of thinking about a recent conversation with the dentist about one's teeth. It is important also that a stimulus can evoke any response similar to a response which has been learned. This adds to the variety of the behavior that occurs in response to a stimulus. Thoughts as responses can be almost infinitely various, since there is virtually no limit to the similarities possible between thoughts.

To use another example to indicate a different sort of complexity in responses to stimuli, if I see a sign saying "Grocery Store," this may evoke the behavior of thinking about whether I need to shop for food. Such thinking is evoked because in the past it has been reinforced by its utility. If I am hungry, my thinking about food will be strongly reinforced. But if I am absorbed in a conversation, a line of thought, or an activity, I may turn my eyes toward this sign and barely respond to it at all, because I am busy responding in my thoughts, words, and actions to other stimuli and being reinforced for that behavior.

Skinner explains that we experience behavior caused by operant conditioning as voluntary. When we make a rational voluntary choice, we consider the causes for action by examining the situation and the benefits or penalties likely to result from various actions. We covertly try out (think about) these actions and covertly respond to (gauge how we feel and think about) their likely outcomes. Such thinking is operant behavior responding to the situation in the way our learning history leads us to do because in the past such thinking has been reinforced by the successful outcome of behavior chosen with its help.

Operant behavior is caused and yet may not be "determined" in a philosophical sense. Operant conditioning increases the *probability* that a response will be repeated, and each of us has a hierarchy of responses for a given set of circumstances. Several responses may be almost equally probable, and occasionally even an improbable response occurs. We may make a wholly new response or an earlier learned response – a regressive one. Several responses may be experienced covertly if they are all strong (Skinner writes of behavior as being "in strength" when it is in progress or has been strongly learned for a situation). A new response is likely when no learned response fits our circumstances, for then a novel response is more likely to be reinforced. A regressive response is likely when a more recently learned response is too difficult or when the regressive behavior will be strongly reinforced, perhaps by getting attention or by annoying someone we want to punish.

So far I have explained the concept of reinforcement only in a common sense way. Anything that increases the probability of a behavior is a reinforcer. Most reinforcers are pleasing, but their effect does not depend on this. That is, we do not necessarily feel pleasure when we survey our environment to look for danger, though doing this reinforces the behavior leading up to it. In addition, pleasure does not cause behavior. For example, we may enjoy a candy and want to eat more of it. The pleasure of eating the candy and the wish to eat more can act as discriminative stimuli to guide our behavior, yet, as I have explained, such stimuli do not cause behavior. Thus we may enjoy the candy but eat only a few pieces because our learning history makes it more reinforcing to have a slender body. We learn to think of the pleasures of many reinforcers and to behave in ways to obtain these pleasures. Yet our behavior can be reinforced without our *feeling* pleased, and we can resist pleasure and be reinforced by other outcomes instead.

There are two types of reinforcers, those inherited by a species and those that acquire their reinforcing power through conditioning. We inherit the capacity to be reinforced by food and drink, by comforting bodily contact and sex, and by opportunities to observe and manipulate the environment. The second type of reinforcer becomes reinforcing through a kind of conditioning not yet explained here: if we associate one of the inherited reinforcers with a stimulus that has no effect as a reinforcer, this neutral stimulus becomes a "conditioned reinforcer." As a child is fed, physically comforted, and lovingly smiled at by adults, the accompanying voice sounds, expressions of affection, and other behavior become conditioned reinforcers. As smiles and affection and social rewards of all kinds are used to express approval, any accompanying words of approval also become conditioned reinforcers. Whereas food may only reinforce a hungry person, affection, social approval, money, and the submissiveness of others are called "generalized" reinforcers because they can reinforce a person in almost any condition. And when hearing words of approval has become reinforcing, self-approval will also be an important reinforcer. (Most conditioned reinforcers are specific to a culture.)

In some theories of behavior it is said that humans "have" needs or drives for dominance and approval. Such a view makes it difficult to explain, without positing an organic deficiency, why some people do not seem to have such drives. In the behaviorist formulation, there is an inherited capacity to be reinforced for dominating behavior, for example, because such a capacity has had survival value, but if a person's situation in life never leads to dominance, then the reinforcement of dominating behavior does not occur and the behavior does not become strong. In the behaviorist view – and in the view of most psychologists as well as experts in genetics – behavioral and emotional tendencies depend on the interaction of the inborn with the environment, on nature *and* nurture. A genetic factor may predispose a person to schizophrenia, depression, or a life of crime, but in most cases much still depends on what happens in the person's life.

Through learning, a person can come to find listening to jazz, fishing for trout, fantasizing, or almost any other experience reinforcing. In addition, behavior leading up to reinforcement, what Skinner calls "precurrent" behavior, becomes a conditioned reinforcer. As the dinner bell preceding a meal can elicit mouth-watering, so behavior immediately preceding a reinforcing event becomes reinforcing. Once *this* behavior is reinforcing, the behavior immediately preceding *it* becomes reinforcing, and so on. Although the reinforcing strength diminishes with each remove from the final reinforcer, these conditioned reinforcers help us to keep going through a series of thoughts and actions when the ultimate reinforcement will come much later.

The reinforcement of precurrent behavior gives us our feelings of incentive and pleasurable anticipation. The important effects of joyful anticipation should thus not be seen as opposing the behaviorist view. We feel joy and anticipation, we formulate plans and intentions, and a behaviorist analysis explains the causes but does not deny or "reduce" our experience. Anticipatory thoughts and intentions are caused, but they also participate in the causal process as discriminative stimuli and reinforcers which guide following thoughts and actions and give them their emotional tone.

We are very active beings because we have inherited a capacity to be reinforced for activity in general – an obvious advantage for a creature that must move about for its food. We are centers of warm life and energy, not passive, and as Skinner says in *About Behaviorism*, our behavior at any moment depends on what *we are*, even if this depends on our previous interaction with the environment (249). In reflex behavior, however, which includes emotions, our responses seem to be forced on us by stimuli. An event such as a loud noise can cause the glandular and muscular responses of fear to occur instantly and without our first *thinking* that something frightening is happening. These responses occur as "automatically," as much apart from "willing," as does the contraction of the pupil of an eye when a light shines into it.

Thus in Skinner's terms emotions do not cause behavior because the emotions are involuntary responses to whatever causes *them*. Moreover, most of our behavior when we feel an emotion depends on our learning history. That is, the event causing the emotion is also a discriminative stimulus for whatever behavior has become our response to that event. If a child frightens an adult by jumping out from behind a door, the adult may reproach the child or pause a moment and laugh. A culture may reinforce its young people for striking anyone who strikes them or for turning the other cheek or for both. A person in therapy can learn to relax, or to be more assertive, when feeling the physiological symptoms of anger or fear.

It is easier, however, to teach us to strike back than to turn the other cheek because emotion changes what reinforces us – when we are angry we have an inherited tendency to be reinforced by signs of weakness and injury in the person who has provoked us. Still, most causes of emotion are *learned*, acquired through the process by which we come to have a physiological emotional response to events that initially do not elicit such a response. If an event that compels an emotional response – an "unconditioned stimulus" – occurs in the presence of a neutral stimulus, the neutral stimulus comes to elicit at least part of the emotional response to the unconditioned stimulus. Thus if a loud noise elicits fear, a bell that rings just before the loud noise will come to elicit some fear. The initially neutral stimulus may be the kind of place where the emotion-generating events occur, or the persons or kind of persons present, and so forth. Symbols of all kinds acquire their emotional power through this process of pairing a neutral stimulus with an unconditioned stimulus. The name of a beloved person acquires an emotional aura. A flag can come to elicit an emotional response if emotional events or rhetoric focus on it. Conditioned emotional responses are very important in propaganda and in coming to like or dislike a person or a product or a kind of experience. (The conditioning of emotional responses to texts is discussed in Chapter 3 in relation to the psychology of acting.)

For conditioned responses to occur, we need not be aware of their causes. We may recognize we are in a place where we have experienced sadness, and if we do, this may well affect what we feel, acting as an additional stimulus. We feel the emotion, however, whether we see this connection or not. And the "connection" can be tenuous, for a stimulus similar to one that arouses emotion elicits some of the strength of our response to the original stimulus. If Tom has a hostile relationship with his father, he may feel uneasy, without knowing why, with a person who is in some way like his father – perhaps in having authority over him. This phenomenon is familiar from psychoanalytic theory, and behaviorist psychology takes into account such manifestations of the "unconscious," but without positing a mental entity called "the unconscious." Instead, Skinner explains that we think of things or do not – are conscious of them or not – depending on our learning history, our current state, and the present circumstances.

Thus whether Tom recognizes why a man like his father makes him feel uneasy depends on *operant* conditioning: the man functions as a conditioned stimulus to produce an emotional response, but also as a discriminative stimulus to which Tom, depending on his learning history, may or may not respond operantly by thinking of the connection with his father. Even if Tom responds operantly by rebelling or submitting as he would toward his father, the operant response of recognizing the cause of this behavior and the emotion will not be likely if the recognition would be painful: we have an inherited tendency to do what is positively reinforced and not to do what produces painful or "aversive" results.

So far I have explained positive reinforcement, but here we need to consider also what happens when behavior produces aversive results ("aversive" is used instead of "painful" because not all negative conditions affecting behavior are noticeably painful). If behavior that has been positively reinforced simply stops being reinforced, it undergoes "extinction" – the behavior gradually ceases. But when behavior is punished – has aversive consequences – it tends to be immediately suppressed (Skinner uses "punishment" only to refer to aversive stimulation that is thus contingent on behavior).

Distinct from punishment is the use of aversive stimulation to motivate behavior: a person beaten until he or she does something is being aversively stimulated. The result of aversive stimulation depends on what is called "negative reinforcement." Both positive and negative reinforcement increase the probability of a behavior (as the term "reinforce" indicates), and punishment decreases the probability of a behavior. The concept of "negative" reinforcement can be better understood if we see that negatively reinforced behavior becomes more probable because the behavior is followed by the *removal* of a *negative* (aversive) stimulus, whereas positively reinforced behavior becomes more probable because the behavior is followed by *addition* of a *positive* stimulus. Tom will pick apples if he is paid *or* if picking apples ends whippings: in either case the outcome reinforces apple-picking. Generally speaking, aversive stimulation causes negative reinforcement of any behavior which will end or diminish the aversive condition.

Punishment is of course aversive, so punishment and aversive stimulation have important results in common. Neither is a very effective means of controlling behavior. Unless positive measures are also taken, moderate punishment only temporarily suppresses behavior, and both punishment and aversive stimulation cause anger and fear, which interfere with healthy behavior. Anger disposes a person to retaliate, and fear conflicts with effective behavior of any kind and disposes a person to escape from the situation. To summarize in technical terms, punishment causes anger, fear, and guilt, and temporarily causes any behavior that competes with the punished behavior to become stronger. By conditioning an emotional response, punishment causes guilt or fear the next time we do what we have been punished for, and so our own behavior becomes aversive to us. By this same process, any behavior associated with the punished behavior, the place where the punishment takes place, and whoever is present all become aversive.

Skinner points out that this explanation supports Freud's observations on a number of phenomena related to repression (*Science* 184). Skinner's account of repression explains that we may lose our awareness of a tendency to engage in strongly punished behavior because this awareness would be aversive. We *escape* an aversive awareness when we first experience such awareness but then its aversive quality makes it negatively reinforcing to do or think something less aversive (perhaps we think about the aversive situation in a way that makes it less aversive). We *avoid* an aversive awareness when the thoughts that typically precede the aversive awareness have come to have an aversive quality, and so we think or do something else *before* we think of punished behavior. Even when we repress awareness completely in this way, what we think and do instead may yet express the repressed behavior in a disguised form. This is Skinner's version of Freud's idea that repressed wishes remain active.

For example, if young Tom has been punished by his father, he may do things that annoy his father yet not be aware that his anger causes him to be reinforced by the annoyance his father suffers. In this case the hostile behavior is not repressed but the behavior of recognizing that the behavior is hostile is repressed. His father may not only be annoyed but infuriated because he thinks Tom is acting deliberately to vex him. When he accuses Tom of this, Tom is infuriated in turn because no such intentions have crossed his mind. Tom denies the accusation and may go into an aggrieved sadness "to make his father sorry" he mistreated him so unjustly.

In this last behavior Tom may become aware that he is hurting his father and *rationalize* it to himself as justified by his father's outrageous accusations. When we rationalize we do not repress punished behavior – here hostile behavior toward the father – and we do not repress awareness that it is behavior ordinarily punished. Instead we think of a way the behavior is justified under the circumstances, or we think only of the causes for our behavior that enable us to avoid anxiety. Thus Tom's father may become angry enough at Tom's annoying behavior that he decides to correct the boy's conduct by spanking him. As Skinner says, the father tells himself he punishes Tom for his own good, rationalizing the hostile behavior of spanking, and repressing awareness that the spanking is especially reinforced because he is angry at the child.

I will give a more specific example to illustrate the analysis of complex behavior. Suppose that Tom's father has just punished him, but indicates that good behavior will result in parental approval and affection. Tom's response depends on his learning history and all the factors in the situation, and he may respond positively to the offered affection. But because of the punishment, Tom's responses will tend to include anger and resentful thoughts, even if his overt behavior is compliant. Tom may overtly rebel or, if his resentment has caused very harsh thoughts toward his father, Tom may find these thoughts aversive and escape from them by deciding to obey. Suppose he smiles and says "I was angry at you because you punished me, but I've decided to be more grown up, as you ask, and put my anger aside." Tom can respond in various ways to his own behavior of saying this. It may be most reinforcing to praise himself silently for growing up, or he may be more reinforced if he says to himself he's a scaredy-cat to have knuckled under. This latter response is possible if punishing his father would still be quite reinforcing for him and if calling himself a scaredy-cat stimulates him in a way that rallies him to resist the aversive control that has angered him.

Thus even after acting and speaking obediently Tom might feel rebellious, but he probably would not overtly rebel insofar as this would undermine his claim to being grown up and so would not be reinforced by his own thoughts. This example illustrates the way behavior can form a "chain" in which we respond to our own thoughts, actions, and emotions as well as to other factors in a situation. Note that a thought can respond to a thought, perhaps also reinforce it, and act as a stimulus for a further thought or action. It is important to note, too, that a thought can reinforce other behavior – for instance, we can say Tom finds it reinforcing to think he is being grown up.

The example also illustrates other important phenomena. Frequently there are two or more responses competing to result in behavior, and the winner is the one that is stronger ("prepotent") at the moment because of the situation and the condition of the person. In Tom's case we can see how the balance between two competing behaviors can change: as the prepotent behavior achieves some of its purpose and is reinforced, it may be weakened by satiation and give way to the still strong competing behavior. One result may be oscillation between two competing behaviors.

Competing behaviors may, in Skinner's terms, manifest competing selves. Skinner defines a self as "a functionally unified system of responses" – the inter-connected behavior (both thoughts and actions) and emotions that we acquire for a particular function or situation (*Science* 285). Thus we have many selves and each self has a subjectivity that is at least subtly different from the subjectivity of our other selves. As subjects we are no more unified than autonomous:[3] "The pious churchgoer on Sunday may become an aggressive, unscrupulous businessman on Monday. He possesses two response systems appropriate to different sets of circumstances, and his inconsistency is no greater than that of the environment which takes him to church on Sunday and to work on Monday" (*Science* 285–6).

As Skinner notes, however, the man in this example may think he has an integral self or character (cf. Anselm L. Strauss 152–3). As a functionally unified system of responses, the Monday businessman self may not think about how Monday's conduct contradicts his Sunday self-concept. Such thinking would be aversive and so any competing behavior – for example, thinking about how to maximize profit – would be strengthened. Alternatively, on Monday the businessman may think of Sunday's sermon but in such a way that there is no contradiction – he has socially accepted rationales justifying his behavior: "the more money I make the more I can invest to create new jobs. . . ." Thus people in our culture are in effect taught to rationalize: we are sometimes strongly reinforced by material well-being for exploitive behavior, and we are also strongly reinforced for being able to interpret our behavior as conforming to ethical ideals (cf. Sullivan, *Interpersonal* 200, 207–8).

Further complicating this picture, if the unscrupulous businessman acts and the pious church-goer rationalizes the action, then together they constitute a sort of self, a *"functionally* unified system of responses" combining aspects of these two selves. A person develops characteristic ways of thinking and acting that can be seen in many selves, including characteristic defenses for many situations – rationalization, repression, projection, and so forth. And a person's selves may change under the impact of experience.

Much of this complexity arises from the interaction between the selves or systems of responses organized around primary reinforcers such as sex and the selves created by parents and the community to control these responses.[4] The strongly reinforced responses of sexual behavior tend to influence behavior in all areas of life. We may not be aware of the effects, however, if to notice them would be aversive. Thus our speech may include Freudian slips and our reactions to others may include responses stemming from childhood parental attachments and conflicts without our being conscious of the sources of these responses. Likewise, we are not conscious of most of the workings of the system of responses that controls the responses of the sexual self. These controlling responses include responses due to punishment, and since the punishment can cause awareness of the sexual responses to be repressed, we may also avoid awareness of the repression and of the process of repression.

The resulting behavior will in part be shaped by the strongly reinforced but punished responses (e.g. sexual or aggressive responses), and in part by the system of responses which controls the punished behavior in the sense of displacing it or, as in dreams, disguising it.[5] Thus a person's sexual responses may be manifested in caring for others or in artistic expression (Freudian sublimation: see *Science* 376–8). But we can be conscious of conflict between punished responses and controlling responses, with the result that our "conscience" tells us we are doing wrong – or does so until we can rationalize our behavior.[6]

Skinner uses "self" only as shorthand for his technical terminology (*Science* 285), and he usually dispenses with the term in his analyses. It is not ultimately very helpful to say that a man's church-going self has an effect on his businessman self. This language creates a misleading implication of homunculi with minds and wills of their own, active as independent causes. It will be clearer to say that a *person's* thoughts as a result of going to church on Sunday may affect his or her behavior on Monday.

A behaviorist explanation can then show how the person's thoughts and actions function as a system of responses, without having to use the term "self." But we need "self" to refer to the person in "self-control" and "self-esteem" or to a person's understanding of his or her character and status in "self-concept" and "self-fashioning" or to the character enacted for others in "the presentation of self in everyday life."

In our culture it is important to believe we have autonomous self-control, and our feeling that we have such control can prevent us from seeking more realistic self-control. The limitation of our thinking creates the illusion of autonomy. We cannot see how our learning history causes us to think and act as we do, but we see ourselves considering alternatives as we make decisions, and it is reinforcing to regard this as evidence of freedom because it makes us feel potent – any behavior allowing us to think we have surveyed and can control the environment is reinforced because of our genetic endowment.

We also feel free because we can resist efforts to control us. Our resistance is caused not by freedom, however, but by our tendency to experience overt efforts to control us as aversive. We feel free, too, when we use great "will-power" to do what we do not wish to do. Such a choice can seem to deny that we are subject to contingencies of reinforcement. But a behaviorist analysis is particularly helpful because it explains the conditions under which we submit ourselves to something we find unpleasant, or even to pain or death. First, painful behavior may be less painful than other behavior it displaces and so represses. If we are tormented by guilt, we may punish ourselves if this enables us to feel less guilty. We may allow ourselves to suffer from our own ineffective behavior because changing ourselves is arduous work. If something troubles us that is too salient to ignore or repress, it may become strong behavior to try to escape this aversive condition by thinking about it at length. These "worrying" thoughts are aversive because they deal with troubling matters, but we may return to them again and again to seek a way to end the trouble or find a less aversive way to think about it. We will endure a painful experience if it is a necessary condition or a discriminative stimulus for behavior that brings reinforcement. We risk danger to achieve a valued good. We may hurt ourselves to prove we have free will. A social group can so strongly reinforce altruistic behavior that persons become willing martyrs or heroes rather than act for self-preservation.

The ability to endure pain for a greater good is a key to our ability to learn a better self-control than that based on a delusory sense of freedom. We can learn to endure a critical self-examination and to question our beliefs so we can consider choices in a more informed and open way, though we can never completely transcend the thinking of our group. We may need the help of others to see that a new way of behaving, including thinking, yields better results than our current behavior. The results of improved behavior reinforce our being open to further change, and so progressively we can come to have effective self-control.

Skinner writes that "The evolution of a culture is a gigantic exercise in self-control" (*Beyond Freedom* 215), and this is the key to his idea of how we can be agents of social change even though we are subject to our culture's practices. Thus the community can educate people to look beyond immediate reinforcers by reinforcing them for thinking about what should be done in the future for the sake of those who will outlive them (*Beyond Freedom* 134–7, 143–4, 214). Skinner notes that "The designer of a new culture will always be culture-bound, since he will not be able to free himself entirely from the predispositions which have been engendered by the social environment in which he has lived" (*Beyond Freedom* 164). Still, Skinner also says "Novelty or originality can occur in a wholly deterministic system," as can be seen in the diversity of life forms produced through evolution ("Creating" 339). One theory explaining why young animals of certain species engage in novel play activities that do not continue when they are adults is that some behavior seen in play may become important for survival if conditions change (Herron and Sutton-Smith, "Comparative Approaches," and Ellis 114–17).

Human play and fantasy know virtually no bounds. Thinking of new possibilities is pleasurable in itself, and the novel possibilities conceivable on the basis of the known is enormous, as we see, for example, in science and in science fiction. Experimentation and training people to break conventions and to try variations from accepted methods can lead to further innovation (Skinner, "Creating" 339–40). Operant conditioning as a cause of behavior always allows for wholly novel responses to occur, especially if other responses are not producing desired results. Thus in several ways our inherited capacity to find it reinforcing to control the environment can be linked to innovation and change. But what will move a social group to change, or even to educate people so they will want to design for the future? Technologically advanced societies, in which the need for new information and the ease of access to such information have made it increasingly difficult to maintain control by aversive means, are already engaged in various sorts of social evolution, and even aversive control tends to cause us to imagine the conditions for a better future.

Still, although we can achieve positive control of ourselves and our societies, there is much in the preceding discussion to suggest that we generally tend instead to think and act in ways that serve our more immediate personal interests or the interests of those who control the contingencies of reinforcement within which we act. Given the powerful effect of these interests on what we find it reinforcing to think and do, we tend to be egocentric and easily self-deceived in the sense that it is difficult to enter into the viewpoint of those with different views or to look critically at our own views and actions. We will find it very reinforcing to think of arguments defending our accustomed ways in order to escape the aversive experience of doubting ourselves, and we may well fail to see weaknesses in our arguments. The great relief we feel when we escape anxiety can make our thinking seem absolutely right to us even when it seems preposterous to those with different views.

We are taught that moral thinking is the application of a certain set of values – albeit sometimes contradictory values – that our group approves, and so when we think about what we do we may, without realizing it, merely construct justifications that bridge the gap between these values and our actions. We can believe fully in our justifications and become absorbed in our activities and roles, or, at the opposite extreme, if we doubt our group's values, we can merely pay lip service to them and play our roles with cynical detachment. As we see throughout this study, although radical behaviorism does away with the traditional mentalistic division between cognition and other behavior, it can provide a detailed analysis of the ways thought and action may be joined – or disjoined – in the complex dynamics of human behavior.

3

Character Formation and the Psychology of Role-Playing and Acting

This chapter employs modern psychology to analyze the way character and cognition are shaped in social roles and the way theatrical roles affect actors. The analysis especially focuses on the causes of our identifying or not identifying with the selves we enact in social roles and the causes of the sense actors have that they "become" or do not become the characters they play. To provide a synthesis of these aspects of the psychology of acting and social role-playing, the discussion will draw on the observations of writers in areas ranging from sociological role theory to developmental psychology to the training of actors.

As all men and women are "merely" or entirely players, all human behavior and character can be thought of as being shaped within social roles (Brim 141; Goffman, *Presentation* 235 and *Frame* 293–300, 573–6). Social psychologists usually define role as the socially scripted behavior for a certain identity (office manager, mother, son, teacher; my examples will all be drawn from Western culture).[1] The behavior for a role is different for different situations. Thus the role of mother scripts different behavior for mother-with-child's-teacher than for mother-with-child, and traditionally mother-with-son has differed markedly from mother-with-daughter. These examples illustrate that, as R. D. Laing emphasizes in *Self and Others*, role is a term for complementary identity (82–3). Social psychologists think of roles as socially scripted because we learn from others, and from sources provided by the social group, how we should think, feel, and act in our roles. But since a role created or modified by an individual may have the same psychological effects as one that is entirely socially scripted,[2] I will use "role" to refer also to individually scripted behavior.

If our behavior for a role is scripted, the behavior, at least at first, may be consciously rule-governed in some ways: we think of what we should do and these thoughts guide our behavior. For example, a man just learning to be a father may need to remind himself of what the role calls for.

Such a man's behavior may differ from the behavior of a man who does not think self-consciously, but intuitively thinks of and does loving and caring things. Central to the difference are their different ways of thinking and the ways thought and action affect each other. The relation between thought and action is crucial to our questions about the psychology of acting and role-playing – questions about why we do or do not identify with the person we present to the world, perhaps changing our thinking in the direction shaped by our actions, hence "becoming" what we do. (By "identify with" I mean to sense no conflict between what we feel ourselves to be and the person we present to the world.)

There are many ways we may think of what we are doing. For example (1) we may be absorbed in doing something intuitively and not think self-consciously of our mode of action, (2) we may be conscious we are behaving as we are learning or have learned to do and, hence, think about how to behave appropriately, (3) we may do as in (2) but with conscious concern for self-esteem in doing what we have learned and practiced, (4) in our self-concern with behaving appropriately we may have a sense of an audience watching us – whether actual others or an imagined "reference group" on whom we depend for esteem and so for self-esteem, (5) in thinking of being seen we may have concern to be sure to perform with appropriate expressiveness, and (6) our concern for showing proper expression may become greater than our concern for behaving effectively.[3] As we proceed through this series, our behavior becomes more and more "theatrical," moves closer and closer to being a contrived self-staging, yet even in the last cases described we may not think of ourselves as playing a role in any sense that makes us less than sincere, for we may not think our expressiveness is at all false.

The nature of roles in a complex society may cause people to think consciously of their behavior as detached or even cynical role-playing. Erving Goffman's analyses are particularly astute in showing that many social roles have a front-stage routine and a back-stage routine, because they call for different ways of thinking and acting with different people. Thus the attitude sales clerks project in selling to customers and the attitude toward customers shared with colleagues may differ in a way that makes the role-playing with customers seem cynical to the clerks and heighten their tendency to rationalize the manipulation of customers (*Presentation* 170–5).

This brings us to an important principle in sociological role-theory, the need for a "definition of the situation" so that the participants in an interaction can know which of their identities are relevant and what role-behavior is called for. Knowing how to behave appropriately in an interaction also involves taking the role of the other, or "role-taking," through which we acquire an understanding of the viewpoints and roles of the others in a situation. Needless to say, role-taking is most important for successful role-playing.

Goffman and other sociologists have ably explicated the various ways in which the situation may be defined and have analyzed basic patterns of interaction that ensue (see, for example, Goffman's *Encounters* 17–81). I believe, however, that works of drama and fiction may illuminate human behavior even more than most discussions of social psychology do, and that bringing literary analysis and social psychology together can yield new insights for both fields. The social psychologists are right that we learn to be adept at responding even to the subtlest cues in order to maintain norms in interactions with others, but the plays of Shakespeare show how interactions take interesting directions precisely because people do not merely perform appropriate roles in response to cues. If we are preoccupied with private goals and anxieties, we respond to situations in quite remarkable ways. Especially in emotional situations, Shakespeare reminds us, people tend not to respond according to social role norms.[4] A Shakespearean character is often absorbed in a very subjective view of self and others. Some characters have idealized self-concepts that they enact or attempt to enact, with consequences ranging from the heroic in a character such as Hotspur to the comic in a character such as Malvolio.

At the opposite extreme from self-belief in role-playing an ideal character are hypocrites such as Richard III or Iago who only pretend to have a certain character. The social psychology of such figures, too, is complex, and between the extremes are even more complex ways to play or be oneself, as we see in characters such as Hamlet, Prince Hal, and Rosalind: all the world's a stage, and all men and women are players.

Let us consider gender identity as a crucial aspect of self-concept that we enact as a sort of role, whether intuitively or self-consciously. Most students of gender agree that biological factors and learning work together in forming gender identity,[5] and there is persuasive evidence that the effects of biological factors can be overcome by learning.[6] Virtually all students of developmental psychology agree that children learn how to think of themselves as boys or girls and how to behave in a gender-differentiated manner, and that the learning comes through the way adults behave toward them, through interaction with other children and imitation of children of the same sex, through play, and of course through other sources of information about gender roles.[7] At every stage of development children are given subtle or not-so-subtle responses from adults and from other children indicating whether their behavior, including their thinking, is appropriate.

These responses reinforce the desired behaviors and shape the children accordingly. A boy learns he is a boy and which other people around him are boys, including big ones like daddy. In a traditional society, everyone reinforces the boy's efforts to imitate males, and he comes to reinforce himself with self-approval for behaving as he has learned a boy should. Typically he learns different sets of role-behaviors for interactions with adults and with his peers.

An important part of a child's imitation of male or female models is expressed in playing house as daddy or mommy. However, Jean Piaget and some other students of play say that whereas in imitation children *learn*, by accommodating to the norms that others express in their behavior, in play children assimilate experience to their existing modes of thought.[8] That is, in play the boy can imagine he is just like daddy, identifying his own childish feelings in the role of daddy with the feelings of the adult, and so he may learn to think mistakenly about what it is to be an adult male and a father. On the other hand, play enables children to try out identities and see if they feel appropriate. Children expand their sense of control and of having the capacity to carry on a variety of activities, even though in doing these things they may learn ways of thinking about themselves and their roles in which there is an element of make-believe. In sum, play makes becoming "grown-up" more comprehensible to a child, but in a way that can lead to becoming a childish grown-up or turn being an adult into something of a role to be "played," whether for good or ill.

In considering how we learn to enact ourselves, let us look at some of the factors tending to induce us to believe we are or are not the social self, character, or person we present to the world.[9] Although few of us feel profoundly alienated from the person we present to society, it is important to understand what may cause such an outcome (cf. Laing, *Divided Self*, esp. 79–105). Children who do not want to give up unsocialized behavior and whose parents are punitively strict will find it reinforcing to retaliate by resisting efforts to change them. Such children can obey their parents to avoid punishment, while being reinforced with self-approval for thinking that rebels against coercion. They can think of the self that obeys as a mask, and be pleased with themselves for being able to fool their parents. As in the case of a hypocrite, the self-manipulation here is for the sake of manipulating others, and these children must think about their role-playing in order to keep from expressing what they really feel when they are with their parents.

Under certain circumstances, however, all of us feel some detachment from our social selves. When we are in unaccustomed social situations, when we must seem to be more interested in what someone says than we actually are, when we are especially nice to someone we want to please, and even when thinking about how to respond to what someone says, we may feel that our overt behavior is rather contrived. Then we may feel that the way we think "within" ourselves is the "real me." Instead we can simply think we have learned to control our behavior. We are likely to think this way unless we are in situations that do not allow us to express ourselves truly so much of the time that they come to control our attitude toward the self we present (see Greenblatt on Thomas More, *Self-Fashioning* 11–73). A man who works with men who expect him to be "one of the boys" may act like one of the boys around them while feeling detached from this self-presentation. Similarly, women in male-dominated workplaces have traditionally been expected to "take a kidding" smilingly, to endure sexual harassment.

There can be some tendency to become alienated from the social self we *wish* to be if we are deliberately putting this self forward to others in order to please them. In school and at work we want to earn reports saying things like "accepts criticism well, is cooperative with others." It is so reinforcing to have others say such things about us that, even when we think the criticism is unfair or we are being exploited by co-workers, we may put on the appearances desired. Our behavior will be consciously rule-governed ("I should take criticism well") and so will not be experienced intuitively as self-expression.[10] To generalize, beginning in childhood we learn socially-scripted rules of good behavior so that we can act the character of a socialized person in all our roles, and we may sometimes feel detached from this character.

Any sort of self-consciousness, even the useful kind found in self-knowledge and self-control, can thus make us feel we are at least ever-so-slightly not at one with the self we present to others. Consider the example of a woman whose self-control and self-knowledge are of the most positive kind, who sincerely wishes to make her dealings with others serve everyone's best interests. She will need to think about how to conduct herself, since she will know that we may act selfishly without realizing it if we act intuitively. As a self-knowing person, she may worry that her thoughtful responses to others are calculating and that her efforts to please others are insincere, since she knows she wants something for herself, too, if she is honest with herself. This woman may also see that her social self is somewhat different with different people, and hence she may think that no one of these social selves is truly her. In Skinnerian terms, the *private* selves that do the self-knowing in each role or situation are strongly reinforced for seeing the self-knowing and self-control as constant – for seeing a unified, autonomous self. The difficulty of seeing that one's self changes from one social situation to another is made greater by the fact that in different situations one does have some consistency in personality defenses and other characteristics.

Self-conscious reflectiveness about behavior is certainly not necessarily a problem, however, and it does not necessarily occur in many situations. We are often absorbed in un-selfconscious thoughts about what we are doing – or in thinking about what we have done or will do or wish we were doing. Mostly we do not think much about ourselves in the doing unless something evokes such thoughts because of our learning history. The person who has learned to behave intuitively in formal social gatherings with polished social graces will not experience the self-consciousness felt by the person whose behavior must be consciously rule-governed in such a situation.

As we shall see shortly, the successful actor is also mostly absorbed in performing a character, and for many of the same reasons that people in everyday life are absorbed in what they are doing. Here, having explored factors that may lead us to feel we are not quite the person we present to others, let us look at the factors inducing us to feel that we *are* our social selves. Most people, as I have suggested above, do identify with their social selves most if not all of the time and see little cause to question the differences in their behavior with various others. Nor do their private thoughts about how to respond to others make them think they are at all phony. This is the way they have been raised to think and act, so there is nothing about these phenomena that prompts them to question how to think of themselves.

Insofar as a major function of culture is to give people a sense of meaning and value, social groups virtually demand belief in the self one presents to others.[11] The person who fails to present a self he or she believes in and can enact convincingly may be labeled psychotic. Hence a failure to identify with one's social self is an aversive condition and will tend not to occur. We *want* to "be" our social selves that are approved by others, and it is frequently said that we and our sense of self and of self-reality are created through learning and enacting identities and roles assigned to us as we are socialized.[12]

Indeed, many elements of our basic nature are transformed into second nature before we are old enough to understand what is happening. Bertolt Brecht offers a succinct description of the process:

> One easily forgets that human education proceeds along highly theatrical lines. In a quite theatrical manner the child is taught how to behave; logical arguments only come later. When such-and-such occurs, it is told (or sees), one must laugh. It joins in when there is laughter, without knowing why; if asked why it is laughing it is wholly confused. In the same way it joins in shedding tears, not only weeping because the grown-ups do so but also feeling genuine sorrow. This can be seen at funerals, whose meaning escapes children entirely. These are theatrical

events which form the character. The human being copies gestures, miming, tones of voice. And weeping arises from sorrow, but sorrow also arises from weeping.

It is not different with grown-ups. Their education never finishes. Only the dead are beyond being altered by their fellowmen. Think this over, and you will realize how important the theatre is for the forming of character. (152)

Thus we tend to think and feel according to what we do, and it may follow that as our behavior changes we tend to repress knowledge of what we have been and of how we have changed (cf. Goffman, *Presentation* 80–1, 158–9). For example, as a boy grows up, the selves he presents to others undergo great changes, yet usually it will be reinforcing for him to feel that his character has been continuous, even as he goes from good little boy to teenage hellion to cool young adult in going from his parents to his peers as reinforcing reference groups (Anselm Strauss 144–7). At any time of life when we have undergone change, it is aversive to remember how childish or ignorant or socially awkward – or whatever – we were before. Nicolas Evreinoff, in *The Theatre in Life*, quotes Nietzsche's aphorism: "'I did it,' said my memory. 'I could not have done that,' said my pride, and remained inflexible. In the end memory yielded" (51).[13]

The process involved here is not merely that as we change we selectively forget the discrediting aspects of what we were before and of the arduous process of change. The idea found in Plato's objection to acting, that we become what we start out pretending to be, has found support in a number of modern studies. For our interest in the psychology of acting, it will help if we can differentiate changes in a person caused by what might be called ordinary social learning in social roles from changes occurring through more contrived or temporary role-playing. In the ordinary course of life a person who becomes a business manager, for example, will usually learn to think in a way that is shaped by this position. If the person develops conservative socio-economic attitudes, it will be not only because consistency between behavior and attitudes is reinforcing or because of reinforcement by financial rewards and by peers, but also because the person's position makes salient the burdensome aspects of government and labor unions, etc. All these causes may explain the results of a study by Seymour Lieberman showing that when a group of workers became foremen, their attitudes changed markedly toward those of management, and when later some of them returned to being workers their attitudes reverted to what they had been before (cf. Breer and Locke 11–21, 28–9; Stires and McCombe).

Thus through a change of role a person may simply learn from experience how to act and think in new ways. In behavior modification therapy, people overcome phobias by gradually learning to engage in activities in the situations that have caused them fear. Or a socially awkward person may be taught to behave more gracefully with others through role-playing rehearsals in a therapeutic setting.[14] George A. Kelly describes results going beyond what can be fully explained in these terms, however. In his therapeutic practice he rehearsed clients in roles designed to counteract the behavior causing them difficulty (1:326–7, 374–5). He reports not only that clients frequently would say of their new behavior that "I feel as if this were the *real* me," but also that some who changed greatly thought that most of the change was not in themselves but in their situations (1:416, 412). Especially striking, Kelly says a client in this sort of therapy would tend "to forget what he originally came in for" (1:413; cf. Montgomery and Haemmerlie).

These facts suggest four processes at work: (1) we tend to become absorbed in what we are currently doing, and so other thoughts are displaced, (2) as we rehearse and learn a role-behavior, we come to experience it as intuitive, (3) because we experience positively reinforced behavior as voluntary, we will experience behavior producing successful results as arising from our own nature as an agent; (4) in any case, if the behavior is successful, we will find it reinforcing to think it is our own. Thoughts opposed to these will be aversive, so that our earlier self is "forgotten," and thoughts that the earlier self is still the "real" me will be especially aversive if this earlier self was unhappy enough to want the help of a therapist.

Thus attitudes and the sense of self may change when behavior changes, or rather when changed contingencies of reinforcement change all behavior, including the way we think. If contingencies provide positive reinforcement for changed thinking and other behavior, and if these contingencies do not appear coercive, we will tend to behave in the new way and experience the change as voluntary. On the other hand, if the changed contingencies are openly rather coercive – if we perceive that we are under peer pressure to conform, for example – the aversive character of the coercion may cause us to rebel, or we may only pretend to go along while feeling resentful. Many people, however, change their views even when social pressure is obvious, as indicated by studies done some years ago showing that most Bennington College students entered the college with conservative views but became more radical by the time they graduated. Typically the students said they changed their views partly to win greater acceptance, and they knew this meant rejecting their parents as a reference group, but they evidently did not think of their new views as coerced or false (Bem 82–4).

The degree of voluntariness required for attitudes to change can be coercively or at least artificially induced. Contingencies can be arranged so there will be great reinforcement – whether positive or negative – for a change of belief, and then it will be most reinforcing if we can think we change voluntarily because the new view is right, not because of rewards or threats. People being "brain-washed" are reduced to infantile dependence, anxiety, and terror, and then are induced to confess the weakness they feel and to participate in discussion, group self-criticism, and the persuasion of others. They hear only one view and are under intense pressure to change their thinking, but real change seldom takes place unless they can be induced to participate in the process (see esp. Holt; cf. Cushman; Lifton). Erik Erikson writes that in rituals of initiation and confirmation social institutions seek "to combine some badge of sacrifice or submission with an energetic push toward sanctioned ways of action – a combination which, where it works, assures the development in the novice of an optimum of compliance with a maximum sense of free choice and solidarity" (*Identity: Youth* 184).

Entering into a role in a simulated "real life" situation and interacting with others can create a sense of reality. This may especially happen when the interaction is emotionally absorbing. Irving L. Janis and Leon Mann asked smokers to role-play persons suffering the ill effects of smoking who are told by an experimenter playing the role of a physician that they have lung cancer. "This role-playing procedure proved to be an extraordinarily disquieting experience," and it led to more decisions to stop smoking than did a procedure in which smokers were given the same information with no role-playing (Janis 583).

Some experiments studying "cognitive dissonance" yield attitude change through role-playing when the issue is less emotional. In a classic experiment by Leon Festinger and J. Merrill Carlsmith, subjects were asked to do a boring task. Then they were told that the person who was to introduce the next subject to the task would not be able to come, and were asked if they would help. They were told that the experiment required them to say to this new subject that the task was interesting. At this point half of the subjects were offered one dollar for their assistance, the others twenty dollars. After they had talked to the next subject, an interviewer asked them to rate the interest of the original task. Those paid twenty dollars tended to say it was boring, whereas those paid only one dollar tended to rate it as more interesting.

How to explain these results has been much debated, but many interpreters agree that self-esteem is a controlling factor. In behaviorist terms, persons paid twenty dollars think they are paid so much to induce them to be willing to tell another person something they know is not true. This thought functions as a discriminative stimulus to help them remember that the task is boring even when they say it is interesting. Their behavior is reinforced by the money, and their self-esteem does not become involved in what they know is an experiment. In contrast, persons paid only one dollar regard this as a token payment for voluntary cooperation, and their main reinforcement will be self-approval, which requires thinking they told the other person the truth. It would be aversive to remember they found the task boring, so they will tend not to think of this. Instead they may come to think they were mistaken to find the task boring in the first place.[15] In such cases it seems that the disposition to believe we *act* the way we *think* can lead us to infer we have done so, with the ironic result that instead we *think* the way we have *acted*.

Not all people think this way, however. Psychologists have used questionnaires based on Machiavelli's *The Prince* to distinguish between people who have a "Machiavellian" outlook on how to behave with others and people who always want to be sincere and act morally – between "high Mach" and "low Mach" individuals. These two types of individuals respond differently in cognitive dissonance experiments and in similar experiments involving counter-attitudinal role-playing. Gilda F. Epstein asked students who favored the fluoridation of water to participate in discussions on fluoridation and then placed them "in a role-playing situation in which they were asked to improvise talks against fluoridation for possible use on radio programs." Low Machs shifted "toward anti-fluoridation attitudes after role playing more than after silent reading only. High Machs showed the opposite pattern by becoming more anti-fluoridation when presented with factual arguments than in the role playing condition" (Macpherson 390–1).

High Machs thus apply reasons to guide their attitudes and conduct; also, their reinforcement by self-approval does not depend on believing they always say what they think, for they know they may have reasons to say things they do not believe. In contrast, a commitment to sincerity on the part of the low Machs induces them to deceive themselves in order to maintain their belief that they do not deceive others. In playing games involving interaction with team-mates and opponents, low Machs usually lose to high Machs because they attend less to strategy than to emotional involvement with their side's cause and with their team-mates. On questionnaires low Machs say they will not be dishonest, but they do lie or cheat when urged to do so by a team-mate. As Florence L. Geis and Richard Christie observe, "In answering questionnaires low Machs may be influenced by implicit assumptions, or what they expect of themselves. Then, in action situations they can get carried away from these private (and sincere) assumptions in going along with particular others in the process of interaction" (308).[16]

The discussion in this chapter so far suggests some ideas about why actors might remain detached from characters they play or might instead

come to identify with the characters. Actors will not identify with characters if they do not think they should, and the choice of whether to try to
identify depends on the director and actor's view of the art of acting.
Some actors believe they should use technique to create the *illusion* of
emotional reality, and in this view actors who feel the emotions of their
parts have lost control and are likely to be self-indulgent hams (the classic
exposition of this view is by Denis Diderot).[17]

Actors who believe they should portray but not feel emotions will rehearse an expressive smile, not react with amusement. They will be reinforced for responding to what other actors do and say as cues for their
well-practiced behavior, not for responding directly to what happens. Since
they are reinforced for maintaining a sense of conscious control, they will
think self-(as-actor-)conscious thoughts, and these may absorb their attention enough to further reduce their direct responses to what happens
around them. Carried to an extreme, this mode of performance can result
in self-absorption and even ham acting. Nevertheless, actors who rely on
technique are capable of polished performances, and in some plays the
effects called for are so shallow, artificial, or psychologically incoherent
that it would be foolish to expect an actor to identify or "fuse" with a part.

It is easy to understand how actors can remain aware of themselves
as persons apart from the characters they play, and what needs to be
explained is how anyone could cease to be aware of this, no matter what
I may have shown about the effects of role-playing in social life, since
there we have much more reason to identify with the self we present to
others – we present ourselves as *ourselves*. Many actors, however, have
experienced identification with a character; as noted in Chapter 1, we
have testimony starting with Plato that actors can feel they become the
characters they play.

Before looking more closely at what may cause this to happen, I should
say what is experienced when an actor fuses or identifies with a character.
It is not that an actor suffers a psychotic delusion that he is Hamlet,
although there are reports of actors getting so caught up in their roles that
they stayed in character backstage between scenes, or even killed other
actors (for examples of such violence, see Plutarch, *Cicero* ch. 5, sec. 3–4;
Heywood E3v). What it means for an actor to fuse with a character is that
he or she thinks the thoughts and feels the emotions the script creates for
the character and responds to what happens on stage as if the action were
real. Constantin Stanislavski, the great director of the Moscow Art Theater,
wrote that such fusion should be the goal of the actor's art. He reports
that he sometimes experienced a complete fusion in his acting, but that
most of the time an actor using his techniques retains some self-consciousness. Stanislavski believed this self-consciousness is of the kind we all
commonly experience, and hence should not interfere with the sense actors

have that their thoughts and feelings are those of a character (*Building* 167; cf. his *Actor* 252).

Stanislavski is most interested, however, in teaching actors how to achieve and use the state of fusion with a character. He writes that even a brief period of fusion produces a sense of reality which will open up the actor's "subconscious" so he or she will feel at one with a character. Stanislavski describes the state marking the onset of this condition: "Your head will swim from the excitement of the sudden and complete fusion of your life with your part. It may not last long but while it does last you will be incapable of distinguishing between yourself and the person you are portraying." And then "truth and faith will lead you into the region of the subconscious and hand you over to the power of nature" (*Actor* 278). Similarly, in defining acting as an art, Stanislavski says that "the very best that can happen is to have the actor completely carried away by the play. Then regardless of his own will he lives the part, not noticing *how* he feels, not thinking about *what* he does, and it all moves of its own accord, subconsciously and intuitively" (*Actor* 13).

Shortly we will look at Stanislavski's techniques for creating the sense of fusion and so of working on the actor's "subconscious," but first let us consider the condition in which actors remain conscious of themselves along with feeling what their characters feel. Through the processes of conditioning, such experiences on stage could cause actors to regard their personal emotions off the stage with some detachment. François Talma said that when he was in "deep distress" in his personal life, "my histrionic obsession was so overmastering that, crushed as I was by a genuine enough unhappiness, in the very moment of shedding tears I took involuntarily a quick, fleeting notice of how my voice altered . . ." and he found himself "thinking automatically how I could make use of this. . . ." Similarly Albert Lambert said that in his personal life, "Whatever distress I may be feeling, in spite of myself I watch it all, listen to it all, take note of it all; and doing so does not lessen my emotion. It seems to me that the same thing must happen to everybody, and that its absence would constitute a mental limitation" (William Archer 147, 149).

Whether or not this happens to everyone in some degree, these passages suggest that actors may experience a divided consciousness more than most people, and this brings us to an important point in the psychology of acting and role-playing. Actors may experience being themselves in the way they experience being characters partly because their mode of being themselves changes through acting. That is, through becoming a character in a self-conscious way, an actor may also become histrionically self-conscious in social life. We are affected by what we specifically do, and if we play roles self-consciously, we become self-conscious players of our roles rather than the character the role would

suggest. Since in social life we all are self-conscious on occasion, as discussed earlier, we may all approach the condition of the self-conscious,
self-observing actor. Although Jean-Paul Sartre evidently regarded all
actors as people who are inauthentic and therefore become actors, and
although a psychoanalyst may say actors are exhibitionists compensating
for inadequate selfhood,[18] we might propose instead that the experience
of acting may cause people to *become* inauthentic or exhibitionistic if they
become self-conscious through acting and so experience their personal
emotions as unreal or for display.

On the other hand, a balance of strong emotion and self-awareness may
lead to an imaginative mode of acting and becoming. In *An Actor Prepares*,
Stanislavski writes of what happens as the actor gradually merges with a
character: "Our type of creativeness is the conception and birth of a new
being – the person in the part. It is a natural act similar to the birth of a
human being." He says that as actors grow into their roles they "are
influenced by their parts, which affect their daily lives." The actors' past
"daily lives" should also affect how they play their parts, so there is a
convergence of influences between role and life leading to the birth of
the person in the part (294–5). In *Creating a Role* he describes this new
being as having a "quivering, live soul, the soul of the human-being-
actor-character" (232).

When actors fuse with a character, they experience the character's
thoughts and emotions, and also their own are somehow displaced. At
least as long ago as 1900 it was noticed that this state of consciousness
is much like that of trance or hypnosis (Kjerbühl-Petersen 175–6), and
experiments have shown that the ability to play roles correlates with
hypnotizability (Sarbin and Allen, "Role-Theory" 519–20). In recent years
students of origins of drama and writers on performance theory have
shown that participants in tribal dramas of possession by spirits of divine
or animal natures experience either a double-consciousness or a fusion
that is interpreted as a trance state.[19] Charles Marowitz writes of our
contemporary Western theater, too, that the actor uses "a mild form of
self-hypnosis" (98–100).

These observations are helpful, but there is little agreement among
experts about what hypnosis is, and a leading theory holds that it is a
form of absorbed role-playing like that experienced by the Stanislavskian
actor.[20] The circularity here suggests that these two phenomena may have
a common explanation. Both the actor and the hypnotized person closely
concentrate their attention on controlling stimuli which originate outside themselves. A term occurring frequently in descriptions of hypnotic
concentration is "absorbed," and the absorbed person is said to reduce
self-conscious thinking greatly.

The external stimuli for the actor are of course the script and then the staged action of the play. Through these there arise the stimuli of the actor's own performance – speech, movement, gestures, thoughts, and emotions. Marowitz thinks the hypnotic state is induced by repetition of the performance of text and action in rehearsals (99–100). Charles McGaw writes of actors' total concentration and their "belief" in their enactment (16–17, 56). Peter Brook, Peter Hall, and others write of actors' concentrated responses to their own speech, or say that a script functions as a score does for a musician, virtually demanding certain responses (Brook 110–11; Hall 424). We saw in Chapter 1 that Elizabethans regarded the written text of an actor's part in much the same way: from Cicero and Quintilian on it is said that if actors give their full attention and imagination to a powerfully written text expressing passion, they will feel the emotion. This absorption in the script does not need to be total ("hypnotic") in order for actors to experience a degree of fusion with their parts that reduces interfering thoughts greatly (cf. Goldman, *Actor's Freedom* 85).

B. F. Skinner rarely refers to the psychology of acting or role-playing and he provides no extended discussion of these as specific topics. His brief references to acting are helpful, however, and his discussions of our responses to texts of all kinds are applicable to the actor's response to a script. In analyzing responses of listeners and readers, Skinner explains the importance of factors creating a context reinforcing belief in what is heard or read. In *Verbal Behavior* his comments on hypnosis clearly apply to the actor's absorption as well:

> Hypnosis is not at the moment very well understood, but it seems to exemplify a heightened "belief" in the present sense. The world is for a time reduced to verbal stimuli which are in practically complete control of the hypnotized subject. Behavior characteristic of listeners appears in a dramatically intensified form. The sharply localized reaction to verbal stimuli in hypnosis is similar to absorption in a book. Macaulay claimed in his last illness that an interesting book acted as an analgesic. (160; cf. 409–10)

Skinner's explanation of how a reader may identify with a character in a book can also be applied to an actor. Skinner accepts Freud's view that in part a text expresses attitudes and feelings the author is not conscious of, and that similarly readers respond to a text according to tendencies they are not conscious of. Thus strongly reinforced behavior that has been punished and hence is repressed may lead to identification with a character who performs similar behavior, though perhaps in a disguised form (*Verbal* 273–4; *Science* 216–17). Readers may also identify with a character because of their *conscious* feelings and behavior: people in love may identify with a fictional lover. And we may be drawn to characters who do things that are strongly reinforced but that our lives do not permit us to do.

In absorbed reading we are drawn into an imaginative or "vicarious" enactment of what characters do, performing their behavior at a covert level and being reinforced by the same outcomes as they are. Skinner notes that readers especially enjoy dialogue partly because its use of the first person facilitates identification. The skillful writer can prepare us for what the character will say so we can anticipate the saying and feel what is said as our saying (*Verbal* 275–6). Through this technique, readers can be induced to identify with many characters. As Stanislavski says, identification depends partly on a matching of selves between actor and character (*Actor* 279), but it may depend even more on the writer's creation of a character and a script that induce identification. In social life, too, how much a person identifies with a role depends partly on the initial congruity between self and role, and partly on whether the person finds the role absorbing and reinforcing and is therefore shaped by it.

Skinner also explains how emotional responses become conditioned to words. Individual words can elicit emotional responses if they have been used in emotional situations. The effects are weak, though, unless enough words are used to create an imagined scene or a vivid emotional expression stimulating strong feeling.[21] Passages that do not at first cause an emotional response can come to do so through conditioning if they are experienced repeatedly in a context causing emotion. In the case of a speech in a play, since the situation in which it is performed is based on the text, the emotions of text and situation will strengthen each other.

Stanislavski, however, believed the force of the text alone could never induce an actor to feel the emotions of a character. He held that if an actor's emotions become involved with a character's through the use of a partly improvised "script," then learning the character's speeches can be a discovery of what the *actor* wants to say (*Creating* 95, 100–1, 207–8; cf. 266). As a result of this process, the emotions the actor has already come to feel can be conditioned to the scripted speeches. The basic principle Stanislavski employed to generate emotion was to make the actor's life as the character as "real" as possible, for he knew that we cannot will ourselves to experience an emotion: in Skinner's terms, emotional responses cannot be operantly conditioned (*Science* 169). We respond emotionally only to what actually causes us as persons to feel emotion: to feel in a situation on stage, actors must feel as themselves.

Stanislavski taught actors to use what he called the "magic if": actors should not ask what a character would feel but what they would do if they were in the circumstances of the character (*Actor* 42–9; *Building* 30; *Creating* 201, 222). As they respond to the "given circumstances" of a character's situation, actors can gradually become caught up in a sense of reality as they respond to what happens on the stage. An actor's own responses, however, are in a sense only a starting point, for as Stanislavski states repeatedly, actors should work to make their responses more and more similar to a character's as scripted (*Actor* 14, 168, 178–9, 196, 269). Stanislavski taught actors to use their "emotion memories" to arouse feelings in themselves analogous to a character's. From there little is required to create the sense of fusion which in turn causes a continuation of the intuitive, "subconscious" sense of reality (*Actor*, esp. 196).

Actors' intuitive sense of reality in roles will not be destroyed by artificial aspects of the theater if they learn to think in the appropriate way. The "given circumstances" to which they are to respond include all the conditions of staging that impinge on their attention (*Actor* 48). Thus they are not asked to believe they are not actors on a stage, but to respond to their surroundings. In rehearsals, however, actors concentrate on limited areas of the stage and especially on the other actors and on their own words, thoughts, feelings, and actions, so that they are aware of the theatrical setting and the audience mostly as background contingencies of reinforcement for their work. Although a good audience will evoke a good performance, a good actor will not directly respond to the audience (see, for example, *Actor* 191–3).

Stanislavski taught actors to compose a stream of thoughts and emotionally-charged visualizations to accompany their speech and action on the stage. These thoughts and images are derived from the actor's imagining of the earlier life as well as the stage life of the character, and are – like all else in Stanislavski's techniques – designed to heighten the sense of reality and to elicit real feeling. Stanislavski called the resulting stream of feelings, purposes, and other thoughts and visualizations the subtext. In his view, the subtext represents what characters think and feel that causes them to speak and act as they do.[22]

Stanislavski also taught actors to make their interactions as real as possible. To this end, actors should think of their characters' purposes, since in "real" life we act for the sake of purposes, and our emotions arise as our purposes are thwarted or otherwise responded to by the people around us (cf. McGaw 26, 28–9). If an actor pursuing a character's purpose behaves in a way that provokes real responses from the other actors, the reality of these responses heightens the first actor's sense that his or her own behavior is real: a circular effect is created that can greatly increase the sense of reality for all the actors.[23] Another cause of a sense of reality here is that since in everyday life the act of speaking evokes a sense that what we say is our own utterance, the act of speaking to someone on stage can evoke this sense as well.

One of Stanislavski's most important techniques for creating a sense of reality is the "method of physical actions," which he developed as his system evolved, especially, according to Pavel Simonov, when he came under the influence of the behaviorist psychologist Ivan Pavlov.[24] If an actor concentrating on thinking about what to do in the character's given circumstances improvises natural actions connected with carrying out the character's purposes, the reality of this physical behavior creates an intuitive sense of reality and hence fusion with the character.[25] The "real" activity need only last a few moments and can even be extraneous to the character's purpose – Stanislavski mentions the example of righting a chair that has been accidentally overturned on the stage (*Actor* 133, 270). And the improvisation can be mostly in thinking rather than in physical behavior (*Actor* 275, 278). If an actor whose character faces a crisis not only responds to the given circumstances but also imagines other, related circumstances that might make the situation even more critical, he or she may respond as Stanislavski's Kostya does: "At the very thought my heart was in my mouth" (*Actor* 274).

Although he says a few moments' reality of action can induce a sense of fusion with a character, Stanislavski taught actors to construct a series of such actions to give physical form to an entire part. Actors who put themselves in their characters' given circumstances and respond to these circumstances intuitively and with improvisations in action and thought can create a sense of emotional truth in all they do (*Actor* 136–9). Then repeated rehearsals of the sequence of thought and action with full attention to the naturalness and detailed reality of what is done heighten the emotion and the sense of reality (*Actor* 289; *Creating* 240–9).

Rehearsals make the behavior and the interactions more intuitive and natural and hence more likely to arouse emotion. This emotion becomes conditioned to all that is happening and to the setting and the other actors. Further, emotions become conditioned to emotional behavior. Every time an actor becomes angry, for example, the postures, gestures, voice tones, and facial contortions of anger become more able to elicit the emotion.[26] Finally, in emotional contexts we tend to interpret a state of physiological arousal as the emotion appropriate to our situation (Schachter and Singer). This suggests that Stanislavskian actors in an aroused state and behaving angrily, for example, in situations that are supposed to cause anger, will tend to interpret the arousal as anger, and will do so all the more because this interpretation is reinforced by the sense that they are experiencing the emotion of the character. Some actors deliberately "work themselves up" for an emotional scene, but the anticipation of such a scene may well cause arousal, and the enactment of strongly emotional behavior should itself add to the arousal experienced.

Through such techniques as Stanislavski's, then, there are many ways in which an actor may come to think and feel as a character does – or to believe that this is happening. Acting can also have physical effects: studies show that Stanislavskian actors experience heightened emotionality and an increased ability to use their faces expressively.[27] An actor may even turn pale, a response that is more difficult to elicit by consciously controllable means than the production of tears or an angry or blushing redness. Of special interest are changes in character and attitude that carry over into an actor's off-stage life. According to Kenneth J. Gergen, seventy percent of a large group of actors reported such effects: "The person comes to develop an identity based on the role and to use this identity in his behavior over a wide variety of circumstances" (*Concept* 55; cf. Hammond and Edelmann). An actor of my acquaintance is a very gentle man and a feminist, but when he played a "macho redneck" character, his wife noticed that in posture and voice he took on the manner of the character with her and began to express sexist attitudes. When she objected, he saw how the role was affecting him. As part of this, he felt a connection between the way he had come to hold his body and to speak and his coming to think and feel in a way that intuitively went with that physical manner.

It is tempting to conclude of actors exposed to all the influences considered here that the wonder would be if they were *not* to experience some fusion with the characters they play. Stanislavskian actors in performance will be thinking, speaking, and doing what they believe the character would. Concentration on these activities leaves little room to think of oneself as a person apart from the role. Stage-fright is usually experienced only before a performance, since once the action is under way the activity is so absorbing that self-conscious thoughts tend not to occur. Stanislavski says that sometimes an actor actually cannot remember what has transpired on stage (*Actor* 46–7, 275). As Skinner points out, the suppression of self-awareness when success depends on intense concentration can be explained by the principle of prepotency (*Science* 290). One's actions and thoughts become so absorbed in what must be done that the competing responses of self-observation do not occur. Self-conscious perception and thought are behavior, and they are necessary as a basis for later recall: if we do not observe ourselves while we do something, we lack the basis for repeating the behavior of self-perception later in memory. Of course we usually do have some self-awareness, and actors will as well. Yet precisely because people generally have some self-awareness, actors can expect characters as imagined persons to have some, too, and so can experience their own self-perception as that of their character. Indeed, any self-consciousness, insincerity, or other form of self-detachment scripted for a character is part of what an actor can become absorbed in through Stanislavski's techniques.

Thus for actors on the stage and for people in social roles, absorption is one key to a sense of reality and belief in one's own performance. In any situation in life we tend to become absorbed in activities that are interesting or important to us, and we tend to think self-consciously only insofar as such thinking is related to what we are doing or insofar as there are influences from our past or factors in our present situation that evoke self-conscious responses. On the stage, circumstances that might distract actors are ever-present, but there are also potent techniques that can help actors to become absorbed and to create a sense of reality.

Absorption and the sense of reality depend, too, on our having the sense that our behavior is truly ours. There is a reciprocity of cause and effect as the sense that our behavior is ours facilitates the sense of reality and the absorption, while the absorption displaces thoughts doubting that our behavior is ours. Feeling that our behavior is our own depends most fundamentally on the lifetime's conditioning that usually gives us an intuitive sense that what we do and say is what we want to do and say in the prevailing circumstances. Even if the circumstances in which we act are manipulated, so long as they allow it to be reinforcing to think of our action as voluntary, we experience it as our own. Much depends on the way others behave, but the sense we have that our behavior is truly ours also draws on our deeply conditioned responses to our own expressive behavior, through which we feel what we say and do.

"All the world's a stage, / And all the men and women merely players" attests to more than a general analogy between the stage and the world. The players hold the mirror up to nature in a specific sense: the relation between the psychology of acting and the psychology of social life illuminates how our cognitions as well as our actions are shaped, including the ways we are affected by our own feelings, thoughts, words, and deeds.

4

Hamlet

In some influential post-structuralist commentary on Shakespeare's representation of character, Hamlet is regarded as psychologically incoherent, and humanist critics are said to project onto the inscription of this character the notions of inwardness and an essential self which were fully developed only in the century following the composition of the play.[1] Francis Barker argues that Hamlet is unable to define the truth of his subjectivity directly and fully because his interiority is merely "gestural," so that at his center there is "nothing" (36–7; cf. Belsey, *Subject* 41). Contrary both to the views of the post-structuralists and to the view attributed to humanist critics, I will argue that Hamlet is not psychologically incoherent but has the divided and only partially self-aware and self-controlling subjectivity that in Shakespeare's time was said to characterize human beings. Hamlet is unable to define the truth of his subjectivity directly and fully because he has a complex interiority that makes self-knowledge difficult. Thus this character is himself able to think about how his thinking may be in error. After all, his own statements that his inaction is caused by cowardly thinking are the main source of the theory that he rationalizes to delay revenge (esp. 4.4.32–46; cf. Belsey's opposed view of how to interpret Hamlet's soliloquies, *Subject* 50, 52).

Regarding the general question of how to think of the text of a play in responding to a character, there is certainly a sense in which a character exists only in the performance of an actor; but on the other hand insofar as we are aware of the actor performing, we are aware, too, that he or she is performing a text. The text is the starting point for both actor and reader. As Harry Berger argues, we infer a character from the text of a play, and this has an important corollary: "a character or dramatic person is the effect rather than the cause of his or her speech and of our interpretation" (147). Whether we are actors, audience, or readers, however, according to the Elizabethan ideas developed in Chapter 1, our imaginations will mostly assimilate scripted speeches and actions to imagined persons who, like real persons, are the cause of their speech and action. And because we respond to imagined persons *as if* they were real, we infer "inner" thoughts and feelings from scripted words and deeds in the process of interpreting the characters as the effect of these phenomena in the way Berger says.[2]

As explained in Chapters 1 and 3, the text is – and was for the Elizabethans – a score for a performance, and a critic who has seen many
performances may be able to perform the analysis of the psychology of
a character by responding to the text and to memories of performance
as evoked by reading the text. My readings have been arrived at in this
way, but what I write is based on the potentialities and the constraints
for any kind of interpretation that I find inscribed – or implied by what
is inscribed – in the text. When I say a character thinks or may think this
or that, I mean that the text implies such thoughts, and I do not assume
that the character is a real person. The "I find" and "may" here indicate
my recognition that any interpretation is inevitably subjective and uncertain, however much one tries to achieve objectivity by taking into account
the interpretations of many others and all of the relevant contexts.

In sum, when I infer what Hamlet thinks and feels, I regard him as an
imagined person created by Shakespeare to be entered into imaginatively
by an actor and imagined or construed by an audience. The audience
needs to be able to respond to Hamlet as an imagined person in order to
respond appropriately to the play *Hamlet*.[3] For the tragic effect, we must
remain sympathetic even when Hamlet does dreadful deeds, and this
requires an understanding of his character and situation so that we can
see both the qualities that move him and how these lead to tragic error.
Hamlet intends to act for the sake of dignity and integrity and the obli-
gations of love, duty, and justice. If he acts wrongly, it is because, as he
responds to his very complex and painful situation, his sensitivity and
intensity distort his concern for these values, resulting in an error he is
unable to see. He has keen awareness, but paradoxically this awareness,
joined with his sensitivity and intensity, results in a self-absorbed blindness in crucial situations.

Of course this is only one possible interpretation of Hamlet's character,
even using a behaviorist analysis. One strength of a behaviorist analysis is that it suggests that motivation is multiple as well as complex –
that thought and action have as many motives as they have reinforcing
consequences – so that a single reading can include a number of interpretations usually found only in competing readings (or such motivation
is sometimes referred to without much analysis as "overdetermined").
Because a behaviorist analysis focusses on what a character specifically
experiences from moment to moment, it is an analysis that could be
especially helpful to an actor seeking a psychological understanding to
use as a basis for performance.

The explication of text in a behaviorist interpretation occupies so much
more space than does the accompanying technical psychological analysis
that at times the interpretation may appear not to be specifically behaviorist. I have tried to strike a balance between showing that a behaviorist

analysis can be written without excessive use of technical terminology, and explaining phenomena in technical terms sufficiently to show how a behaviorist analysis works. I will count on a reader's recognizing that certain terms having a common-sense meaning have a similar but more specific meaning in behaviorist psychology. In Chapter 2 I have explained Skinner's powerful analysis of the relations between emotions, thoughts, and actions. That chapter explains the technical use of terms such as "avoidance," "escape," "aversive," "reinforced" or "reinforcing," and "evoke": an event or thought evokes a "response" a person is "disposed" to because it has been made probable by conditioning. "Disposed" is used similarly in the proto-behaviorist tradition – we are disposed to act a certain way because of our habituation. Readers will also be able to tell that my analysis is behaviorist in its ways of discussing what a character sees and does not see, how certain thoughts are displaced by others, how absorption in a point of view affects thinking, how intentions arise and change, how intentions and emotions affect and are affected by actions, and so forth. Thus it should be clear that a distinctive psychology is being used even when technical terms are not employed, as is also the case in some psychoanalytic essays on literature.

I analyze Hamlet in detail in order to demonstrate how his character is psychologically coherent throughout the play. I discuss the play *Hamlet* first because none of Shakespeare's works has more to do with ideas about intention, motivation, and action, with the psychology of role-playing and the link between the psychology of acting and of personal life,[4] and with the proto-behaviorist ideas about habit and character. The play contains statements that refer to all the most important ideas in the proto-behaviorist tradition. Early in the play Hamlet draws on the traditional idea that we are creatures of nature but also of habituation. He explains that as a custom which is a vice causes a whole people to lose the respect of others, individuals lose respect "for some vicious mole of nature in them," or "By their o'ergrowth of some complexion," or "by some habit, that too much o'erleavens / The form of plausive manners . . ." (1.4.24–30). When Hamlet arraigns his mother in the closet scene, he suggests that her habitual vice may have "braz'd" her heart so she cannot feel the evil of her life with Claudius (3.4.34–8). In the graveyard scene, Horatio refers to the related principle that habituation makes unpleasant activities become easy in explaining that the Gravedigger sings because he has become accustomed to his work (5.1.65–9). The closet scene, again, has the most complete statement of the psychology of habits in Shakespeare. When Hamlet urges his mother not to go to bed with Claudius, he

explains that although custom or habit is a monster in making us unaware
of the evil in our vices, by the same token if she acts virtuously she will
come to think virtuously, too (3.4.162–72). Attitudes follow behavior.

Each of these passages poses a question about Hamlet. Is he one in
whom a "complexion" such as the humor of melancholy "o'ergrows" to
break down "the pales and forts of reason" or in whom "some habit . . .
too much o'erleavens the form of plausive manners"? In the closet scene,
is Hamlet becoming "braz'd" so that he is callous to the death of Polonius
as he turns from stabbing him to speak daggers to his mother about *her*
sins? Does such conduct as the role-playing of the antic disposition change
him? In the graveyard and at the end of the play have gravemaking and
thoughts of death come to have "a property of easiness for him"?

Now, I am certainly not the first to suggest that the psychology of
habits may be important in *Hamlet*.[5] A. C. Bradley repeatedly uses the
word "habit" in discussing Schlegel's and Coleridge's ideas about Hamlet.
He says that in their view Hamlet's excessive thinking "proceeds from an
original one-sidedness of nature, strengthened by habit, and, perhaps, by
years of speculative inaction" (85). Bradley's thesis is that Hamlet's "imaginative and generalising habit of mind" causes his melancholy over his
mother's conduct to affect "his whole being and mental world." Hamlet's
"speculative habit" helps cause him endlessly to dissect the proposed
deed, and the frustration and shame of his delay make him even more
melancholy (93). Bradley sees Hamlet becoming caught up in a vicious
circle of thought, feeling, and inaction that deepens his melancholy and
renders him less and less able to act. Bradley tends to attribute most of
Hamlet's feelings, attitudes, and behavior to his melancholy (99), regarding the antic disposition mostly as an effect, as a form of inaction, not also
as an important cause, an "act" having an important effect on Hamlet.

Some nineteenth-century interpreters of *Hamlet* did think of the psychology of habits in connection with the antic disposition as an "act,"
however. C. A. H. Clodius wrote in 1820 that Hamlet's pretended madness "eventually becomes a habit" so that he is "really melancholy and
insane" (2:280), and this view was echoed by Hartley Coleridge in 1828
(2:198). Clodius's reading is an interesting effort to synthesize the poles of
the nineteenth-century debate on the question of whether Hamlet's madness is real or feigned. This question could then – before Freud's thinking
displaced the older psychology – still evoke the answer that what is feigned
may become real through habituation. Although I do not think Hamlet
becomes mad by pretending to be mad, I will argue that his "habit" of
mourning and his antic disposition do affect him, directly in a way related
to the psychology of habits and indirectly through his interpretation of
others' responses to his behavior.

It is a convention of dramatic literature that the audience should make inferences about characters' dispositions and motives and even about some influences in their earlier lives based on what they do and say and what others say about them: consider what is conveyed by Hamlet's anguished "Must I remember?" (1.2.143). Hamlet's first soliloquy expresses dispositions that we see repeatedly in the play and that we can only imagine have been shaped by his upbringing and education (1.2.129–59). His life at Wittenberg may have heightened a disposition to reflect on experience. He has also developed a concern for Christian values and for the values of noblemen, and it is important that in his situation these two sets of values oppose each other. Hamlet's earlier life has also of course shaped his attitudes toward his father and mother. Hamlet regards his father as noble, and he remembers his mother to have seemed so until she wed Claudius (139–45). In its context, Hamlet's exaggerated idealization of his father as a "Hyperion" is especially reinforced because it emphasizes the baseness of Claudius as a "satyr" (139–40).

Hamlet's ways of thinking and acting have depended on his being reinforced for regarding his father and mother as ideal models whose position held great promise for their son, "Th'expectancy and rose of the fair state" (3.1.154). Because his father is dead and the monarchy is now corrupted by his mother and uncle, the activities of a prince are no longer reinforced for Hamlet. This, along with his grief and outrage, has caused him to fall into a lethargic depression in which "all the uses of this world" seem "weary, stale, flat, and unprofitable" (1.2.133–4). Further, his mother's conduct, especially, has made noble thoughts aversive as they remind him of what she has done (143, 146). In proto-behaviorist terms, we see that it is his character – his disposition ingrained in habits – to think idealistically, valuing honesty, loyalty, love, and noble action. Because he is strongly disposed to think in this way – reinforced by self-esteem – he continues to do so, which means that now his own thoughts add to his torment.

The offensive behavior of Claudius and Gertrude moves him to such great shame, scorn, despair, and rage that in the soliloquy he does not directly express grief for his father. However, real grief must accompany what he says to let him be reinforced by a sense of justification in his outrage over his mother's having mourned so briefly. And Hamlet's grief itself is indirectly expressed in his sense of loss and his idealization of his father.

Hamlet's expression of a wish to die is evidence less of self-rejection than of concern for self-respect – the wish is reinforced as a thought of escape from life's anguish and indignity. The Prince's outraged sense of honor clashes with his Christian values as he finds it reinforcing to think he does not kill himself only because God forbids it. The thought of suicide seems mostly a gesture of protest: he articulates it only in explaining why he cannot do it. Hamlet does not blame himself for any of the wrongs that have occurred. On the contrary, there are hints of self-righteousness in his attitudes. His princely concern for self-respect and noble ideals makes it especially reinforcing for him to think that all the shame comes from his mother and her world.

Yet Hamlet does feel his life has been stripped of value, does feel some contempt for himself because he feels helpless, unable even to speak to remedy what his mother has done. Hence this soliloquy expresses a peculiar mingling of contempt for self with self-respect and self-righteousness. Hamlet's thoughts of how he is sullied primarily evoke a heightened bitterness and vehemence of response from his disposition to affirm his ideals and to scorn those who are truly base. The scorn he expresses is strongly reinforced when it generalizes to all the world and all women because then it all the more expresses the superiority of his father and his ideals and justifies his thinking that he cannot prevail against his foes. This kind of thinking creates the danger that Hamlet will find it reinforcing to think everyone associated with his mother's world is corrupt, or to exaggerate their actual corruption. Also, insofar as he may respond to attacks on his self-respect by seeking grounds to affirm it, he will be strongly reinforced for selectively seeing what he himself does and thinks in an approving and even self-righteous way.

There is no clear evidence that anything Hamlet says here is specifically shaped by Oedipal or pre-Oedipal motives; that is, there is no evidence that his strong idealization of his father is a reaction formation or that his emotional agitation over his mother's conduct is a result of repressed sexual wishes or anxieties. It is impossible, however, to rule out such interpretations, since his feelings about himself and his mother and father and about what his mother and uncle have done may support them. Perhaps we should conclude that here the pre-Oedipal and Oedipal background from Hamlet's early life does not contribute much to the specific shape of what he expresses beyond the conscious manifestations of idealizing his father and being emotionally involved with his mother's nature and behavior.

There are indications that Hamlet avoids reaching the most aversive conclusions about his mother. He may say all women are frail because it is less painful to think this than to think his own mother is an exceptionally frail woman. Also, he could have interpreted Gertrude's brief effusion of tears before her speedy marriage to Claudius as less frail than hypocritical. Such an interpretation could then have led Hamlet to suspect adultery and, given his hatred of his uncle, murder. Hamlet's strong emotional absorption in his response to the open wrong he sees – his mother's hasty remarriage to a base man – may also contribute to blocking any suspicious thoughts that might occur if he were more detached. He wants to believe the worst of his mother because she has hurt him so terribly, but because she is his mother and can hurt him so much, he does not want to believe the very worst of her.

Hamlet's not dwelling on his grief when alone prompts us to compare his emotions in the soliloquy with his earlier protestations to his mother that he feels grief to the depths of his being (1.2.76–86). Hamlet's continued mourning is customary, for Claudius concedes as much in his first speech (1–4). But is it only his father's death that motivates Hamlet's mourning in defiance of his mother and uncle? This question goes to the heart of the play's exploration of the causes of human behavior and the connection between an intention and an act. In traditional terms, we want to know whether Hamlet intends or has an "unconscious wish" to punish Gertrude and the King by constantly reminding them that they are wrong to have mourned so briefly and married so hastily. If we infer an intention to punish, we may see hypocrisy in Hamlet's claim that he knows not seems and is grieving to the very core of his being. That is, he does not explicitly say he feels only grief but implies this while merely saying he has inside him more than can be shown. If we see what "passes show" as including an intention to punish Gertrude and Claudius, we may think Hamlet is a sly role-player in his speech claiming he knows not seems.

A behaviorist reading can provide a different kind of answer. Hamlet's mourning is reinforced by several consequences, among them punishment of his mother and Claudius, though he may only think of his feelings for his father. Thus mourning is reinforced because Hamlet does indeed feel grief, and mourning for his father is the only expression of his ideals and character that he feels he can enact. However, the mourning does vex the King and Queen, and Hamlet is aware of this. Hence, since his anger at them causes punishing them to be reinforced, their vexation inevitably reinforces Hamlet's mourning. If it would be aversive for Hamlet to think he mourns in order to punish them, then it is not likely that this thought will occur to him or, if it does, that he would believe it. His protestations that he knows not "seems" indicate that it would be aversive for him to think his mourning is not wholly for the sake of his father.

Here I think the play strongly evokes empathy with Hamlet, and a behaviorist analysis validates this response by saying that while his mourning is motivated partly because it punishes the King and Queen, Hamlet is not necessarily conscious of this at all, that his scorn of seeming, along with everything else he says here, indicates he is not a conscious seemer himself. But Hamlet's character may change as a result of the combination of his painful circumstances and his own disposition and behavior. His mourning may become obsessive through a process that proto-behaviorism related to becoming habituated to the behavior, as is perhaps implied in the reference to Hamlet's "customary suits of solemn black" (1.2.78).[6] Hamlet may be caught up in a vicious circle, something like the one Bradley proposes, in which (1) his father's death motivates sincere grieving, (2) this behavior becomes strong because it is reinforced by several results, as explained above, (3) these strong expressions of grief induce more grief (as a conditioned response) and an increased tendency to be unsocial and solitary, and (4) solitariness in turn increases melancholy. And so on and on until Hamlet is completely obsessed with his grief and anger, at which point, in Elizabethan terms, the habit or "aduston" of melancholy and choler would make him not only sad and angry but long in deliberation, full of doubts but obstinate once he has made up his mind, deceitful, and suspicious or fearful of others without factual basis, and so forth – all the symptoms of melancholy that scholars have made familiar to us because they seem to fit Hamlet at times (e.g. see excerpt from Bright in Hoy 110–11).

When Horatio and the soldiers enter at the conclusion of Hamlet's soliloquy in 1.2, it takes a moment for Hamlet to recognize his friend (160–1). Then as he greets Horatio we see that Hamlet's disposition as a noble prince and a friend is still strong. He is gracious to Horatio, interpreting generously his embarrassed answers about why he has come to Elsinore, inviting him to criticize Gertrude's behavior and then quickly confirming his friend's reply (163–83). Hamlet's response to the news that his father's spirit has appeared shows that in these circumstances he can make a quick resolution to act in a risky way. He immediately decides to join the watch that night, saying "If it assume my noble father's person, / I'll speak to it though hell itself should gape / And bid me hold my peace" (244–6). There is a note of bluster in this, as though Hamlet is rising to meet a challenge rather than expressing a resolution habitual to his character, but meeting a ghost is not the sort of challenge one accustoms oneself to meet. Hamlet is eager especially because in his frustration he finds it very reinforcing to take action that links him with his father and confirms his feeling that the world is corrupt (255–8).

As they wait that night for the ghost to appear, Horatio's question about the King's drinking is answered by Hamlet in terms that, as I suggested earlier, may apply to himself (1.4.12–38). Many critics have suggested this, of course, and sometimes the speech is interpreted as an explicit statement of something like a theory of the "tragic flaw." Interestingly, it becomes such a statement through the way it is only indirectly such a statement. That is, Hamlet is not explaining how "one defect" in a trait or habit causes the doom of men who are otherwise noble. Rather, his point is that such a flaw causes such men to suffer dishonor. Hamlet's disposition to be a noble prince causes such loss of nobility to be the kind of doom that moves him to feel the tragic qualm.

The Ghost appears, and Hamlet responds in fear, love, and awe, as we would expect on the basis of what we have seen of his characteristic dispositions. Hamlet rejects his companions' warnings of danger and follows the Ghost because he is strongly disposed both to be with his father and to think he has nothing to lose in dying (64–5). Hamlet may also be brave in his habitual character, but it takes more than habitual courage to follow a ghost into the midnight darkness.

In the next scene, once he understands that Claudius has murdered his father, Hamlet is eager to obey the call to revenge. His cry of "O my prophetic soul! My uncle!" (41), does not necessarily indicate that he has earlier suspected his uncle of murder, however. Each of Hamlet's responses to the Ghost before this line indicates more a questioning attitude than an eager suggestion that the Ghost should quickly confirm what he already thinks (7–8, 25–6, 29). Hamlet may speak of his prophetic soul thinking or wishing he had suspected his uncle of murder, or perhaps he means that his hatred of his uncle was an intuitive response to the man's villainous nature. "O my prophetic soul!" may refer specifically to his suspicion at the end of 1.2 that there has been "some foul play" (256). Foul play may be what was prophesied, and "My uncle!" may express a mixture of surprise and confirmation of an intuition that is reinforced because of his hatred.

Hatred of his uncle makes it very reinforcing for Hamlet to believe the Ghost and to accept the command to revenge (1.5.92–112). Hamlet's passionate tone here can be explained by his fierce hatred of Claudius, by the overwhelming nature of what he has just experienced, by his gladness to be released from frustration in having a noble deed to perform, and by his being able to act for his father. As a result of all these reinforcing consequences, Hamlet represses whatever doubts he might otherwise feel. Thus he is not consciously whipping himself into a vengeful rage. There is a highly theatrical quality to his reaching for hyperbole, his rhetorical questions and assertions, and in general the near-fustian quality of the entire speech. But I think this character, who is now so strongly disposed to nobility and honesty, will speak in such a hyperbolic way only if he is entirely absorbed in the feeling and its rhetoric. The speech is an immediate response to an overwhelming experience and he is in a state of vengeful rage from the start.

What Hamlet swears in this speech is to obey the Ghost's final injunction, "Remember me" (91). Both he and the Ghost mean that he should remember his father partly in order to remember to take revenge. Ironically, Hamlet keeps this vow and yet delays revenge: cognitive acts do not in themselves produce physical action. That Hamlet assumes a person simply does what he thinks to do is also suggested in his earlier asking the Ghost to tell him about his murder quickly so he can "sweep" to revenge "with wings as swift / As meditation or the thoughts of love"

(29–31). The irony here is very clear – Hamlet does sweep to his revenge on wings as swift as meditation; he does not yet realize that meditation and the thoughts of love can move slowly. The obviousness of this irony is a sign we should take the error into account as implying a question about the relation between thoughts and deeds.

In Hamlet's vow to think of nothing but the Ghost's command and to wipe out of his mind all he has ever learned, there is a danger he will become obsessed. In his excited state, Hamlet is strongly reinforced for thinking that absolute single-mindedness regarding his purpose is fitting. Such single-mindedness would not only be dangerous psychologically but also morally and practically in making him unable to gain perspective on what he is to do. However, Hamlet's vowing to think only of revenge is part of his excited hyperbole, and once his excitement passes, he can be expected to recover the disposition to reflect on his situation.

Until nearly the end of this scene Hamlet remains in an excited, almost hysterical state. The forceful assurance he gives Horatio and Marcellus that the Ghost is honest shows he continues to be powerfully reinforced for believing the Ghost's story. Hamlet's belief is actually strengthened by his past thinking, which he has *not* wiped away, including his own earlier hatred of his uncle. Indeed, Hamlet's phrasing suggests that he affirms the Ghost's honesty so forcefully in part because the Ghost has validated this hatred, though Hamlet does not indicate awareness of such a motive:

> HOR.   There's no offence, my lord.
> HAM.   Yes by Saint Patrick but there is, Horatio,
>   And much offence too. Touching this vision here,
>   It is an honest ghost, that let me tell you.
>   (141–4)

When Hamlet finally comes down from his state of excitement, his words suggest that his speech to the Ghost also helps to calm himself: "Rest, rest, perturbed spirit" (190). Following this he is more gracious to Horatio and Marcellus, more the friend he was in 1.2. As he begins to think less excitedly of what he has vowed to do, Hamlet's feeling about his mission changes: "The time is out of joint. O cursed spite, / That ever I was born to set it right" (1.5.196–7). He accepts the necessity of taking revenge but sees what he is to do as a vast and burdensome undertaking. This is a realistic perception, and so we can easily sympathize with him. These words may go far toward explaining the difficulty he experiences in bringing himself to kill Claudius.

It is just before Hamlet becomes calm that he tells Horatio and Marcellus that he may "put an antic disposition on" (1.5.180). As many critics have suggested, Hamlet may say this first of all because in the continuing excitement of his "wild and whirling words" he is already in an antic disposition (139). Whether he also has a purpose related to his revenge in saying this is uncertain, since he never explains why he puts on the antic disposition. To explain the behavior, then, we can look for the consequences that reinforce it, with the understanding that Hamlet may not be aware of all these. This understanding can help explain how Hamlet can say in his soliloquy at the end of Act 2 that he does not know why he has not yet killed Claudius. If he could see how the antic disposition interferes with turning himself toward revenge, he might be able to understand his delay.

Let us review the possible reinforcing consequences of the antic behavior, any of which Hamlet may think of as a purpose for it at some time. First, Hamlet may hope that the antic role will protect him, though its actual effect is to draw the King's questioning attention. Second, it may be Hamlet's intention to move the King in this way so that his reactions will reveal his guilt. Third, the King's indulgence of the antic humor may help to catch his conscience by disarming whatever suspicions he might otherwise have regarding Hamlet's staging a play about a royal murder. Fourth, the antic disposition enables Hamlet to feel detached from the Court and to evoke or expose folly, baseness, and treachery in Polonius, Rosencrantz, and Guildenstern. Thus the antic behavior enables Hamlet to manipulate and dominate his foes. It also enables him to speak freely though in a somewhat disguised manner what he really feels, perhaps functioning in this way as a safety-valve allowing him to express his deep bitterness in a form that is less aversive for him than the deep bitterness itself. In addition, the antic role gives Hamlet time to consider what to do, and hence also allows delay of a deed he may find aversive even if he feels strongly committed to doing it.

The antic role may be a way to avoid acting, but of course the antic role itself is an "act," and Hamlet's expressions of scorn in this role could cause him to become absorbed in this activity, tending to displace action as a revenger, a role that calls for using daggers rather than merely speaking them. In behaviorist terms, since the antic role does enable him to speak daggers, it would certainly be reinforced as a form of revenge, and absorption in it might be reinforced very strongly because it also enables him to avoid the aversive aspects of thinking about blood revenge.

Although the antic role is marked by an alienated detachment, this could be more a detachment from others than from self. It has often been suggested that Hamlet is an *eiron* who has a self-detachment enabling him to see himself well. If instead he becomes absorbed in the righteously alienated viewpoint of the antic role, he might see only those of his own faults that allow him to retain a fundamentally self-protective view of himself. The antic role gives Hamlet the impression that he has a detached, objective perspective on others, but this impression could be reinforced because it masks from himself a use of the role to confirm his worst suspicions of everyone. As mentioned earlier, since his feelings about Claudius and Gertrude strongly dispose him to see evil in anyone he links with them, Hamlet would find it reinforcing to interpret any strange responses of characters such as Polonius as evidence they are false to him. Revealing or finding evil in others could further arouse hatred in Hamlet, and his preoccupation with their evil could heighten any tendency in him toward self-righteousness, a tendency reinforced by self-esteem. The more detached and isolated from others he becomes, the less he would be able to engage in role-taking (taking others' points of view) or in fellow-feeling of the sort depending on the acknowledgement of faults or frailties similar to theirs in himself. Thus through playing this role, he might become increasingly suspicious and crafty, hostile and self-righteous, his penetrating intelligence narrowed so that although he expresses profound insights, he fails to consider matters of great importance adequately.

On the other hand, insofar as Hamlet is not absorbed in the antic role's viewpoint, the process of "acting" feelings that are partly sincere and partly "put on" could tend to blur his emotional reality for himself and turn him into one who self-consciously performs his emotions. In this sense Hamlet may become an actor: through putting on an antic disposition he may become less an antic than one who puts on. This would interfere with his ability to identify with any role, and hence help to explain his difficulty in becoming a revenger. But although a number of critics write that Hamlet needs to be able to fuse himself fully with the role of revenger, it is not clear that the play suggests this would be a desirable result either morally or psychologically or even practically. It seems more important for us to see whether Hamlet remains true to his noble character and whether he taints his mind in revenge (1.3.78, 1.5.85).

Turning from hypotheses about the antic disposition to the text, we should consider more specifically the shape of the antic behavior. Although the court thinks Hamlet is mad, we can take it for granted from his behavior when he is alone or with Horatio or the players that he is not simply insane in the sense of being out of touch with reality. Thus Hamlet is pretending to be mad when he seems to be unable to recognize Polonius or remember whether he has a daughter (2.2.174, 182). This episode also suggests an alternative interpretation which has frequently been offered, that Hamlet is not so much pretending to be insane as he is playing the Fool, using his reputation of madness as the Fool uses his reputation of natural "idiocy" as a mask preventing the others from fully understanding and taking offense at his pointed witticisms. I do not mean to suggest that Hamlet has a *playful* involvement with the antic disposition. Even when he may act as if he thinks he does, I think the text shows he is confined by his antic role in a bitterly narrow perspective.[7]

Statements of other characters describing the antic disposition give the impression that at least some of Hamlet's behavior is more mad than Foolish; in the behavior we actually see, on the other hand, Hamlet is more Fool than madman. The most bizarre conduct the audience sees is in 4.2 and 4.3. Then it is not entirely certain that Hamlet controls his behavior fully as he does such things as play hide-and-seek with Rosencrantz and Guildenstern and the others who are trying to make him tell where Polonius's body is. Hamlet's behavior in these scenes, however, comes too late to influence greatly our impression of the antic disposition.

In Act 2 Ophelia's description of his conduct in her chamber especially gives us an idea of the behavior which convinces other characters that he is mad (2.1.75–100). We cannot tell whether Hamlet controls this behavior as part of what he deliberately "puts on" in his antic role. His pallor suggests genuine feeling, but his disordered attire and knocking knees are more "playable." There is a strong expression of what troubles him in his "look so piteous in purport / As if he had been loosed out of hell / To speak of horrors" (82–4). These lines imply virtual identification with the Ghost and its mission, an obsession with "horrors" that is sickening Hamlet's thoughts and emotions. He expresses the depth of his anguish in a "sigh so piteous and profound / As it did seem to shatter all his bulk / And end his being" (94–6). Hamlet thus reveals to Ophelia something of what he cannot put into words for her, his preoccupation with horrors loosed from hell that he feels are ending his being. He is evidently reinforced for sharing his suffering with Ophelia as someone who will pity him. He would also be reinforced for inflicting pain upon her, since she has refused to see him and since his bitterness may now extend to her as a woman and hence frail.

It is clear, then, that Hamlet's conduct is not always and only foolery. During the period of the antic disposition, Hamlet's behavior from the outset has elements of both Fool and madman, as in the near hysteria from which it arose at the end of Act 1. In either of these modes the antic disposition would enable Hamlet to express his emotions in a way that is not well controlled while being reinforced by the thought that this behavior *is* under his control. The behavior is so strongly reinforced by its effect on the court that any thought which justifies it to himself and explains it as sane will also be strongly reinforced: I must be in control of this behavior because I know I am putting it on: "I essentially am not in madness, / But mad in craft" (3.4.189–90). Hamlet means he only pretends to be mad, but he lacks control of this claim itself, since he does not intend the ironic meaning that he may indeed become mad in craftiness, enjoying the "sport" he finds in plot and counter-plot.

We first see Hamlet put on the antic manner in his dialogue with Polonius in 2.2. Hamlet plays the Fool as he says that Polonius is a fishmonger: the joke is that Polonius thinks Hamlet is too mad to recognize him and does not see he is being called a whoremaster (174). But in the light of Hamlet's recent behavior, even a lesser fool than Polonius might think that Hamlet is mad. Indeed, most of Polonius's responses here simply reflect his presumption of Hamlet's madness: if Hamlet says something sane, Polonius can only respond that "Though this be madness, yet there is method in't" (205–6). Polonius has learned to think a certain way and is therefore reinforced for interpreting whatever happens as confirming what he thinks.

But is not something like this occurring in Hamlet's thinking, too? He presumes that Polonius is a fool, and he is strongly reinforced for thinking that the old man's responses merely confirm this conviction (219). For another example, when Hamlet later induces him to say that a cloud is shaped like a camel and a weasel and a whale, Polonius must think he is humoring a madman. Yet Hamlet manipulates Polonius's responses to confirm that he is a fool (3.2.367–75). Each man finds it reinforcing to think himself intelligent and the other mad or foolish, and each is partly right, partly wrong. Hamlet's tone with Polonius in 2.2 suggests that he finds it very reinforcing to give full credit to his wit as the cause of his triumph. Since it would be aversive for Hamlet to see how truly mad he has seemed or to acknowledge any validity in Polonius's point of view, he does not do the role-taking that could enable him to see how his earlier mad conduct affects Polonius's responses.

At the end of this dialogue, Hamlet expresses a death-wish when he says he would not part with anything more willingly than Polonius, "except my life, except my life, except my life" (215–17). Hamlet's feeling about Polonius may partly prompt him to say at this moment that he wishes to die. "These tedious old fools" (219) inhabit the unweeded garden of Hamlet's world and add to his weary despair of life (1.2.133–5). Ironically, insofar as Hamlet is responsible for the mode of his dialogue with Polonius, he is himself the creator of the tediousness. Hamlet's antic behavior contributes to the folly and falseness he rails against in the antic role, so that a vicious circle is created in which he is increasingly alienated and less able to see how he partly causes what he sees as contemptible in others. The more he scorns them, the more he will find it reinforcing to see that he is right to scorn them. This in turn will make it progressively less likely that he will be disposed to see that their behavior with him is in part shaped by his own behavior.

We see this pattern develop further in Hamlet's following dialogue with Rosencrantz and Guildenstern. These friends of his (and Hamlet himself insists that they have been good friends: 2.2.224, 284–6) have been told that Hamlet is mad, and so far as they know, the only purpose of the King and Queen in sending them to Hamlet is to help him recover by finding out what is troubling him (2.2.1–39). There is no hint here that they think of themselves as the King's spies: this is Hamlet's inference and it is important to see how he arrives at it. In the first part of their dialogue he expresses a gladness to see them and a willingness to engage in witty repartee, yet they are aware he receives them "with much forcing of his disposition" and with what appears to them a "crafty madness" through which he evades their inquiries (3.1.12, 8). Hamlet's first greeting seems to express surprise as well as friendliness, and when they respond with witty remarks on their relation to Fortune, he continues the dialogue at the level of banter about the parts of Fortune instead of bringing them closer as friends by asking more personal questions (2.2.224–36). Soon we hear the main tone of the antic voice in the bitterly wise wit of his melancholy assertions that Fortune is a strumpet, that if the world is becoming honest doomsday must be near, that the world and especially Denmark are prisons, and that the seeming great of the world are but the outstretched shadows of beggars (235–65).

In the midst of this, Hamlet explains that the reason he sees Denmark as a prison is that his thinking has made it so (249–51). In saying this, Hamlet implies that the cause of his suffering is more in his mind than in the facts of his situation, distorting if not falsifying what he believes. He again implies that his problem is only in his melancholy state when he says he suffers from "bad dreams" and not from thwarted ambition (254–6). Clearly Hamlet holds his friends at arm's length, concealing the true causes of his griefs. Yet he suddenly demands that they "deal justly" with him and "be even and direct" in answer to his question about whether they were sent for by the King and Queen (276, 287). Because they hesitate so long in answering this question, he begins to think of them as being on the King's side and against him (290–1, 294–5). There is no sign he takes into account that his supposed madness, his forcing his disposition, and his failure to be even and direct have made it difficult for them to be even and direct.

Hamlet sees himself from his own point of view, as a sane person justified in self-concealment and suspicions of others, and his righteous tone suggests that he does not take their role in order to observe himself from their point of view. Hamlet himself needs what he expects the players to provide for the King and Queen, a mirror to be held up so he can see all the features of his antic behavior that so strongly influence others' responses to him. He creates the impression that he is mad, but evidently expects his friends to respond to him as a normal person. Rosencrantz and Guildenstern do not know what to expect or how to deal with a friend who is mad, and it is reasonable to infer that they should be played as anxious in their repartee from the start.

If Hamlet errs here, the error is a main cause of the deaths of Rosencrantz and Guildenstern, so let us look more closely at the evidence that Hamlet judges them unfairly. When he asks if they were sent for, his choice of words in asking them to "deal justly" implies that he will regard an acknowledgement that they were sent for as a confession (2.2.274–6). This makes it difficult for them to answer honestly, and as they hesitate to speak, he says their looks confess that they were sent for, implying that this fact taints their friendship (278–9). In addition, Hamlet apologizes so strenuously for the poverty of his thanks for their visit that they may find what he says unconvincing (272–4). If the Prince were to take the role of these two "indifferent children of the earth" (227), he might not speak of himself as a beggar. Moreover, there is a sarcastic thrust at them in his remark that "sure, dear friends, my thanks are too dear a halfpenny" (273–4). Although this may mean his thanks are of little worth, the words imply that even such thanks are too good for them if they were sent for. Addressing them as "dear friends" in the midst of all this can make Hamlet seem an insincere friend himself, and he is surely dishonest if he exaggerates the closeness of their friendship to coerce them to be honest: "by the rights of our fellowship, by the consonancy of our youth, by the obligation of our ever-preserved love . . ." (284–7).

Rosencrantz and Guildenstern's responses to Hamlet's questions show they have been put on the defensive and are uncertain how to answer. They do not lie: "To visit you, my lord, no other occasion" is not a lying answer to his question "what make you at Elsinore?" (270–1). The answer equivocates about whether they were sent for, but they do finally acknowledge that they were (269–92). They are only as false to Hamlet as he is to them in not being "even and direct." Their reluctance to be more direct can perhaps be largely explained by the nature of the truth: they believe he is mad and they want to help his family cure him. Alas, Rosencrantz and Guildenstern "have not craft enough to colour" their discomfort (280), nor Hamlet, absorbed in his craft, enough perspective to interpret their discomfort justly: "there is nothing either good or bad but thinking makes it so" (249–50). The result is truly tragic, for Hamlet's disposition to be concerned for honesty and loyalty is what heightens the crafty wariness of his antic attitude so that his perception is severely narrowed.

As the scene continues, Hamlet behaves in a friendly manner with Rosencrantz and Guildenstern, but this manner appears to mask a preoccupation with his private concerns. In the dialogue about the players,

Hamlet immediately hints at the reason why he warms to this topic: "He that plays the king shall be welcome" (318). A little later he commiserates with the boy actors because they are required to "exclaim against their own succession" (349). Also, he compares the triumph of the boys over the adult actors to Claudius's succeeding his father in the affections of the people (357–64). When he then formally welcomes Rosencrantz and Guildenstern to Elsinore, the terms he uses suggest more concern for social propriety than a wish to be truly a friend (366–71). Next he hints that his madness is not real, but his words about hawks and handsaws are mystifyingly antic enough to confuse his friends and perhaps even to make them think he is mad (372–5). The hint that he merely feigns madness is probably lost completely when he then plays the antic strongly for Polonius.

Hamlet again lays aside his antic manner when he welcomes the players and asks for a recital of Aeneas's narrative of the revenge slaying of Priam. As the First Player performs, the text does not indicate whether Hamlet's conscience as a revenger is caught, or whether he sees how Gertrude's conscience might be caught by the grief of Hecuba for her slain husband. However, when he stops the Player, he comments on how the theater reflects the realities of the time, and he sets in motion the use of a play to catch the conscience of the King (519–36). This suggests that in his request for a recital about Priam's slaying, Hamlet continues to be preoccupied with his own situation.

When Hamlet is alone a few lines later, he does not respond directly to the grief of Hecuba or to the ruthless action of the revenger, but to the passion of the actor. Hamlet may seem to say it is "monstrous" that the Player has been moved so greatly by the "force" of a mere "conceit" in a fiction (545–54), but I think the context of these words suggests that this is not his real point. In saying that the actor forces his soul to his conceit and thereby produces emotion, Hamlet says no more than writers on rhetoric and poetry said about the power of vivid language to move a speaker, as explained in Chapter 1. What Hamlet finds monstrous is that he himself has not been moved even though he has great personal cause, and the monstrosity of this is especially revealed through comparison with the actor, who is moved by a mere fiction. This comparison, and the self-judgment it prompts Hamlet to make, is indicated at the start of this speech, as he begins to speak of the actor: "O what a rogue and peasant slave am I! / Is it not monstrous that this player here . . ." (544–5). Hamlet uses the comparison to lash himself with thoughts of how the actor would be moved to an amazing height of passion if he had cause for revenge, while he, Hamlet, has been dull and muddy-mettled, peaking like John-a-Dreams (561–4). Hamlet attacks himself vehemently because doing so is less aversive than failing to oppose his shameful state. That is, because he is strongly disposed to be noble, he feels guilty, which makes it negatively reinforcing for him to punish himself.

When Hamlet asks himself what has caused him to delay his revenge, all he thinks of is cowardice, but he *asks* if he is a coward: he speaks of cowardice as what "must" be holding him back, since he has failed to act, not as what he knows he has felt (566–76). This invites us to try to see for ourselves why he has delayed, and, needless to say, critics have offered many possible explanations, usually explanations suggested by the whole pattern of his action in the play. In my reading, the speech suggests that the psychology of acting helps to account for Hamlet's delay and his inability to explain it to himself.

The key to this idea is to see how Hamlet has not so completely differed from the actor as he thinks he has. I have argued that Hamlet is absorbed in his antic role and that this absorption could tend to displace the thoughts that might lead to his taking revenge.[8] In effect, there has been a re-shaping of vengeful behavior into the expression of hostile suspicions and witty verbal attacks that are reinforced strongly because they punish his foes and avoid more aversively bitter thoughts about his dreadful situation. Since he is making his foes suffer, an act of blood revenge can seem less urgent except when he stops to reflect. He can think and speak hatefully, but the role in which he does this is not one that leads to plotting and acting revenge. While Hamlet is absorbed in the antic role, he cannot see the full effect of the role on himself: "Am I a coward?" (566).

It is not true, then, that Hamlet has failed to act; he has acted, but more as an actor than in acts leading to violent revenge. What an actor actually does and does not do points to another aspect of Hamlet's relation to the actor that he does not seem to see. When he speaks of what the actor would "do" if he had a revenge motive, he seems to mean that the actor would do terrifying deeds, but all he literally says is that the actor would display great emotion. Actors emote and they speak daggers, but the theatrical mode of action does not include actual stabbing. This may imply that any role undertaken in an actorly way will not lead to "real" action even if strong emotion is felt. Condemning himself for not being like the actor, Hamlet suggests the way he is like the actor in asserting that he "can say nothing" (564), as if speaking is what is demanded of him. Of course he means that he cannot even say anything against the evils he sees, let alone do anything. If he saw the opposite irony, that he has said a great deal, he would attack himself for it at this point, rather than later in the speech when he does see it. In this again he shows how absorbed he is in his own conceit as he does not see how he is like the actor in the way his conceit moves his soul to "say" much in a great outpouring of passion.

It is sometimes suggested that in this soliloquy Hamlet attempts to whip himself into a passion so he can "put on" the revenger role. But in concentrating on how he is unlike the actor, Hamlet does not suggest that he thinks he is imitating the actor in his passion. Indeed, nothing Hamlet says suggests he has the deliberate intention of working himself into a vengeful passion, and in such a passionate tirade, what is said expresses what is felt and thought unless there are indications to the contrary. It is true that his expression of rage is reinforced because it works up his hatred of Claudius, but if Hamlet were *thinking* of working himself into a vengeful passion, he would likely emphasize his reasons to hate his foe more than he does. He does mention early in his self-condemnation that a "damn'd defeat was made" upon his father, but the passive construction implies that his anger even in saying this is not immediately directed against the agent of this damnable act (566), and following this for several lines his anger is entirely directed against himself. At this moment Hamlet's thought and feeling are turned away from pursuing revenge because, ironically, thoughts about his failure to take revenge absorb him in an expression of shame that threatens to perpetuate the failure it reacts against.

Hamlet expresses his shame by imagining someone insulting him as a nobleman might mock a coward. If this shows that Hamlet is especially concerned about how others judge him, it may suggest that his self-condemnation is not fully internalized. It seems clear, however, that the person who insults Hamlet is Prince Hamlet himself. Up to this point, the text gives no hint that anyone else alive knows he has any reason for such shame. Thus he evidently attributes his view of himself and his ideals of noble action to an imaginary interlocutor (his father?) in order to punish himself severely for his shameful inaction. In the process of condemning himself, Hamlet finally states what he has failed to do, and so his anger is more or less automatically directed against Claudius, too (574–7). But immediately he rejects such passionately vengeful verbal assaults as inappropriate (578–83) – another likely indication that he has not been intentionally whipping himself up into such a passion thinking that it would move him toward revenge.

Hamlet's reason for rejecting his passionate speech is not that he thinks his emotion is like an actor's and hence invalid and unlikely to lead to action. Instead, he continues to focus on how his behavior is shameful, saying he has been "like a whore" in unpacking his heart with words (581–3). Hamlet's repetition of base terms for prostitutes implies that he means they are base, weak people who curse their lot but do not change what they do, and he thinks that his cursing shows him to be like them, that his cursing will not lead to action. Thus Hamlet does not consciously relate his rejection of unpacking his heart with words to his ideas about the actor, does not think he has behaved like an actor. He has not been

markedly histrionic here in an unconscious sense, either. He has the motive
and the cue for the passion he expresses in the soliloquy and is not responding with emotions in excess of what his whole situation provokes.
All the world's a stage at this moment especially in the sense that Hamlet
as the tragic character he is – and is becoming – feels and thinks in a way
that absorbs him in a perspective preventing him from seeing fully how
this very absorption affects him.

Hamlet rejects his passion when his guilt and shame, which first turned
him toward passion, turn him away from passion as itself shameful. There
is psychological complexity here, as Hamlet first responds to the actor
and then to his own response to the actor. A secondary cause of Hamlet's
rejection of passion may be that the strong expression of a behavior causes
it to weaken so that another becomes prepotent and replaces it. Or in
Elizabethan terms, perhaps Hamlet has expended his passion so that he
only has the energy needed to *think* of what he should do (cf. 3.2.191–2,
4.7.113–17).

As Hamlet withdraws from absorption in passion into cool thinking,
he examines his idea of using "The Murder of Gonzago" to catch the
conscience of the King. As many critics have suggested, it may be that
Hamlet no sooner finishes condemning himself for having delayed
revenge than he finds a rationalization for further delay. This view does
not depend on his rationale for the delay being a poor one; rather, even
if a rationale is sound, it is a rationalization if it is in part reinforced as
an avoidance of behavior that would be aversive. Yet our suspicion that
Hamlet rationalizes should be tempered by relief that he has thought to
raise the question whether he can trust the Ghost's word, and hence for
the first time moves toward a resolution of the moral issues concerning
the revenge (2.2.594–600).

Interpreters often assume that delay is bad, if not because it prevents
revenge, then because for Elizabethans it was a sign that Hamlet has a
weak character. However, most writers in the tradition I have reviewed
say furious anger, not delay, is a weakness and they recommend delay in
order to gain time to cool off and think better about what to do – even if
revenge is still to be pursued as a result of careful thinking. Some writers
recommend almost any rationale or rationalization to prevent angry,
unthinking revenge.[9] Thus although in the *Nicomachean Ethics* Aristotle
recommends a moderate anger that can be controlled by reason to carry
out forceful actions such as revenge (1125b–6b, 1149a–b), most writers
thought anger is difficult to restrain, that it tends to become immoderate
and take control from reason.

Seneca writes on the danger of injustice to others in anger because in
that emotional state we defend harsh judgments and resist any evidence

or thought opposed to our hostility ("On Anger" bk 1, ch. 18, sec. 1–2; ch. 19, sec. 1). In anger a person acts rashly, meaning in haste and without due consideration. In his essay on "How One Ought to Governe His Will," Montaigne especially condemns angry, rash action as lacking discretion and therefore being ineffective, but he too couples angry indiscretion with injustice, and this second fault of rashness is important in the long tradition of writings on this subject (3:259; cf. Plutarch "On the Control" 458c–60c). Hamlet makes an issue of rashness by going against the traditional view and praising it as having assisted him in sending Rosencrantz and Guildenstern to death (5.2.6–11). The issue is whether rash "indiscretion" does serve him well when he judges others, or whether his anger makes it reinforcing for him to condemn those he thinks are evil on the basis of inadequate evidence.

In his exposition of the Sermon on the Mount, Augustine writes of rashness as the sin of condemning others for the mote in their eye while ignoring the beam in one's own eye. He says that "those parties especially judge rashly respecting things that are uncertain, and readily find fault, who love rather to censure and to condemn than to amend and to improve, which is a fault arising either from pride or from envy . . ." (bk 2, ch. 19, sec. 63). If anger is of long duration, it hardens into hatred, and then a person "cannot wish to convert" his foe (sec. 63). When men who hate reprove evil in others, "they are acting a part which does not belong to them; just like hypocrites, who conceal under a mask what they are, and show themselves off in a mask what they are not" (sec. 64). Especially troublesome are those "who, while they take up complaints against all kinds of faults from hatred and spite, also wish to appear counsellors." And then follows a passage which scholars think Shakespeare might well have drawn on for important statements on this theme in *Measure for Measure*:

> And therefore we must piously and cautiously watch, so that when necessity shall compel us to find fault with or rebuke any one, we may reflect first whether the fault is such as we have never had, or one from which we have now become free; and if we have never had it, let us reflect that we are men, and might have had it; but if we have had it, and are now free from it, let the common infirmity touch the memory, that not hatred but pity may go before that fault-finding or administering of rebuke. . . . (Sec. 64)

Jesus's statement that how we judge others determines how God will judge us means that the "very same rashness wherewith you punish another must necessarily punish yourself" (ch. 18, sec. 62).

Hamlet's behavior repeatedly invites comparison with Augustine's hate-filled reprover who does not see how his hatred compromises the integrity of his view of others and who is finally punished through his own rashness. In Act 3 his preaching as "Virtue" to his mother's "Vice" while he stands unrepentant over the body of a man he has rashly killed may be an instance of reproving another for evil while disregarding a greater evil of one's own. I will especially argue that Augustine's ideas about rashness help to explain the psychology of Hamlet's dooming Rosencrantz and Guildenstern and how he is then killed when he judges Laertes to be like himself and a noble youth.

In considering Hamlet's soliloquy at the end of Act 2, however, my main point about rashness is that the dangers of indiscretion probably justify Hamlet's delay. But the dangers of indiscretion are also manifest in the thinking Hamlet does when he cools off in this soliloquy and speaks of his scheme for using "The Murder of Gonzago." He speaks more coolly, but his hatred for Claudius is still at a peak. In wanting to test the conscience of the King, Hamlet thinks well insofar as it is true that the Ghost might be a devil lying to him in order to tempt him to murder. But Hamlet does not think of the corollary to this that Elizabethans would easily have thought of, that the devil can tell truths to tempt us to evil – as Macbeth learns, for example. Even if his uncle is guilty, it may be damnable for Hamlet to kill him, especially if this is done as a hate-filled act of private revenge and not as a political act to displace a regicide from the throne.

Hamlet's failure to think this through can be explained as avoidance. In the first part of the soliloquy he reaches a passionate conviction that he must take revenge, and he has a scheme to allay his anxiety that he might damn himself. But his hatred of Claudius makes it reinforcing to think in a biased way: he says not that he will test the conscience of the King, but that he will "catch" it – he speaks as if he has already found the King guilty (2.2.601). Claudius needs only to flinch at the sight of a staged murder to doom himself (593). When Hamlet is thus disposed it would be aversive for him to consider further whether his scheme will really resolve the moral question about revenge. Now, especially, when he has felt great shame for taking no action, and when his hatred of Claudius has been roused to a peak of intensity, it will be reinforcing to think only of actions which clearly lead to revenge or clearly end the need for revenge. He feels good about this resolution of his dilemma, and it would arouse great anxiety to think that his scheme may fail in some way.

This reading does not preclude the possibility that while Hamlet is strongly disposed to *think* here that he wants to take revenge, the plan he has hit upon is reinforced also because it rationalizes avoiding revenge. The strong conscious desire to kill Claudius may thus co-exist with factors tending to cause Hamlet not to kill him. Hamlet may have a revulsion against killing, he may hate the thought of the whole sordid business, he may fear failure and death, or death as a result of killing, as he evidently fears damnation. And he may delay because he unconsciously identifies Oedipally with his uncle.

In the "To be or not to be" soliloquy, Hamlet is still in the relatively calm if intensely absorbed state that marked the end of the 2.2 soliloquy. Just before Hamlet begins to speak in 3.1, we learn that Claudius, the villain, has a conscience which functions in a straightforward way, causing him pain when he is reminded of his guilt (49–54). Hamlet, however, questions the value of conscience by arguing that it prevents the enactment of important undertakings (56–88). This contrast of course does not show that the villain has a better conscience than the protagonist, but it raises an interesting question about how to compare them. The King's speech may mostly serve to show that a suffering conscience is no guarantee of moral behavior and so prepare us to accept Hamlet's probing toward a more sophisticated view of conscience in the soliloquy.

Because this soliloquy has been interpreted in many ways, it will help to provide a summary of what I think is the most obvious way to read the surface meaning of the speech, as a basis for further discussion.[10] Ostensibly, the question is whether to live or die, and the criterion for the answer is which is nobler if to live is to suffer life's torments passively and to die is to fight against myriad evils and be killed in the unequal contest against the King (56–60). Hamlet finds death desirable so long as he can think of it as a peaceful state of dreamless sleep (60–4). He is perhaps too absorbed in his reverie to think of the Ghost (78–80), but perhaps Hamlet's experience with that spirit evokes the thought that death can be a state of nightmare torment (65–8). The fear of this torment is all that keeps us from committing suicide to escape life's pains (66–83). Thus conscience makes cowards of us all by making us fear punishment for suicide or for carrying out "enterprises of great pitch and moment" such as "taking arms" against a foe. The resolution to act is sickened into pallid thinking about the possible consequences of our actions (83–8).

Although Hamlet's judgment of conscience is negative, it may arise from a more honest conscience than most. Hamlet acknowledges that he longs to escape the evils of the world and that he refrains from suicide or revenge not because he feels they are morally wrong, but because such acts may be punished after death. In this Hamlet is honest about his conscience, saying he does not deeply accept its moral judgments, yet is afraid to disobey it. Hamlet errs, however, in saying that fear makes "us all" obey conscience. Since Claudius has just mentioned his conscience, we note that it has not kept him from doing evil, and various enterprises proceed apace in Hamlet's world undaunted by conscience.

Indeed, Hamlet reveals here a more potent conscience than most. Although his frustration may make it reinforcing to condemn his conscience as mere cowardice, he says he has felt compelled to obey it. His concern not to cause his own damnation is serious, for he has referred to it in each of his major soliloquies, in 1.2, at the end of 2.2, and again here. Originally this concern may have been an opportune rationalization to justify the avoidance of deeds – suicide or revenge – he could not bring himself to perform for other reasons. But in order to work as a rationalization, this concern had to be believable to Hamlet as an intention. Therefore as an intention it can act as a rule guiding his behavior as long as it and the behavior it guides continue to be reinforced. There may be another rationalization here, too. Torn between his nobility and his morality, Hamlet's saying all humans suffer his malaise lets him see his problem as a general one he should not blame himself for too much.

Perhaps Hamlet is both drawn to and diverted from taking revenge because it will lead to his death: drawn to revenge because it will lead to death as escape (60), diverted from it if this makes him see revenge as a form of suicide and hence a cause of damnation. Also, he may think of a mode of revenge that will result in his death (taking arms against a sea of troubles), because suicidal behavior – not including consciously suicidal thoughts – is strongly reinforced even when he intends to think of a revenge action. In this sense suicide may be a theme from the very beginning of the speech, and it can be linked with Hamlet's desire for nobility, which is also expressed in the heroic imagery of taking arms against a sea of troubles.

The strength of noble thoughts for Hamlet can perhaps especially be seen in his discounting conscience as mere cowardice. His disposition to be concerned about integrity and virtue suggests that he would usually value conscience, but when behavior that violates his conscience is strongly reinforced as noble, his thinking alters. Hamlet illustrates very richly the way thought and action can change with changing circumstances and with changes in the behavior that is prepotent.

A psychological analysis should also take into account Hamlet's agony of soul in this soliloquy. Conscience in the sense of "consciousness" achieves a victory here as Hamlet is able to open his eyes wide to the painful conditions of human life as he sees them. Even if he has unknowingly made his world seem worse to him than it is, he shows the tragic figure's capacity to question deeply and to suffer heroically. Hamlet exemplifies Marsilio Ficino's tragic conception of Promethean man, great in his intellectual capacity, but in his use of intellect "uncertain, vacillating, and distressed," "made wretched by the . . . most ravenous of vultures, that is, by the torment of inquiry" (208).

This is the first of two scenes in which Hamlet speaks a monologue while another character seems to be praying (cf. 3.3). Comparison of the two speeches leads to the question of why Hamlet no longer thinks of fears of damnation in the prayer scene. The scene with Ophelia that follows the "To be or not to be" soliloquy is also paralleled in the scene with his mother that follows the prayer scene. Comparison of Hamlet's bitter attacks on Ophelia and Gertrude strengthens the impression that his disposition toward his mother at least partly shapes his response to Ophelia: "Frailty, thy name is woman" (1.2.146). Hamlet does not attack Ophelia only because he is bitter at his mother, however. Ophelia returns his love-tokens, and he shows that this hurts him when he replies by denying he has ever given her anything (3.1.93–6). This reply hurts Ophelia, and her response appears to be an effort to retaliate, since she says he has proved "unkind" (97–102). Then this speech of Ophelia's, in turn, may well evoke Hamlet's attack, which begins immediately in his line "Ha, ha! Are you honest?" (103). He may think she is dishonest because she accuses him of being unkind when she is the one who ended their courtship, or because he senses the falseness of her pose of religious devotion when she has brought all the tokens he has given her and has a self-righteous couplet ready that rhymes her "noble mind" with his having proved "unkind" (100–1).

Hamlet's feelings toward his mother and Ophelia heighten each other here. His mother's behavior has disposed him to be angry at all women as frail, and hence to be reinforced for attacking them. Then he is hurt by Ophelia's rejection and angered by her dishonesty, which in turn may make him think more specifically of his mother. Thinking of his mother presumably increases his anger, and it evidently contributes greatly to the specific things he says – many of his particular accusations seem to be much more strongly evoked by his mother's conduct than Ophelia's (esp. 111–15, 136–51). Thus Hamlet and Ophelia at first attack each other in a vicious circle of hurt provoking greater hurt, and Hamlet's bitterness toward his mother feeds his responses to Ophelia and is fed by Ophelia's responses to him, so that his attack is savagely in excess of anything Ophelia has done to provoke him.

Insofar as Ophelia's rejection hurts Hamlet, it appears not only that he loved her once, as he says at one point (115), but also that he still feels love for her. In telling her to go to a nunnery, he intends to help her escape from corruption and from the evil he feels welling up in himself (121–31). Although "nunnery" could mean "brothel" here as part of his attack on Ophelia, the context each time he uses this word suggests that she should go to the nunnery to *escape* from evil. Hamlet is profoundly ambivalent toward Ophelia here: he knows their love cannot survive what is to happen, and he is bitter at his mother, Ophelia, and himself for complicity in creating their hopeless situation. Indeed, his attack on Ophelia may be an expression of ambivalence, since it may partly be reinforced as behavior that will end her love for him and so lessen her suffering as well as his for the loss of their love. Hamlet's behavior can be reinforced both by this consequence and by the hurt inflicted on Ophelia.

This analysis of why Hamlet unleashes his tirade against Ophelia obviates the need to assume that at some point he realizes they are being spied upon: if Ophelia's behavior seems dishonest to him, he may infer on this basis that they are being watched. But does Hamlet behave as though he thinks they are being watched? Does he shape his attack to create a certain impression on an audience, perhaps the usual impression that he is mad? The evidence that he tries to affect a hidden audience more directly, such as his reference to his vengefulness and the statement that one who is married will not live, can instead be used to argue that he is *not* aware of having a hidden audience, since these lines betray his secret purpose (125, 150). But the crucial point is that if Hamlet pretends at all, this does not prevent his becoming caught up in an emotional tirade. In this scene he is first so absorbed in his meditation that he does not notice Ophelia; then when he does notice her, he is drawn from his meditative mood into a nearly hysterical state, and he remains at this pitch of intensity until just before his exit.

Hamlet's instructions to the actors and his dialogue with Horatio in 3.2 show that when he is not with those who provoke his passion or evoke his antic role he is capable of normal behavior. He may especially urge the players to hold the mirror up to nature in their acting (1–35) because their performance must be natural enough to catch the conscience of the King by mirroring his guilty image. Although Hamlet is moved in expressing his admiration and affection to Horatio, his emotion is not unbalanced and it subsides immediately when he begins to explain his purpose for staging "The Murder of Gonzago" (54–87). Hamlet is presumably moved to praise Horatio as a man who is not passion's slave partly in response to the pain of his own passionate behavior. Yet, whatever regret he feels for his passion does not seem to include regret that it has most recently hurt Ophelia. He plays cruelly with her feelings as part of his antic performance for the court following this dialogue with Horatio (108–49). Telling Horatio that "I must be idle" as the others enter (90), Hamlet indicates that he quite deliberately puts on the antic disposition, yet his wit has a hectic quality suggesting he is caught up in the excitement of his expectation of triumph over Claudius. In this excitement he finds it especially reinforcing to gloat in the power of his wit to make everyone squirm, and Ophelia is easy for him to victimize.

Hamlet identifies the murderer in the play-within-the-play as the "nephew to the King" (3.2.239). In some interpretations this reveals that

Hamlet unconsciously identifies with Claudius as the murderer who killed his father. This is possible, but there are also more immediate causes to consider. Hamlet now thinks that he wants to kill the King and so may speak in a way that identifies himself with the murderer of the King because it would be reinforcing for him to kill King Claudius, and he may not notice the import of his words if it would be aversive for him to see that he reveals his purpose. He can be unaware that he identifies himself as the murderer, for his statement about the murderer's identity is evidently a fact in "The Murder of Gonzago," and he need only see this to explain his behavior to himself. Further, his excitement and his hatred could make frightening the King so reinforcing that Hamlet blurts out these words without noticing how they undermine his avowed purpose in staging the play by making it uncertain whether the King's emotional response to the play is guilt or fear.

Once again it is also possible that Hamlet, without being aware of it, recoils from killing the King, so that the statement that the murderer is the nephew of the King is reinforced because it warns Claudius of the threat Hamlet poses. Since Hamlet thinks he wants to kill the King, however, he would find it aversive to think he recoils from the deed, so awareness of this will likely be repressed. Saying the murderer is the nephew of the King may then be reinforced because frightening the King is one kind of revenge still possible for Hamlet. According to this view Hamlet is ambivalent: two opposed behaviors are strong in him, to revenge and not to revenge, and each controls what he says and does in some degree.

Others in the court think the play threatens or falsely accuses Claudius, and the only reason Hamlet can be so sure of his interpretation of Claudius's reaction is that he knows what others do not, that the play mirrors the Ghost's story. But this suggests that Hamlet's interpretation is at least partly based on a prejudgment and on his hatred of the King which makes it reinforcing for him to find confirmation of the King's guilt. Horatio's agreement with Hamlet's view might show that the King's reaction is unambiguously a guilty one except that Hamlet has shared his knowledge and his prejudgment with his friend. Horatio is not embroiled in Hamlet's personal passions, but he has the same "reasons" to see the King as guilty. To Horatio, as to Hamlet, the King's reaction to the play itself is the thing to watch and there is no reason to relate Hamlet's remark about the nephew of the King to the moment of testing the King's con- science. When the King reacts strongly to the murder, Hamlet and Horatio therefore see no reason to doubt that his reaction is guilt and not fear, or horror that Hamlet should falsely accuse him of so awful a crime. Yet the courtiers who are ignorant of the Ghost's "facts" and Hamlet's reason to focus on the play by itself will interpret the episode as a whole, so that

Hamlet's remarks about the play appear to convey his purpose for staging it. The play scene shows how much our responses to events depend on complex contingencies of character, situation, and point of view.

Although Hamlet's situation may lead him to err about the King's re-action to the play, the King is nevertheless guilty and presumably should be punished. But Hamlet's thinking about Claudius also affects his think-ing about others, and his actions against them are not so justified. His treatment of Rosencrantz and Guildenstern here seems especially erring. Between 2.2 and late in the play scene, they have reported their observa-tions of Hamlet to the King and Queen (3.1.1–28), but in that episode there is no sign they are evil spies or that their report is not intended to help the King and Queen cure their friend. Rosencrantz and Guildenstern think Hamlet is suffering from melancholy and hence needs to be helped by friends in a manipulative way,[11] and nothing the King and Queen say to them suggests any motive other than to restore Hamlet to health.

The dialogue of Rosencrantz and Guildenstern with Hamlet following the play-within-the-play shows how tragedy arises from mutual mis-understanding. Hamlet thinks he has proven the King's guilt, and in his excitement he does not seem to understand that his friends think he has threatened to kill the King instead (as they say in 3.3.8–23). Their speeches to Hamlet have a tone of impatience and rebuke. In the first part of the dialogue, Guildenstern's impatience gradually increases as Hamlet inter-rupts with what his friend can only perceive as irresponsible wit (3.2.289–310). Guildenstern feels that Hamlet has behaved outrageously and he dares to be openly critical of these interruptions (300–1, 306–10). On his side, Hamlet is offended by his friends' manner and by their taking what appears to be the King's point of view. Unable to see the possible alter-native causes of his friends' conduct, Hamlet evidently infers betrayal. This inference would be reinforced because it fits his earlier suspicions of them and his general view that all at court are corrupt.

The episode reaches its crisis when Rosencrantz half-exasperatedly and half-imploringly says "My lord, you once did love me" (326). But it is too late – Hamlet now interprets everything by his inference that his old friends have betrayed him (327–63). What seems a sincere if desperate and pathetically ill-timed plea for Hamlet to let his friends help him evokes a response that they are only trying to trap him and to play upon him. Guildenstern's last effort to reach Hamlet is "O my lord, if my duty be too bold, my love is too unmannerly" (339–40). This statement expresses the traditional idea that an honest friend or courtier who loves his prince should tell him boldly but courteously when he does wrong and should seek to help him improve his conduct (Castiglione 297; bk 4). The state-ment is certainly not too hard to explicate for a person of Hamlet's wit – Guildenstern claims that he has been doing his duty and that if he has been too bold in doing it, he is motivated by his love of Hamlet, which transcends mere courtesy and custom. Hamlet's response epitomizes the tragic theme of the scene: "I do not well understand that" (341). When Polonius enters, once again there is mutual misunderstanding caused partly by Hamlet's absorption in his own point of view. As explained earlier, Hamlet thinks he shows Polonius to be a fool by playing the Fool while Polonius evidently thinks of himself as humoring a madman (367–76). Hamlet remarks that these men are pushing him to the extremity of the role of Fool (375), but once again his absorption in the narrow viewpoint of his antic disposition, coupled with his excited and threatening behavior, contributes to the folly of what happens.

Thus Hamlet is tightly enclosed in his alienated vision by the end of the scene, when he asks to be left alone. The first lines of his soliloquy echo the imagery of hellish midnight in the speech of Lucianus, suggesting that Hamlet has now come to think as the murderer does, that the nephew of the King has become Lucianus (249–54, 379–83). This parallel prompts comparison of the revenger's psychology with the murderer's, and we may wish we could find that Hamlet is exaggerating his murderousness as a way to work himself up to kill Claudius. But Hamlet is already worked up to a demonic pitch at the start of the soliloquy, and in his second sentence he begins to cool as drinking hot blood is something he merely says he "could" do (381). Following this he thinks only of how he should behave when he goes to his mother.

But why does Hamlet go to Gertrude instead of killing the King now that he is convinced his revenge is just and he feels ready to do bitter business? The first lines of the soliloquy imply that he takes for granted that in his present mood he is already prepared to act vengefully, and it seems this is why his attention so quickly focusses on the need to separate his violent intentions regarding the King from his purposes regarding his mother. Hamlet sees the danger of killing her, too, in his rage, but not the reverse of this, that thoughts about not using daggers on his mother, but speaking them, may divert him from stabbing the King.

The vehemence of Hamlet's attack on Gertrude in the closet scene suggests that the main cause of his deciding, in this soliloquy, to go to her and not to the King is that speaking daggers to her is powerfully reinforced. Then, too, his mother has asked to see him now. Her request could function as a conscious pretext for delaying his revenge if going to her is partly reinforced because it enables him to escape from anxiety associated with killing his uncle. Nothing Hamlet says in this soliloquy suggests, however, that he perceives himself to be delaying revenge in a sense that casts doubt on his strength of purpose.

Hamlet's monologue in the prayer scene is an extreme example of absorbed thinking that narrowly focuses only on one way of analyzing a situation (3.3.73–96). He analyzes what revenge demands if he is to seek full retribution for what his father has suffered, but the analysis becomes more and more passionate as it proceeds, and he does not consider what he will do to himself by deliberately seeking to damn Claudius. Since Hamlet is familiar with ideas about self-damning acts, we may infer that he has heard (or could figure out for himself) that to seek someone's damnation is such an act. Earlier he has repeatedly expressed a concern that he should not damn himself. Now, however, his newly confirmed hatred of Claudius makes it so reinforcing to think of damning his foe that such thoughts are entirely absorbing, entirely prepotent over thoughts which would lead away from such a goal, so that any concern about damning himself is repressed.

Nonetheless, killing Claudius could still be aversive to Hamlet for any or all of the reasons reviewed earlier and also, at this moment, because it would be horrible to kill a person in the attitude of prayer. Hamlet's passionate determination to damn his uncle may then be regarded as a rationalization, enabling him to delay revenge and also to avoid thinking he does so for any purpose except to punish Claudius more severely. If, however, Hamlet's idea that he wants to damn his uncle is at all a rationalization, it is a passionate one and may become his purpose. Indeed, even if this rationale were a totally false explanation of Hamlet's behavior, once it occurs to him and is strongly reinforced as his purpose because of his anger and because it justifies his delay, it can guide future behavior as an intention – a discriminative stimulus. The reinforcement of this way of thinking could cause it to become strong behavior for Hamlet to seek the damnation of his foes.

The view that Hamlet spares the King at prayer partly because he so urgently wants to confront his mother appears to be confirmed in the closet scene. Hamlet's purpose and his anger so totally absorb him that he is nearly oblivious of all else. He brushes aside his mother's efforts to lecture him (3.4.8–19); her wrongdoing, not his, is the issue. He says he will set up a mirror to show her the innermost parts of herself, but he has no mirror to show him how his rage might evoke her cry for help (3.4.17–21). In some performances, Hamlet draws his sword to keep his mother from leaving, or still has it in his hand from the preceding scene, and he unthinkingly holds it up so its blade can be like a mirror turned toward her. Somehow it seems to Gertrude, as she cries out, that Hamlet's speaking daggers is about to become physical action. Then Polonius, too, cries out, startling Hamlet in his rage so that he reacts "rashly" and stabs through the arras. The act of stabbing is powerfully reinforced because Hamlet is in such a rage, and the person stabbed might be almost any of the several people he now hates. This stabbing could also be reinforced because it strikes at a foe while avoiding the aversive process of preparing a purposeful revenge. Indeed, this stabbing could conceivably be reinforced as well because it might allow Hamlet to avoid a purposeful revenge altogether by resulting in his being restrained from future action. In any case, Hamlet's words suggest that he does not consciously think it is the King behind the arras as he stabs. His mother asks him what he has done and he says he does not know; then he asks whether it was the King (25–6). At most he hoped it was the King as he stabbed.

When his mother reproaches him for his "rash and bloody deed" (27), Hamlet minimizes what he has done, not only to avoid guilt but also because he is now so strongly reinforced for speaking daggers to her that he will not let anything divert him. His deed is, he allows, "Almost as bad" as hers of killing a king and marrying his brother (28–9). His absorption in her evil will not let Hamlet see how his killing Polonius undercuts his righteous indignation, showing him to be rash in the sense of attacking others' vices while overlooking his own. Gertrude's surprise at the accusation of murder (30) appears to convince Hamlet that she did not know of that crime, since after this he reproaches her only for her marriage to Claudius. If Hamlet no longer thinks she is guilty of murder, then evidently his thoughts about her relationship with Claudius are enough to absorb him intensely. On the other hand, if he continues to think she is guilty of murder, his preoccupation with this relationship is so strong that thoughts of the murder are crowded out.

Hamlet also judges rashly in putting all the blame on Polonius for his own death. Hamlet says Polonius was a "wretched, rash, intruding fool" (31), but if he saw how these words could apply to himself he would not use them so scornfully of Polonius. Hamlet's statement that Polonius has been too "busy" may also apply to himself (33). In the Elizabethan translation of Plutarch's moral essays by Philemon Holland, a person who looks for evil in others while not seeing his own faults is called a busybody ("Of Curiosity").

"I took thee for thy better" again reveals more about Hamlet than about his victim (32). Hamlet now finds it reinforcing to believe that when he stabbed he thought it was the King behind the arras. Moreover, these words say the King is Polonius's "better," suggesting that Hamlet vaguely rationalizes Polonius's death as not very significant because he is a social inferior. Hamlet's thinking here is at least as strongly rooted in princely ideology as in morality, since he does not believe Claudius is morally better than Polonius. Later the same kind of judgment is part of Hamlet's attitude toward Rosencrantz and Guildenstern, when he speaks of their "baser nature" as contrasted with Claudius as well as himself (5.2.60–2).

Hamlet brushes aside his mother's anguish over what he has done and insists that she should let him wring her heart (3.4.34–5). Hard as his own heart has been toward Polonius, he now suggests that "damned custom" has "braz'd" her heart so it is "proof and bulwark against sense" (36–8). Especially in the context of the other ironies here, these lines suggest that as "custom" or habit is hardening Hamlet to hate and scorn most of the people in his world, he is losing his sensitivity to others' suffering and his ability to see from any point of view but his own.

Gertrude's responses show that he "roars" and "thunders" in his tirade against her (52; cf. 39–40). Later in the scene Hamlet claims that he is "cruel only to be kind" (180), that he speaks daggers only to bring Gertrude to repentance. But he does not assert this intention until the Ghost makes him look to his own behavior as well as hers. Before going to her chamber he has said he would be cruel to her, would speak daggers to her so she would be "shent" (3.2.387–90). Editors have usually been kind to Hamlet by glossing "shent" as "rebuked," "reproved," or "censured." The *Oxford English Dictionary* tells us, however, that to shend is to disgrace, to put to shame or confusion; to blame, revile, or scold; to destroy, ruin or injure, including to disfigure, corrupt, infect, soil, and defile. That Hamlet intends something like this in saying he will shend her is clear when he says the shending must be only in words and not also in murderous deeds that would confirm the thrust of his words (389–90).

Before the Ghost comes, there is no indication Hamlet intends to do anything except force his mother to see her inmost evils in order to hurt her. He may also have a dim intention to bring her to repentance, but if he does have such an intention, it is in some degree a rationalization, since in his extreme anger his behavior is of a sort that seems more calculated to "Make mad the guilty" than to enlighten her (2.2.558). Hamlet gives no hint of any compassionate understanding; indeed, he takes the view that Gertrude's behavior has been well-nigh incomprehensible in human terms (3.4.63–81). When she says Hamlet has succeeded in making her see her corrupt nature, he continues to stab with his imaginings of her vile sexual encounters with Claudius (88–94). She replies that his "words like daggers enter in my ears," confirming that he has sufficiently spoken daggers to her if he is attacking her only so she will repent (94–96). Yet when she says this, Hamlet intensifies his attack (96–103).

If Hamlet's purpose were to bring her to repentance, he would by now begin to preach as he does later in the scene when this becomes his stated purpose. As it is, his attack is ended only by the Ghost, who expresses fear for what the "conceit" Hamlet has forced on his mother's soul may do to her, and urges him to help her (112–15). To argue thus that Hamlet's attacking Gertrude is reinforced because it punishes her is not to say this is the only cause of his behavior. The Oedipal attachment makes speaking daggers to her be reinforced as a way to create emotional intimacy between them as they break down together. In addition, hurting his mother, especially speaking daggers to her, could be reinforced as a form of sexual sadism.

The re-appearance of the Ghost causes thoughts of using daggers to become prepotent over speaking them for Hamlet. Even before the Ghost speaks, its presence reminds Hamlet of its command and he thinks of how he has been "tardy" in his revenge (107–9). Hamlet's saying he is "laps'd in . . . passion" is interestingly ambiguous: he probably means he has let the passion for revenge lapse in himself, but part of the cause for this is that he has lapsed into passion, has failed to act as much because of the passions he *has* experienced as because he has lacked passion.

The Queen sees no Ghost and so her thoughts are turned from her own sins to Hamlet's madness. The situation is similar to the start of the scene, as Gertrude and Hamlet see each other to be erring, but they are now more compassionate toward each other and more aware of a need to respond to the other's point of view. Gertrude pities her son for his madness, and because she does not see the Ghost, Hamlet thinks he must explain his behavior to show that he is sane and therefore to be listened to when he tells her about herself (142–51). It would be very reinforcing for Hamlet to believe his explanation that his purpose has only been to move her to repentance (151–7) – especially after the Ghost has urged him to help her – and not that he spoke earlier in vengeful rage.

Thus Hamlet may sincerely think he was cruel "only" to be kind (180), yet his thinking this is also a defensive rationalization. His rationalization becomes extreme when he asks Gertrude to forgive his "virtue" and personifies himself as Virtue in deploring how Virtue must beg pardon and bow and "woo" to be allowed to help Vice reform (154–7). He did not speak in a submissively courteous tone earlier, and the body of Polonius lying on the stage shows that Hamlet is wildly mistaken to regard himself as so near to Virtue.

Hamlet urges Gertrude to reform by habituating herself to sexual abstinence (159–72). He knows that being moved to repentance is not enough, that if she is really to change, her sexual behavior must be habituated so she will no longer desire Claudius. Ironically, Hamlet's statement also applies to the way he himself is changing through his own actions and thoughts, becoming brazed to killing and perhaps "mad in craft" (190). At the moment, however, his intention to reform Gertrude and his thinking of himself as virtuous make it reinforcing for him to repent the killing of Polonius (174–9). Hamlet accepts responsibility for his deed (178–9), and he also speaks of his revenge as a punishment of himself. In this he shows how aversive he finds the Ghost's command: "heaven hath pleas'd it so, / To punish me with this and this with me, / That I must be their scourge and minister" (175–7).

This part of what he says also weakens his repentance insofar as he claims that he did Heaven's will in slaying Polonius. For the first time Hamlet hints that revenge requires the death of more than Claudius, and it seems he thinks this way chiefly because such thoughts allow him to

feel justified for killing Polonius. It would be much less aversive to think
Heaven has used him to punish Polonius, and through him the King, than
to think he has killed a foolish old man in a wild rage. It may even be less
aversive to think of himself as a damned agent of God – one meaning of
"scourge" – than to think he is a damned agent of his own murderous
rage in an act that foolishly dooms himself and has no moral or political
value at all. If this reading is correct, Hamlet's concern with his mother's
repentance and his turning to repentance himself have deeply ironic consequences insofar as his repentance leads him to see the death of Polonius
as providential.

The plurality of evil ones who are to die is next expanded to include
Rosencrantz and Guildenstern. Hamlet thinks they know he is to be
killed when they reach England, for he speaks of destroying them with
the weapon they mean to use against him (206–11). Their dialogue with
Claudius in 3.3 shows, however, that they believe Hamlet is to be sent to
England because he has threatened the King: there is no evidence anywhere
that they think the King's sealed commission orders Hamlet's death.

The nature of Hamlet's error in wanting to kill Rosencrantz and
Guildenstern is revealed when he takes pleasure in anticipating their
destruction, speaking of the "sport" of hoisting the engineer with his own
petard, and saying "'tis most sweet / When in one line two crafts directly
meet" (208, 211–12). To find it "most sweet" to pit deadly craft against
deadly craft is to be essentially "mad in craft" in proto-behaviorist terms,
for the pleasure shows that such craftiness is becoming a habit and therefore a characteristic of Hamlet. By the end of the scene, these thoughts
have led Hamlet away from repentance for slaying Polonius: as he removes
the body he expresses a sportful, mocking contempt that minimizes the
importance of the slaying (213–18). In addition, once Hamlet's preoccupation with his mother is out of the way here, his intensely pleasurable
anticipation of destroying Rosencrantz and Guildenstern is prepotent over
any movement toward killing the King. Hamlet accepts his being sent to
England, and here he seems almost to welcome it as an occasion to kill
his former friends. Thinking of this kind may well be reinforced partly
because it allows him to avoid killing Claudius.

This analysis of the closet scene illustrates how a behaviorist interpretation can unfold the moment-to-moment dynamics of a drama. Particularly valuable is what such an analysis suggests about the importance of
thoughts and intentions and how they change. At one moment Hamlet
may not have a very clear intention in mind, as perhaps in his rage at the
beginning of the scene. Then when the Ghost has prompted him to cease
this rage and his mother's doubts of his sanity make it highly reinforcing for him to explain himself, he thinks of an acceptable rationale for
his behavior. He is reinforced in believing this rationale by the assurance

it gives him that he has behaved sanely and even virtuously. Hence it becomes his sincere intention to reform his mother, and this intention guides his behavior as he tells her how to reform. This brings him to thoughts of his own need to repent, but then he finds it reinforcing to think his actions are fulfilling the intentions of Heaven and he widens his revenge to include Polonius. Once Polonius is seen as having fallen under Heaven's doom, the revenge can widen further, to include Rosencrantz and Guildenstern. Thus intentions can control behavior, but the intentions are part of the behavior and are subject to the same contingencies of reinforcement as other activities.

This view of Hamlet does not mean he is insincere in his concern for virtue or his mother. He intensely feels what he says at each moment; indeed, it is the intensity of his sincere thinking which so absorbs him. And it is not that Hamlet behaves in merely contradictory ways. The changes in his behavior reflect a coherent character, a character having the complexity to be moved in complex ways as the action unfolds.

In my initial discussion of the antic disposition I said that some of Hamlet's behavior in Act 4, scenes 2 and 3 may be out of control. Thus his saying that he has "Safely stowed" Polonius's body seems out of touch with reality if he thinks he has adequately disposed of the body by putting it in the lobby upstairs. Hamlet has evidently been absorbed in hiding the body and thinking about its being safely stowed, for when he is called he expresses surprise, as if he has been wakened from preoccupation: "Safely stowed. [*Calling within.*] But soft, what noise? Who calls on Hamlet? O, here they come" (4.2.1–3). Most of what Hamlet says in these scenes, however, has the tone of the antic wit at its highest pitch of controlled intensity, and any element of apparent madness may reflect hectic excitement. Certainly Hamlet now has cause to play the antic disposition as madly as possible to give the impression that he has not "murdered" Polonius but killed him in a mad fit. Hamlet's concern with seeking cover by hiding the body of Polonius and then hiding himself in his antic disposition blocks any action against the King. Hamlet's anxiety about confronting his foes after he has killed Polonius evidently makes self-concealment prepotent over other behavior.

Hamlet's soliloquy in response to the sight of Fortinbras's army invites comparison with the soliloquy at the end of Act 2. Again Hamlet's disposition to act nobly makes it reinforcing to punish himself when he sees someone who acts vigorously with less cause than he himself has to act (4.4.32–66). As before, he suspects himself of cowardice, but now he denies that he lacks will and strength and more explicitly blames his disposition, as an intellectual and a Christian moralist, to think about outcomes. As a subject in the psychological sense, he is divided between the disposition to nobility and honor and the disposition to think morally.

He defends reason as given by God, but disparages careful foresight as more cowardly than wise. Hamlet does not question the validity of the reasoning he did earlier so much as he suggests that his thinking was to justify a delay caused mostly by fear: "some craven scruple / Of thinking too precisely on th'event – / A thought which, quarter'd, hath but one part wisdom / And ever three parts coward – " (40–3). Hamlet here accuses himself of what we call rationalization. There are references to rationalization in other works of Shakespeare,[12] but Hamlet is one of the few characters to ever see it in himself.

Yet Hamlet has little insight here. When he thinks of cowardice as an explanation of his delay, he examines himself no further. The accusation of cowardice is especially painful to a prince, and hence is especially reinforced as punishment. Hamlet wants to discredit himself, but his conclusion that he has been a coward, though it may have some truth, allows him to avoid probing for other causes of delay, some of which might discredit him more. Thus he uses Fortinbras as a model to torment himself with the thought that he has failed to act greatly when his honor is at stake: "a father kill'd, a mother stain'd, / Excitements of my reason and my blood" (57–8). His emotion makes it reinforcing for him to think that henceforth his thoughts must "be bloody or be nothing worth" (66) – he does not want any "thinking too precisely on th'event" to block the bloody deed of revenge. Evidently he intends no longer to think of how he may damn himself or others in what he does, since such thoughts about consequences have especially delayed his revenge. But Hamlet's passionate concern for honor in thinking about "th'event" makes it reinforcing for him to renounce the kind of thinking necessary for truly honorable action. Ironically, to avoid the dishonor of thinking himself a coward, he may think in a way that leads him to act dishonorably in the treacherous means he uses to destroy Rosencrantz and Guildenstern.

Hamlet does not appear again until he returns from the voyage to England, but in 4.6 his letter to Horatio shows he is not a coward in the ordinary sense, for he was the first to board a pirate ship when it attacked. We cannot say, however, that he did this in order to return to Denmark for revenge. Hamlet's apparent purpose was to help repel the pirates, and he became a prisoner when the pirates then broke off the fight (4.6.15–18).

Hamlet and Horatio enter in the graveyard scene as the First Gravedigger sings of his youth and love while digging Ophelia's grave:

HAM.   Has this fellow no feeling of his business a sings in grave-making?

HOR.   Custom hath made it in him a property of easiness.

HAM.   'Tis e'en so, the hand of little employment hath the daintier sense.

(5.1.65–9)

These lines refer to the proto-behaviorist idea that the most unpleasant activities become easy and even pleasant through habituation. The passage recalls Hamlet's suggestion that his mother has been so "braz'd" or hardened to sin by habit that she may be incapable of sensing the evil of what she has done (3.4.35–8). In 5.1 perhaps more than in the closet scene the statement about habituation raises a question about Hamlet, inasmuch as the Gravedigger is less a character than a figure whose primary function is to be a mirror held up to Hamlet's antic disposition as this disposition fades.

Thus the statement about the Gravedigger's habituation leads to the question whether Hamlet now finds it easy to jest about death, too. If Hamlet comes to terms with death here, he does so on the basis of a hardening of his sensitivities in which he excludes awareness of matters that might cause him pain. By now Hamlet has killed Polonius with his own hand, has used his hand to write Rosencrantz and Guildenstern's death warrant, and has fought the pirates in hand-to-hand combat, so perhaps his hand is no longer the "hand of little employment" that has "the daintier sense" of death. Hamlet may be insensitive in part because he avoids thinking of the deaths of Polonius and his father: the graveyard evokes no remark at all about either of them.[13]

Hamlet's response to death here shows no grief or compassion until his personal relationship with Yorick begins to bring death closer to him. Until then, the single exception tends to confirm this generalization, for it comes at the start in what Hamlet says about the Gravedigger's insensitivity that lets him treat a skull as though he did not know it "had a tongue in it, and could sing once" (74). After this through line 115 there is no sign that Hamlet responds to death as destroying a creature capable of song. Hamlet's comments on death in these lines take a sardonic view of life as a base pursuit of worldly goods that death shows to be futile. Although a similar view is found in Christian thinking, there the idea is to renounce worldly values for the sake of the soul. Nowhere in this scene does Hamlet express any hope, or any concern for the human soul. In this part of the graveyard scene, Hamlet's only regret seems to be that death ends all distinctions of social class. He comments that the Sexton's spade striking Lady Worm's skull is "fine revolution," and he continues, "Did these bones cost no more the breeding but to play at loggets with 'em? Mine ache to think on't" (87–91). We hear this complaint again when the Gravedigger insolently equivocates in answering his question of who the grave is for, and Hamlet says that "the age is grown so picked that the toe of the peasant comes so near the heel of the courtier he galls his kibe" (135–8). Yet even in these complaints Hamlet gives the impression that he feels detached from individual human lives and deaths.

Hamlet shows he is detached, too, in the way his concern about the Gravedigger's insolence diverts him from the question about whose grave is being dug, immediately after he has been told it is for a woman, to the question of how long the fellow has been digging graves (130–8). We know that this is Ophelia's grave, and as we respond to the structure of this scene we are waiting for Hamlet to be jolted out of his impersonal attitude by the news of her death. Hence the statement that a woman has died prompts us to think Hamlet should ask who it is – not be so easily diverted – if he is really concerned and not merely curious in his questioning.

Even when the Gravedigger unearths the skull of Yorick, Hamlet responds with personal feeling only briefly. Soon Yorick's skull becomes an impersonal symbol to use in expressing the traditional warning that the life of the flesh is transitory, that we should remember death (178–89). Again, Hamlet says nothing of the soul; instead he follows the skull into the earth and comments on the "base uses" to which "we may return" (196–209). Hamlet's thinking continues to be narrowly focussed even in the words that express the part of the traditional *memento mori* idea he does utter: "Now get you to my lady's chamber and tell her, let her paint an inch thick, to this favour she must come. Make her laugh at that" (186–9). Hamlet has no intuition that *his* lady is already dead. Only his ignorance lets him speak this way: he has not fully hardened into a person who can laugh at death, for when Ophelia's body is brought in he is overcome with emotion.

Hamlet's use of Yorick's skull as a symbol and his speaking of his lady as a social type lead him back to his concern about how death makes noble bones ache: "Dost thou think Alexander looked o' this fashion i'th' earth?" (191–2). Hamlet's perception that death brings human greatness to "base uses" moves him to a deep sense of loss that he counters with irony: "O that that earth which kept the world in awe / Should patch a wall t'expel the winter's flaw" (208–9). These lines do not express an acceptance of death that frees Hamlet to act but a tragic prince's concern with death as the destroyer of human greatness. Paradoxically, Hamlet's disposition as tragic prince has displaced concern for the soul, choked off compassion for the loss of song, and provoked scorn of petty worldlings.

When Hamlet asks "Why, may not imagination trace the noble dust of Alexander till a find it stopping a bung-hole?" (196–8), Horatio's reply, "'Twere to consider too curiously to consider so" aptly indicates how Hamlet's thinking has led him away from what he most needs to think about if he is to act effectively or greatly (199). In ancient, medieval, and Renaissance writers "curiosity" is often used to mean a vice of inquiring about things in a way that leads to the wrong kind of knowledge. Even so free a thinker as Montaigne sometimes uses "curiosity" in this sense (esp. "Apologie" 2:199, "Upon Some Verses" 3:95, 97). Hamlet's thinking that minimizes character and spirit as essential greatness does not lead him to think about the fundamental moral and human qualities which his particular greatness depends on. The narrowness of Hamlet's thinking is emphasized by the juxtaposition of his concern for greatness with the entrance of Ophelia's funeral procession. She is a pathetic, not a tragic figure, a victim of the struggle between "mighty opposites." As her body is carried on stage, Hamlet's sensibility could not be further from an intuition of her death.

When he sees that Ophelia is dead, Hamlet becomes so emotionally distracted that for a time he loses his ability to recognize how his killing Polonius has affected Laertes and Ophelia (5.1.239–42, 247–56, 283–5). That Hamlet actually cannot think how he may have offended Laertes – "Hear you, sir, / What is the reason that you use me thus? / I lov'd you ever" (283–5) – may also show how strongly he represses awareness that he has killed Polonius. Laertes has forcefully reminded Hamlet that he killed Polonius (239–42), and it may be part of the point that Laertes's description of Hamlet as a "cursed" one who has committed a "wicked deed" presents the Prince with an image of himself which he cannot recognize. When he later says that the image of his own cause shows him the portraiture of Laertes's (5.2.77–8), Hamlet sees the parallel between himself and Laertes as revengers, but evidently does not see how from Laertes's point of view he appears only as Claudius does to himself, as the murderer of his father – Laertes knows nothing of Hamlet's revenge cause. Again Hamlet interprets a mirror held up to him in a way that reflects his absorption in his own point of view.

Insofar as Hamlet's failures in 5.1 are caused by the overwhelming shock and anguish he feels upon learning of Ophelia's death, sympathy for him is evoked throughout this episode, even in response to his seemingly empty protestations of what he would do to show his love for her. Hamlet is reinforced for thinking and speaking in a way that powerfully expresses his love for Ophelia and thereby not incidentally denies any guilt for her death. This is not to say, however, that he deliberately puts on emotional shows, since Hamlet most needs to convince himself, and he will not be convinced by emotional protestations he sees he is putting on. At the end of his tirade he realizes that he has spoken rant – it has become characteristic of Hamlet to recoil from his own emotionality – but it is in his next speech that he is least in touch with reality, asking Laertes how he has offended him (283–5).

The crucial evidence that Hamlet feels what his words claim he feels about Ophelia is the way he speaks with righteous indignation as though he were simply a faithful lover who has a right to object when his lady's grieving brother expresses great love for her (261–6). In this Hamlet is so preposterously oblivious to the realities that he is probably sincere. In saying he will match Laertes's expressions of grief, Hamlet does not see that Laertes's grief is heightened to a furious passion by vengeful anger. Hamlet says "I will fight with him upon this theme / Until my eyelids will no longer wag" (261–2), meaning the theme of who loved Ophelia more, but this is not the theme upon which Laertes wishes to fight.

Hamlet is calm at the beginning of 5.2, perhaps partly because of the influence of Horatio and partly because passion spends itself (see esp. 5.1.279–83; cf. 3.2.189–92, 4.7.109–14). Here a crucial question is what to make of Hamlet's belief that he has been guided by providence in having Rosencrantz and Guildenstern killed in England. I have explained that according to the traditional meaning of rashness, it is doubtful that Hamlet should praise rashness as a mode of providential action. Hamlet's belief that Rosencrantz and Guildenstern have betrayed his friendship is what makes him so bitter toward them. The evidence, however, does not so clearly support Hamlet's suspicions as to justify sending them to death with no chance of defending themselves. And if they did not know the content of the King's sealed orders, once he destroyed those orders Hamlet had no need to have them killed for fear they would have sought to contrive his death in England.

The text of 5.2.6–48 and the relation of this to what Hamlet says at the end of the closet scene indicate that Hamlet was guided by habit, not providence, when he stole the King's commission and forged a replacement. In part Hamlet believes he was guided by providence because before he could address his "brains" regarding what they should do, they began to write a new scenario (30–1) in the forged commission: that is, he wrote intuitively, without thinking first. But his action here carries out his earlier intention to use craft to destroy Rosencrantz and Guildenstern through the means that were to be used for his own destruction (3.4.206–11). The thought of forging a commission for their deaths is precisely what could be expected to occur intuitively to Hamlet when he finds a commission for his death and is disposed to hoist the engineer with his own petard. There is also evidence that Hamlet acted intuitively on the basis of habit in the suggestion that he took pleasure in forging a new commission – he certainly is excited and pleased as he tells Horatio about it (5.2.38–55). Hamlet's pleasure suggests that he was "mad in craft," habituated to its "most sweet" "sport," so that he is insensitive to the reality of what he has done.

Hamlet's thinking seems paranoid when he says he was "benetted round with villainies" (29). Although the sealed commission has proven only the King's villainy, Hamlet forged orders that would harm only Rosencrantz and Guildenstern. This was an opportunity for Hamlet to act as the rightful King of Denmark, but what he says does not indicate he thought of this, and what he wrote was a parody of the voice of Claudius in the original commission, using fair words to cover a treacherous deed (32–47). Hamlet indicates no awareness that he has come to be at all like Claudius in craftiness or that his actions have been base. He especially shows insensitivity to the substance of his act when he emphasizes the style of handwriting he employed. His perception of what is base here is that he once thought it "baseness" to write clearly, so he labored to un-learn his ability to write in a clear hand (32–6). Yet his earlier learning – the habit of being able to write clearly – still survives, and this habit enabled him to write "fair" or clear copy. That he applies his concern for what is "fair" only to clarity of handwriting parallels the insensitivity of his reference to "baseness." And perhaps it is significant that even fairness in handwriting was an earlier habit Hamlet has practiced to overcome.

When Hamlet turns to "Th'effect" of what he wrote (37), his concern is more with the statesman's rhetorical style than with the substance of his command (38–47). Hamlet is gleeful as he tells of piling up clauses to parody this style, and as he puns on "as" and "ass" (43). This speech contains eight lines of mock-rhetoric and one-and-one-half lines telling what he commanded, that Rosencrantz and Guildenstern should be "put to sudden death / Not shriving-time allow'd" (46–7). Horatio's question about how he sealed the forged commission evokes the response that "even in that was heaven ordinant" (47–8). The "even" here suggests Hamlet finds it reinforcing to think Heaven was ordinant in the action he has just been narrating. He feels that Heaven has approved of what he has done when he says his indiscretion has served him "well" and this shows there's a Divinity that shapes our ends (8–10). Moreover, his entire narrative has a self-satisfied tone, and he goes on to say that the fate of Rosencrantz and Guildenstern does not "come near" his conscience (58).

But if Heaven was ordinant in Hamlet's sending Rosencrantz and Guildenstern to death without shriving time – an evil if not Satanic act – this could only mean that Heaven used Hamlet as an evil instrument of its vengeance. Since Rosencrantz and Guildenstern may have been guilty of betraying Hamlet, he may have been justified in having them executed and also in having this done "Without debatement further more or less" so they could not argue that he was the one to be killed (45). But Hamlet could have stopped here or he could have used other words to emphasize and enforce his point than "not shriving time allow'd." In their context these words go beyond callousness to suggest that Hamlet feels some gratification at having found justification for letting Rosencrantz and Guildenstern be damned. He draws attention to the nature of his act by his following claim that Heaven has guided him. However guilty Rosencrantz and Guildenstern may be, in a Christian context they should not be deprived of a rite that *they*, at least, might think could save their souls. Hamlet's judgment is deeply tragic as his sense of destiny and right lead him into this dreadful error.

Hamlet does not claim that when he acted on board the ship he thought Heaven was guiding him. He says he did not think about what he was doing, but simply did it intuitively. This may suggest that his idea about providence is a rationalization after the fact to explain and justify his intuitive behavior. Once he has sent Rosencrantz and Guildenstern to death, Hamlet would find it very reinforcing to believe that Heaven directed his actions, but he indicates that he was conscious of his crafty wit at the time he forged the lethal commission, and this challenges his claim that he was not guiding his own conduct. Yet his self-satisfied tone indicates Hamlet is sincere now in thinking providence guided him, and because he believes this, faith in providence can guide his future action.

Ironically, Hamlet's reliance on rashness as providential contributes to his doom. As we saw in the earlier discussion of rashness, Augustine wrote that the rash judge is doomed through his rashness: he judges unjustly, not seeing the "beam" in his own eye while condemning others for "motes," and he is punished through his rash misjudgment of others. Hamlet is killed through his blind trust of Laertes, which is partly caused by his adoption of rashness as providence. Convinced that there is "special providence in the fall of a sparrow," Hamlet now refuses to avoid the potential danger of the fencing match with Laertes (208–20). Hamlet trusts Laertes in a way that expresses the most erring aspect of his rashness. In the graveyard scene he spoke of Laertes as "a very noble youth" (5.1.217), and now he confirms that opinion in saying to Horatio he is sorry he "forgot" himself to Laertes in the graveyard and will "court his favours" (5.2.75–8). This shows that Hamlet still forgets himself to Laertes: Hamlet's reason for being sorry about his earlier behavior is that he sees himself and Laertes to have causes which are the image or portrait of each other, suggesting that Hamlet is inclined to identify with Laertes and to judge him accordingly. But if Hamlet saw his own actions in a clearer light, he would know that he has destroyed Rosencrantz and Guildenstern not nobly but treacherously, so if Laertes is the image of Hamlet, he may be expected to be treacherously vengeful. Thus Hamlet does not expect Laertes's treachery partly because he does not see his own.

To recapitulate the entire ironic pattern of Hamlet's rashness: he judged Rosencrantz and Guildenstern rashly, interpreting their conduct without enough attention to the effect of his behavior on them, assuming they knew they were taking him to his death in England and presuming the nobility and hence justice of his own view. Then this rash judgment led him to doom them rashly, and to avoid guilty thoughts of this he finds it reinforcing, according to the psychology of cognitive dissonance reduction, to think even more strongly than before that his judgment of them was right. This intensifies his sense of himself as noble and hence helps to induce a rash misjudgment of Laertes when he identifies with him. In this sense, the too-harsh judgment of Rosencrantz and Guildenstern is part of what leads to the too-uncritical view of himself and Laertes. To look at it another way, Hamlet's rash judgment of himself helps to induce his opposite misjudgments of Rosencrantz and Guildenstern as base and of Laertes as noble.

In the dialogue with Osric, the subject is for a time Laertes and his fine qualities, but Hamlet mostly attends to Osric's affectedly elaborate style of speech. In a peculiar way, Osric is another mirror in which Hamlet does not see himself. It is partly because they are both admirers of Laertes that, instead of questioning the substance of what Osric says, Hamlet imitates and parodies his speech (106–23). This echoes Hamlet's account of how he parodied the rhetoric of royal commissions, in which he did not consider the deeper implications of imitating the King. Hamlet says that Osric has collected many things to say by rote or habit, but has no character that can be the source of things to say when he is tested beyond what he has collected (184–91). This, like the play's other statements about habit, invites us to consider whether it applies to Hamlet. Whatever habits Hamlet may have, as his trial reaches its climax in the duel scene what do we see has become of his character? Habits of virtue and vice become characteristics, but has Hamlet become a person whose words and thoughts, however sincere, are habitually rationalizations and other forms of self-justification? Has he become evil or false through the ways he has treated others?

Let us take a wider look at Hamlet's thinking in the last scene. He now insists he should kill the King; indeed, he says he would be damned if he did not end the King's evil deeds (63–70). Here Hamlet comes close to claiming a right in law to execute justice on Claudius. But in giving Claudius's original commission to Horatio to read "at more leisure" (26), Hamlet apparently does not think of using this proof of the King's treachery and criminal injustice to further his cause. Evidently Hamlet's new belief that "divinity" "shapes" his course lets him think he does not need to plan any action of his own (10–11, 73–4, 215–20). His thinking that providence will guide his revenge would be strongly reinforced not only because he has been unable to plan revenge but also because thinking that providence is guiding him enables him to avoid anxiety about what he has done to Rosencrantz and Guildenstern.

Yet even if it is in a sense "self-deceiving" for Hamlet to believe he has acted nobly and that providence guides him here, the most important question is whether these beliefs help him to confront his final trial with integrity and courage. Hamlet is aware of peril and he shows courage in his statement that "The readiness is all" (208–20). On the other hand, because Hamlet's disposition to regard death as a state of "felicity" (352) may be one cause of his readiness, his trust of the King and Laertes in the fencing match might be more suicidal than courageous. Now, it appears to me – as to most interpreters – that following the dialogue with Osric the play primarily emphasizes Hamlet's nobility. His rash judgment of Laertes as noble may be predicated on a faulty self-perception, but – again – even an erring notion sincerely believed in can become an intention guiding future action, and so his perception of Laertes and himself as noble guides him back toward nobility. The one constant in all this, and it is a crucial one, is that Hamlet is always disposed to do what he *thinks* is noble.

In his speech asking Laertes's forgiveness for slaying his father, Hamlet is noble to Laertes in acknowledging he has done him wrong and in appealing to Laertes's own gentlemanly honor and "most generous thoughts" for pardon (222–3, 227, 238). Still, this could be rhetoric calculated to manipulate Laertes by appealing to his vanity. Also, there seems to be more self-exculpation than honesty in Hamlet's saying his madness and not he killed Polonius (226–35), even though Hamlet could have come to believe he was mad when he killed Polonius because this enables him to avoid more aversive explanations of the act. The most important basis for believing that Hamlet intends to make a true peace with Laertes is that he has stated this intention to Horatio in a context suggesting sincerity (75–80). In sum, although Hamlet's apology to Laertes is surely in part reinforced because it placates a man who might kill him, Hamlet's intention is almost as surely to give an accounting that will be acceptable to a noble person and will preserve his own image of himself as noble. Thus Hamlet may use manipulative rhetoric but avoid the aversive awareness that he is being manipulative.

Of course in this speech Hamlet conceals crucial facts because he thinks he cannot publicly explain that his cause is the image of Laertes's and that he killed Polonius in a moment of vengeful rage at the King and his mother. Even if Hamlet thinks he deliberately lies in saying his madness and not he killed Polonius, he could be reinforced as a person disposed to be noble if he thinks this is a guiltless lie because the real truth, if he could tell it, would put him in an even better light. Perhaps because Hamlet cannot demonstrate his nobility by explaining to Laertes the facts of his past action, he speaks in a way that expresses his noble character in tone and manner.

Hamlet also acts nobly in fencing with Laertes, showing courage and bending his best efforts to win the match. His not examining the foils despite his suspicion that he is in peril (208–20) may indicate that his conduct is reinforced partly because he is disposed to die. However, not examining the foils also shows he trusts Laertes and so is further evidence he is the noble man the King counted on him to be (4.7.133–5). Hamlet's surprisingly aggressive fencing suggests that despite his brotherly intentions he is strongly reinforced for attacking Laertes. The possible sources of reinforcement here are many: Hamlet intuits his danger and the King's purpose; also, the fencing is an opportunity to take violent action showing the King what he can do and indirectly attacking the King. Hamlet could even attack Laertes as an image or portrait of himself, if this would be reinforcing, without conscious awareness of this as a supplemental source of strength for his action.

Hamlet acts aggressively, too, in things he says. It is disingenuous for him to say that Laertes's skill will contrast brilliantly with his own ignorance (5.2.252–4), for he has told Horatio he expects to "win at the odds" (206–7). More significant, when he has scored two hits to none for Laertes, Hamlet tauntingly suggests that Laertes wants to shame him by not fighting his hardest (301–3). This remark comes at a crucial moment, for Laertes has just indicated in an aside that his conscience makes him reluctant to stab Hamlet (300). In taunting Laertes, Hamlet intends to provoke him to his best effort, but he does not know of this conflict of conscience. Laertes is evidently angered by the taunt (304), tries again to score a hit on Hamlet, fails, and then immediately stabs him when they are not fencing (305–6). If Laertes's determination to stab Hamlet has been strengthened by Hamlet's taunt, there is tragic irony in Hamlet's success as a fencer moving him to a moment of hubristic insolence that seals his fate. The tragic irony is intensified in the way the blindness of Hamlet's hubris is caused by his inability to take the role of the other, to put himself in the place of the very man he thinks is an image of himself.

Until Laertes treacherously stabs him, Hamlet has been trusting, and the violation of that trust moves him to a controlled anger and a disposition to take revenge that governs his behavior through the killing of Claudius. Obviously when Hamlet kills Claudius his revenge is for himself and his mother as well as for his father, which allows us to speculate that Hamlet might not have taken revenge even now for his father's death alone or if he himself were able to continue living. But such speculations should not be allowed to obscure the main impression created in Hamlet's slaying of the King, that he acts in a purposeful and composed manner with a sense of full justification. He is noble in his exchange of forgiveness with Laertes, in his concern that Horatio should report his cause "aright," and in turning his dying thoughts to the future of Denmark (337, 344–5, 360–3).

Whatever changes Hamlet undergoes in the course of the play, it is most important that it is always his characteristic disposition to act nobly: he never becomes unjust in Aristotle's sense of *being* such a person. There is something to the Gravedigger's assertion that an act has three branches, "to act, to do, to perform" (5.1.11–12). In the *Nicomachean Ethics* Aristotle writes that it is "possible for a deed to be unjust without yet being an `unjust act' if the element of voluntariness is absent" (1135a). Hamlet would act unjustly only if he performed an unjust deed in the way an unjust person does – for the sake of what he knows is an unjust end because he thinks he should act unjustly for the sake of a wrongful motive. In this sense Hamlet never acts unjustly and therefore never becomes an unjust person. Although his deeds and thoughts may become unjust, he never intends to act or think unjustly as an unjust person would. He may acquire the habits and therefore the characteristics of judging rashly and acting craftily, but he does not acquire the habit of thinking he is right to act unjustly – indeed, he does not ever think that what he does is unjust.

These ideas are important, I think, for understanding the complexity of Hamlet's divided subjectivity – the way his intentions and his thinking, his underlying character and his habits, relate to each other in complex and dynamically variable ways as he responds to his changing circumstances. Moreover, if the analysis here has been persuasive, it will be clear that to respond to Hamlet with tragic compassion we must understand him as an imagined person whose behavior can be studied for what it reveals about how and why he thinks, feels, and acts as he does. Only with such an understanding, whether arrived at intuitively or through a psychological analysis, can we see how profoundly erring deeds and perceptions can arise from an intense, sensitive, and anguished concern for love, duty, nobility, and justice.

5

Prince Hal – King Henry V

Critics generally agree that Prince Hal, later King Henry V, is Shakespeare's most penetrating characterization of a master politician. Because Hal is a politician, his psychological development as an imagined person especially focusses on his mode of engagement with his roles.[1] A behaviorist approach, by providing a specific analysis of how modes of role-playing in various situations affect what characters see, feel, think, and do, yields particularly valuable insights into Hal and his career. In this chapter technical behaviorist terms are used less than in the chapter on Hamlet, yet each important mode of thought and behavior is explained fully at least once. The chapter traces Hal's career through the three plays on his life, with special emphasis on *Henry IV, Part 1* as the play in which the direction of his psychological development is established.

I will begin by comparing Hal with Hotspur, a comparison Shakespeare invites by changing history to make them the same age. Hotspur's character provides a perspective on Hal that helps define the issues regarding the Prince's conduct. Critics have generally seen Hotspur as the one character in *1H4* who is so emotionally involved with his thinking and conduct that he has very little self-detachment. He hardly seems able to think[2] of using pretenses: he must speak his mind even if to do so hazards his head or offends a powerful ally (1.3.124–6, 3.1.142). Because of the rank dishonesty of some other characters in the play, we may find Hotspur's raw candor appealing and infer that his lack of pretense, if not his harebrain, is a standard by which Hal is to be judged. This would be a mistake, however, for although Hotspur speaks and acts without pretense, he deceives himself, and his self-deception makes him dishonest with others, too.

Hotspur is an extreme example of the character who thinks he simply *is* his self-ideal. He never reflects on his conduct except with the assumption that it expresses his strong sense of honor. Hal, on the other hand, reflects on how he should best present himself as his self-ideal, and is usually more detached from what he is doing. At one time or another, as we shall see, Hal exemplifies nearly all the varieties of acting between the extremes of Machiavellian hypocrisy and absorbed, sincere playing. In his tavern role as a "lad of mettle" (2.4.12), Hal's premise seems to be that in order to show himself as the "true prince" he should first present himself as a "false thief" (1.2.150–1), pretending to be a thief as a foil for his later princely conduct (1.2.190–212). The paradoxical suggestion that truth emerges from falsehood depends on the logic of a double negative: a false thief is a true man. Such ingenious logic is dubious, but to see why it may seem plausible to Hal we need only to look at Hotspur to see how truth can be falsified by the simply true man.

Hotspur thinks of himself with single-minded passion as the perfect man of honor. To him this means that he should do everything for the sake of winning honor, and he exemplifies the danger that a person who seeks honor for its own sake may not attend sufficiently to what it is honorable to do, may too easily find it reinforcing to think that the actions which win praise must be honorable. Hotspur is especially self-deceived in his claim that the Percies' rebellion is honorable, and what he says repeatedly betrays the falseness of his thinking (1.3.158–85).

In his anger at Henry IV, he finds it reinforcing to attack his father and uncle for making Henry king. He says "you" or "both of you" (172) are shamed for serving Henry; he never says "we" are shamed, even though later in the scene he says he was a supporter of Henry and received his promises (239–51). For the purposes of Hotspur's attack, Richard II, whom the Percies despised when he was alive, becomes a "sweet lovely rose" (173). His father and his uncle did wrong in helping depose Richard, but they are especially dishonored because they have not been rewarded as Henry promised (158–9, 175–7, 182–3, 247–51). They can redeem their dishonor in deposing one king by attacking another king (178–82) – and this the very man they have made the king and have presumably sworn to uphold. Hotspur's opinions of Richard and Henry and of the actions of the Percies have changed radically as the contingencies of reinforcement have changed.

Late in the play, in a public justification of the rebellion on the night before the battle of Shrewsbury, Hotspur claims that the Percies did not intend to help Henry depose Richard and become king (4.3.59–65, 74–6, 90–2, 101). This contradicts what he says in private to his father and uncle in 1.3 (158–9, 170–4), but it is possible that he has come to believe in the Percies' innocence as the need to believe in the rightness of the rebellion has become critical. Hotspur's strong susceptibility to reinforcement by self-approval for thinking he behaves honorably could make even this self-deception possible. If we ultimately remain sympathetic to Hotspur, it is partly because we see that his passionate self-involvement "blinds" him – that is, makes it extremely aversive and hence impossible for him even to question his own conduct, much less to see it as not entirely honorable.

If Hotspur exemplifies how zealous devotion to a self-image of being honorable can lead to betrayal of honor, we can sympathize with Prince

Hal's desire to find directions out more indirectly through something like an antic disposition. Hal's tavern role may make us think of Hamlet, and, as in studying Hamlet, we must look closely to see whether Hal actually plays a role which enables him to have insight. A key to understanding Hal's motivation is the soliloquy in which he reacts to his dialogue with Falstaff and Poins (1.2.190–212). Although some critics believe that Hal steps out of character in this speech and that Shakespeare's purpose is merely to tell the audience that Hal will reform in good time, most critics today agree that the speech does express Hal's own thinking, or at least part of his thinking.[3]

If the soliloquy reveals character, we must still ask whether Hal conveys the sense that he has a good understanding of himself. It has been frequently argued that the soliloquy is a rationalization, that Hal really enjoys the tavern life and his companions, or that he has really fled the court for Oedipal reasons or in condemnation of his father's usurpation, or that he simply wants an excuse to delay acceptance of the burdensome duties of an heir apparent. Of course all these motives may strengthen his disposition to stay in the tavern, and they would all add to the reinforcement of any rationalization that would justify this result. But even if it is a rationalization, the speech reveals that Hal is also strongly motivated by pride in his royal identity. His upbringing, which has led him to regard himself as a person of the highest worth, makes it very reinforcing for him to think he will fulfill a royal identity and hence to justify staying in the tavern by thinking it to be consistent with this identity. Thus my statements that Hal finds it reinforcing to think a certain way will assume that the context makes clear that the immediate reinforcement is self-approval or approval by others, or the avoidance of self-contempt.

Hal's desire to prove royal is so strong here that he insists his loose behavior itself serves his future royalty. We may sense self-deception in this insistence, for Hal seems to "protest too much" in saying he is like the sun in appearing ugly to the world. Alvin Kernan has argued that when Hal says he will "imitate the sun" he sees himself as an actor, and that his strength is that with this self-awareness he can choose the right roles for himself and play them effectively (*Playwright* 83–4; cf. "Henriad" 274–5). This is an important idea, but I think Hal's use of "imitate" here supports it only indirectly.

Hal's meaning, as he explains it, is that he will imitate the sun by following its example in the way he makes his glory as a royal person visible. Thus what he refers to as imitation when he says "herein" he will imitate the sun is the "loose behavior" which conceals what he thinks he *is* (195, 205). Such actorly behavior will continue until he is ready to reveal his inherent brilliance, when he, like the sun, will break through the clouds in order "to be himself" (195). He varies the figure in a more theatrical metaphor when he says he will "throw off" his "loose behaviour" and show what "I am" (203–5). There is no suggestion that he is consciously intending to say that "to be himself" or to be what "I am" will also be an imitation or artful performance. When Henry IV later speaks of "sun-like majesty" in a passage paralleling this one (3.2.79), he means that to imitate the sun is to be a king, not to play the role of king in an actorly sense.

Hal's soliloquy is related to his later approaching the roles of prince and king in the way an actor might insofar as thinking of behavior as something to be thrown off becomes a characteristic as he is "taken with the manner" or habit (2.4.311). Another element in the soliloquy that may cause him to become like an actor is his great concern for appearances (1.2.207–10). This concern may divert his attention from what his country needs to what will enhance his royal image. Thus, he may "imitate" the sun by putting on a fine show in which the duties of a king are neglected and he is only an imitation king.

There may be no serious wrongdoing in Hal's prodigal life, but when he reviles his companions in this life, he prompts us to question the honesty of his view. He evidently thinks that the life of thief and roisterer constitutes the being of such men as Falstaff and Poins, whereas his own being is princely and whatever he does in pretense is not really a part of him, is merely "loose behavior" that he can "throw off." In his imitation of the sun he is hardly even involved in loose behavior. The sun "permits" base clouds to hide his beauty, and in Hal's words here the baseness is less in his behavior than in his companions (190–8). Hal thus heightens his glory to a sun-like level by heaping degradation on his companions. In this, his thinking is similar to Hotspur's in denouncing "you" – his father and uncle – for their dishonor. Hal knows "you all" and will awhile uphold "your" idleness. Another dubious elevation of himself is betrayed by the illogic of his metaphor of working days and holidays. Surely he is on holiday now and will be at work when he behaves in the way royalty should, yet his metaphor equates his tavern life with work (199–201).

Hal's thinking that takes too favorable a view of himself and judges others harshly in support of this view is not hard to explain. By joining in the tavern life, he has put himself in a situation that causes defensiveness. The soliloquy shows that at least in such a situation he cares greatly about what others think of him. Hal's exaggerated view of the distance between himself and the others in the tavern and his anticipation of future glory are reinforced because they minimize his anxiety about how his loose behavior is perceived. His defensiveness about his conduct is like that of an insecure person, though Hal is actually very capable. Indeed, his main reason for doubting himself has arisen through his conduct in the tavern world. Yet this is enough to make him feel that he must explain, justify, and especially prove himself. He knows the cynicism of the world, and so he speaks of how he will "falsify men's hopes" when he shows himself to be a true prince (206).

This defensive determination to show that others are wrong about him may make it difficult for Hal to have much freedom in playing the role of king. If he thinks he must prove himself to others, he will have to measure up to their expectations and be "The mirror of all Christian kings," not his own man. If he behaved well as a prince, he might depart from others' expectations in being a good king without losing their confidence before he could show his conduct to be praiseworthy. If he has been a prodigal as prince, however, any conduct as king thwarting what others wish would likely be interpreted as faulty. Thus his freedom now to play in base roles may cause him to lose a more important freedom later when he is king.

Hal shows that he takes a considerable interest in honor in saying he will "attract more eyes" because his loose behavior will serve as a foil for his noble self when he reforms (209). We notice first the great differences between Hal and Hotspur, yet their attitudes toward honor are more similar than has sometimes been observed. Both defend themselves against the imputation of dishonor, and both want to glitter and attract eyes but tend to neglect the importance of the traditional idea that one should seek honor only through honorable actions. A great difference between the two is that whereas Hotspur seeks honor for its own sake – for the immediate gratification of self-love – Hal wants honor to come only later, when he proves he can fulfill his royal identity.

Another difference between Hal and Hotspur's attitudes toward honor is that Hal will behave in a way he recognizes to be less than noble and Hotspur generally will not. Hotspur's refusal to behave dishonorably results in his not thinking he does so; comparably, Hal's concern for honor causes him to minimize the dishonor of his conduct. Hal will "so offend, to make offence a skill" (1.2.211). The underlying principle here is that the end justifies the means. Hal shows no concern for the psychological danger traditionally associated with this proposition, that while we hope for the good end, what we do is evil, and by doing evil we may become evil. We may come to enjoy the means as an activity so that it becomes habitual and the good end is forgotten or reduced to the merest rationalization.

The "offence" in which Hal may become entangled will not simply be the pleasures of the tavern life. So long as he thinks as he does in this soliloquy, those pleasures will be accompanied by thoughts that they are base and that he engages in them for the sake of his future royal image. The continuation of the tavern life might be marked by a high degree of ambivalence as it is reinforced by the tavern pleasures and by self-approval for thinking that he does not stay in the tavern for the sake of pleasure. He would learn to do as he pleases and rationalize that he acts in a way that ultimately enhances his image as prince or king. He might also learn to be dishonest with others and use them to enhance his image, perhaps treating them unjustly in the process. Through his role of "false thief" in the tavern, Hal may learn to steal, but only with a justifying rationale connecting the stealing to his destiny as "true prince." Through such behavior he may become a king who seizes others' kingdoms while providing noble justification for his actions.

The soliloquy itself can only suggest possibilities. Hal may be moved to think as he does by what has just transpired with Falstaff and Poins, and so what he says may not express a settled disposition. The soliloquy may not provide the key to Hal's course of action because a rationale – whether it is a rationalization or not – can give way to a better plan if a new situation develops. At any time Hal might discover a better way to make himself an object of wonder as a prince.

In the tavern world Hal cannot show himself directly to be royal while engaging in "loose" activities, but he does try to prove his superiority by showing that the tavern people are "base." Thus, although he enjoys Falstaff's company, Hal repeatedly puts him down. Treating Falstaff this way may be reinforced partly because the older man evokes responses Hal would direct at his father for Oedipal reasons or in disapproval of his conduct in becoming king. Yet these cannot be the chief causes of Hal's aggressive behavior in the tavern, since he also puts down Francis and (in *2H4*) Poins, who are not father figures. Hal chiefly puts them all down for what they have in common, that they are the base denizens of the tavern world. Indeed, putting them down must be strongly reinforced for Hal, since he does it consistently and it holds his attention so strongly that he fails to see how his success in putting them down depends on lowering *himself* in a way that undercuts his success.

It may appear, however, that Hal and Falstaff engage in games of wit for their mutual pleasure, so that what I have termed aggressive behavior is understood by both of them to be part of their fun. Anthropologists have shown that aggressive joking relationships are common in some cultures when the relationship is socially strained (Becker 105), as it is between persons of high and low status. This is close to my view, since the aggressive joking expresses tension or ambivalence in such relationships. To be sure, Hal's keeping company with Falstaff is partly motivated by pleasure and by some degree of affection, but an insulting mode of joking can also be reinforced as a put-down.[4]

There may be collusion between Hal and Falstaff of the sort described by R. D. Laing in which people support each other's illusions about themselves and their relationship without awareness that these are illusions (*Self and Others* 108–9). An example in *1H4* is the dialogue between Hotspur and Douglas in which each flatters the other in return for being flattered himself (4.1.1–12). The collusion between Hal and Falstaff would be a mutual understanding that all they say shows what good fellows and sharp wits they are and how much they enjoy each other's company, a view that enables both to avoid acknowledging any real tension between them.

The text suggests, however, that Hal is sometimes consciously hostile to Falstaff, but acts in a way that lets Falstaff think he is only kidding. Falstaff evidently does believe that Hal loves him, and as a result he finds it disconcerting when Hal's behavior is so hostile that it is hard to think he is only kidding. Falstaff is no innocent victim, though, for his belief that Hal loves him is evidently reinforced by hopes to profit when Hal becomes king. In 1.2 the reinforcement due to such hopes seems strong, since Falstaff thinks it acceptable to allude to his ambitions in a way that assumes Hal will tolerate corruption when he is king. Or rather, Falstaff alludes jokingly to these things, so that he can say he is only kidding if Hal should take offense.

Falstaff wittily urges Hal not to call thieves "thieves" when he is king, but "squires of the night's body . . . , gentlemen of the shade" and "men of good government" (1.2.23–7). When Hal's reply starts out with seeming encouragement ("Thou sayest well") but ends with an ominous reference to the gallows (30–8), Falstaff counters with jesting references to Hal's corrupt sex life in the tavern (39–56). Hal in turn counters Falstaff's imputations with a veiled threat of imprisonment (41–2). Falstaff returns to the question about thieves, urging Hal not to hang any when he is king (56–60). When Hal ambiguously turns this aside by saying that Falstaff will hang the thieves, Falstaff's hope leaps to interpret this: "Shall I? O rare! By the Lord, I'll be a brave judge!" (61–2). Falstaff perhaps states his hope extravagantly here so that Hal can understand him to be only joking. Hal puts his hope down, saying he meant Falstaff will be a hangman, but he, too, uses a jesting tone and so it is not clear how seriously he means this (63–5).

Falstaff senses that his relationship with Hal, and Hal's status, will not allow plain talk about his hopes. Knowing that Hal will never openly promise him advancement, Falstaff finds it plausible (because reinforcing) to interpret Hal's remarks in a way that does not end his hopes. On his side, Hal seems more aware of Falstaff's thinking than Falstaff realizes (see, e.g. 69). Hal toys with Falstaff's hopes in a way that may appear honest to himself because to him it is obvious that he is saying no to Falstaff and putting him down. In this toying Hal seems to be amused partly because he thinks Falstaff misreads his intentions only as a result of self-deception. The Prince must sense that Falstaff's words of affection are at least partly flattery: three times in this episode Falstaff addresses Hal as "sweet wag" and follows this phrase with an appeal or question about "when thou art king" (16, 23, 56–8). All doubts that Hal sees through

Falstaff in a general way are of course ended by his soliloquy, by which time Hal has been provoked to reject totally Falstaff's imputations about the sort of king he will be.

The cause of Hal and Falstaff's only communicating with each other in a jesting way is not necessarily that their characters will not allow more direct communication under any circumstances. Although perhaps this is becoming true of them, their situation and kind of relationship keep them from being more open. Even if Falstaff were not hoping for advancement, Hal would have to suspect he is, and although Falstaff cannot dream he is to be the foil for Hal's royal glitter, he may be uncomfortable with Hal because he senses that Hal must be at least a little suspicious of his motives in loving the heir apparent (cf. *R2* 5.1.59–68 regarding mutual suspicions).

By letting Falstaff deceive himself in his hopes of advancement, Hal contributes to the corruption of the kingdom, though there is no evidence he intends to do so. Hal is disposed to think that as long as he is a false – a pretended – thief and not a true thief he does no serious wrong. But by appearing to be a thief, he encourages the corruption around him. Several times in 1.2 questions arise about whether Hal is somehow false and a corrupter of others. Just after the dialogue we have been examining, Falstaff pretends to think Hal is corrupting him and claims he will reform (79–95), perhaps because Hal's responses have suggested he is aware of Falstaff's efforts to corrupt *him*. If Falstaff can make a joke of the idea that one of them is corrupting the other, this will pre-empt any move on Hal's part to accuse him. Knowing Falstaff is merely pretending he will reform, Hal proposes that they should steal a purse (96). If Falstaff wished to pursue his pretense, he could reply that this shows how Hal plays the devil to tempt and corrupt him. Instead, Falstaff's avarice and spirit of good fellowship dispose him to accept the proposal eagerly, and Hal puts down his claim that he will reform as a ridiculous bit of hypocrisy (97–100). Falstaff wittily replies that thieving is his vocation and "'tis no sin for a man to labour in his vocation" (101–2), implicitly raising the question whether Hal is laboring in *his* vocation.

If Hal has succeeded in putting Falstaff down, does it not matter at all that to do this the Prince has stooped to the low pretense of proposing that they rob? Granted, this is all said in jest and Hal is not "really" tempting Falstaff, but since this "not really" is the mode of most of their communications, the interchange is worth noting. It is noteworthy especially because it has the same pattern as later episodes in which it is clearer that Falstaff replies to Hal's put-downs by challenging the way he has acted to achieve the put-down.

Hal's criticism and Falstaff's defense of his stealing is the cue for Poins's entry. Poins tempts Hal as Hal has just tempted Falstaff. (Then in the soliloquy at the end of the scene the parallel between Hal and Falstaff continues as Hal vows to reform even though he intends to engage in stealing for the sake of his vocation.) When Hal is asked if he will participate in the highway robbery Poins proposes, he says "Who, I rob? I a thief? Not I, by my faith" (134). The scene provides evidence that he has robbed, however. Hal speaks of "us that are the moon's men," not "you" thieves (31). And he asks Falstaff where "we" shall "take a purse" (96). This phrasing and Falstaff's reply leaving the choice to Hal suggest that Hal has joined in thievery. If he has never done so, Falstaff should be surprised to hear him say these things. In addition, Poins's initial proposal of the robbery seems to include Hal as a matter of course (120–9).

The context and the tone of what Hal says also suggest he is not fully serious in saying he will not rob. He has just used Falstaff's eagerness to steal against him, and he does not want the tables to be turned. Hal's triple protest "protests too much," as does the shocked outrage of its tone: "Who, I rob? I a thief? Not I, by my faith" (134). The righteous tone registers a mock protest, as if to say he will not yield so foolishly as Falstaff does to temptation but that they should not ultimately leave him out of the adventure. Evidently Hal has not participated in all the robberies, however, since Poins and Falstaff respond to his hint that he must be wooed by wooing him rather than by laughing at his protest. Yet they give no indication that if Hal assents to go it will be for the first time (135–53). Hal continues his coy pretenses when he responds to their persuasions first with seeming reluctance – "Well then, once in my days I'll be a madcap" – and then a moment later says "Well, come what will, I'll tarry at home" (138, 140).

It is revealing that Hal says he will "be a madcap" in going. The soliloquy shows that Hal would never see himself to "be" a thief, and Poins persuades him to join only in robbing the robbers on this occasion. This is truly to act as a "false thief," a phrase that especially applies because Falstaff has just used it in encouraging Poins to be persuasive so that "the true prince may (for recreation sake) prove a false thief, for the poor abuses of the time want countenance" (150–2). Falstaff probably uses the phrase "false thief" to emphasize the falseness of thieves, but Poins's proposal to rob the robbers implies that the phrase can mean pretended thief, a thief false to thieves. Hal says later that he will repay the stolen money to its rightful owners, showing that through his thieving the pretended thief can undo the original theft and so may prove himself to be an honest man and true prince (2.4.540–1).

It is not certain, however, that Hal intends to repay the money before he is endangered by the Sheriff's coming to the tavern looking for the robbers. Earlier Hal's intentions have seemed to be only to enjoy the adventure and the fun of putting Falstaff down as a coward. Even if his purpose all along includes repaying the money, what Hal has been *doing* is robbing. Although robbing robbers is presumably not a seriously corrupting activity, it is not very princely, either, to pounce on people from ambush when their guard is down. For reasons explained in connection with his soliloquy, however, Hal finds it reinforcing to take very lightly the means he uses to gain his ends. The thought he relishes and becomes absorbed in is what fun it will be to prove Falstaff a coward and a liar, and it does not seem to occur to him that the outcome will be flawed if he has to lie and perhaps act in a cowardly fashion himself to achieve it. Either Hal does not see his own base acts in the robbery, or they do not matter to him because in his view these acts are just for fun or for the good purpose of showing up Falstaff, merely "loose behavior" ultimately in the service of a sun-like royalty.

Other characters, however, may justly regard Hal as encouraging corruption and as repaying the money to protect himself. This view is suggested in the emblematic scene at the inn which, like England, has been "turned upside down" (2.1.10). Gadshill says that "nobility" join thieves "for sport sake," and that his great allies "do the profession some grace" (69–70, 74–5). Hal's paying back the stolen money after the Sheriff has questioned him will not make Gadshill think he is a true prince. Rather Gadshill will see that when "matters" are "looked into," the nobility "make all whole" for "their own credit sake" (70–2).Gadshill's speech thus links Hal with other "nobility and tranquillity, burgomasters and great onyers" who "ride up and down" on the commonwealth and "make her their boots" (74–5, 81).

Gadshill promises, "as I am a true man," a share of the thieves' "purchase" for the Chamberlain. When the Chamberlain tells him to promise instead as he is "a false thief," Gadshill replies "Go to, *homo* is a common name to all men" (90–3). The thief sees that the great men's claims of nobility are false, but he dignifies his thieving by calling it a "profession," his booty by calling it "purchase" (70, 91). Everyone thinks himself a true man (or prince) and the others false thieves. It is the essence of the times that "homo" is a name for all men: all men are human and therefore they are all true men. To call a man a true man is not to say he is honest but to say he is human. Humans in this time are most truly human when they are most truly false yet think in some way that allows them to see themselves as honorable and their foes as thieves.

Insofar as this is the condition of their world, we should not make severe moral judgments of characters such as Hal or Hotspur. For my purposes, what is important here is to see Shakespeare's understanding of the human tendency to act and think in ways that are self-serving and therefore often self-deceiving. The issue confronting Hal, and us, is especially the way he is learning to see his actions from a point of view shaped by the contingencies of reinforcement for a prince among thieves.

The misnaming of true / false continues in the scene of the robbery when Falstaff expects thieves to "be true one to another" and when he attacks their victims as "villains" and "whoreson caterpillars" (2.2.27–8, 80–1). The final confusion of true and false here is, as Hal says, that in their panic each thief "takes his fellow for an officer" (102), which may indicate that Hal thinks of himself more as an officer here than as a "fellow" of the thieves.

Following the robbery, Hal is in high spirits as he waits for Falstaff in the tavern. He has been drinking with the tavern waiters, and he laughingly tells Poins of his exploits among them. Hal says he humbled himself to the level of the waiters as a "brother" and a "good boy" (2.4.5–12). Yet with Poins now he expresses scorn of the waiters, speaking of them as "loggerheads" and even a "leash of drawers," as if they were dogs (4,7). He seems amused by his condescension: "I have sounded the very base-string of humility" – and by their presumption: ". . . a good boy (by the Lord, so they call me!)" (5–6, 12–13). He claims he has learned the language of the people "in one quarter of an hour" (18), but he is not necessarily learning appropriate attitudes toward them. As Hamlet says to Polonius, a nobleman should treat inferiors with respect according to his own dignity (2.2.526; cf. Guazzo 1:192–5).

Of special psychological importance here is the way Hal's conduct may change his attitude toward the commoners and then his altered attitude may in turn affect his conduct with them. The dialogue between Hal and Poins is what Erving Goffman discusses as "backstage" action (*Presentation* 112–40, 170–5). As Goffman explains, a major element of backstage behavior is denigration of the persons we have had to treat with respect in an on-stage performance. In behaviorist terms, we can escape the aversive quality of maintaining a front that expresses respect we do not fully feel by sharing a denigrating attitude with colleagues.

According to this psychology, if Hal felt uncomfortable in lowering himself to the level of the drawers, this could lead him to express an exaggeratedly scornful view of them to Poins. Looking again at Hal's soliloquy at the end of 1.2, his scorn of his companions then, too, may have been heightened by the backstage effect – in Goffman's terms, Hal is a team of one in his soliloquy (*Presentation* 80–1). Backstage denigrations of others tend to cause acute awareness of the discrepancy between the attitudes expressed when with the others and the attitudes expressed in their absence. The backstage attitudes seem more sincere because they are expressed in private, although they have a heightened cynicism because of the dynamics of the situation. Once an attitude has been expressed backstage, thoughts supporting it and affirming sincere belief in it are reinforced by self-approval – we want to believe that somewhere, at least, we are honest. Then thoughts that the backstage attitude is sincere function as discriminative stimuli to increase our sense that the attitudes of respect expressed frontstage are insincere.

After telling Poins of the episode with the drawers, Hal manipulates Francis to prove his backstage assertion that the fellow "never spake other English in his life" than what is required in his role as a waiter in the tavern (2.4.24–77). When the manipulation ends, Hal repeats this conception of Francis: "That ever this fellow should have fewer words than a parrot, and yet the son of a woman!" (96–7). Hal thinks he has shown Francis to be virtually a subhuman being, but he overlooks crucial facts. Clearly Francis can speak as a person apart from his tavern role, for he begins to answer each of Hal's personal questions and stops only to respond to Poins's calling him (42–4, 49–52, 54–6). Francis is prevented from truly speaking for himself by his social role, which requires him to respond to Poins's calls as well as the questions of the Prince.

Hal's view of Francis is unjust partly because Hal does not have a clear view of his own and Poins's roles. Hal may take into account that if Francis's speech is limited it is because he has learned to conform to his role and not merely that he was born this way. However, Hal does not seem to take into account the degree to which a tavern waiter is coerced in the work-place by his master and by customers' calls for service. If Hal were more aware of how his own social position and his manipulation cause the behavior he sees in Francis, he could see Francis better: a failure of self-perception causes a failure to perceive another person justly.

Hal asks Francis questions about himself, yet takes no real interest in the answers. Hal seems to have made up his mind about Francis and merely anticipates Poins's call of "Francis!" as Francis starts to speak. Although Hal has learned to speak the tavern lingo of a drawer, he evidently has not learned to speak to such a person's humanity or to listen to him. Hal puts Francis down as subhuman because his speech is limited; ironically, the limitations of Hal's speaking and listening show how much Hal's understanding of himself and Francis is constricted by what his own role-situation makes it reinforcing or aversive for him to see.

There is a parallel between Francis and Hal as young men with roles they should perform who are called away from those roles. It seems certain, however, that Hal does not see the parallel, since he so totally fails to take the role of Francis. Hal focusses so narrowly on the perception of Francis as a parrot, disregarding what he actually says, that it would be surprising if Hal could see a similarity between himself and Francis. Hal says nothing to dispel this understanding of his point of view; if he sees the parallel, he sees it only with concern for his own plight, for he scorns Francis's humanity from start to finish.

When Falstaff arrives at the tavern, Hal relishes his role as the one who exposes false pretenses. As Falstaff boasts of how many men he fought in the robbery, Hal pretends to be impressed, leading Falstaff on in his lies until they are "open" and "palpable" before revealing the truth (159–251). Actually, of course, Hal gives no credence to any of what Falstaff says, since he is disposed to think Falstaff is lying about everything. If Falstaff calls him and Poins cowards, this is simply false in Hal's view; he does not think of his and Poins's staying out of the robbery or their striking from ambush as caused by fear (but see 1.2.176). Since he and Poins have anticipated Falstaff's behavior, Hal can respond to Falstaff's accusations and boasts with amused detachment, thinking mostly of the fun he will have in putting the fat knight down. Although Hal may think more of the fun than of the putting down, he indicates what I have suggested is a major reinforcing outcome of his tavern role-playing when he says at his moment of victory "mark now how a plain tale shall put you down" and concludes by asking "What trick, what device, what starting-hole canst thou now find out, to hide thee from this open and apparent shame?" (250–61).

There is nothing in Hal's gloating tone to suggest that he expects Falstaff to invent a "device" that can enable him to escape shame. Falstaff's reply that he recognized Hal but did not fight him because "the lion will not touch the true prince" evens the score with Hal, if it does not free Falstaff from shame (267–8). The text does not indicate that Hal ever gets Falstaff's point, but Falstaff emphasizes it when he expands on what he has said: "I shall think the better of myself, and thee, during my life – I for a valiant lion, and thou for a true prince" (269–71). The question about false thief and true prince helps to explain what Falstaff says: "If I have not acted as a true, valiant knight, have you acted as a true prince?" Hal does not see how he leaves himself open to counter-thrusts such as Falstaff's reply here because his lowering himself in the tavern makes it so reinforcing for him to focus his attention defensively on ways in which others are inferior to him.

Falstaff concludes with a merry appeal embracing all of the tavern crowd in "good fellowship" (274–5). He proposes a "play extempore," and Hal says the subject should be Falstaff's "running away" (276–8). Hal has contrasted himself with Francis and Hotspur, men concerned with only one matter, saying he is of all humors, but his actions of putting Francis and then Falstaff down limit him in a way comparable to Francis's role or Hotspur's mind (90–106).

For a second time in this scene, Hal's proposal for the subject of a play extempore is turned aside (cf. 106ff and 277ff), raising the question of how much he controls the script for his own acting. Even in the episode with Francis, in which Hal is very much in control, he merely exploits the coerciveness of a script society has created. In his first proposal for a play extempore, Hal wants to play Percy to Falstaff's Dame Mortimer (107–8), but Falstaff determines the play they will act by throwing himself into the role of the brave but sadly betrayed warrior-robber. Of course this role plays into the script controlled by Hal and Poins, in which Hal plays the controlling role, but this role is mostly limited to encouraging Falstaff to follow his own histrionic inclinations. Also, the script for this play has been invented by Poins, not Hal, right down to a knowledge of the boasting role Falstaff plays and the conclusion that "in the reproof of this lives the jest" (1.2.156–85).

Following the "reproof," when Falstaff proposes a play extempore, Hal's suggestion that the "argument" for their play should be Falstaff's running away is pushed aside by a message from the King that Hal "must" go to the court in the morning (2.4.276–85, 329–31). The script for the larger play of the rebellion in which Hal must perform is one he has had no hand in shaping because he is a truant from his "place in Council" (3.2.32). It is Falstaff who suggests that Hal should "practise an answer" for the scolding he must expect from the King. Hal, however, takes control in suggesting that the practice should be in the form of a rehearsal with role-playing and in casting Falstaff to act the King opposite his own enactment of himself (2.4.368–72).

Falstaff as the King quickly turns from scolding Hal to defending Falstaff, since his overriding concern is to induce Hal to defend their relationship when he talks with his father. It appears that Falstaff's light-hearted self-flattery is offensive to Hal, for when Falstaff is finally turning from self-defense to require Hal to speak for himself, Hal demands that they exchange roles (425–8). This action of Hal's and his conduct earlier in this scene with Francis and Falstaff suggest that Hal exerts control through making himself the director of the play, the one who controls the conditions of the role-playing situation. This is a role for a king to play.

Hal plays King Henry – starting with his deposition of the previous king – in a way suggesting how closely he will follow his father's script for the part (439–75). To be sure, he is expected as part of the pretense to speak like his father, but as his attack on Falstaff develops he becomes more strident and less witty in his abuse, so that he seems to become absorbed in the emotion he expresses. When he says "I do, I will" in response to Falstaff's plea not to banish him, the second phrase suggests that Hal speaks for himself as well as the King. Hal's power-play in taking over the role of the King thus enables him to defend himself without having to speak directly in self-defense. His defense is to show that he has a conventionally correct attitude toward Falstaff and can play the role of king. Yet he is also Prince Hal still, for again he plays his tavern role in putting Falstaff down.

Hal is not yet ready to act on his judgment of Falstaff, however. "I do, I will" is more than an assertion that as Henry IV he banishes Falstaff within the play extempore and that as Henry V he will one day really banish him. It also suggests that although his denunciations have brought him to a present will to banish Falstaff, he then reflects that he does not really want to banish him now, and so he temporizes by saying "I will." In playing the role of his father Hal can be reinforced for giving full sway to his disposition to put Falstaff down while also telling himself that he is "only pretending" and thereby escaping the aversive effect of feeling that he is harshly attacking Falstaff. In this reading, as he ends his tirade and steps back from the King's part, he feels that he has gone further than he intended and he recovers himself to his role as Prince Hal in the tavern in "I will." These words thus express Hal's ambivalence and his own recognition of it. The role-playing situation would also cause Hal's tirade against Falstaff to be reinforced if Hal is disposed to attack his father or himself, since Falstaff has been playing the King and is now standing for Hal. Hal would presumably not be aware of these motives, as he may also be surprised at the vehemence of his attack on Falstaff.

Prince Hal's "I do, I will" is the cue for the Sheriff to knock at the door. For the second time in the scene, the larger world intrudes into the tavern play, and this time Hal is called on not merely to practice an answer but to make an answer to the figure of the King's authority in the person of the Sheriff. Hal tries to collect himself, but his playing at being a false thief has compromised his ability to play the true prince to the Sheriff: "Now, my masters, for a true face, and good conscience" (494–5). A true face is an appearance that can be composed, but can a good conscience be summoned in this manner and be expected to act effectively or does it need more regular exercise? Hal seems to think of himself as an actor might in collecting his thoughts about how a true prince's conscience would cause him to behave.

Although Hal's equivocating answer to the Sheriff's question about Falstaff may be the closest to good conscience that the contingencies of reinforcement will allow, it is also very close to a lie: "The man I do assure you is not here, / For I myself at this time have employ'd him" (505–6). But actually Hal has merely sent Falstaff to the side of the room to hide behind the arras. Hal also engages his "word" to send Falstaff to answer charges the next day (507–10). Hal's word, however, has been equivocated, and there is no sign that he intends to act on this promise, for when the Sheriff has left, Hal says he will "procure ... a charge of foot" for Falstaff to lead. Hal evidently finds it reinforcing to think he will show sufficient integrity if he repays the stolen money with interest (538–41). It may be that Hal acts with generous intent here in risking his word and honor to protect Falstaff, but the dialogue between Gadshill and the Chamberlain suggests that Hal is also protecting himself.

The conference between Prince Hal and King Henry in 3.2 demonstrates how much the father and son think alike about the need to project a royal image. The King sees only the difference between his son's behavior and his own before he became king. But the more he holds his own conduct up as a model, the more his language indicates that Hal has followed him, for he says he kept his royal nature hidden in order to win an "extraordinary gaze, / Such as is bent on sun-like majesty / When it shines seldom in admiring eyes" (78–80). And both men are willing to steal to get what they want, for the King says that he "stole all courtesy from heaven" in order to "pluck allegiance from men's hearts / . . . / Even in the presence of the crowned King" (50–4).

In the tavern Hal is not trying to steal allegiance but is creating a basis for appearing better only than himself, not the King. To be sure, Hal as heir apparent might be assumed to have no motive to threaten his father's reign. According to the historical sources, however, the Prince was rumored to want to supplant his father, and hence it is significant that the text gives no hint of Hal's having such an intention. Here the King speaks of Hal's tavern life as a threat to himself only in thinking of the baseness of it as a punishment (4–17), as a cause for the downfall of his royal line (30–8), or as a sign that Hal might fight for Hotspur "through vassal fear, / Base inclination, and the start of spleen" (124–6).

This last accusation is evidently intended to shame Hal so deeply that he will be strongly moved to reform. Hal has said in his 1.2 soliloquy that he will reform "when men think least I will," suggesting that he will control his own actions. However, his passionate response to the accusation that he might be disloyal suggests that his father has chosen the time and has controlled the nature of his response. In addition, the time is hardly "when men think least" he will reform: if Hal is ever to rise to his royal identity, he needs to now when his family's future is at stake. Hal's disposition to prove himself causes him to become very emotional when his father shames him, and this emotion makes it reinforcing for him to promise everything. Hal is thus like the actor whose own feelings support those of the character the script calls on him to play, but the script is authored more by his father's manipulation, by political exigencies, and by the vulnerability Hal has because of his tavern life, than by Hal's own calculations and self-control.

Although Hal's own style of calculation is heard in this speech vowing his redemption, the hyperbole of the calculation shows how much it is an emotional response to his father's accusations. Hal says he wishes Hotspur had "multitudes" of honors for each one he has and that his own shames were "redoubled" (142–4). In the following lines calculation dominates emotion as he explains his arithmetic of honor, yet even here there is hyperbolic excess – not only will he gain all Hotspur's honors by killing him, but also Hotspur will have to bear all of Hal's "indignities" in exchange (145–6). The rhetoric of hyperbole is still heard even in the most calculating lines of all, in which he speaks of Hotspur as his purchasing agent (147–52). The calculation here is all in excess, not balanced and controlled. Hotspur will be forced to render "every" glory up, and this exaggeration is then expanded in a whole line that begins with a strongly emotional word of avowal: "Yea, even the slightest worship of his time" (150–1).

Hal proposes to hold Hotspur to a strict account, but he is not strict in his accounting regarding himself, and this can be a key for interpreting his use of commercial language to discuss honor. The emotional intensity of the whole speech suggests that at least for the moment Hal has an overwhelming desire for honor. In this context, his metaphor of the "factor" is mostly an extreme reaching out for a term to express his hope that he can gain the honors Hotspur has won in many combats by the single brave deed of killing their bearer. Thus the metaphors of purchasing and accounting do not show Hal speaking in a calculating way that coolly expresses a detached view of honor as a useful political commodity. Rather, Hal speaks unguardedly and his language reveals that he may lack concern for honor's deeper import. He speaks of honor as the emblems bedecking a hero's helmet, the outward shows that can indeed be gained and lost like a commodity (142ff), but what this expresses is his longing to have all the praise that his father and others lavish on Hotspur.

In the first speech of the next scene, set in the tavern, Falstaff says "Well, I'll repent, and that suddenly, while I am in some liking; I shall be out of heart shortly, and then I shall have no strength to repent" (3.3.4–7). This comments neatly on Hal's repentance as having come in an emotional moment which led him to vow strongly. But Falstaff soon loses his heart for repentance when he gets into a quarrel with the Hostess in which she asks him to pay the money he owes for the purchase of a dozen shirts (3.3.50–68). Falstaff's unwillingness to pay what he has promised in the past shows his unwillingness to make a true promise to God about his future conduct, and this failure raises the question whether Hal's reformation will be undercut by his past deeds and commitments.

When Hal enters, Falstaff has been complaining about his pocket being picked, and he has just said the Prince is a "sneak-up" (83). Hal, however, is intent on shaming Falstaff, not to evoke a strong response as his father has done with himself, but in a tone which – however much his intention is to be "only joking" – suggests that Falstaff could not possibly redeem himself:

> sirrah, there's no room for faith, truth, nor honesty in this bosom of thine; it is all filled up with guts and midriff. Charge an honest woman with picking thy pocket? Why, thou whoreson impudent embossed rascal, if there were anything in thy pocket but tavern reckonings, memorandums of bawdy-houses, and one poor pennyworth of sugar-candy to make thee long-winded, if thy pocket were enriched with any other injuries but these, I am a villain: and yet you will stand to it, you will not pocket up wrong! Art thou not ashamed?   (152–63)

Falstaff first tries to defend himself as an especially frail but essentially typical victim of Adam's fall, and then he thinks to add: "You confess then, you picked my pocket?" (164–8). Hal is evidently taken aback by this query, for the only retort he musters is "It appears so by the story" (169). This is the most glaring example in the play of Hal getting so caught up in a mock but also righteously mocking expression of contempt that he does not see what he confesses about himself. Surely if he sees what he confesses and is only pretending to accuse Falstaff, knowing that his vehemence is making himself look ridiculous, he would at least expect Falstaff's rejoinder and would have a better comeback prepared.

In his confidence that he has Falstaff trapped, Hal uses a self-betraying turn of speech which Falstaff earlier used in a similar way. Hal says that if Falstaff's pockets contained anything of value, "I am a villain" (161). During his boasting in the earlier tavern scene, Falstaff repeatedly says things like "I am a rogue if I were not at half-sword with a dozen of them two hours together" (2.4.162–3; cf. 149, 177, 183, 185, 190, 202). In the last of these instances, Falstaff's phrase is "I am a villain else," which is very close to Hal's phrase in 3.3. In Falstaff's use of these phrases the joke is that his vehement claims that he is not a villain actually carry the meaning that he is one, since in fact he is lying. Ironically, Hal is right in what his facts show about Falstaff, yet blind to what the way he came to know these facts suggests about himself. It is especially revealing that Hal's account stresses that nothing of monetary value was taken from Falstaff's pockets. Hal is so disposed to see himself as greatly superior to Falstaff that he avoids seeing how having Falstaff's pockets picked matters more than what was found there.

The parallel between his father's shaming of him for his tavern life and his own shaming of Falstaff here suggests that Hal may be taking out on Falstaff what his father did to him, and that he is doing so partly because he finds it reinforcing to blame Falstaff for his own shames: "I am a villain else." This may partly explain the vehemence of Hal's attack on Falstaff, though Hal is not likely to think in such terms. In saying "it appears so by the story" Hal evidently means that the simple facts show he has had Falstaff's pocket picked (169). This way of saying it, however, implies a further meaning, that in his own story he has unintentionally revealed the action he confesses. There is an implication here that Hal is not as fully in control of the show he projects to the world as he would like.

In telling what he has done about the robbery, Hal is as affectionate as he ever is to Falstaff: "O my sweet beef, I must still be good angel to thee – the money is paid back again" (176–7). Yet the affection in "sweet beef" is nicely balanced by derision, and Hal's claim that he has played the role of Falstaff's good angel in repaying the stolen money, though perhaps sincere, overlooks the fact that Hal was protecting himself as well as Falstaff in repaying the stolen money. Perhaps in part Hal's flattering himself as a good angel makes it reinforcing for him to think of the one he saves as worthy of his own goodness, hence "sweet." This somewhat parallels the way Falstaff has just assumed the pose of the innocent person who forgives the wrong done by the Hostess, hoping to induce her to forget he still owes her money (170).

The scene ends with Hal telling Falstaff that he will command a unit of foot soldiers in the war (185, 198–201). At the end of the first tavern scene Hal joked that Falstaff's "death will be a march of twelve score" (2.4.538–40). Now, however, Hal seems intent on the war's business, so perhaps he expects Falstaff to exercise his command responsibly. But if Hal has procured Falstaff a charge of foot soldiers with the half jesting expectation that it will be the death of the fat knight, he is careless of the likelihood that such an officer will be the death of his men. That Hal may be characteristically disposed to have a careless attitude toward common people is suggested by his spontaneous outburst about the women of the land when he first heard of the rebellion: "Why then, it is like if there come a hot June, and this civil buffeting hold, we shall buy maidenheads as they buy hob-nails, by the hundreds" (2.4.357–9).

At the parley before the battle of Shrewsbury, Hal's reformation to the true prince is well under way, and a crucial phase of this change occurs in this scene. Earlier Hal has spoken derisively of Hotspur, as of everyone else he puts down (2.4.99–108). Now, however, speaking before his father and the noblemen on both sides of the civil conflict, Hal gives honor to Hotspur by praising his courage and noble deeds, then chides himself as a truant to chivalry. As climactic proof that his truancy has ended, Hal concludes by proposing that he and Hotspur engage in single combat to determine the issue of the war and so to save lives on both sides (5.1.83–100). In doing these things, Hal is especially reinforced because he demonstrates his nobility. The praise of Hotspur may be fully sincere, yet it and the self-dispraise also serve Hal's end of winning praise of himself. As he foretold in his soliloquy in Act 1, Hal's audience admires his reform especially because of its contrast with what went before.

The importance of the audience's response is suggested in Vernon's recounting this scene to Hotspur in the rebel camp (5.2.51–68). Vernon's account not only shows how greatly Hal's conduct has impressed even his foes, but also indicates that Hal has learned a paradox of honor which Hotspur's envious response shows he has still not learned (69–71). Although Hotspur can be chivalrous in his praise of Douglas as long as Douglas will praise him in return even more highly as "the king of honour" (4.1.1–12), Hotspur still wants no "corrival" in honor (1.3.204–6). As Hal spoke of his reform in 3.2, he did not want to share honor with Hotspur, but Vernon's speech tells us that Hal has now learned that he can gain honor by taking it from himself as well as by giving it to Hotspur. He "chid" himself "with such a grace / As if he master'd there a double spirit / Of teaching and of learning instantly" (5.2.62–4). The idea here is evidently that as Hal learns to chide himself as part of honoring his rival, he also teaches the value of this behavior and shows that it expresses the Prince he is coming to be. The grace of Hal's speaking shows that this conduct is both becoming to him and becoming natural for him (60). His grace confirms his learning and makes his self-expression convincing as a demonstration of his new princely character.

Through his speech, Hal simultaneously creates and expresses a princely self. At first in this speech he may calculate how he will demonstrate his reform if he praises Hotspur and dispraises his own former behavior. As he proceeds, however, the effect of his speech on his audience (*vide* Vernon) reinforces his performance strongly, causing him to throw himself more fully into his role so that his manner is more confident and graceful. He masters a "double spirit / of teaching and of learning instantly" in simultaneously realizing the effect of this behavior on others and the rightness of it for himself. These are simultaneous largely because Hal's sense that his behavior is right especially depends on his awareness that the others see it to be right for him. Indeed, even his initial intention here is partly evoked by the expectations of the noblemen he wants to prove himself to.

Hal's lesson here is of great importance for a prince. Renaissance writers emphasize that giving honor is a special role of the king, and that through giving honor the king especially establishes his supremacy. Annibale Romei in *The Courtiers Academie* writes that when a superior honors an inferior, this shows a "supereminency in the superior" (113). In "An Inquisition Upon Fame and Honour," Fulke Greville states the frequently repeated principle that honor always comes from others, so that the most a person can do to receive honor is to act so as to be worthy of it: "the essence of this glorious name, / Is not in him that hath, but him that gives it . . ." (stanza 47). Stephano Guazzo's *Civile Conversation* uses language which relates this idea to notions about imitating the sun: "he which honoureth, receiveth more honour, than he which is honoured, for like unto the sun, the beams of honour by reflection, as it were, do shine back again upon him" (1:165).

As long as a man must contend with others and keep proving himself worthy of honor, he does not control his possession of honor. The way to escape this condition is especially open to a king – he can simply rise above the contention for honor and graciously bestow honor on the contenders. By behaving as if he has an endless supply of honor, he shows that he does have such a supply, since no matter how much he gives he has more: the act of giving honor creates honor in oneself. When Hal has learned this lesson, however, he must still contend for honor with Hotspur, still prove himself in terms of the vow he made to his father.

In the battle, Hal proves himself by continuing to fight even when he is wounded, by saving his father from Douglas, and climactically by killing Hotspur (5.4.1–13, 38–56, 62–85). During and after the battle, Hal also finds frequent occasions to exercise his new learning by bestowing honor. He gives honor to his brother John, to the dead Hotspur, to Falstaff, and finally to Douglas and to his brother John again. In each case there is an indication that Hal is taken with bestowing honor but has not learned how to do it appropriately. In behaviorist terms, Hal may not look carefully at what he is doing because self-approval and the honor he receives in return reinforce him so strongly for giving honor. By the same token, it would be aversive for him to question what he does.

There is at least a little presumption in the way Hal praises his younger brother John for his fighting spirit: "By God, thou hast deceiv'd me, Lancaster / I did not think thee lord of such a spirit" (5.4.16–17). Since this is precisely what others might say to Hal himself, the speech prompts us to question his right to have doubted and now to judge his brother. I think Hal's words suggest that he does not reflect on how his earlier conduct might make these words sound inappropriate. The alternative interpretation, that Hal honors his brother in a calculating way, is unlikely because calculation would enable him to avoid phrasing what he says in a way that raises a question about himself.

Hal again seems sincere in his speech over the body of Hotspur (5.4.86–100). Hal praises Hotspur's great heart, spirit, and courage, but in the middle of this praise Hal becomes self-conscious about the appropriateness of his behavior in honoring his foe. His self-consciousness leads Hal to speak awkwardly as he visualizes a scene of role-playing in which he presumes to speak for Hotspur by honoring himself for honoring Hotspur:

> If thou wert sensible of courtesy
> I should not make so dear a show of zeal;
> But let my favours hide thy mangled face,
> And even in thy behalf I'll thank myself
> For doing these fair rites of tenderness.
>
>   (93–7)

A little later Hal allows Falstaff to claim the honor of having killed Hotspur, saying that "if a lie may do thee grace, / I'll gild it with the happiest terms I have" (156–7). This willingness to lie is generous to Falstaff, but is it honorable? – and especially is it honorable or generous to Hotspur to let everyone think that he could be overcome even by old, fat Sir John Falstaff? Hal may conceive on the moment a scheme to demean Hotspur for political ends, but the text suggests more that in his happy success Hal is strongly reinforced even for a half-joking bestowal of honor, so that he does not think of what he is doing to Hotspur's memory, which he has cherished in private a little earlier. Hal's nonchalance about honor here is not the true grace of a chivalrous prince insofar as his conduct shows that he still lacks mastery of true honor. Moreover, although Hal may be jesting in offering to lie, Falstaff takes him seriously and in his final speech suggests that Hal's rewarding him reveals a truth about all noblemen, implying that even those who "live cleanly as a nobleman should do" are able and willing to do so chiefly because of such "gilding" as he hopes to receive (5.4.161–64).

In his last bestowal of honor, Hal honors several men simultaneously. He brings honor to himself in wanting to free the captured Douglas in order to honor a valiant foe, and he gives his brother John the "honourable bounty" of freeing him (5.5.17–31). This shows how honor can be multiplied as it is passed along, since both Hal and John are to be honored for a single act. In addition, through delegating to John the role of bestowing honor, Hal elevates himself further in the hierarchy of honor. He speaks like a king, but not in a way that threatens his father, for he honors his father by asking his permission to dispose of Douglas (23–4). Henry IV gains honor himself through the honor of his sons, and he asserts his authority over them by giving them commands in the final speech of the play.

Thus the end of the final scene presents a tableau of a unified royal family sharing honor with each other and also with a valiant foe. Hal is the chief creator of this tableau, and it is likely that he plays his role here with intentional artistry, since he simultaneously secures his brother's loyalty, appeals to Douglas to become a friend, and impresses his father and Westmoreland with his royally chivalrous character. There seems to be an element of contrivance especially in Hal's praise of Douglas. In saying that Douglas has taught them to "cherish" a foe's "high deeds" of valor, Hal may feel sincere – perhaps partly because to say this is so strongly reinforced by its effects – but it appears that what he says about Douglas is not entirely warranted or honest. To be sure, Hal's calling Douglas a "vile Scot" in the heat of battle (5.4.38) need not cast doubt on the later praise, but when Hal engages Douglas in combat, the stage direction tells us that "*Douglas flieth*" (5.4.42 s.d.). And in the last scene, before Hal praises Douglas's valor, he describes how at the end of the battle the "noble Scot," seeing "all his men / Upon the foot of fear, fled with the rest, / And falling from a hill, he was so bruis'd / That the pursuers took him" (5.5.17–22). In this description Douglas appears to be an almost ludicrous victim of panic, and it is against this background that Hal distributes the honors which depend on Douglas's "high deeds."

Hal's praise of Douglas is also put in doubt by its ironic relation to a dialogue in the first tavern scene. Word of the rebellion has just come, and Falstaff teases Hal about the fearsomeness of his foes, including "that sprightly Scot of Scots, Douglas, that runs a-horseback up a hill perpendicular" (2.4.338–40). A few lines later Falstaff says "that rascal hath good mettle in him, he will not run," and Hal replies "Why, what a rascal art thou then, to praise him so for running!" (345–8). Falstaff explains that he praised him for running on horseback, adding that "afoot he will not budge a foot," but Hal says "Yes, Jack, upon instinct" (349–51). The verbal parallels between this passage and Hal's description of Douglas's behavior at the end of the play may help us understand Hal's conduct in each situation. In Act 2 he was defensive and denigrated everyone, and now he has gone to the opposite extreme in his remarks about Douglas, "to praise him so for running," or rather to praise him so and ignore his running. The contrast between his two views of Douglas suggests that Hal's praise in 5.5 is at least a little politic.

There is thus good reason to think Hal deliberately seeks to make himself appear ideal at the end of the play. Yet there is also reason to think he sometimes gets caught up in what he says so that he is fully sincere. According to the view of Hal's character taking shape here, it will be especially reinforcing for him to prove that he *is* a true prince. Therefore, even when he performs his role as prince consciously, he will be reinforced by self-approval for seeing his conduct as real, not merely simulated, and for seeing himself acting according to the norms of filial piety, loyalty, and chivalry, not as failing those norms in some degree because of a truant's ignorance and carelessness. Perhaps we should see Hal as a character who can uphold noble values when he is well prepared to perform, whether in condemnation of baseness as in the tavern scenes, or in fulsome praise, as in honoring Douglas. In his last encounter with Falstaff, however, Hal is quite taken aback to find the fat knight still alive, and surprised again to hear him insist that he killed Hotspur. Hal has no prepared responses, and the resulting offer to "gild" Falstaff's lie may taint his performance in the final scene through which he gilds Douglas, Prince John, and himself.

The remainder of this chapter will survey more briefly the continuing development of Hal's character in *Henry IV, Part 2* and *Henry V*. Because *2H4* is a new play, we do not need to account for Hal's return to the tavern world, which otherwise would appear to be inconsistent with his character at the end of *1H4*. In *2H4* Hal behaves with the people of the tavern world much as he did in *1H4*, with the important difference that he seems to see more clearly how he lowers himself in being with them (2.2.134–5, 167–9; 2.4.358–9). Hal also acknowledges more fully than before that he lowers himself in order to put the tavern people down, but he still does not seem to see – or perhaps does not care – how ugly his own conduct may become in doing this.

In Act 2, scene 2 of *2H4*, Hal's attitude is epitomized in his saying that his desire for "small beer" makes him "out of love with" his "greatness," and then saying to Poins "What a disgrace is it to me to remember thy name! or to know thy face tomorrow!" (10–14). His love of small beer disposes Hal to be reinforced for reacting against his "greatness," but his deeper love of his "greatness" reinforces him for rejecting small beer in the form of Poins, who has put him on the defensive by suggesting that his weariness and his desire for small beer put his greatness in doubt (2–3, 7–8). When Hal finishes saying how much he despises himself (and Poins) because he knows all about Poins's wardrobe, Poins thrusts back by reproaching Hal for "talking so idly" when his father is very sick (28–31).

Hal's response again shows how strongly reinforced he is for defending his behavior, and how much this defensiveness causes him to take others' opinions of himself into account in shaping his behavior. (Poins's adroitness in putting Hal on the defensive in this scene suggests that he is well aware of the Prince's vulnerability.) Hal replies that he wants to show sorrow for his father, but cannot let himself do so because, as a result of his "keeping such vile company" as Poins is (47), "every man" (even Hal himself?) would think him a hypocrite (52, 53, 55). His reasoning here reverses the rationale for not going to join his father and the court world in Hal's soliloquy in Act 1 of *1H4*. According to that rationale, Hal should think that if he reformed and showed true sorrow for his father, his previous baseness would enhance the brilliant appearance of his reformation. Now, however, he says that his tavern life would make going to his father look false. Of course the situation has changed so that Hal's earlier plan for his reformation is no longer feasible. His going to his father now might indeed appear hypocritical: by waiting to reform until his father is dying, Hal has lost the ability to choose the time and the terms of his reformation – in both *1H4* and *2H4* we see that his father's situation and not his own choice controls Hal.

Hal seems to have advanced toward the moment of final reformation insofar as he now acknowledges a direct conflict between his tavern life and his ability to act as a true son and prince should. Admitting this to himself may lead to a reformation in which he will be less reinforced for concern about appearances than he was when he was guided by the rationale that there was really no conflict between his tavern life and his destiny as a true prince. He is still not ready to reform, however: according to his "own" thinking about himself, he should grieve for his father, but what others think creates contingencies allowing him to express public sorrow only in explaining to Poins why he cannot express sorrow to people such as Poins.

There is a question here of how sad Hal feels about his father's sickness. At one point Hal says "my heart bleeds inwardly that my father is so sick" (45–6), but before Poins provokes him to this strong statement he has merely said that he "could be sad, and sad indeed too" (41). In most of this dialogue Hal seems only to sense as a rational possibility that he "could be sad." His adding "and sad indeed too" suggests a need to insist on the strength of the emotions he is capable of feeling because he now feels little more than the potential for such emotion. Yet when he is provoked to say that he "bleeds inwardly" for his father, his phrasing suggests that he does feel sorrow. Poins's mocking attitude could make Hal unwilling to express – and perhaps unable to feel at this moment – much more than vexation.

If Hal does not have enough sympathy for his father, it is especially to be seen in his failure to take the role of his father – to look at his behavior from his father's point of view and take into account how he grieves his father by not going to him. Strangely, Hal seems more concerned here with the opinions of people whose thinking "keeps the roadway" of what "every man thinks" than with the judgment of his father and the noblemen. It is difficult to see how Hal can believe that his father would think he more truly grieves if he stays in the tavern than if he comes to the court and expresses sorrow. Perhaps Hal is afraid his father and the noblemen think as the masses think, so that if he were to go to his father now he would be rejected. Such a fear would show how little Hal understands his father's desire to have faith in him. This episode with Poins as a whole raises questions about Hal's present emotion, his capacity for emotion, and his way of regarding and controlling his emotions. He speaks of them as available but to be turned on and off according to a reason that seems so detached from spontaneous feeling – so much a defensive reaction to what others think – that love and sorrow may have little chance to develop.

At the end of 2.2, Hal and Poins plot to go to the tavern and "steal upon" Falstaff as he dines with the Hostess and Doll Tearsheet. Poins says they can do this if they disguise themselves as drawers, and Hal sees he will be lowering himself to play such a role: "From a prince to a prentice? A low transformation, that shall be mine, for in everything the purpose must weigh with the folly" (167–9). The emphasis on folly is heard also in what Hal said a little earlier as they talked about Falstaff's letter to Hal: "Well, thus we play fools with the time, and the spirits of the wise sit in the clouds and mock us" (134–5). Although Hal speaks of the judgment of the wise as coming from outside himself, this judgment is becoming an aspect of his own thinking about his tavern life, rather than a view to ignore because his reformation will give his follies positive value. In these speeches Hal seems lighthearted, however, and criticizes only the folly in what he does, suggesting that he still finds it reinforcing to suppress or laugh off more serious questions about his behavior.

In 2.4 Hal and Poins play the role of Francis (15–17, 278–9). In *1H4*, Francis felt compelled to obey the commands of Hal and Poins as customers, and so Hal was easily able to see him as shallow and witless in not speaking for himself. Now Hal and Poins sneak in on Falstaff's dinner with the Hostess and Doll, and for the sake of their plot they must listen to Sir John describe them as shallow and witless without speaking back to him (233–52). When Falstaff calls "Some sack, Francis," Hal and Poins echo Francis in *1H4* as they say "Anon, anon, sir" in coming forward (279). Unlike Francis, however, they can step out of their roles as drawers and attack their mocker.

The strategy by which Hal attacks Falstaff is to say it was wrong to slander him in the presence of "this honest, virtuous, civil gentlewoman!" – sarcastically referring to the prostitute, Doll (298–9). A little later Hal turns to Doll for her reaction:

PRINCE.   You, gentlewoman, –
DOLL.   What says your Grace?
                    (346–7)

Falstaff's retort that "His Grace says that which his flesh rebels against" (348) suggests that Hal pauses because as a prince and spiritual being ("your Grace") he finds it difficult to call Doll a gentlewoman when his fleshly being knows she is a prostitute (not that he has ever had sex with her himself: cf. 2.2.145–6, 159–61).

The neat pairing of "gentlewoman" and "your Grace" as terms of ad-dress in two successive short lines implies the same sort of comment on Hal's behavior as Falstaff's statement in *1H4* that coupled his own "val-iant lion" with Hal's "true prince," for if Doll is no gentlewoman, Hal is showing little grace. He is only *pretending* the grace of good manners in addressing Doll as a gentlewoman, and he does this to dis-grace Falstaff and ultimately her as well, at least in jest. This device might be entirely acceptable if Hal were willing to acknowledge that he really behaves gracelessly here, but he does not seem to admit this to himself, for it is evidently his princely sensibility and disdain that will not let him con-tinue to address Doll as a gentlewoman. As so often before, the reinforce-ments maintaining his disposition to see himself as superior cause Hal to see his behavior in a way that overlooks some aspect of it which undercuts his view. He toys with others' feelings as if he has left his princely sen-sibilities behind when he came to the tavern, then he indulges these sensibilities when they express his superiority over others.

A moment later there is news that the King has gathered his leaders and has sent to find Falstaff (352–7). Hal again acknowledges that his tavern life simply interferes with what he should be doing. There is now no idea that spending time in the tavern may help him to "redeem the time" when he reforms: "By heaven, Poins, I feel me much to blame, / So idly to profane the precious time" (358–9). The tavern life is now aversive for Hal as the demands of his princely identity make him feel guilty, not justified, in such behavior. The next time we see him he has left the tavern world forever to go to his dying father.

As Hal arrives at court he exhibits an inappropriate levity, optimism, and loudness which bespeak a self-conscious feeling of being rather out of place (4.5.7–16). When his brothers and Warwick withdraw, Hal stays to watch by the sleeping King, and his attention is immediately drawn to the crown. Hal's meditation on the crown shows that he regards kingship as "troublesome," and the speech as a whole suggests he is thinking of a king's need to be watchful against efforts to overthrow him as well as of the cares of rule (20–46).

When Hal thinks that his father has died, he speaks of his mourning in terms that make his grief sound less like heartfelt emotion than an oblig-atory payment made in exchange for the crown he should receive:

> Thy due from me
> Is tears and heavy sorrows of the blood,
> Which nature, love, and filial tenderness
> Shall, O dear father, pay thee plenteously.
> My due from thee is this imperial crown,
> Which, as immediate from thy place and blood,

Derives itself to me. [*Putting it on his head*] Lo where it sits,
Which God shall guard; and put the world's whole strength
Into one giant arm, it shall not force
This lineal honour from me. This from thee
Will I to mine leave, as 'tis left to me.

(36–46)

The grief Hal promises to pay "Shall" be paid, suggesting it is not felt strongly now, yet "O dear Father" seems heartfelt. In any case, the emotion he chiefly expresses at the end of the speech is a defensive determination to keep the crown even if the whole world tries to take it from him. Here an Elizabethan audience might well have responded with the thought that there is no guard that can prevent death itself from coming at any time, independently of any human force, to take the crown from a king. Hal thinks this has happened to his father now, but in his defiance of "the world's whole strength" he seems to have no inkling that he could die of disease as a young man after triumphing over his human foes.

Hal soon expresses grief, for a little later Warwick tells the King that he found Hal weeping with a "deep demeanour in great sorrow" (83–4). Although Warwick puts a good face on Hal's conduct in talking to the King (cf. 4.4.67–78 with 5.2.14–18), there is no reason to doubt that Hal weeps, for he soon points to his tears to defend himself against his father's condemnation (4.5.138–42). The King, however, scolds Hal as if the tears mean nothing, accusing him of taking the crown because he cares only about it and wishes his father were dead (92–137). In saying that Hal's wish caused him to think his father was dead when he took the crown, the King invokes the principle that people think in the way that suits their own interests. This is the traditional explanation of behavior that contemporary behaviorism explains in terms of reinforcement. But however we explain Hal's thought, the King's thought that Hal wanted him to be dead is probably fathered by fear. Ironically, Hal's thinking that his father was dead may also have been linked to fear, since the misperception of his father's condition came when he had just been speaking of the peril of kings.

The effect of the King's scolding is similar to that of its counterpart in 3.2 of *1H4*. Again Hal's response shows how much his tavern life has put him in a position where he must prove himself, only now he must also try to prove that his taking the crown was innocent. Hal's situation and his defensive emotion are so extreme that they make it reinforcing for him to claim that when he took the crown he only "upbraided" and accused it, and put it on his head solely to "try" and "quarrel" with it as "an enemy / That had before my face murder'd my father" (157–68). Hal gets so carried away in his self-vindication that he comes to a remarkably hyperbolical climax:

But if it did infect my blood with joy,
Or swell my thoughts to any strain of pride,
If any rebel or vain spirit of mine
Did with the least affection of a welcome
Give entertainment to the might of it,
Let God for ever keep it from my head,
And make me as the poorest vassal is,
That doth with awe and terror kneel to it!
(169–76)

Certainly Hal's wish to convince the King of his innocence is father to this thought about his wishes when he addressed the crown in private, for then the climax of his speech had a rather strong "strain of pride" and "affection of a welcome . . . to the might of it." As he put the "imperial crown" on his head, his "Lo where it sits" had a proud and welcoming ring to it, as did also his assertion that, albeit with God's help, he could defeat the whole world's effort to "force / This lineal honour from me" (40–6).

In speaking to his father, Hal may be sincere when he denies that he said anything like this, since the hyperbole of his denial is a sign of his being carried away, as suggested above. Thus he seems to feel his sincerity strongly as he creates it through his speech. He could feel sincere because he had no conscious wish for his father to be dead and because the demand for him to vindicate himself makes it very reinforcing to remember his earlier statements selectively in order to support the image of himself he is presenting to his father. In this he may be like an actor absorbed in a role. On the other hand, the hyperbole of his denial may be evidence that he protests too much, so he could be consciously pretending. He could think the lie is a "white" one because it does not merely defend himself but is so kind to his dying father. I think Hal comes to be a character who slips very easily from one of these modes of acting to the other, becoming sincere in what starts out as at least partly a pretense. This capacity is very useful for a politician.

Impressed by Hal's speech, the King accepts him as a worthy heir and proceeds to explain the political situation to him. The theme of the King's thinking is how to keep oneself in power. He says that Hal should "busy giddy minds / With foreign quarrels, that action hence borne out / May waste the memory of the former days" (213–15). The context suggests that the King refers to obliterating the memory of his own former wrongdoing in obtaining the crown by "indirect crook'd ways" (184), but Hal can add to this the desire to make everyone forget his own former days. Hal is powerfully reinforced for intending to do as his father urges because he has just been moved so greatly to prove he is a true son who will fulfill his father's hopes. There is no indication that father or son explicitly thinks about the good of the people in thinking a foreign war is the best way to end the civil wars. Henry IV has always thought mostly of his own good, and at the moment Hal, too, is strongly reinforced for being concerned about his own self-interest.

When Henry IV has died, the new King enters the court to present himself to his brothers and his father's friends and officers. The scene is comparable to what would happen if an actor should come on stage and explain how he will play the role he is to perform and then start to perform it (5.2.44–145). Hal, now Henry, speaks of "This new and gorgeous garment, majesty" as not sitting easily upon him and he says to his brothers that their sorrow for the death of Henry IV "so royally in you appears / That I will deeply put the fashion on, / And wear it in my heart" (44–5, 51–3). According to the Elizabethan psychology of acting, thinking of emotion as at first something that is put on, like the costume of a king, does not mean the emotion will not reach the heart. Such thinking does, however, suggest that the emotion may not *originate* in the heart for Henry V. At least in his present state of self-consciousness, he is so busy thinking what he should say about what he feels that such thoughts will certainly interfere with more intuitive, direct responses. In Chapter 3 I discussed how self-consciousness can interfere with the sense that our thoughts and feelings are "real" and sincere, but as noted there, such self-consciousness may be only temporary and can especially be expected in a person who is in an unfamiliar and formal social situation, as Henry V is here. Therefore his statements here are not evidence he will always feel this way: Shakespeare dramatizes what it feels like to be a certain person in a certain situation and he often shows how a change in situation can change a person. Yet it is possible that for a king with Henry's experience in the tavern world, the role of king will always be played with some self-consciousness.

Henry's main purpose in this scene is to convince the court that he will be a good king, and to do this he must reassure them about his past behavior. Again he is strongly reinforced for proving himself, and his past misdeeds specifically influence the shape of his reform. Henry has seemed the enemy of the Lord Chief Justice, so now he will take him as a "father to my youth" and will follow his "wise directions" (118, 121). However, the only matter we know of in which Henry follows the Justice's will is the rejection of Falstaff. There is no indication that the Justice urges the new King to make war on France, yet in the last speech of this play Prince John says that Henry has heeded the prompting of someone to this end (5.5.105–8). Henry IV was the father who first prompted Henry V to make war on France, and in his effort to prove himself, the new King Henry evidently exaggerates how much he intends to be guided by the Lord Chief Justice.

In their dialogue in 5.2, the Justice himself suggests that Henry should imagine he is Henry IV (92–101). Henry accepts this, and in the speech in which he adopts the Justice as his father (118) he goes on to imply that his kingly father's spirit is actually his guide (125–6). Although Henry may well be sincere in saying he will be prompted by the Justice's "wise directions" as his new father (121), he has never sought fatherly advice. Instead, in his great concern for his political image, Henry is very similar to his father.[5]

Henry echoes his soliloquy of long ago in which he said he would "falsify men's hopes" in his reformation when he now says he will "mock the expectation of the world" (*1H4* 1.2.206; *2H4* 5.2.126). Both speeches show that in situations causing him to be powerfully reinforced for putting himself in a good light, Henry does not see that his words can be taken ironically. In the past he did not see that "men's hopes" could include his father's and his own hopes; now he does not see that to "frustrate prophecies" (127) may include frustrating his own prophecies. His father's promised crusade is the counterpart of Henry's campaign in France, and the prophecy his father depended on, that he would die in Jerusalem, was thwarted by his failure to make peace at home. Henry V's first prophecy is that "God consigning to my good intents, / No prince nor peer shall have just cause to say, / God shorten Harry's happy life one day!" (143–5). This prophecy is frustrated insofar as Harry's life is shortened by many days in his untimely death and insofar as the princes and peers of France, if not of England, have just cause to ask God to shorten his life. The epilogue to *H5* may indicate that God has not consigned to his good intents when it emphasizes that following his early death during his second campaign in France, England suffers more terrible civil strife than he undertook to end by making war on France. Henry's certainty about his "good intents" may be interpreted by the light of the traditional idea that men believe so strongly in their own self-interested positions that they start unjust wars with the conviction that they are just (see, for example, Erasmus, *Education* 251; ch. 11).

As he approaches the end of his long speech about his coming rule, Henry says he will henceforth conduct himself in "formal majesty" (133). Then for the first time he uses the royal "we," signalling that he has completed his statement of how he will play the king and has begun to speak in the role of king (134 ff.). At the end of the speech he reverts to the first person singular and refers to himself as "Harry," thus stepping out of his role as "formal majesty" in asserting the hope that God will endorse "my good intents" (143–5). This emphasizes the distinction between the man and the role of king, and Henry's acute awareness of the distinction, too, at this juncture.

In the rejection of Falstaff, we may hear the guidance of the Lord Chief

Justice, whom Henry first asked to speak to Falstaff for him (5.5.44), but
we also hear the voice of Prince Hal in *1H4* caught up in the role of his
father condemning and banishing Falstaff (2.4.440–75). The first part of
the rejection speech is very harsh and its curt moralistic rhetoric suggests
that Henry is deliberately speaking in a way that will show how greatly
changed he is. In this, however, Henry is Henry still: he does not so much
sound as if he thinks he has turned away his former self as that his
formerly hidden self has "throw[n] off" its "loose behaviour" (*1H4* 1.2.203).
It is uncertain whether Henry is becoming a person who intuitively con-
ducts himself uprightly and royally, or whether his actual character
continues to be hidden, in the sense that he is becoming a person who
throws himself into the role of the moment. Although he is presumably
quite self-conscious in his rejection of Falstaff because it is such a public
test of his reformation, Henry's harsh rhetoric conveys a sense of urgent
belief. Again I think we see a character who can believe and feel what he
needs to in order to play his role convincingly. As noted earlier, this
ability can be useful in politics, but it is also perilous insofar as it invites
self-deception.

In *H5*, Henry again seeks to prove himself in a way that is partly governed by the standards others propose. In Act 1 it is clear that Henry
wants to make war on France. He is also urged to make war by the
bishops and noblemen, whose first appeal is that he should show himself
to be the true heir of his great ancestors (1.2.102–10, 115–19, 122–4). This
of course is an appeal that Henry's disposition to prove himself makes
very reinforcing for him to accept.

Yet the degree to which he acts because of the others' wishes is uncertain, since there is evidence he invites their appeals in order to be able to
say he acted on their advice. Thus he demands that Canterbury sanction
the war before he will commit himself to it (1.2.4–32, 96), and in the first
scene, the churchmen have shown their willingness to collude with Henry
and support his war on France so he will protect their interests (1.1.1–23,
69–89). This collusion contributes to the impression that in 1.2 Henry, the
churchmen, and the noblemen deliberate a decision the outcome of which
they already know. But there is also evidence that Henry is stirred by the
appeals of the prelates and noblemen, for his performance goes beyond
mere calculation and has what increasingly becomes his characteristic
mode, an actor-like mixture of calculated intent and strong feeling in
which the dominance may slip from the one to the other from moment to
moment.

There may be an indication that Henry counts on the Archbishop to bless his French war when, in ostensibly instructing the Archbishop to say *whether* to make war, he says that "God doth know how many now in health / *Shall* drop their blood in approbation / Of what your reverence *shall incite* us to" (1.2.18–20, emphasis added). Also, neither Henry nor Canterbury attends very well to Canterbury's argument in favor of Henry's claim to the French throne based on his descent from Isabella, daughter of Philip IV. Repeatedly Canterbury indicates that the claims to the throne by kings of France who have traced their inheritance through women are regarded as tainted (65–85). It seems that Henry merely waits for the end of the Archbishop's argument as his cue to ask for the declaration he wants: "May I with right and conscience make this claim?" (96). Canterbury's reply shows little regard for right in quoting Numbers 27.8, which says a daughter should inherit when her father dies without a male heir (98–100), while ignoring Numbers 36, which says the daughter loses her right to inherit if she marries outside her tribe. Evidently self-interest makes it difficult for Canterbury and Henry to have a fully responsible concern for what is right in this situation.

A crucial issue for a psychological analysis of Henry is how much the specific features of his behavior are shaped by a disposition to do what is right, how much by a disposition to serve the interests of his kingdom and his people, how much by a disposition to busy giddy minds and so secure his crown, and how much by a disposition to prove himself in the eyes of his prelates and noblemen. As the scene progresses, Henry shows concern for what England may suffer from attacks by the Scots while he is in France (136–54). He is presumably reinforced for this expression of concern by a sense that he is doing what is best for the kingdom and by the approval of others for doing this. Hence, he is also reinforced because he has strengthened his own position in serving agreed-upon interests of the kingdom. It is impossible to disentangle self-interest from service to country in such speeches.

Once he is satisfied that England can be defended if he invades France, Henry resolves to conquer France and only then calls in the French Ambassadors, indicating that hearing the reply of the French to his claims to "certain dukedoms" is a mere formality (221–48). Moreover, Henry's having already decided on war before hearing the Ambassadors makes it obvious that he pretends when he says to the Ambassadors that the Dauphin's insulting gift of tennis balls is the cause of his war to win the French crown (261–97). Henry uses the Dauphin's insult as a cue for how to shape his declaration of war against the French. Henry is calculating – in the pretense and in the ingenious rhetoric turning tennis balls into gunstones – yet characteristically he also seems to be moved by the Dauphin's insult and his own emotional rhetoric.

The Dauphin's insult strikes at the root of Henry's defensiveness about proving himself, and as usual when he is put on the defensive, Henry's emotional reaction causes him to overstate his reply in a way that is glorious in its eloquence yet also self-betraying. He says that in his "wilder days" "We never valu'd this poor seat of England; / And therefore, living hence, did give ourself / To barbarous licence; as 'tis ever common / That men are merriest when they are from home" (267, 269–72). He means that in his wilder days he lived barbarously "hence" or away "from" his "home" at the royal palace, so that "this poor seat of England" is not the country but the throne in the palace (as most editors agree). Emotionally absorbed in his own point of view, he sees only this intended meaning and not that his words are general enough to refer to the country of England and therefore can describe his present attitude and the behavior he proposes. Even now he does not greatly value England's throne, calling it a "poor" seat as he anticipates the greatness of France's throne. Ironically, then, Henry's statement raises the question whether in his invasion of France, where he will certainly be "from home," he will "give" himself "To barbarous licence." He goes on in the following lines to describe how he thinks he will appear in France: "I will keep my state, / Be like a king and show my sail of greatness / When I do rouse me in my throne of France" (273–5). And he adds another contrast between his earlier days in England and his future days in France:

> . . . I have laid by my majesty
> And plodded like a man for working-days,
> But I will rise there with so full a glory
> That I will dazzle all the eyes of France,
> Yea, strike the Dauphin blind to look on us.
> (276–80)

Here we have another of Henry's prophecies, coupled with suggestions in the text of an alternative, ironic prophecy. He says his behavior in France will contrast gloriously with that in England, but as noted above, the speech also allows the possibility that he may instead give himself to barbarous license in making war. In addition, his prophecy of glory will not be fulfilled insofar as it depends on his actually rousing himself "in my throne of France."

The possibility of an ironic significance in Henry's speech to the Ambassadors is strengthened when we compare what he says here with his soliloquy at the end of the corresponding scene in *1H4*. In the soliloquy he said his "loose" behavior was for the end of making himself appear more glorious when he reformed and showed himself to be sun-like. Now he says he will not show his full sun-like brilliance until he is King of France. In both speeches, Henry tends to look beyond the moment to the future as the time when he will prove himself.

The soliloquy in *1H4* is echoed in *H5* not only in the imagery of transformation into a sun-like glory, but also in the claim that he had "plodded like a man for working days" when he was not behaving as a royal prince (1.2.277): in *1H4* he had compared his loose behavior in the tavern with working-days, contrasting it with the holiday effect his reformation would have (1.2.199–200). In both plays his implication that he has been like a working man in his tavern life is part of a general exaggeration of the merit in his looseness and in the amazing radiance of his sunrise into majesty. In both speeches there is the suggestion that in his concern to *appear* glorious, Henry may not quite *be* what a king should be: in the soliloquy he said he would "imitate" the sun, and now he says he will be "like" a king (274). Before, he said he would "throw off" his loose behavior, now he says he had "laid by" his majesty (276). Henry does not intend to imply in *H5* that he is not essentially a king, for the emotional exaggeration of the speech as a whole indicates that he intends strongly to say he will be fully a king in his French throne. He thinks of himself as the sun, not as like the sun, when he says "I will rise there with so full a glory / That I will dazzle all the eyes of France" (278–9).

In his speech to the French Ambassadors, then, Henry reminds us of his performances in the earlier plays, for in striving to appear glorious he reveals things about himself that prompt questions about his conduct. Once he had Falstaff to put down, and now he very effectively puts down the Dauphin, but he expresses little sense of his own responsibility as he blames the Dauphin for the carnage he himself threatens (281–8). As Canterbury says, meaning to praise Henry: "List his discourse of war, and you shall hear / A fearful battle render'd you in music" (1.1.43–4). A man who speaks musically of a fearful battle may not have a deep sense of the "fearful" nature of his subject. As Prince, Henry said "I'll so offend to make offence a skill," and as King he again may be in danger of looking past the dark means he uses, fixing his eyes on the bright sunrise to follow.

From the rest of the play I will discuss only a few important passages to show how Henry's character continues to develop along the lines already indicated. In Act 2 he deals with the traitors as he did with the French Ambassadors. He has already made up his mind to condemn them, but he uses what they say as pretext and cue for the condemnation (2.2.1–83). Calculated as the condemnation is, Henry is hurt and angry, especially because one traitor, Scroop, has been a close friend (79–142). Henry's tone of righteous amazement at this personal betrayal reaches a hyperbolic climax as he compares betrayal of himself with Adam's disobedience to God (141–2). After the traitors are taken away, Henry commits his power "into the hand of God, / Putting it straight in expedition" to France (184–91). In these lines he evidently thinks that to do what he himself wants is to do what God wants. This kind of thinking is echoed when he wins the battle of Agincourt and commands that soldiers who boast of the victory, taking "that praise from God / Which is his only," should be put to death (4.8.116–18). The kings in Elizabethan history plays are generally wont to claim that God supports their actions, and so Henry is "the mirror of all Christian kings" (2. Prologue 6). To see in each case whether the particular king who is speaking is politic or believes what he says, we must look at his character and the context of his assertion. Perhaps Henry has learned the supreme lesson Bacon teaches in "Of Honour and Reputation," that "Envy, which is the canker of honour, is best extinguished by declaring a man's self in his ends rather to seek merit than fame; and by attributing a man's successes rather to divine Providence and felicity, than to his own virtue or policy" (505).

A closer look at 2.2 prompts us to question Henry's thinking further, for it appears that he does not see how the words he uses in denouncing the traitors may imply a question about himself. He says the traitors' own words, condemning a man who railed at him, now condemn them (2.2.82–3). Then he condemns Scroop for having been tempted by "glistering semblances of piety" (117). His speaking of "glistering semblances" recalls his earlier words about the goodly "show" of his "reformation, glitt'ring o'er" his "fault" (*1H4* 1.2.208–9). The echo raises the question whether he, too, has been tempted by what glisters and seems pious, in his case the "dazzle" and "glory" of being King of France as justified by the Archbishop of Canterbury. If Henry perceived these ironic meanings, he would presumably use words that do not raise questions about himself. His failure of perception thus suggests a lack of calculation and tends to confirm the impression that his zeal in denouncing the traitors is sincere, or becomes so as he is caught up in a role that is very reinforcing in its self-righteousness.

At the siege of Harfleur, Henry gives two brilliant performances as the personification of Mars that the Chorus said him to be at the start of the play (3.1.1–34, 3.3.1–43). In each of these scenes Henry throws himself into a role in order to manipulate his audience, and for the sake of this manipulation he again finds it reinforcing to speak in extreme terms. In concentrating on the effect he has on others, he does not seem to notice (or be concerned about?) the brutality of the character he creates for himself in what he says. In 3.1 he virtually describes the way he is at this moment throwing himself into his role as he speaks like a theatrical director and tells his men to throw themselves into the role of warrior by imitating ferociously inhuman models and contorting their faces and forcing their emotions accordingly. They are to become unnatural composites of the tiger and the cannon to prove their *nobility* in battle (3.1.5–25). The powerful poetry of the speech and this appeal to nobility remind us again of Canterbury's praise of Henry's eloquence: "List his discourse

of war, and you shall hear / A fearful battle render'd you in music"
(1.1.43–4).

In 3.3, the second of these scenes with Henry as Mars, he threatens to
let his soldiers rape and massacre the people of Harfleur if they do not
surrender. Yet the instant the town surrenders, he becomes a figure of
reason and mercy. He evidently threatens in the most dreadful terms he
can imagine in order to induce the French to surrender. He may think that
since he threatens for the good end of saving lives and so is "only pretending," what he says (the means he uses) does not really show anything
about himself. Such threats and such actions as Henry threatens were
allowed by the laws of war, but Henry endangers himself insofar as his
imagination becomes engrossed in his vivid description of rape and
butchery. To "imitate the action of the tiger" in rhetorical performance
can become second nature, for imitation passes into habit as the action
shapes the man.

An important episode is the scene in which, dressed as a common
soldier, Henry talks with Court, Bates, and Williams (4.1). Although this
encounter reminds us of his earlier life in the tavern world, the differences are striking. This scene is Henry's only dialogue ever with common people in which he conceals his identity and attempts to be one of
them. It is also his only dialogue with common people who are not tavern
denizens. Before, his role-playing was sometimes false to the commoners
because he concealed his true attitude toward them or himself, though
he revealed his true identity. Now his role-playing is false because he
conceals his true identity, thereby making it impossible for him to speak
straightforwardly.

Henry explains to the soldiers that the King is only a man and therefore is afraid as they are but must not show it because that would dis-
hearten his army (101–13). He evidently wants them to give him a little
touch of sympathy in the night, and he is taken aback by Bates's saying
that the King's fear may get the better of him and make him wish himself anywhere at home rather than here (114–21). This puts Henry on the
defensive and there ensues another version of his effort to prove himself.
His role-playing takes on an added degree of falsity as he speaks wholly
to defend himself, yet still pretends to be a commoner speaking his "conscience" (119). It is such strong behavior for him to defend himself, and
what Bates says evokes defensiveness so greatly, that Henry evidently
does not see the falseness of his conduct.

When Williams questions his claim that his cause is "just and his quarrel honourable" (128–30), the slippery logic of Henry's reply suggests that
what he thinks and says is primarily shaped by powerful reinforcement
for compelling a favorable response (135–84). As a number of critics have
argued, Henry's reply does not respond effectively to Williams's argument

that if the King's cause is not good he has "a heavy reckoning to make" (135–49). Further, in denying responsibility for his men's deaths (159–63), Henry seems to forget that in 1.2 he himself suggested that he would be responsible, and even culpable, if his cause is unjust (13–28, 96). He may speak hypocritically now, or he may have changed his mind, but it would be easy for him not to recall a view that would be highly aversive to think of when he is being challenged. To account more readily for his forgetting, we might also infer that in 1.2 he spoke as he did less because he believed what he said than to show himself to be a responsible ruler and to have the Church endorse his cause.

Williams and Bates accept Henry's arguments, and then when Bates adds that he will fight lustily for the King, Henry characteristically encourages them further in a way that invites approval of himself by saying "I myself heard the king say he would not be ransomed" (4.1.197–8). Long ago Prince Hal said he had learned in a quarter hour to speak the language of the tavern so well that he could drink with any tinker during his life. Yet he still has not learned to listen to the common people, as he did not listen to Francis's efforts to reply to his questions. If he had really heard how these soldiers think, he would have had a better intuition of the effect of saying he had heard the King state that he would not be ransomed.

Henry has learned the effect of praising his heroic capacities when he is speaking in his role as the King, and here he seems to expect a similar statement to have the same effect when he speaks about the King while playing the role of a commoner. Henry evidently fails to take into account that people applaud him as King especially because subjects strive to please their rulers and learn to accept a king's self-aggrandizing statements. Henry also seems to misperceive his role-playing situation in not realizing how weak it is to say the King has said he will not be ransomed. This is not the same as uttering the words "I will not be ransomed." The reference to speaking invites Williams's skeptical response that talk is cheap (199–200). In reply, Henry says "If I live to see it, I will never trust his word after," again misperceiving what is credible to say about himself in his present role-situation (202), and soon he has allowed himself to become so angry that he exchanges challenges with Williams to fight after the battle (203–27).

The soldiers exit and the rest of the scene is virtually one long soliloquy in which Henry's being put on the defensive once again disposes him to think in a way that avoids self-critical perceptions and is reinforced by self-approval. In his soliloquy he is out of touch with his own and the commoners' reality. He minimizes the power of kings, saying a king cannot command a subject's health, but it is more to the point here that Henry *can* command a subject's death (262–3). And he assumes that peasants never suffer sickness or hunger that keeps them from sleeping in Elysium all night (274–80). Henry has just experienced the anguish of Williams and Bates on a sleepless night, but already he has forgotten or discounted this. His defensive self-pity allows only kings to be kept awake by cares. He discounts the cares of peasants partly because his social perspective lets him think they are mere "slaves" with "vacant" minds (274–5, 287–8). The most transparent self-deception is his remark that the "gross brain" of the peasant keeps him from knowing "What watch the king keeps to maintain the peace . . ." (288–9). Henry would likely not say this if he could see the irony of his claim that the king keeps a sleepless watch to maintain the peace, when he is keeping watch the night before a battle he has labored to bring on.

In the prayer that follows, Henry asks God to pardon the sins of Henry IV "in compassing the crown," but does not think to pray about his own intents and deeds in compassing the French crown (295–311). This striking omission prompts us to question his thinking. When he prays for the "sense of reckoning" to be taken from his men, we may remember that Williams used the word "reckoning" in speaking of the King's responsibility to see that his cause is just (296–7, 136). Henry's prayer is thus perhaps answered ironically in his losing his own sense of reckoning of what he should most pray about. In behaviorist terms, if he ever doubted his cause, as perhaps he did when he demanded that Canterbury vouch for it, he would not do so now because such thinking would be especially aversive just before the battle.

After the victory at Agincourt, Henry resolves his quarrel with Williams in a way that mingles honesty and dishonesty, using modestly dubious means for a modest good end which he at least partly achieves. The episode begins when Fluellen asserts that, as a fellow Welshman, "I need not to be ashamed of your majesty, praised be God, so long as your majesty is an honest man" (4.7.117–19). These words are the cue for Williams – who has questioned the King's honesty – to enter with the King's glove on his cap. The most honest way for Henry to act would be to confess that it was he who quarreled with Williams and to return Williams's glove to him. Henry evidently decides, however, that he must allow Williams the satisfaction of his sense of honor in striking the wearer of his glove. We may question the great value that Henry and his men place on this kind of honor, but from the beginning it has been one of the most powerful forces (reinforcements) that control their world. In effect, Henry chooses honor for Williams over honesty for himself, because he must now lie to get someone to wear Williams's glove whom Williams can strike without committing a high crime.

The question about Henry's honesty is emphasized when he chooses to lie to Fluellen, the very man who has just expressed concern for honesty. Henry asks him to wear Williams's glove and tells him it was the Duke of Alençon's so that the man who challenges it will be "an enemy to our person" (157–62). Henry's manipulation here is reminiscent of his prankish ways as Prince Hal, which suggests that insofar as his lies and manipulations demean Fluellen's dignity and Williams's honest courage, Henry has not thought very much about what would be most appropriate for their sake. He has chosen a course of action which is reinforced in part by pleasure in doing what he has learned to enjoy in the past: such manipulation has become his characteristic (habitual) approach to others.

When Henry enters upon the altercation he has caused between Williams and Fluellen, he confesses it was he whom Williams promised to strike, but he puts Williams in the wrong for having given his King "most bitter terms" in their quarrel the night before (4.8.42–3,46,50). This is evidently more manipulation, for in what follows it seems clear that Henry has accused Williams in order to let him complete his vindication by saying that if anyone acted wrongly it was Henry (51–8). Henry must have wanted Williams to say this, since he responds to Williams's blaming him with a generous reward and not a trace of defensiveness (59–62). Henry has ceased to be defensive because he has just proved himself gloriously by winning the battle of Agincourt, and his attention is focussed on enabling (and requiring) Williams to prove himself. Filling his glove with gold coins for Williams and telling him to wear the glove as an honor is the best thing Henry can do to prove himself in the situation he has created with Williams. In causing Williams to chide his truancy from the role of King and then honoring him, Henry behaves in something like the way he did in praising Hotspur and chiding himself before the battle of Shrewsbury, and in praising the Lord Chief Justice for disciplining him. In all three situations Henry's generosity reflects well on himself.

Or, at least, so it appears as Henry speaks. But his last line in this episode, telling Fluellen he "must needs be friends" with Williams (63), reminds us that he has given all his care to the entanglement of his own and Williams's honor, and has overlooked how he has manipulated his Welsh captain, whom he could so easily praise now for his loyal and courageous service. As Fluellen attempts to make the best of his awkward situation, in effect he imitates the King by offering Williams money – twelvepence, enough to mend his "not so good" shoes (65–6, 71–3). Williams, resenting Fluellen's earlier accusations and his patronizing manner, says "I will none of your money" (70). This little coda to the episode comments on what has gone before. Williams did not say anything when Henry gave him the glove full of crowns, so "I will none of your money" are his first words since the gift. Williams's failure to thank the King may indicate resentment, and he can express resentment openly when Fluellen, too, condescends to honor him for taking a risk that would have been avoided if the King had behaved properly the night before. Williams may resent as well that the King's way of making up for the night before has wronged him again by inflicting first Fluellen's accusation of treason and now his condescension on him.

Fluellen's advice to Williams to stay out of brawls and quarrels and dissensions raises a question about much that happens in the play (66–9). Fluellen himself is disposed to engage in dissensions, and Henry and his men are in France to brawl, of course. Henry seeks to end civil wars at home by making war on the French, yet his people do not become entirely unified. Although they all serve Henry loyally except Pistol and the others of his "nation," there is friction among Englishman, Scot, Irishman, and Welshman that can be compared with that among the French princes and noblemen. These episodes suggest that human quarrelsomeness over honor and crowns (coins and kingly) can move from civil war to other modes of conflict, but as long as king and captain and commoner alike think blows must be struck for honor's sake even in a matter such as that between Henry and Williams, the world will never be free of "prawls and prabbles." Indeed, in such a world giving advice to avoid quarrels may be a provocation because, as in Fluellen's case, the speaker does not practice what he preaches and cannot look at the quarrel from the point of view of the person to whom he gives the advice. Prideful egocentrism and the self-deception it causes underlie the quarrels and undercut the resolution of the quarrels, as throughout the episodes with Williams.

Henry's last role-playing scene is his courtship of Princess Katharine of France. He tells her that he is a plain-talking "plain king" and "plain soldier" who knows no arts of wooing (5.2.125–53). Actually, however, he creates this character for her. Earlier in this play he has never spoken as he does here, but he reminds us of the Prince Hal of *1H4*. Henry evidently feels awkwardly self-conscious about how to woo a Princess brought up in a most sophisticated court. Therefore he re-creates a character based on an earlier role in his life that will in no way invite comparison with her courtly norms of behavior. If she laughs at him, it will be because he has created an amusing character and wants her to laugh. He will be safe from any humiliation because he can think it is not really himself she laughs at.

Henry's role-playing is not merely protective, however. He takes his cue from something Katharine says early in the dialogue and then appears to sense her responses as he plays the character he creates to make himself appealing to her. Thus he begins haltingly to use a plain manner, stating flatly that she is an "angel" and adding even more flatly that having said this he "must not blush to affirm it" (109–10, 113–14). This wooden style of plainness is plain flattery, and the Princess's generalizing response shows that Henry has not separated himself from the mass of men in her eyes: "O bon Dieu! les langues des hommes sont pleines de tromperies" (115–16). This prompts him to try the finer *tromperie* of a more colorful manner of speech in presenting himself as a roughneck farmboy-king and soldier who has no eloquence to win a lady by rhyming (121–73). Actually, of course, he uses his prose eloquently to present himself as a figure of rugged masculinity. He says he lacks cunning, yet while seeming to dispraise himself, he strives to make his supposed defects as charming as possible.

How much Katharine sees what he is doing and enjoys his wooing as an ingenious conceit we cannot be sure, for her responses are mostly quite non-committal. But as he begins to play the farmer-king, she says "me understand well" (133). Because her understanding of English is none too good, Henry may sense that the general impression of a character that he creates is more important than the specific things he says. She could miss much of his verbal meaning and still "understand well" his body language and manly tones. Nevertheless, his words are clever and charming, and this scene is one of Shakespeare's great successes in writing a wooing scene that is unconventional yet triumphantly fulfills the conventions. Henry insists on the truth of his plain prose as contrasted with the false eloquence of rhyme, but then he uses prose to assert in an unconventional form the conventional conceit of the poet–lover that his love is as constant as the sun (156–70). Although Henry claims that the plain prose wooer can be trusted because "he hath not the gift to woo in other places" (159), his combination of wit and rough charm is likely to be as generally appealing as any rhymer's speech.

The physical power Henry projects as a wooer is of course largely based on his great military victory over Katharine's countrymen, and he repeatedly refers to this, speaking of his soldiering and his conquest of France and saying how well he could woo "if I might buffet for my love" (138–45). Both he and Katharine know that although for political reasons he must make himself attractive to her, for the same reasons she must find him to be charming. In a sense, then, the wooing is an elaborate little play with a foregone conclusion. Still, Henry's speeches suggest that, as usual, he gets caught up in his part so that his wooing becomes more than contrived. He evidently finds Katharine's shy responses as appealing as she finds him to be, and his enjoyment of her enjoyment reinforces his involvement in his playing. In the confidence his victory and her responses give him, Henry is perhaps more winning than ever before.

Presumably he is confident also because he plays a character like one he has played earlier. Now he can play such a character more winningly than before because to win he does not want to put his hearer down in the same way he did when he was a truant. Although he wants Katharine to feel politically and sexually submissive, he knows that to achieve this he should create positive impressions of the submissive role required and therefore also of himself as a man and a king to look up to. The result of all this is that Henry does not significantly undercut the appeal of the character he presents by miscalculations which would show him up. To be sure, as Henry gets caught up in the role, he also gets carried away to extremes of coarseness or self-praise at times, but these generally support his self-irony: he says he speaks like a farmer and he is ostensibly stressing his defects, not praising himself.

If Henry's speeches are subject to an irony he is not aware of, it is because of our knowledge that he is to die so soon, and this gives a poignant pathos to his character which heightens his emotional appeal to the audience. Earlier, in response to his situations as heir apparent and as new King of England, Henry has said that the future would prove his true worth when he would shine like the sun in his reformation and then finally rise like the sun on the throne of France. Now that he is the prospective King of France, it is his "good heart" which "is the sun" because it will not change with age. Like the sun, he says, his heart "shines bright and never changes, but keeps his course truly" (168–70). Once again he is unaware of an ironic meaning of his prophecy when he says that "old age" will "do no more spoil upon my face" (242–3). He gives his word for his English half of a son who will "go to Constantinople and take the Turk by the beard" (215–18). He asks "shall we not?" beget such a boy, but it is evident that he means his questions only in the rhetorical sense (219). This entire dialogue reveals a man who is full of his own life and success and hopes, and who has no inkling that he will die while his son is a helpless infant, leaving his kingdom doomed to defeat in its foreign ambitions and headed more furiously than ever toward a terrible civil war. Shakespeare wants us to feel the triumph of this man, but in a perspective that shows how he is confined in a "small time" (Epilogue, 5). To the very end, Henry is Henry still as his words make us ponder the value of his existential mode, a mode in which he projects himself more toward a future fulfillment than toward self-realization in the present.

6

As You Like It

In *As You Like It* Shakespeare dramatizes many modes of self-enactment on the stage of a world in which all the men and women are players. At one extreme are characters who play out stereotypical social and literary roles but do not see themselves as players at all, and at the other extreme is Rosalind, who creatively enacts herself as an imagined person.[1] Rosalind's self-enactment is in a mode similar to the actor who uses Stanislavski's "magic if" not to induce complete absorption but to keep an "iffy" self-awareness along with a degree of absorption in a role. Rosalind thus achieves a wisely playful balance of detachment from and engagement with the self she enacts, a state Maynard Mack regards as Shakespeare's ideal ("Engagement and Detachment" 287).

In *As You Like It* Shakespeare develops his own idea about "if" in relation to acting roles and to self-enactment.[2] In the last scene, just before the resolution of the play's conflicts, Touchstone says "Your If is the only peacemaker: much virtue in If" (5.4.102). He explains that even when a duel seems inevitable because one man has insulted another and the second man has accused the first of deliberately lying in his insult, the two parties can make peace by saying "If you said so, then I said so" (100–1). Although they have indeed said things which the rules of honor require them to fight a duel over, the men tacitly agree to pretend that their saying was not so actual and unconditional as in fact it was. In saying "if you said so, then I said so" they manage to assert what has been said in a way that makes it less than a "Lie Direct," closer to the "Lie Circumstantial," which does not necessitate duelling (80–1, 94–6). A factual description of what they have said is rendered ambiguous by the "if," which makes it seem hypothetical, enabling the quarrelers to *act as if* they had not said what they said.

In this way "if" can be used to suggest the transformation of actual events into pretense and fiction. In Touchstone's example, "if" may also suggest the attempt to transform pretense into reality, for the quarrelers were deluded in thinking they were courageous men governed "by the book" of honor – the test of real peril showed them the limits of their ability to play such a role.[3] In these terms, "if" can mediate between the actual world and a fictional world and between actual character and pretense. An author can adapt actual events and persons to the uses of

146

fiction, or use fantasies as the basis for verisimilar fictions. Correspondingly, actual people and fictional characters often think or pretend that
they are other than they are. In general, "if" can be a sign that the "real"
or fictional status of an event or person is ambiguous in some way or to
someone.

In *As You Like It* these ideas of "if" are especially associated with the
role-playing of Rosalind and its effect upon others. Pretending to be the
boy Ganymede, she proposes to Orlando that they enact a little play to
cure him of love's madness: "I would cure you, if you would but call me
Rosalind and come every day to my cote and woo me" (3.2.414–15). When
her role-playing of Rosalind and Ganymede has caused frustration for
Orlando and a conflict for Phebe and Silvius, she proposes to resolve all
problems in a series of "ifs" (5.2.111–22; 5.4.5–25). Thus to Phebe she says
"I will marry you, if ever I marry woman, and I'll be married tomorrow"
(5.2.114–15). The logic of "if" here seems to necessitate Ganymede's
marrying Phebe – and it would do so if Ganymede were not a fiction,
Rosalind's pretense. So in 5.4 Rosalind can use "if" in a way that gives
Phebe confidence to commit herself unambiguously: "if you do refuse to
marry me, / You'll give yourself to this most faithful shepherd? / PHEBE.
So is the bargain" (13–15). Phebe thinks the logic of the "if" will give her
a free choice of whether to marry Ganymede, not realizing that her own
and Rosalind's "real" sexual natures will determine her choice for her so
that she will marry Silvius. Rosalind's proving "a busy actor" as Ganymede
in the play of Silvius and Phebe brings Phebe to discover love and to
know what it feels like to suffer unrequited love, and at the end Rosalind's
ability to transform herself from Ganymede back to Rosalind causes Phebe
to join her love with Silvius's. It is important that at the end Rosalind does
not merely come forth as Rosalind but that everyone is able to recognize
her as Rosalind-who-has-appeared-to-be-Ganymede. This recognition is
implicit in the repeated use of "if," especially Phebe's:

DUKE SEN.   If there be truth in sight, you are my daughter.
ORL.   If there be truth in sight, you are my Rosalind.
PHEBE.   If sight and shape be true,
             Why then my love adieu.

                                                    (5.4.117–20)

The comedy's ending of weddings for Silvius and Phebe and for Rosalind
and Orlando thus depends on Rosalind's ability to present herself as a
woman, specifically as Rosalind-who-has-played-Ganymede. The ending
also depends on her way of playing Ganymede's Rosalind for Orlando
and herself earlier, as I will argue.

Although it is important for the weddings that Rosalind is a woman, the speeches of Duke Senior, Orlando, and Phebe quoted above, and Rosalind's own series of "ifs" in reply, suggest a continuing ambiguity about her identity (5.4.117–23). The god of marriage, too, suggests some lingering ambiguity about identities when he says the four couples "must" wed "If truth holds true contents" (127–9). The Epilogue, spoken by "Rosalind," provides a key to this ambiguity which indicates how important it is that the role of Rosalind is designed to be played by a boy actor. In the first part of the Epilogue, Rosalind apologizes because it is not conventional for a woman to speak an epilogue and because she does not know what approach or role to employ (198–208). Then she asserts that her way of playing the epilogist is to play the conjurer (208), recalling that she pretended to use magic in producing Rosalind at the end. The magic, of course, is theatrical transformation, and in the Epilogue Rosalind is transformed in the opposite direction right before our eyes as in mid-conjuration "she" says "If I were a woman . . ." (214–15).

Earlier the magical transformation from Ganymede back to Rosalind required an off-stage change of appearance, but now the transformation of Rosalind back to the Ganymede-like boy actor can take place while the boy still appears to be a "lady" (198). In the first of these transformations, a character is dropping a pretense within a play; in the second, the boundary between the world of the play and the actual world is marked by an actor dropping out of character while still in the character's costume. The first change maintains a sense of illusionistic "reality" about the change of sexual identity; the second destroys the dramatic illusion and invites us to contrast our world with the play's world. According to all the "if sight and shape be true" statements, sight and shape were less true in our "real" world when Rosalind appeared to be a female. The weddings are possible only *if* we enter into the imagined pretending of the play's world, for in our world all the people on the stage are males and "Rosalind" would have to be Phebe's mate, not Orlando's – except that Phebe, too, is a boy.

In the use of "if" to link the transformation of Rosalind from male to female with that of the boy actor from female to male, *AYL* suggests a parallel between the character and the actor. It has been argued that some of the meanings of Rosalind's lines belong more to the boy actor as a boy than to Rosalind, as when, speaking as Ganymede, she thanks God she is not a woman (3.2.339–40). But I think it is more in keeping with the conventions of Shakespeare's dramaturgy to see that this statement is wittily in character for Rosalind as speaker, and also to see that the witty irony of the speaker's actually being a boy actor should be attributed to the author. Thus there is metatheatrical commentary, but I think we can always hear the characteristic voice of Rosalind in the lines that convey meanings for the boy actor as well. Before Rosalind plays Ganymede, the text does not evoke responses to the boy actor as a boy. And when Rosalind plays Ganymede, she is herself playing a boy actor, hence her part contains his. This is not to deny that the boy actor's appeal as a potential object of sexual desire was played on in a role such as Rosalind. What I think the audience primarily sees when Rosalind plays Ganymede, however, is not the boy actor behaving in a feminine manner, but an androgynous Rosalind playing up the boyishness of her creation of Ganymede.[4]

The relation I see as the most important between Rosalind and the boy actor is a parallel that creates complementarity or reciprocity between them. Thus, as Rosalind pretends to be a young man pretending to be herself, the boy actor pretends to be a young woman pretending to be a boy doing what he is doing – playing Rosalind. Putting it another way, each of them pretends to be doing what he or she *is* doing: Rosalind with Orlando in 4.1 *is* Rosalind and she pretends to be Rosalind, and the boy actor *is* a virtual Ganymede as he pretends to be Ganymede. Each of them has the chance to approach being or "doing" himself or herself with a sense of artful pretense and with attitudes tempered by an approach to self through a character whose relation to the subject in hand, love, is the complement of his or her own. As a result, their role-playing situations can facilitate empathetic role-taking with a person of the complementary gender and/or sex.

Modern sociological theory emphasizes the complementarity or reciprocity of roles, and we find a similar emphasis in Cicero's use of "officiium," a term which means "reciprocal personal relationship" (Edinger ix). As R. D. Laing explains, the genuine fulfillment of an identity requires a complementary other and a kind of reciprocity in which people find gratification partly through facilitating each other's ability to be gratified in reciprocating (*Self and Others* 82–3). Enacting a role in a way that is more than merely perfunctory or exploitive requires role-taking in which one has a knowledge of the other person's role, character, and human needs that is empathetic and dynamic, sensitive to the nuances of the other's responses during an interaction.

Shakespeare explores the relation between role-playing and role-taking in *AYL*. The Elizabethan word for "role" is "part": "all the men and women" are "merely players" and "one man in his time plays many parts" (2.7.140, 142). "Part" is not only a theatrical term, for it refers literally to a person's allotted portion in life, his or her social identity and situation. Thus Shakespeare's characters sometimes use the expression "for my part" to mean "from my point of view" or "for my success in this situation." Correspondingly, Shakespeare's characters speak of role-taking as taking someone's part. This expression has several meanings that are important for understanding men and women as players. It can be used to refer to role-taking in the sense of an empathetic sharing of another person's point of view and feelings, as in Le Beau's description of the scene after Charles the Wrestler has nearly killed three young brothers: "Yonder they lie, the poor old man their father making such pitiful dole over them that all the beholders take his part with weeping" (1.2.119–22). In this context the expression suggests not only the compassionate role-taking expected of any human being in response to another's suffering, but also the role-taking expected of "the beholders" at a play in response to an actor whose emotional role-playing is designed to move the audience.

"Pitiful" in this passage seems to mean both that the old man was full of pity for his sons and that his weeping was pitiable. "Pity" is an Elizabethan counterpart of our "empathy," for it carries the sense of compassion or fellow feeling. As Aristotle says, to feel pity for a person we must be able to imagine that we may suffer what he or she is suffering (*Rhetoric* 1385b–6a). In a loving friendship or erotic relationship, the two persons should become as one so that each feels what the other feels, and the role-taking may include imagined role-playing of advocacy for the other. Celia urges Rosalind to resist her love for Orlando by wrestling with her affections, and Rosalind replies "O they take the part of a better wrestler than myself" (1.3.21). Here there is also a pun on "part" as sexual part, implying Rosalind's desire for erotic as well as emotional intimacy with Orlando.

Taking someone else's part can also combine empathetic role-taking with actual role-playing of advocacy for another person. The most complex instance of this in Shakespeare is probably Kent in *King Lear*, whom the Fool calls a fool "for taking one's part that's out of favour" (1.4.104). Thus Kent was Cordelia's advocate when she was out of favor, as a banished man he plays the role of one out of favor, and he is undertaking to assist Lear when the Fool speaks. Kent's own suffering enables him the better to pity Lear, and Lear, in turn, learns to empathize with others only when he suffers what they suffer (3.2.68–9). Taking someone else's part connects our feelings with the other person's, and through this can help us see our behavior better.

But there is another sense in which one person can take another's part, the literal sense of stealing his or her place. The end of the first scene of *AYL* suggests that this meaning is important in the play and that a person can also attempt to steal another's "good parts" in the sense of good qualities. Oliver wants Charles the Wrestler to think Orlando is a villain, so he says that Orlando is "an envious emulator of every man's good parts, a secret and villainous contriver against me his natural brother" (141–3). As soon as Charles has left, Oliver muses to himself about his hatred of Orlando, and he reveals that the hatred is motivated by envy of Orlando's good qualities or rather of the esteem that Orlando's good qualities have won for him (162–70). Envy is a feeling of sorrow or pain because of a sense that another person's good harms oneself, as suggested in Corin's statement that "I . . . envy no man's happiness; glad of other men's good . . ." (3.2.71–3). Oliver says he feels "misprised," undervalued, because of Orlando's good qualities. Hence it is Oliver who is the "envious emulator" of his brother. Aristotle writes that "Emulation makes us take steps to secure the good things in question, envy makes us take steps to stop our neighbor having them" (*Rhetoric* 1388a). Emulation can be virtuous if it inspires imitation of the good qualities of another person, but an "envious emulator" would evidently be one who wishes to secure qualities for himself by taking them from another person. Oliver describes himself when he speaks of Orlando to Charles, and he "imitates" Orlando only in pretending that he is the sort of person Orlando actually is. Oliver steals Orlando's part or role in order to move Charles to maim him, hoping to acquire his brother's good parts, or rather to be "prized" as his brother is.

In the traditional view, envy is the antithesis of pity. Citing Aristotle's *Rhetoric* (bk 2, sec. 9), Aquinas for example writes that "the envious man grieves over his neighbor's good, whereas the pitiful man grieves over his neighbor's evil, so that the envious have no pity, . . . nor is the pitiful man envious" (II–II.36.3 ad 3). There are two ways to take another's part, then: one with pity and the other with envy. Pitiful role-taking is an imaginative putting of oneself in another person's place, an expression and cause of fellow feeling and self-knowledge. Envious role-taking is role-stealing, a usurpation of another person's place that shows a lack of fellow feeling and self-knowledge. Self-love makes a just judgment of the relative merits of self and others too aversive for the envious to accept, and therefore they avoid seeing the truth even about their feeling of envy. Oliver says he does not know why he hates Orlando: he immediately describes his envy, but apparently does not recognize this as the cause of his hatred.

The importance of role-taking and Oliver's lack of self-knowledge as a brother are also seen in the episode with Orlando early in 1.1. Orlando complains to Adam of the "part" (6) he has been reduced to under his brother, who has deprived him of the rights bequeathed by their father (1–4, 6–15). In his role as the successor to his father, Oliver has certain rights over Orlando, but he also has the duty to educate his younger brother as a gentleman. Oliver, however, rejects the idea that there is any reciprocity of this sort required of him. When Orlando complains, Oliver treats him as an inferior who does not remember his place:

OLI. Know you where you are sir?
ORL. O sir, very well: here in your orchard.
OLI. Know you before whom sir?
ORL. Ay, better than him I am before knows me.
(40–3)

Oliver's egocentrism allows him to think that his own presence defines where Orlando is. Egocentrism also prevents Oliver from taking the role of Orlando and so from choosing words that would not so easily allow witty rejoinders showing up his arrogance. In behaviorist terms, Oliver's self-love makes it reinforcing for him to see what happens only egocentrically.

The usurping Duke Frederick parallels Oliver as a foolishly envious villain (1.2.230). As Le Beau says, Frederick is displeased with Rosalind simply because "the people praise her for her virtues, / And pity her for her good father's sake" (1.2.270–1). Frederick expresses the envious man's feeling that the good of others harms himself when he tells Celia that in winning the pity of the people by patient acceptance of her lot, Rosalind "robs thee of thy name" (1.3.74–6). Of course it is Frederick who has actually been the robber in usurping his brother's dukedom. Here is the ultimate form of envious role-taking in which one man actually takes another's social role for himself.

Charles the Wrestler exemplifies another variety of egocentric role-playing. He twice claims to speak out of empathy for Oliver in warning him against letting Orlando wrestle (1.1.128, 130). Yet clearly Charles is especially concerned to save himself from punishment by Oliver in the event that he injures Orlando, and the claim that he acts for "love" of Oliver is a ploy. Charles is a pitiless man who has so depersonalized his role as a professional wrestler that he thinks it credible to say that if Orlando wrestles with him and is hurt or disgraced, "it is a thing of his own search, and altogether against my will" (133–4). Charles's reasoning seems to be that when he wrestles to maintain his standing and honor as the Duke's prize wrestler he has no freedom to refrain from employing his strength and skill to their most brutal effect. Needless to say, in willing to maintain his role, he does in effect will his brutal acts, but he claims he is the unwilling victim of what his role demands. Such thinking is obviously reinforced because it enables him to avoid responsibility for harming others.

The dialogue between Rosalind and Celia at the beginning of 1.2 affords a striking contrast with the attitude of Oliver toward his brother in the first scene. Oliver's pretense that his envious feelings are his brother's is followed by Celia's claim that she can take her cousin's role and know what Rosalind should feel (7–13). Celia, unlike Oliver, is sincere and well-intentioned; she loves Rosalind and wants to make her happy. Celia has less than full empathy, however, in saying that Rosalind's unhappiness shows "thou lov'st me not with the full weight that I love thee" (7–8). Celia thinks she can take Rosalind's role and know what it feels like to have a banished father and live on the dole of the man who banished him. But if she really knew, she would understand that Rosalind can love her and still be sad for her situation and for her father. Effective role-taking would especially tell Celia that she will not make Rosalind happy by starting her appeal with a statement that Rosalind does not love her enough. Celia's concern about being loved as much as she loves thus reveals her to be somewhat too egocentric to take Rosalind's role with full empathy. Yet Celia states a willingness to act on her role-taking, promising that when she inherits her father's dukedom she will give it to Rosalind (16–22). As it happens, Celia instead shares Rosalind's role as a banished person, so that she exposes herself to suffer what Rosalind suffers in experience and not merely in imagination as before.

Shortly I will study Rosalind's modes of role-taking and role-playing in some detail, but first I want to provide additional context for this study by looking at the role-taking and role-playing of more of the other characters. The Fool sometimes plays others' roles to parody the foolish things they do, and he does this out of empathy with his audience, to reveal the nature of folly. In 1.2 Touchstone directs Rosalind and Celia to parody the behavior of a knight who swore by his honor when he had no honor. Touchstone instructs the women in their roles and interprets his little play for them (67–74). In the forest Touchstone parodies the behavior of Silvius, Orlando, and Jaques, and his courtship of Audrey seems to be played as a parody of what the lovers are doing: "I press in here sir, amongst the rest of the country copulatives, to swear and to forswear, according as marriage binds and blood breaks" (5.4.54–7).

Touchstone's treatment of Audrey especially suggests that the role-taking needed to play the Fool's role in his way does not require much empathy. In wooing her, Touchstone confesses only to sexual desire; there is no respect or love in his parodic courtship or his hope not to be well married to her. No empathy accompanies his knowledge of her simplicity, for he uses this knowledge to mock her. He seeks less to communicate with her than to demonstrate his wit at her expense by saying things she will not understand (3.3).

For his parodies of Jaques and Silvius, Touchstone does not capture more than the outward shape of their folly. Parody as a mode of enactment tends to lead away from empathetic thoughts toward complete detachment by creating an exaggeratedly ridiculous form of the other person's behavior. The detached wit required for the role of Fool is in Touchstone's case almost entirely subordinated to the role. In using his courtship of Audrey to parody the other lovers, he allows his Fool's perspective to crowd out his perspective as a human being, so that he does not see (or care?) how mean and ultimately foolish he is in his relationship with her.

Jaques wants to take Touchstone's role in the sense of becoming a Fool himself, and he thinks he has an empathetic understanding of the role as he imagines playing it (2.7.34–87). But Jaques is so egocentrically absorbed in his self-created role as the man of melancholy (4.1.10–19) that he is almost entirely incapable of empathetic role-taking. It is an expression of his egotism that Jaques should want a role such as that of the melancholy man or the Fool which detaches him from ordinary social life and ordinary social roles. Through his melancholy role he loses self-detachment, however. As I have argued earlier in this study and have suggested is true to some extent in the case of Touchstone, when an outlook on life is adopted as a role to be played, it can become reinforcing to see only from its single point of view, confirming its sense of life and so deepening absorption. Perception is then further limited as a vicious circle is created. What begins with an intention to free oneself from ordinary roles and perceptions can result in deep confinement.

Jaques's melancholy is more scornful than sad; the failure of humans to transcend folly and vice does not move him to true pity. Although he is not altogether lacking in sympathy for others, his sympathy is indiscriminate and sentimental because his role does not invite him to enter into the point of view of others in order to respond to their actual needs. His sympathy is usually limited to attempts to disabuse others of their optimistic illusions. He sees no value in what others think and he wants to cure the world by imposing his views on everyone.

Jaques is especially comical because his egocentrism blinds him to how egocentric he is and causes him to misinterpret others in a way that shows further how poorly he sees himself. Thus Jaques's own description of Touchstone moralizing on the time shows that Touchstone was parodying Jaques, but Jaques gives no indication that he sees this (2.7.12–34). That Jaques should accept a parody of himself as the basis for thinking he can fuse his "deep–contemplative" role with the role of Fool shows just how blind he is to himself and to others' views of him.

Jaques's failure in role-taking and self-perception is especially clear in his dialogue with Orlando, a dialogue that is also important for what it reveals about Orlando. Repeatedly in his own attempts at mockery Jaques leaves himself vulnerable to Orlando's witty rejoinders. Thus he assumes that his dislike of Rosalind's name is an effective put-down. Orlando's reply neatly points out the absurdity of such egotistical thinking: "There was no thought of pleasing you when she was christened" (3.2.259–63). Jaques especially seems foolish because he fails to see how different Orlando is from himself (271–9). Jaques does a sort of reverse role-taking in seeing Orlando's wit as the basis for inviting him to join in his own egocentric activity of railing against the world. Orlando's statement that he will chide only his own faults is a model statement of the self-knowledge that should keep people from proudly attacking the motes in others' eyes while blind to the beams in their own. If Jaques were capable of empathy, he should respond in kind, and he does not see how arrogant and foolish he appears as he takes Orlando's statement instead as an invitation to tell the other man what his fault is. Orlando's reply that he will not exchange his fault for Jaques's "best virtue" is an ironic use of role-taking: he knows that Jaques thinks of himself as compounded of virtues.

The final failure of Jaques's wit in this episode is also the most revealing of his egocentric blindness, for he fails to see how he is set up by Orlando to proclaim himself both a fool and a figure of Narcissus in one stroke (280–5). Because he is a Narcissus, Jaques is, paradoxically, unable to see how self-love blinds him: his egotism will not let him think that anyone would see him as a fool, and hence he shows himself to be a fool. Like William, Jaques thinks he has a "pretty wit," and Touchstone's reply to William fits Jaques, too: " 'The fool doth think he is wise, but the wiseman knows himself to be a fool' " (5.1.28,30–1). Knowing that he can be a fool, a wise man will not make a fool of himself simply by failing to see that someone suggests he is a fool.

In this episode with Jaques and the episode with Oliver in 1.1 discussed earlier, Orlando shows that he has insight into himself and a witty ability to play upon the self-absorption of egocentric characters. His perception and his wit make him worthy of Rosalind's love, although his love for her renders him by turns wordlessly witless or witlessly wordful (1.2.239–50; 3.2.1–10, 86–93, 122–51). To preserve the sense that Orlando is worthy of Rosalind even when love drowns his wit, Shakespeare uses the device of the foil, portraying a more extreme form of the hapless lover in Silvius. In his dialogue with Corin in 2.4, Silvius's self-absorption results in a most ludicrous failure of self-perception (19–40). Silvius is so overwhelmed by his love that he is not able to take Phebe's point of view and think about how to make himself attractive to her. Corin indicates that he can take the role of Silvius and know how it feels to be so much in love, but Silvius denies that an old person could successfully empathize with a lover even if he has been a "true" lover in his youth (21–4).

Here Silvius seems to think of being a lover as a role, and he claims that no one has ever loved as he has, referring for proof to the "many actions most ridiculous" his love has drawn him to (25–40). Although Silvius is proud of his ludicrous behavior, the pride prevents him from seeing the import of his saying that his love compels him to behave ridiculously (28,32,38). It is as though his love plays him, making him a pathetic stereotype of the infatuated lover. Most tellingly, Silvius is as infatuated with himself as a lover as he is with Phebe. He says that "now," since he has entered and has "sat" with Corin, he has been wearying his hearer in his "mistress' praise" (34–5); actually he has not praised Phebe but is praising his love for her at length. Like Jaques, Silvius is so narcissistic that he does not see how he reveals his narcissism.

Because of his concern with his own feelings, Silvius also fails to take the role of the other in his dialogue with Phebe in 3.5. Instead of trying to make himself attractive to her, he expresses mostly self-pity while begging for her pity (1–7, 27–31, 84, 86–9, 99–104). Phebe is as narcissistically incapable of role-taking as Silvius. She does not praise herself, but she cannot resist using her power to hurt him with her scorn. I think her falling in love with Ganymede is also an expression of narcissism. Ganymede mirrors Phebe's scorn, and in really being Rosalind, Ganymede mirrors Phebe's own femaleness as well. Silvius and Phebe are tightly locked in their roles partly because of the perversity of the script for their sort of "pageant" (3.4.48–50). Phebe constantly rejects Silvius's behavior as a lover, yet according to the rules of love as "truly play'd" in their pastoral world, Silvius is supposed to continue playing the lovesick swain in the face of such rejection.

Rosalind is the only character whose role-taking comes very close to being entirely positive. She responds to others with an empathetic understanding and a witty self-detachment which suggest that she can see both others and herself from their point of view as well as her own. Rosalind's first speech, saying "I show more mirth than I am mistress of . . ." reveals her awareness that oneself can be a role to play in the sense of a presentation of self which requires self-control (1.2.2–3). When Celia reproaches her for her sadness, Rosalind responds to her loving good intentions, taking Celia's view of what Celia says and disregarding the way her behavior is offensive (7–15).

Despite the sadness caused by her father's exile, Rosalind's characteristic disposition is to be sportful (23), as she is in wit play with Celia, Touchstone, and Le Beau in Act 1. In this act she is also assertive in love, strong in her own defense, and quick to take a male disguise. Her character can thus be seen as androgynous, as disrupting gender stereotypes, but whether we see her this way depends on how much we see this behavior as masculine. Among Shakespeare's comic heroines, she is less aggressive than Kate and Beatrice or even Portia, but more disposed to a happily shared playfulness in love.

When she falls in love with Orlando, Rosalind shows that she will not be limited by the conventions of the woman's role. If Orlando cannot play his part because his "better parts / Are all thrown down, and that which here stands up" – his phallus and his body – "Is but a quintain, a mere lifeless block" (1.2.239–41), Rosalind will take his part and incorporate it into her own, as it were, to be the active wooer. She is forthright in offering her chain, and when he can only mumble helplessly about his parts, she takes his part by imagining a speech for him and responding to that: "He calls us back. My pride fell with my fortunes; / I'll ask him what he would. Did you call sir? / Sir, you have wrestled well, and overthrown / More than your enemies" (242–5).

In her dialogue with Celia at the start of the next scene, Rosalind simultaneously confesses her strong love for Orlando and shares Celia's feeling that one should be amused by such "sudden" love (1.3.25). Even when Celia asks Rosalind to say "in good earnest" whether she has fallen in love with Orlando, Rosalind answers with humor in the transparent falseness of her justification of the love: "The Duke my father loved his father dearly" (24–7). After Celia dissects the illogic of this absurd bit of role-taking, Rosalind appeals to Celia for a more serious effort at role-taking, asking her to love Orlando "because I do" (34–5).

Nowhere does Rosalind show her strength and her awareness of the importance of self-knowledge more than when Duke Frederick banishes her (1.3.41–61). In reply to his irrational attack, she defends herself with an appeal to reason that is duly respectful of his view and calls upon him to take her role and respect her self-knowledge as a basis for judging her. Frederick rejects Rosalind's arguments, and Celia takes her part to defend her, describing Rosalind as an *alter ego* with whom she shares all experiences and perceptions (68–72). After Frederick has gone, Celia insists on taking Rosalind's part by suffering banishment with her, and again reproaches her cousin for lacking empathy in thinking she would not do this (92–3).

Rosalind, crushed by the shock of her banishment, needs to be led in thinking about their escape until Celia suggests that they disguise themselves (96–110). Then Rosalind's playful disposition is evoked as she sees the possibility of turning a necessary disguise into a sportful enactment of a gallant male protecting Celia with "a swashing and a martial outside" (116). Essential to her confidence in proposing to play such a role is her sense that a man would also play and not simply "be" the role. In her imagination she can play the role of the gallant male because she realizes that success in the role, even for a man, may depend on outfacing fear with "semblances" (115–18). Here Rosalind shows an awareness that differences of behavior between men and women depend more on costume and custom than on biology. Male attire evokes courageous "masculine" conduct and causes it to be reinforced by the wearer's and others' sense of decorum. The corollary that female attire evokes "feminine" behavior should also come to mind here if we wish to speculate about the experience of the boy actors playing Celia and Rosalind.

When Rosalind arrives in the Forest of Arden she is dressed as a male, and she speaks again of how male attire requires typical masculine behavior: "I could find in my heart to disgrace my man's apparel and to cry like a woman. But I must comfort the weaker vessel, as doublet and hose ought to show itself courageous to petticoat; therefore courage, good Aliena" (2.4.3–7). There is no sense here that by wearing male clothing and pretending to be a man Rosalind is coming to feel "manly" in a stereotypical sense. Rather, she jokingly reminds her "womanly" self to "show" courage to Aliena, then lets this showing be merely to tell Aliena to be courageous. Rosalind is still very much the individual *person* Rosalind, wearing a male disguise and looking at its implications with a witty and playful eye.

Although Rosalind has not deeply entered into playing the role of a "manly" character, the following episode shows her readiness to take the emotional role of a lover without regard to gender differences. She responds to Silvius's outpourings about his follies as a lover by saying "Alas, poor shepherd, searching of thy wound, / I have by hard adventure found mine own" (2.4.41–2). When Touchstone responds by parodying Silvius in order to warn Rosalind against an extreme of love that is "mortal in folly" (43–53), Rosalind acknowledges the wisdom in the warning, but continues to identify her feelings with Silvius's: "Jove, Jove! this shepherd's passion / Is much upon my fashion" (54, 57–8). At this point, Rosalind, like Silvius and Orlando, is romantically infatuated and is thereby drawn to romantic fatuity. Touchstone's attempt to mock her out of fatuity appeals to her good sense and her playfulness, but as yet she does not let it affect the way she speaks of her love.

In Rosalind's next scene, however, she comes to use something like Touchstone's parodistic role-playing for her purposes as a lover. When she enters reading one of the sappy love poems Orlando has left hanging on a tree, Touchstone deflates her pleasure with a bawdy parody of love poetry and asks her why she infects herself with such verses (3.2.86–112). Rosalind reacts defensively to Touchstone's mockery and to the suggestion that she has been infected by the verses, a metaphor implying that she read them with empathy (97,113,115–18). Then the role situation alters as Celia is the one who reads a love poem by Orlando. This time Rosalind plays the mocking role that Touchstone has just played when she was the reader (122–75). (Touchstone has now completed his role's function in relation to Rosalind and is not seen with her again until the end of the play.[5]) No doubt the fatuity of Orlando's verses and Celia's amused reading of them provoke Rosalind to mock, but she is also helped to laugh by not having "infected" herself with these verses through reading them and by having the role of an audience, which invites her to play the critic.

Celia knows that Rosalind suspects the poet to be Orlando, and Rosalind knows that Celia knows this. Hence as Celia teases Rosalind by withholding the name of the love poet for as long as it is fun to do so, each of them is able to take the role of the other and know how her own response will affect the other and how to interpret what the other says (176–214). Each of them engages in a playful pretense. Rosalind pretends that she does not at least strongly suspect who the poet is, and that Celia is not confirming that it is Orlando. Celia in effect tells right away who the poet is by saying he wears Rosalind's chain (178), but when Rosalind pretends not to know whom she means, Celia plays along with the pretense while giving rather obvious clues to his identity. Rosalind's pretending not to know is evidently motivated in part by concern not to appear too eager to believe it is Orlando, lest Celia should mock her even more. Celia knows this and withholds Orlando's name in order to force Rosalind's eagerness from cover. As she succeeds in this, Celia delights in tantalizing Rosalind. Although it seems that Celia is mostly reinforced in teasing Rosalind by their shared fun, Celia may also find this behavior reinforcing because she is a little envious of her cousin's having a handsome wooer or because she finds love's fatuity distasteful – not being in love herself yet.

Rosalind delights in her excited emotional state, and her pretense at least as much expresses this delight and her amusement at her own excitement as it does her wish to avoid Celia's mockery. Rosalind can both relish and laugh at her own tone as one of "most petitionary vehemence" (186-7). Her feelings are strong, but the self-detachment she gains through role-taking makes her feel, too, the absurdity her love could drive her to if she were to express her faining – desiring – with no feigning. Thus she makes a witty effort to blame her eagerness on her nature as a woman (191-3). She shows she is not so much serious in saying this as amused by it as an evasion when she says she is only "caparisoned" like a man, a term that treats her as a horse, not a woman (192). When Celia finally tells her that the poet is Orlando, Rosalind asks ten questions about him in an eager rush which might show she is utterly carried away by excited emotion except that she concludes with·"Answer me in one word," wittily mocking her excess (215–20).

By acting out her pretense with Celia, Rosalind discovers that she can give her faining the strong expression she yearns for through a comic feigning. Indeed, she can feel the absurdity of her feigning as an expression of the very faining it is used to conceal and control. To summarize in behaviorist terms: the combination of Rosalind's love and Celia's mockery makes it reinforcing for Rosalind to express the emotion in exaggeratedly comic role-playing that makes the mockery a shared pleasure. However, Rosalind's self-mockery is reinforced not only because it avoids Celia's playful punishment, but also because Rosalind is a person of sportful disposition, and her role-taking enables her to see herself and her love as delightfully absurd:

CELIA.   . . . I found him under a tree like a dropped acorn.
Ros.   It may well be called Jove's tree, when it drops such fruit.

CELIA. Give me audience, good madam.
Ros. Proceed.
CELIA. There lay he stretched along like a wounded knight.
Ros. Though it be pity to see such a sight, it well becomes the ground.
CELIA. Cry holla to the tongue, I prithee; it curvets unseasonably. He was furnished like a hunter.
Ros. O ominous! he comes to kill my heart!
CELIA. I would sing my song without a burden. Thou bringest me out of tune.
Ros. Do you not know I am a woman? When I think, I must speak. Sweet, say on.

(230–46)

In Rosalind's commentary on Celia's descriptions there is a tone of parody that places the romantic excess *as* an excess. Particularly comical is Rosalind's "O ominous! he comes to kill my heart!" (242). Here she strikes a pose as the woman in love, speaking a romantically conventional cliché; the pun on "hart" and the tone of deliberate exaggeration show that she does not really become absorbed in this romantic stereotype. In the context of this parody of a romantic pose, when Rosalind attributes her constant interruptions to her being a woman, she is playing with the stereotype of women's behavior, not seriously saying that her excited speech is caused by her gender.

By the end of the following dialogue between Orlando and Jaques, Rosalind realizes that it will be fun to continue to play-act her love in a comic role: "I will speak to him like a saucy lackey and under that habit play the knave with him" (290–2). Touchstone and Celia have mocked and teased her; now Rosalind will play a mocking role in response to Orlando's romantic lover. Playing Ganymede with Orlando need not deny love's romanticism, however, for this role can express the style of romantic exuberance she has been developing, an exuberance that knows its own folly and rejoices in it as great good fun.

Before analyzing Rosalind's conduct as Ganymede with Orlando, let us consider the possibilities in this role-playing situation. Rosalind could pretend to speak as a saucy boy but use this voice to express her playful character, her own ideas and feelings. Or, in the spirit of a "magic if" she could enter imaginatively into her boyish "habit" (291) in the sense of disposition or character and try out what it feels like to be a Ganymede, what love looks like to such a "saucy lackey." Or thinking about the absurdity of pretending to be a male could mostly serve to heighten her sense that what she is doing is comical. Or she can do now one and now another of these, or feel her own emotions and the point of view of Ganymede in a state of conflict or dynamic tension. In any of these modes, she may improvise as she goes along for the sake of love and its pleasures. This possibility seems especially likely in her circumstances, and can produce particularly fruitful results for her in not being calculating and hence being open to her intuitive responses to the thoughts and feelings of herself, Ganymede, and Orlando.

The possible outcomes for Rosalind thus include conflict leading to affirmation of a strictly "feminine" character, change toward a more androgynous outlook, or even transcendence of gender- or sex-related viewpoints. Rosalind could come to see both male and female from a detached perspective, with a wise knowledge of life and human nature, perhaps seeing the world as a stage and all the men and women as mere players. It is likely that Rosalind will experience each of these outcomes to some extent if she is as alert as she seems to be to all the possibilities in herself, her situation, and the others she play-acts with. An important question for all these possibilities is whether Rosalind has any clear purpose of having some particular effect on Orlando. Is she at all serious in saying she will "cure" his love, and if so, what does she want to cure him of? Beyond this, what is the actual effect of Rosalind's play-acting on Orlando?

In Rosalind's remarks about time that begin her dialogue with Orlando, she evidently seeks to make Ganymede interesting to him. In speaking first of how time passes for a young maid waiting for her wedding, she describes someone who is like herself (307–11). She alludes to her sexual longings in a series of bawdy puns, but this punning works with the light tone of her other descriptive terms to indicate the amused detachment of this self-description. In her sketches of people in relation to time, Rosalind establishes the perspective of Ganymede as a person who, like Touchstone, looks with detachment on all people as at least faintly ridiculous (302–27). Rosalind expresses an awareness, probably heightened through some degree of taking on Ganymede's perspective, that all perspectives are subjective and relative to one's situation and character: "Time travels in divers paces with divers persons" (302–3).

Orlando is intrigued and curious about the person presented by Rosalind. The chief basis for Orlando's interest at this point is expressed in his addressing this person as "pretty youth" (328). Although he does not recognize Rosalind, he can see her beauty within the male disguise. In the last scene of the play, Orlando tells her father that when he first saw Ganymede "Methought he was a brother to your daughter" (5.4.28–9). Rosalind can see how ridiculous it is for Orlando to be attracted to a person he thinks is a male because he is attracted to her. She expresses an outlook hostile to women and love that will provoke him to respond more to Ganymede's personality, while it will also lead her to play out the dialectic of her emotions and attitudes.

In this role-playing she seems not so much to adopt a typical male chauvinist viewpoint as to make use of it to evoke a response and prepare the way for the game she wants to play with Orlando. In speaking of the "giddy offences" of women, Rosalind may especially think of her own behavior at the moment: she is as aware of the absurdity of what she is doing as she is of Orlando's absurdity, and although she delights in this aspect of love, she says she wants to "physic" it (3.2.341, 349). Or at least she pretends to want to cure Orlando of his "quotidian of love" in which he is a "fancy-monger" who is "deifying the name of Rosalind" (353–6, cf. 392–412). It is clear that she does not intend to cure him of loving her because she has no sooner said that she wants to do so than she does her best to get him to insist that he is as much in love as he claims to be (359–86). As she inventories his appearance from cheeks to eyes to chin and down his body, although she is questioning whether he loves, she must also be stimulating her own physical desire, and so there is a climax for both of them in his hyperbolic claim that "Neither rhyme nor reason can express how much" he loves (387).

Rosalind calls Orlando's love beyond reason a madness, but she acknowledges that she, too, feels this madness: "the lunacy is so ordinary that the whippers are in love too" (388–93). This acknowledges also that Ganymede's behavior is ultimately Rosalind's own, for she, not Ganymede, is the whipper who is in love. In whipping Orlando's love, Rosalind can also whip her own love, since she says hers is mad, too. Certainly her emotions as well as Orlando's will be affected by her role-playing as she pretends to "like" him and "loathe" him by turns (403–5). Thus Ganymede can be a role which, through its sauciness, evokes in Rosalind something like what she felt in her dialogue with Celia before Orlando entered – a duality of delighting in and mocking her love's excesses. In both cases the mockery or playful whipping is delightful because it is a stimulus for love's passionate responses. At the same time, however, Rosalind's speaking of whipping suggests that she has some more serious thought, however vague, about what her sharp "counsel" will enable the two mad lovers to see. Rosalind seems to see how much she shares Orlando's feelings and experiences: playing the role of a male may help her to enter into his feelings.

When Rosalind as Ganymede proposes to pretend to be Rosalind, she invites Orlando to pretend as well. Her play-acting will require play-acting on his part: he is to "imagine" (395) her his love: "I would cure you, if you would but call me Rosalind and come every day to my cote and woo me" (414–15). Obviously Orlando agrees to woo not to be cured but because he finds Ganymede interesting and attractive and enough like Rosalind (whether he is conscious of the resemblance or not) to make the pretense a satisfying one for his love: "Now by the faith of my love, I will" (416). If Orlando knew he was talking with Rosalind, his past behavior suggests he would speak only in tedious romantic verses or be mute in sexual arousal. As long as he is pretending she is Rosalind, however, he can be at ease, amused and detached from what he is doing. In this way, his role-playing will in some degree mirror Rosalind's and he can be much more attractive than he would be on his knees reciting bad poetry. And as Orlando becomes attractive in this way, Rosalind's love may increase to an even greater quotidian through the very means she says she employs to "cure" love.

In the next scene between Rosalind and Celia there is a suggestion about how to interpret Orlando's conduct in Celia's comment that he is true in love "when he is in, but I think he is not in" (3.4.25). When Rosalind plaintively reminds her that he swore "he was" in love, Celia adds that "'Was' is not 'is'" (26–7). Celia says this intending to tease Rosalind, but she may also point to the effect on Orlando of his peculiar role-playing situation. When he is with Rosalind and wooing her "as if" she were Rosalind, he may become absorbed enough in his role that he will kiss her (7) even though he is supposed to know she is "really" Ganymede. Certainly his absorption in acting "as if" she were Rosalind is reinforced partly because she *is* Rosalind and so he sees in Ganymede the beauty of Rosalind, as noted earlier. But when he is not actively engaged in their mutual pretense, he is the actor off the stage who can drop his role, think of other matters, and be casual about his life within the role (17–30). He loves "when he is in."

In this dialogue with Celia, Rosalind seems less witty than in 3.2, more in love in an anxious way. When Celia suggests there is "no truth" in Orlando, Rosalind merely replies "Do you think so?" (19–20). And when Celia responds with a series of witty comparisons, all Rosalind can muster is "Not true in love?" (24). Here we have the comical irony that Rosalind's role-playing, which she presumably thought would stimulate and frustrate Orlando, has come near to curing him of love's madness in a way that leaves her frustrated and lovesick. He can satisfy his love for a time "by thinking" in their pretense (5.2.50), and his nonchalance about their wooing causes Rosalind to lose some of her nonchalance as she fears she has lost him.

There may be indications that Rosalind takes out her frustration on Silvius and Phebe. When Corin offers to show her and Celia the "pageant truly play'd / Between the pale complexion of true love / And the red glow of scorn and proud disdain," Rosalind may refer to her present inability to be active in her own play with Orlando when she says "I'll prove a busy actor in their play" – there can be a slight emphasis on "their" to suggest this meaning (3.4.48–55). As she plays the scene with Silvius and Phebe, Rosalind may also feel the analogy between her situation and theirs through role-taking. Phebe's scorn is like the behavior Rosalind has proposed to help cure Orlando, and if Rosalind now feels slighted by Orlando, her self-pity could become like that of Silvius.

Rosalind may be sincere in her expressions of surprise and scornful resistance as Phebe falls in love with her, but there is some evidence that Rosalind intends her scorn to increase Phebe's infatuation. Rosalind comments that Silvius has fallen in love with Phebe's cruelty and that Phebe will "fall in love with my anger," then says "If it be so, . . . I'll sauce her with bitter words" (3.5.66–9). Moreover, in her last speech to Phebe, Rosalind says "I like you not," but then tells where she lives (74–5). The text does not enable us to say whether Rosalind's behavior here is reinforced mostly by a sense of power that helps to assuage her frustration regarding Orlando, or whether she may already see the way to use her role in Silvius and Phebe's play to break open its rigid "pageant" pattern and fulfill its potential as "*their* play" (3.4.48–55, emphasis added).

In her brief dialogue with Jaques at the beginning of 4.1, Rosalind makes an amused effort to cure his melancholy with Ganymede's counsel. She contests his claim that sadness is an appropriate attitude toward life, criticizing it as an extreme that is as bad as being always a laugher (5–7). This plays with the Aristotelian doctrine that we should seek the mean between extremes, but Rosalind's final judgment here regarding sadness is more characteristic of her: "And your experience makes you sad. I had rather have a fool to make me merry than experience to make me sad, and to travel for it too!" (25–7). As she compares her part in life's play with Jaques's, Rosalind may see that she has traveled from her home and has lost her lands, as Jaques has sold his to see other men's – and she has felt sad both at home and in Arden. Yet she sees it is foolish to let experience make her sad when she has a fool to make her merry: Touchstone, sometimes Celia, possibly Orlando, for the moment Jaques, and always herself insofar as she can play the Fool and take the perspective of the Fool to see her own folly. Here, as typically, the Aristotelian mean in Rosalind is less a fixed center with reason in control of passion than a balance and tension between emotion and wit. This state is produced by the interplay between her character and the experiences she is passing through, an interplay evoking exploration of a capacity for complex responses.

As Jaques departs after Orlando enters and greets Rosalind, she does not speak to Orlando until she delivers a mocking critique of Jaques (31–6). This may suggest that she lets Orlando wait because he has kept her waiting, and also that she hopes to intimidate him playfully by showing him how satirical Ganymede can be. She then turns on Orlando and scolds him for his tardiness, accusing him of not loving from the heart (36–47).

Now, we know from 3.4 that this expresses a feeling close to Rosalind's own, and the question arises of how much she plays a "Ganymede's Rosalind" here, speaking as a male-pretending-to-be-Rosalind. I think the text shows that she uses the mask of Ganymede chiefly to free herself from inhibitions, to drop the socially conventional pretense that she is merely a properly socialized young lady. She thus *un*masks and gives creative shape to Rosalind as a witty, playful, intense person, using a style showing that a male is supposed to be presenting this Rosalind.

This is not to say that the style of Ganymede's behavior and outlook have no effect on Rosalind. Even in the first, most emotional part of her complaint about Orlando's lateness, the role of Ganymede affects the way she speaks by giving a boyishly saucy and scornful tone to her scolding (4.1.36–9). This way of speaking may mask or alter her feeling, for she seems more saucy than unhappy as she scolds. The specifically male aspect of her boyish manner of speech seems to be a mask or "stalking-horse," however: there is no indication here that her pretense causes her personal outlook to become stereotypically masculine in any distinctive way (cf. 5.4.105–6 on Touchstone's use of the pretense of being a simpleton). The character of Ganymede seems to engage Rosalind chiefly as a role evoking a playfully teasing mockery that gives her a degree of amused detachment through which she may gain insight as well as pleasure. In this, Rosalind's sportful disposition and her saucy role-playing work together, moving her to become ever more freely sportful and saucy.

Orlando's warm apologies enable Rosalind to see that all is well and she makes fun of her own censure as well as his imagined falseness as a lover in her fantastic analysis of the lover's minute, in her bawdy jest of Cupid's "clap," and finally in her conceit of the tardy lover as a snail (4.1.42–7, 49–50). Orlando's response of curiosity, surely accompanied by amusement, reinforces Rosalind's playful performance, leading her to develop her conceit of the snail further so that the creature finally symbolizes a cuckolded husband (51–9). Here Rosalind playfully punishes Orlando for his lateness and also seeks to amuse him and engage him with the saucy, knavish personality her role as Ganymede evokes from her. Although a "knave" is a boy, Rosalind's sauciness still does not greatly exceed that of her and Celia's way of teasing Touchstone and Le Beau in Act 1 before she undertook to pretend any male behavior.

Generally in 4.1, Rosalind's readiness of reply to what Orlando says indicates that she takes his role to think about what line she should pursue in her role from moment to moment.[6] This does not mean, however, that she takes Orlando's role so that she can say what he wants her to say. She must know that he will protest when she says that wives cuckold their husbands. His "Virtue is no horn-maker; and my Rosalind is virtuous," suggests that although he finds the Rosalind he is playing with engaging, he does not accept her as his Rosalind, the "real" Rosalind (60–1). Through her role-taking, however, Rosalind has seen how to set Orlando up to say this, and she is ready with her reply. Pretense and reality virtually fuse for her as she says "And I am your Rosalind" (62).

But pretense and reality do not easily fuse for Orlando. Rosalind must use her play-acting to induce him to give up the deified Rosalind of his imagining in exchange for the Rosalind of her imagining. She tries to do this by making her Rosalind an exciting person and by rejecting his responses that are based on the romantic idealism generating his fantasy Rosalind. Yet she only seeks to invalidate his romantic ideals and hence his image of Rosalind insofar as these differ from her own style of romantic idealism, in which romanticism is sometimes indulged with a playful sense of the absurdity of love's excessive idealism, and sometimes mocked in a tone tinged with regret that these ideals are impossible, as critics have suggested.[7]

Rosalind says that now she will be in a holiday humor and disposed to consent to Orlando's wooing. She uses the idea of "if" here to move from a shallow pretense to a more absorbing pretense that approaches reality: "What would you say to me now, and I were your very very Rosalind?" (65–8). But when Orlando offers to turn from the hypothetical world of words to the deed of kissing her, the pretense is about to become more "real" than Rosalind wants for her purposes, and she puts him off with cleverly distasteful talk of orators spitting when they cannot think what to say (69–73). Rosalind uses her male role as a stalking-horse in the indelicacy of this talk and in the sexual implications of her following lines. Both Rosalind's courtly socialization and her sexual desire are heard as her talk of spitting restrains sexual expression but she and Orlando provoke their sexual desire by imagining him out of his clothes in her presence (73–83). Such imaginings make Rosalind feel their closeness and the identity of her physical Rosalind with Orlando's Rosalind: "Am not I your Rosalind?" (84).

Orlando's offer to kiss may show he is caught up in their role-playing, though it seems to be chiefly evoked by the physical identity of this Rosalind with his. Given that his desire is for a woman, he would avoid seeing his wanting to kiss a boy as sinful, perhaps by thinking he is merely teasing Ganymede. In any case, her question whether she is not his Rosalind prompts him to recall the limit of his belief in their play-acting: "I take some joy to say you are, because I would be talking of her" (85–6). This may indicate some acceptance of her Rosalind as his Rosalind, but it mostly suggests that there is still a distance between these two Rosalinds. Her response, "Well, in her person, I say I will not have you" seems intended to close that distance by playing on the psychology of strengthening love by rejecting it (87). Read this way, the rejection expresses

Rosalind's character as a lover and the saucy knavishness the role of Ganymede encourages. She uses a strategem characteristic of lovers, yet it is also one of the things Ganymede said he would do to cure Orlando's love (3.2.397–405).

Orlando responds as she evidently wishes in saying "Then in mine own person, I die," and this opens him up to one of Rosalind's more important points, that he should "die by attorney" because no man has ever died in his own person for love (4.1.88–103). This is a speech of wonderful subtlety, for it is simultaneously a witty mocking of the romantic ideal and a wryly humorous lament that what is being said is true: "men have died from time to time and worms have eaten them, but not for love" (101–3). Rosalind again expresses her longing for the romantic ideal while also asserting her criticism of the excesses of this ideal, her awareness that the real causes of human suffering are beyond the understanding of romantic idealism. She may reduce the gap between her longing and her criticism if she also sees that the romantic ideal of dying for love can be *as if* real in the imaginings and fainings/feignings of lovers. She denies the literal credibility of the "chroniclers" who recorded the life of Leander, but such a literalist denial does not touch the mythic truth of his legend. Hence there is not necessarily a denial here that, for example, Shakespeare's Romeo and Juliet died for love within their imagined world.

In the world that is as you like it and in Rosalind's present imaginings, there is room at least to "die by attorney" for love, and in a sense all is done by attorney in this world. After all, when Rosalind says that in Rosalind's person she will not have Orlando (87), she is saying this by attorney, since her ambiguous phrasing implies that she speaks for Rosalind more than it implies that she speaks as Rosalind. And Orlando's "Then in mine own person, I die" (88) is itself spoken in much the same sense – "*If* Rosalind in her own person should reject me, *then* in mine own person I die." Orlando's phrasing may suggest a detached attitude – he takes the role of himself in a hypothetical situation and declares what he would do: he is far from saying "I die" and dying. The ideas about dying or not dying for love are thus the hypotheses of a pair of romantics, but Rosalind's approach to the use of the "if" of play-acting invites her to "whip" them both by making them aware of the limits of love and romanticism in the working-day world.

Orlando says he hopes his Rosalind would not think men do not die for love, for he fears that even her frown could kill him (104–5). Rosalind has heard this sort of thing before in the dialogue between Silvius and Phebe (3.5.10–16), and of course she wants to keep Orlando from becoming another Silvius. Rosalind's love also keeps her from wanting to become another Phebe in her reply. She amusingly reassures Orlando that her frown would not "kill a fly," and she throws herself from the extreme of rejection to the extreme of full acceptance of his love (4.1.106–10). Her assertion of love is presumably heartfelt, yet it is also a bit of playful "whipping," for when Orlando then asks if she will "have" him (111), she takes her acceptance of his love to an extreme that is actually a rejection again. She will have "twenty such" men: "can one desire too much of a good thing?" (112–17).

As the scene unfolds, Rosalind goes back and forth between seeming to reject Orlando and seeming to encourage him. In this she appears to be Ganymede's Rosalind, who was to be changeable in this way to "cure" Orlando of love. However, these changes also result from changes in Rosalind's own feelings and intentions, though these changes are not the same as the alternations between apparent rejection and acceptance. That is, Rosalind loves Orlando all the time, so when she pretends to reject him, she restrains her strong disposition to express love, which strengthens this disposition. Then, as she asserts her love, her playful but perceptive character and the attitude evoked by her role make it reinforcing for her to stimulate Orlando and herself by crossing their love with knavishly skeptical remarks. The result is that Rosalind expresses both her romantic love and her skepticism, either by turns or simultaneously. It is also probable that Rosalind alternates "liking" and "loathing" Orlando (3.2.403–4) in order to keep their love game going: she delights in fooling or playing with love rather than in merely "being" in love.

Rosalind next indulges her love in acting out a wedding ceremony, and here there is only the barest pretense that she is not Rosalind (4.1.117–33). The delight here is especially that the stalking-horse of Ganymede enables her to play herself plainly and anticipate the pleasure of her actual wedding without Orlando's detection. He, however, gets the same pleasure in much the same way, since he too can pretend to pretend to get married, enjoying the marriage *as if* it were real. Thus Orlando and Rosalind share a pleasant imagining of their future joy together. This moment cannot last, though, for their recognition that this anticipation depends on thought being "winged" so it can run before actions prompts Rosalind to think of the swift pace of time (132–8). Again she draws back from virtually "being" Rosalind, referring to herself in the third person: "Now tell me how long you would have her, after you have possessed her?" (135–6). In saying this, Rosalind also detaches herself from their love in the way she shifts her point of view from anticipating their coupling to regarding its climax as past and perhaps even as finished: "after you have possessed," not "when you possess." Rosalind may thus imply in advance that if Orlando says he would have her "For ever, and a day," she will reply that he should "Say a day, without the ever" (137–8).

The speech in which Rosalind then says these last quoted words is another statement on the limits of love; also, however, it expresses a self-realization and a witty rationale in defense of the self she realizes. She explains that he can have his love for only a day because marriage will change them (138–41). Although she employs a male chauvinist view in the terms she uses to describe how women change when they become wives, these terms also suggest that she is thinking of her own present capriciousness and is realizing that she will always be changeable (141–5). Then she says that this changeableness will be linked to Orlando's moods, as now she is playing off his responses and trying to move him along with her (145–8). Next she also articulates the insightful rationale for this, saying that such changeable behavior is wise in its wayward wit: "The wiser, the waywarder" (152–6). Finally she teases Orlando about the implications of this self-ideal for her sexual behavior (159–67).

In this passage Rosalind seems to become absorbed in the flow of her thoughts, so that she does not realize how much she imagines having "forever and a day" with Orlando in her own terms: December as well as May, a time for children and a time for every mood and every play of wit, all in a world where the possibilities for living are limited only by her desire and imagination. Rosalind also paradoxically belies her statement that because of her changeableness Orlando cannot possess her forever and a day: when she fully develops her idea of how she will change, she describes the wittily wayward character her role-playing has helped her to become, and she projects this present self, with its fascinating potentialities, into her future life with Orlando.

In their future together, just as now in their wooing, Rosalind imagines a less interesting role for Orlando than for herself. Insofar as she becomes absorbed in her playful self-ideal, her role-taking weakens here. Thus her talk of how a wife can excuse cuckolding her husband seems to break Orlando's engagement with their pretense that she is Rosalind, for he abruptly announces that he must leave to have dinner with the Duke (168–71). Rosalind has been enjoying an image of herself wittily crossing Orlando's moods and intents, and suddenly Orlando reverses their roles, perhaps quite innocently, as he crosses her mood and intent. Her imagining was of a world existing mostly for play between the two of them and she is reminded that he has other important relationships. Her reply shows how taken aback she is: "Alas, dear love, I cannot lack thee two hours" (169). There is no pretense here – this cry is pure and heartfelt Rosalind. Then when Orlando explains his going, she puts on an exaggerated manner of "I'm pretending" to cover her continued expression of pain at his departure (172–90).

As soon as Orlando has gone, Rosalind confesses to Celia that she is more deeply in love than can be measured (195–207). I have in part drawn on the evidence of these lines in my certainty that Rosalind never does more than pretend to disapprove of Orlando and that her playing with his emotions affects her at least as much as him. Indeed, these lines show that her acting affects her more than it does him. "The wiser, the waywarder" is thus not Rosalind's only self-realization here; she is immediately reminded of her own emotional intensity, which balances the wisdom of her wit.

Her emotions outweigh her wit in the only later moment in which her role-playing as Ganymede has much psychological interest, when she faints on learning that the bloody handkerchief is from Orlando's wound, but pretends the fainting is only pretended. Yet the text does not treat such fainting simply as stereotypically feminine, for Orlando, not Rosalind, faints on seeing his blood. He faints chiefly because of his loss of blood, she faints when she learns that the blood she has already seen is *his* (4.3.93–7, 146–8, 154–9). Also, Oliver's responses to Rosalind's fainting suggest first that this is a common human weakness, then that as a "youth" Ganymede is weak in lacking a "man's heart" (158, 164–5). Celia suggests that there is "more in it" than merely the weakness of fainting at the sight of blood (159), and Oliver is close to the truth when he insists that Rosalind's complexion shows she feels "a passion of earnest" (170–1). Thus Rosalind fainted when she learned that the one she loves has been injured, and because she does not want her passion to give her identity away, she insists she has only counterfeited, comically affecting a masculine tone and playfully hinting at one truth by saying "I should have been a woman by right" (166–8, 175–6). If we must produce gender stereotypes here, we could say that to the man a strong heart is one that resists weakness and passion, whereas for the woman emotional bonds are heartfelt (cf. Marshall's reading).

In conclusion, I want to emphasize a few points about Rosalind's role-playing and role-taking and about Orlando's response to her, especially in the courtship scene examined at length above. First of all, in my reading the play creates little sense that through her role-playing Rosalind comes to have a more androgynous character or outlook than she had at the beginning of the play. Mostly she uses the Ganymede mask to free herself to say what *she* finds it reinforcing to say when her social identity is concealed. Yet through playing Ganymede her own attitude is affected, mainly in three ways. First, insofar as she enters into the outlook of another character in this role-playing, she gains a detached perspective on herself. Second, such a perspective invites her to laugh at and, more important, play with her own absurdity in courting the man she loves while in a male disguise. Finally, the saucy knavishness of Ganymede as Rosalind creates him works with her sportful disposition to move her to become more freely sportful and saucy, culminating in her realization of a self-ideal in "the wiser, the waywarder." In preventing Orlando from knowing that Rosalind is speaking, she refrains from committing herself to be a person like the Rosalind she creates. As she articulates her self-ideal, she is becoming the character she imagines, but this Rosalind is in the realm of "if" for her, and she may change when she is married, as she says she will. Ironically, since it is now that she acts on the principle of the wiser, the waywarder, her saying that she will change can indicate that when she is married she might eventually become a sedate and predictable wife. That is, the self-ideal of "the wiser, the waywarder" is especially reinforced in the excited state her uninhibited role-playing has brought her to at the time she says this. With the passing of this state of excitement, her self-ideal may change as well. In my view, however, the text implies that because of what she is learning here, she will be determined not to relinquish her wit's freedom.[8] The sense that she accepts her subordination to the patriarchy when she gives herself to Orlando at the end is balanced by *her* giving herself: that this is significant is suggested by an earlier insistence on the patriarchal principle that a woman must be given in marriage (3.3.61–4).

Rosalind's excited talk of her self-ideal has the tone of a playful self-love. Her "bottomless" love may be partly caused by a feeling that Orlando finds her to be as exciting as she thinks she is, so that she loves him in part for loving her. The combination of Rosalind's playing her role with such delight and simultaneously taking the role of Orlando to imagine his responses may induce her to believe his responses are the same as her own. Even under ordinary circumstances, what one imagines as another person's response may actually be shaped by one's own response. This tendency would be intensified in a situation such as Rosalind's, since she enjoys her performance very much and is also reinforced strongly for thinking Orlando enjoys it as much as she does.

We can accept Rosalind's self-love, however, because it evidently helps to increase her love of Orlando and because she never loses awareness that the wisdom she praises in herself is the wisdom of high Foolery. Especially important for our judgment of her self-love, we enjoy her for the same qualities she loves in herself and we enjoy her in the same spirit of enjoying playful imaginings *as if*. Orlando, too, certainly enjoys her performance, though he may not enjoy the Rosalind she creates for him as she or we do. He frequently questions whether his "wise" Rosalind will be so giddily changeable, but his responses come to be playful in their skeptical detachment, prompting her to pursue her imagining further. There is possibly a suggestion in his witty tone that he accepts what she says in the spirit she means it – "wouldn't it be delightful if we could always be so excited and have so much fun?" In any case, he is inevitably associating her ideas of Rosalind with a physical being he already half intuits *is* Rosalind, and when he discovers at the end that this Rosalind is the Rosalind he loves, he joyously accepts her. Through the "magic if" of pretense he has imagined that his Rosalind might be like this Rosalind she creates. The "if" of pretending a hypothetical reality enables him to consider this Rosalind in the perspective of detached wit, the perspective in which such a Rosalind is most attractive.

Perhaps the best indication that Orlando sometimes becomes engaged with the pretense that she is Rosalind is in his coming to ask, toward the end of 4.1, whether his Rosalind will do as this Rosalind says she will (149). The question manifests skepticism, yet that he should ask "Ganymede" what his Rosalind will do suggests that he intuitively accepts the Rosalind before him as one who can speak for his Rosalind. When later he says he can "live no longer by thinking" and needs his very own Rosalind, he does not deny that for a time he has lived by thinking (5.2.50). And of course as an imagined person he will always live by thinking.

So far I may have slighted the degree to which Rosalind becomes psychologically involved with the Ganymede role as a male outlook. The "knave's" outlook is an important element of the perspective in her role-playing that enables Rosalind to see love and herself in a comical light and to "shoot" her wit. But the knave's outlook is not stereotypically masculine, for the play typifies boys as being mischievously unstable and androgynous (3.2.401–3). Moreover, the romantic heroine in Shakespeare's comedies can be playfully knavish without resort to male disguise – for example, consider Beatrice in *Much Ado*. To complete the circle, the romantic hero in Shakespeare's plays, if not always unstable or even usually androgynous, is typically something of a boy, as Orlando is. Thus the boyish role Rosalind plays may help her to take Orlando's perspective in relation to herself. Still, the boyish aspect of Rosalind seems to me mostly that of a witty and playful young woman pretending to be a boy. Thus although Rosalind is surely Shakespeare's heroine whom a boy actor should be able to realize the most fully and appealingly with the greatest degree of psychological involvement, she can be played equally well by a woman. The role of Rosalind offers a rich experience for actor and audience alike, if we enter into her character and role-playing in the spirit of playful imagining "as if."

7

Absorbed Action: "Sure this robe of mine does change my disposition"

Absorption in an action can be terrifying, ludicrous, or beautifully moving. The effect of any absorbed action depends on whether the absorption develops the capacity for becoming and so heightens being. Our finest potentialities may be brought to fulfillment through an absorbed enactment that draws together our full experience and several roles. But absorbed action can instead turn us toward self-destroying error as the single perspective of a tragic role narrows our vision. Or the extremely reinforcing consequences of playing certain kinds of roles may seduce us into attempting to become what we can never be.

Needless to say, Shakespeare's plays provide many examples of characters who become absorbed: Malvolio becomes absorbed in trying to play a role for which he is ludicrously unsuited, Othello and Leontes exemplify the tragic and tragicomic terrors of absorption, and Antony and Cleopatra both achieve moments of heightened being. To conclude this study I want to discuss a special moment of heightened being – Perdita's role-playing as the goddess Flora, through which she beautifully fulfills her nature as an imagined person (WT 4.4).[1] Like other female characters in Shakespeare's later plays, such as her mother, Hermione, and Cordelia in Lear, Perdita is concerned to express her truth. But whereas in the tragic or seeming-tragic worlds of Cordelia and Hermione truth is defeated by falsehood, in Perdita's benign world of romance the final irony is that her actual social identity, unknown to her, is the queenly one she is reluctant even to play-act because she thinks[2] it is so far above her.

In Florizel's view, her costume as the goddess Flora makes her a queen of the sheep-shearing, but Perdita feels that this role is socially inappropriate for one of her low status (4.4.5–10). Her opening statement about what "becomes" her shows Perdita's great concern that her conduct should express what she thinks she truly is in social terms. She goes on to say that the "custom" of folly at feasts makes their costumes acceptable, yet she still expresses the discomfort she would feel if it were not for this custom, indicating that even now she would suffer "to show myself a glass"

(10–14). At this point it seems certain that Perdita's self-consciousness will prevent her from "becoming" Flora in the sense of being absorbed in this role in a self-creating way, and it is important to see how she changes so that at the end of her role-playing she says "Methinks I play as I have seen them do / In Whitsun pastorals: sure this robe of mine / Does change my disposition" (133–5).

In the early part of the scene, Perdita's self-conscious concern for social decorum is largely caused by fear. She points out to Florizel that because of his greatness he has "not been us'd to fear"; in other words, he has not formed the habit of fearing superiors as she has (17–18). Thus she indicates that social conditioning has caused her fear, and this social fear now disposes her to become emotionally involved in imagining a socially realistic theatrical scenario directly opposed to the imaginings needed if Flora is to be a "becoming" role for her. She says she trembles to think how his father would look and speak if he should come and see Florizel dressed as a shepherd, and, shifting her perspective, she asks how she should "behold / The sternness of his presence" in her "borrowed flaunts" (18–24).

Ironically, Perdita's humble upbringing enables her to take the role of a royal person toward herself, with the result that she is afraid to play a royal role. Florizel tries to reassure her by defending the lowly role *he* is playing as mythologically appropriate (24–35). Her fears are more for her own role, however, and are based on actual social conditions, not mythological fantasies. She explains that she fears his father will either force Florizel to abandon her or make her "change" her "life" (35–40). She evidently means that the King may have her imprisoned or executed, but the benign irony of romance lets us see another sense in which her life is to change so that she can marry Florizel.

Again Florizel reassures her, this time by saying she should rid herself of these "forc'd thoughts" (41). He addresses her realistic social concerns by promising that he will abandon his royal identity rather than abandon her (42–6). Then he again urges her to rid herself of her fearful thoughts:

> Your guests are coming:
> Lift up your countenance, as it were the day
> Of celebration of that nuptial which
> We two have sworn shall come.
>
> (46–51)

Here Florizel plays a role something like that of a Stanislavskian director to her actress by suggesting that she think of the festive occasion "as" – meaning *as if* – it were their wedding celebration. As Florizel suggests this imagining, it is still *his* imagining, however, and Perdita's immediate response to his suggestion that she play Flora as if it were her wedding day is continued anxiety, though now she is anxious about her hope rather than tending toward despair: "O lady Fortune, / Stand you auspicious!" (51–2). In response to this, Florizel as a director suggests a simpler role to her, that of hostess at the feast (52–3). Then, as the guests take their places at the table, her supposed father, the Old Shepherd, takes over the role of Perdita's director and he has his own idea of how she should think of herself in her role as hostess:

> Fie, daughter! when my old wife liv'd, upon
> This day she was both pantler, butler, cook,
> Both dame and servant; welcom'd all, serv'd all;
> . . . .
> You are retired,
> As if you were a feasted one, and not
> The hostess of the meeting: pray you, bid
> These unknown friends to 's welcome; for it is
> A way to make us better friends, more known.
> Come, quench your blushes, and present yourself
> That which you are, Mistress o' th' Feast . . .
> (55–7, 62–8)

The role-model the Shepherd describes is one that can allow Perdita to resolve much of her social anxiety by including both high and low degrees within a role that is the social norm for a woman of her class. His wife was "Both dame and servant; welcom'd all, serv'd all" as "Mistress" of the feast (57, 68). As Onions's *Shakespeare Glossary* says, "dame" usually means "woman of rank, lady" in Shakespeare. In this passage Onions connects it with "mistress" as a woman in charge of a household. Onions reminds us that "mistress" usually means "chief" or "first" in Shakespeare, and that it can also designate a woman who has a "protecting or guiding influence." It is suggested that something like the power of such a role is achieved by Perdita in this scene when Camillo says he does not regret her lack of instruction in how to act like a lady, for "she seems a mistress / To most that teach" (582–4).

As dame or mistress of the feast, Perdita's role first of all is to welcome her guests, an activity that the Old Shepherd points out has the social function of making people better known to each other and therefore better friends (64–6). The beauty of her welcoming makes Perdita herself known in a marvelous way to her guests, and her self-revelation works with her welcoming to create the basis for a social bond with Polixenes. Thus although Polixenes is not moved to accept her in his family by her beautiful action, he is moved to see her actual character as one "Too noble

for this place" (159). Hence there is no barrier to her becoming his son's
bride once it is discovered that she is a princess by birth as well as in her
conduct.

It is most important that the Shepherd tells Perdita to stop acting "as if"
she were a guest (62–3), to cease her self-conscious blushing "and present
yourself / That which you are, Mistress o' th' Feast" (67–8). Rather than
asking her to block anxious thoughts in a fantasy of a future role as
Florizel has, the Shepherd says she should shape her behavior to be what
the social situation and his invocation of her enactment declare her to be
in realistic social terms. Perdita immediately accepts this invitation to be
herself in the role of the mistress welcoming guests and thereby creating
social bonds. She greets the disguised Polixenes: "Sir, welcome: / It is my
father's will I should take on me / The hostess-ship o' th' day . . ." (70–
2). This speech expresses her conscious turning to the role, but we immediately see that she will not play it in the bustling peasant's manner
suggested by the Old Shepherd's description of his wife. Perdita instead
plays her social role as hostess according to her costume as Flora (73ff),
the character that Florizel has created for her, which we have seen is
imaginatively linked with their love and her future role as a bride. Thus
she manages to enact her role in a way that fulfills the desires of both her
supposed father and her lover, and even, as far as character is concerned,
the desires of the King. This is not to suggest that she becomes merely
their creature, for she fulfills their desires by transcending all their expectations in a mode expressing her own deepest imaginings. Her enactment
is fully her own creation, though her love and her desire to please and
make friends with all are fundamental to her inspiration.

Her thinking becomes engaged in her role, making her truth known, in
her dialogue with Polixenes explaining that she has no carnations or
streaked gillyvors because they are not natural but adulterated by art (82–
8). Intellectually she accepts Polixenes's reply that "The art itself is nature" (97), but to her this is not the issue. Whether the art is natural or not,
it interferes with the sort of absolute integrity she values for herself (99–
103). For her, a love based only on beautiful appearances created by art
is not enough. In her inspired poetry following almost immediately upon
these lines we are awed by the splendor of Shakespeare's art; however,
Perdita's rejection of art suggests that as she becomes absorbed in her
inspiration, she is not herself consciously trying to fashion her speech
artistically. So powerfully does Perdita's imagination create the flowers
and the season of spring that she must not only say they are not present
but repeat this fact lest it be forgotten (113, 127). She distributes to Florizel
and the maidens not so much the flowers of nature as the flowers of
glorious poetry inspired by her own intense maidenly love for Florizel
(118–27). We see that this emotion has come to absorb her completely

when she speaks frankly and innocently before so large an audience of her desire to embrace her lover on a bed of flowers (128–32). Then she detaches herself enough to distribute the flowers she actually has in her arms (132), and finally she expresses her realization that her disposition has been changed by her enactment in play (133–5).

Perdita's inspired action inspires Florizel in turn to state the significance of what she has achieved:

> What you do,
> Still betters what is done. When you speak, sweet,
> I'd have you do it ever: when you sing,
> I'd have you buy and sell so, so give alms,
> Pray so, and, for the ord'ring your affairs,
> To sing them too: when you do dance, I wish you
> A wave o' th' sea, that you might ever do
> Nothing but that, move still, still so,
> And own no other function. Each your doing,
> So singular in each particular,
> Crowns what you are doing, in the present deeds,
> That all your acts are queens.
>
> (135–46)

This is my final text for Shakespeare's ideas about self-creative role-playing. These lines state as no others do the power of the human capacity to achieve a fullness of being in imaginative action. Florizel speaks only of Perdita's actions, yet his words imply the link of action and being. Especially the last lines emphasize that each of Perdita's acts expresses her special way of speaking and moving, and that her manner of acting "crowns" not her but the very deeds themselves in the instant of action so that all her *acts* are queens. Perdita thus does not merely have the capacity to act like a queen or to *be* or *become* a queen through acting as one. At least in the eyes of her inspired Prince, she has the ability to "crown" every act she performs in her doing of it, so that she becomes the potent source of royalty (143–6). As Florizel's imagery and rhythm suggest, the power of Perdita's actions is in the musical poetic grace flowing into her action from her inspired imagining. It would be difficult to think of a way to assert more strongly the capacity of a human being, whether as an actor on the stage or in the theater of the world, to create a powerful reality through the moving performance of an imaginative act.

Perdita's performance, then, is an expression of Shakespeare's ideal conception of the dramatic medium as a great art, an art in which a natural being becomes an art form and then transcends nature and art by fusing their powers in an art that has the breath of life. On the one hand,

Perdita is by nature a princess and so can crown her doings, but on the other hand, as her comment on how she is like an actor reminds us, her royal acts are not performed by a princess, not even by a beautiful young woman, but by a boy actor who must embody Shakespeare's art. This common-born boy is to show he is capable of the self-creative act of a princess.

This study has been in part concerned with how the role-situations of characters enter into the shaping of what they see, think, do, and hence become. The cases of Hamlet and Perdita reveal contrasting possibilities for tragically confining and for romantically liberating involvement with roles – and with the relationships underlying what we call roles. Hamlet's circumstances and the actions of others evoke responses from him as a son that limit and distort his responses as a lover and friend. In his intensely troubled engagement with an alienating role as revenger, he struggles to do and not to do what he says this role requires, and he does not see what he is doing as he destroys Polonius, Ophelia, Rosencrantz, and Guildenstern.

In Perdita's case, on the other hand, the circumstances and the actions of others evoke a response in which she adds role to role so that all the elements of her past, present, and future identities are brought fully into play. Her vision becomes absorbed and intensely focused, but the combination of her several roles gives this vision a heightened multiplicity that achieves a beautiful poetic harmony. In her speech invoking the flowers of spring there are art and nature, myth and natural description, personal passion and formal ceremony, innocence and sophistication, a sense of self and universal observation – and we can trace all of these to her character as a person of integrity and to the potentialities of her roles as goddess, as queen and hostess of the festival, as daughter, as loving maiden and bride to be, as carefully taught peasant girl, and as princess-in-creation. Here in fullness the power of "great creating nature" flows through the imaginations of playwright, actor, and audience to bring into being an imagined person who enacts one of our most beautiful potentialities.

Appendix: The Psychology of Habits

In Chapter 1 I have presented a brief analysis of the psychology of habits in Plato and Aristotle to show the congruity between this psychology and the radical behaviorism of B. F. Skinner. This appendix will explain how passages in Aristotle and Seneca that may seem to give causal force to thoughts do not do so in a sense that conflicts operationally with behaviorism. The appendix will also show that the psychology of habits in St Thomas Aquinas's *Summa Theologica* is fundamentally consistent with the thinking of both Aristotle and Skinner. In addition, the appendix examines some especially challenging or significant passages in other writers from Aristotle to Shakespeare, and concludes with a list of passages that depend on the psychology of habits from a number of writers after Aristotle.

As indicated in Chapter 1, Aristotle generally says that our habits cause us to act and our thinking controls our action in the sense of guiding it – a view entirely consistent with Skinner's regarding the relation between thought and action. We *choose* to aim at a virtuous end in a very limited sense: habituation causes us to love virtue, and hence we think of and want to do good (*Nicomachean* 1140b, 1143b–5a; cf. Anscombe 62; Shute 75–8; Hardie 37). Beyond this, choice is concerned with the means to attain our end. Aristotle says that in order to be a true choice, a selection of means must be based on deliberation (1111b–13a). In choice (and hence in deliberation), virtue is a characteristic "guided by right reason," which in turn is "determined by practical wisdom" (1144b; see 1144a–5a). But reason and wisdom as guides depend on the habituated virtue of *sophrosyne* (temperance or self-control). For Aristotle this habituated virtue is what "'preserves' our 'practical wisdom,'" and if we lose our virtuous habit our thinking will change accordingly (1140b). This is consistent with Skinner's view that reason and wisdom as guides depend on conditioning.

Practical wisdom "deals with what is just, noble, and good for man; and it is doing such things that characterize a man as good. But our ability to perform such actions is in no way enhanced by knowing them, since the virtues are characteristics" – are "acquired by habit," according to Martin Ostwald's explanation of "characteristics" here (1143b). The relation of wisdom to virtue is thus that "virtue makes us aim at the right target, and practical wisdom makes us use the right means" (1144a). Aristotle adds that although he does not believe virtues *are* "rational principles," "forms of knowledge," as Socrates did, he thinks virtues are characteristics *"united with* a rational principle" (1144b). This statement is consistent with the behaviorist view that the way we think about what we do is an integral part of what we do and of our characteristic behavior.

In their unity, right reason and virtue operate together: right reason, guided by practical wisdom, deliberates a choice of means for a good end which has been chosen because of a habit of virtue. The causal relation between practical wisdom and virtuous action is quite evidently that between rules and rule-governed behavior in Skinner's theory. We act virtuously *because* we have been conditioned to do so, and intentions, rules, and plans function as discriminative stimuli to *guide* our actions (see Chapter 2). In addition, the operations of reason in Aristotle's account of deliberation are of the same sort as Skinner's "covert operations" in making decisions.[1]

But if this is the way Aristotle views the relation between thought and action, what does he mean when he states specifically that thought is a cause of action? We know that for Aristotle action is controlled by the purpose and the thinking which precedes and accompanies any undertaking (e.g. Joachim 12–16). I have explained that in Skinner's theory, too, intentions, rules, and plans may be said to guide and control behavior even though these thoughts are dependent variables with respect to the person's conditioning. Is this all Aristotle means? For the most part in the *Nicomachean Ethics* the answer is evidently yes, as I have argued. But in one important passage in the *Ethics* Aristotle may appear to go beyond this view in taking the position that humans are set in motion by thought and that a thought can necessitate action. I want to show that at bottom this has its counterpart in Skinner's idea that a thought can function as a discriminative stimulus to evoke behavior in a way that may virtually "force" a response (*Science and Human Behavior* 107–13, esp. 112). Now of course there is a conceptual difference, and the issue is whether there is a significant *operational* difference.

Aristotle argues in the *Movement of Animals* that the conclusion of a practical syllogism necessitates action (Anscombe 64–6), and the passage in question in the *Nicomachean Ethics* also uses this argument (1147a–b). First Aristotle states the general form of the practical syllogism. A universal that is a current belief is one premise and "the other involves particular facts which fall within the domain of sense perception." If a particular case falls under the universal rule, "the soul is thereupon bound to affirm the conclusion, and if the premises involve action, the soul is bound to perform this act at once." Thus if we believe as a universal that "Everything sweet ought to be tasted" and we know a particular thing is sweet, then if we are able to taste we are "bound to act accordingly at once."

Aristotle offers this argument as part of a defense of Socrates's view that if we truly know the right thing to do we will do it, and his concern is to elucidate the conduct of the morally weak person, who seems to know the right thing to do but does not do it.

Aristotle continues by analyzing a specific example in which a morally weak person has the universal of practical wisdom that sweets should be avoided, and a contradictory universal, based in strong appetites, that all sweets give pleasure. There is also a factual perception that a particular thing is sweet, and, crucially, "suppose further that the appetite <for pleasure> happens to be present." The result is that although one universal tells the person to avoid the sweet thing, "appetite, capable as it is of setting in motion each part of our body, drives" the person to eat the sweet: "Thus it turns out that a morally weak man acts under the influence of some kind of reasoning and opinion, an opinion which is not intrinsically but only incidentally opposed to right reason; for it is not opinion but appetite that is opposed to right reason" (1147a–b). Aristotle adds that "The final premise, consisting as it does in an opinion about an object perceived by the senses, determines our action." The morally weak person "in the grip of emotion" does not have "active possession" of the universal that the sweet should be avoided, or if the person does think of this universal, it is "not in the sense of knowing it, but in the sense of uttering it as a drunken man may utter verses of Empedocles" (1147b). The comparison with drunkenness is literal, for at the start of this passage Aristotle says that "passions actually cause palpable changes in the body" and that "we must attribute to the morally weak a condition similar to that of men who are asleep, mad, or drunk" (1147a).

H. H. Joachim, who holds that Aristotle here "insists that all action results from a fusion of feeling (passion) and thinking," explains what is meant in this specific example as follows. The knowledge overcome is not the universal principle that practical wisdom proposes but the "knowledge of a principle in a particular perceptible embodiment. . . . And this knowledge is perverted, or fails . . . under the stress of temptation, because the temptation itself enforces a vivid recognition of the percept in question as a case of a different major premiss." Hence the morally weak person cannot carry out his or her "good principle" because the percept is seen as a case of the major premise that sweets give pleasure, and experiencing it in this way "is enforced by" desire (228–9).

It seems to me that the paradigm underlying Joachim's explanation is fundamentally congruent with Skinner's ideas about prepotency and about the way thought affects action as a discriminative stimulus. The appetites of the morally weak person are not habituated to self-control, and in the example an appetite is strong. The sweet is a stimulus, and in a state of intense desire the response of thinking that eating sweets gives pleasure is strongly reinforced. This thought then acts as a discriminative stimulus for eating the sweet. The thought that indulging in such pleasures is bad will tend not to come to mind because it will not be reinforced when the body is in such a physiological state, and because the competing response of thinking that sweets are pleasurable is so strong. Or if the virtuous universal does come to mind, the response to it is minimal: the person utters the words but under the influence of intense desire would not find it reinforcing even to think about what meaning they have ("uttering it as a drunken man may utter verses of Empedocles").

It may be argued in rebuttal that because Skinner believes the action of eating the sweet may occur without any verbalized thought at all, his view is essentially different from Aristotle's. We must remember, however, that Aristotle selectively concerns himself with behavior in which there *is* thought of some kind because his philosophical system is most concerned with such behavior. Furthermore, in the passage we are examining he is explaining how even though a person knows a rule of virtue, the thought of this may *not* come to mind, or may come to mind and yet not have an effect. Note too that he says here it is only "some kind" of thinking, "an opinion about an object perceived by the senses," which "determines" the action, and that "it is not opinion but appetite that is opposed to right reason" and which "drives" the person to eat. In such cases the thought moving action might be no more fully articulated than in Skinner's scheme: to a behaviorist, a person who has found eating sweets very reinforcing will need at least to detect that a thing is a sweet in order to eat it as the result of such a history of reinforcement.

I think it can be shown that Aristotle does not mean to say a thought must be articulated in order to produce behavior. I of course concede that there may well be a difference in the degree to which Aristotle and Skinner see an articulation of a thought as usually occurring in connection with human conduct. Again, the important issue here is whether this difference affects the causal relations in a way that makes a significant operational difference. But let us consider a statement in the *Nicomachean Ethics* which may seem to mean that an articulated thought is at least one of the necessary causes of action:

> Now thought alone moves nothing; only thought which is directed to some end and concerned with action can do so. . . . Only the goal of action is an end in the unqualified sense: for the good life is an end, and desire is directed toward this. Therefore, choice is either intelligence motivated by desire or desire operating through thought, and it is as a combination of these two that man is a starting point of action. (1139a–b)

First of all note that desire is said to motivate or act through thought, and perhaps only thus is thought said to participate in "moving" action. Also, as Martin Ostwald points out, in the *Nicomachean Ethics* Aristotle always uses "praxis" (action) to mean "moral action," so that it is evidently part of his point to say that philosophically speaking, "true" human action is to be *defined* as an action in which thought has a function: "animals have sense perception but have no share in action" (1139a, and Ostwald's note 6 there).

A passage in *On the Soul* appears to clarify what Aristotle means when he says that desire motivates or acts through thought and that the two together originate behavior:

> These two at all events appear to be sources of movement: appetite and thought (if one may venture to regard imagination as a kind of thinking; for many men follow their imaginations contrary to knowledge, and in all animals other than man there is no thinking or calculation but only imagination).
>
> Both of these then are capable of originating local movement, thought and appetite: thought, that is, which calculates means to an end, i.e. practical thought (it differs from speculative thought in the character of its end); while appetite is in every form of it relative to an end; for that which is the object of appetite is the stimulant of practical thought; and that which is last in the process of thinking is the beginning of the action. It follows that there is a justification for regarding these two as the sources of movement, i.e. appetite and practical thought; for the object of appetite starts a movement and as a result of that thought gives rise to movement, the object of appetite being to it a source of stimulation. So too when imagination originates movement, it necessarily involves appetite.
>
> That which moves therefore is a single faculty and the faculty of appetite; for if there had been two sources of movement – thought and appetite – they would have produced movement in virtue of some common character. As it is, thought is never found producing movement without appetite (for wish is a form of appetite; and when movement is produced according to calculation it is also according to wish), but appetite can originate movement *contrary* to calculation, for desire is a form of appetite.   (433a)

This passage as a whole states unequivocally that the chain of causality begins in the object of desire, that the next cause is the person's appetite, and that under the influence of these, reason calculates means to the end desired.[2] Operationally this is virtually the same as Skinner's paradigm of the response to a stimulus object. The conditioning and the contingencies that evoke an act in response to a stimulus also evoke the thoughts that may occur assenting to the act and planning how to go about it. The passage in *On the Soul* also indicates, however, that human behavior can occur with no more in the way of thinking than animals are capable of, so on this point, too, Aristotle's view is operationally compatible with Skinner's.

Thus, to recapitulate briefly, the person whose desires have been habituated to choose the good thinks according to the precepts of moral wisdom as "desire operates through thought" in deliberating what to do in order to serve the good end. As Aristotle describes it, such deliberation is a process of calculation which has the basic pattern of "covert operations" for self-control and making plans in Skinner's scheme. Also, the articulations of goals and plans that Aristotle's person concludes upon to guide and control his or her actions have the full force that discriminative stimuli are capable of in Skinner's "rule-governed" behavior, but they have no more causal force than this. And such articulated thoughts are not necessary for behavior to occur.

In the *Institutio Oratoria*, Quintilian describes the process of learning to think the way an orator should as habit-formation. His description is quite specific about this in regard both to "premeditation" in preparing a speech and to improvisation during presentation (bk 10, ch. 6 and ch. 7, sec. 1–18). Premeditation is based on earlier practice in writing, but it is the composition in thought alone of what is to be said and how to say it, down to the very words to be used except for "the finishing touches" (ch. 6, sec. 2). Quintilian says that premeditation requires great concentration, first of all, and secondly:

> we must gradually acquire the habit of thought: to begin with, we shall content ourselves with covering but a few details, which our minds are capable of reproducing with accuracy; then by advances so gradual that our labour is not sensibly increased we must develop our powers and confirm them by frequent practice, a task in which the most important part is played by the memory.   (Ch. 6, sec. 3)

He goes on to say that although orators must have their entire presentation worked out in premeditation, they must always be ready to improvise when they have a "happy inspiration" and then be ready to return to their premeditated speech when the inspiration ends (bk 10, ch. 6, sec. 5–6). For improvisation extempore, practice and habit are again very important:

> We must acquire a store of the best words and phrases on lines that I have already laid down, while our style must be formed by continuous and conscientious practice in writing, so that even our improvisations

may reproduce the tone of our writing, and after writing much, we must give ourselves frequent practice in speaking. For facility is mainly the result of habit and exercise. . . . (Ch. 7, sec. 7–8)

Quintilian adds that for facility we need a "natural nimbleness of mind," but says "it is scarcely possible either for natural gifts or for methodic art to enable the mind to grapple simultaneously with such manifold duties" as thinking ahead with proper regard for "invention, arrangement, and style" while paying "close attention to voice, delivery and gesture" in what one is saying at the moment. So the key for carrying on all these "mental activities" at once is "a certain mechanical knack" like that of the juggler. But this knack must be preceded by practice in the art of how to compose a speech – invention, arrangement, and so on – "so that what is irrational in itself [the mechanical knack of juggling] will nevertheless be founded on reason" (bk 10, ch. 7, sec. 8–12). Now, this is a strongly behaviorist description of complex thought processes. Ways of thinking that are described in terms compatible with Skinner's "covert operations" are learned and applied in the constant practice of the invention and organization of speeches, and on these rationally ordered foundations practice builds up more complex combinations by habituation to produce a high order of mental facility. Passages such as this and the preceding one on acquiring habits of thought show that the use of mentalistic terms does not preclude a view of thinking which has strong behaviorist characteristics.

Habits of thought in the moral sphere are emphasized by Seneca, whose moral essays and epistles especially focus on the use of philosophical wisdom to oppose the false opinions accompanying passions and vices. He says – correctly from a behaviorist standpoint – that our thoughts and actions in emotion are learned. In his essay "On Anger" he explains that although we cannot help being physiologically aroused when we are provoked by what seems to be an injurious action, what we feel is not what he means by anger if we quickly calm down when we think about what has happened. True anger requires the mind's assent to the emotional desire for retaliation, and we *act* angrily because of our erring opinion that we should respond in this way (bk 2, ch. 3, sec. 1–5).

To explain a person's having a false opinion conducive to angry passion, Seneca draws on the psychology of habits. The humors may dispose a person physiologically toward one passion or another; also, anything else which "impairs either body or mind," such as sickness, anxiety, or fatigue, has some effect. "But these are all only beginnings and causes; habit counts for most, and if this is deep-seated, it fosters the fault" (bk 2, ch. 20, sec. 1–2).[3] So children must be trained to have the habit of thinking and acting with self-control to resist passion (bk 2, ch. 21, sec.

1–7). If we become hardened in habitual vice, we cannot be reached by reason, and even if we think we desire to reform, we are only deceiving ourselves ("On Reforming" sec. 3).

But as long as our natural tendency to act in a human way with reason and virtue has not been entirely overcome by hardening in vice, the philosopher can use reason and precepts to correct the erring opinions which cause our vice, and to guide us to virtue ("On the Value" sec. 31).[4] There is in this a faith in the natural goodness of humanity and the power of reason, yet many of Seneca's specific explanations of the way philosophy changes minds, and thereby conduct, are clearly compatible with a behaviorist formulation. In behaviorist terms, the main Stoic use of reason is to point out the "real" contingencies of reinforcement for vice and virtue. For example, the Stoic tells a person who is too desirous of becoming wealthy that he or she should learn to think about the miseries of the rich and the rewards of the spiritual life. To avoid suffering from the vagaries of fortune and nature, we should learn that since only what happens in our own thoughts is under our control, we may lose all the things and people around us. Therefore we should practice thinking in a way that prepares us to bear their loss without suffering. In Seneca's description this especially includes forming habits of thought in the sense that we learn to respond to the death of a loved one with certain well-conned Stoic arguments (e.g. "On the Natural" sec. 16). In behaviorist terms, this activity, if strongly learned, may be prepotent over sorrowful thoughts and therefore tend to suppress them. Also, further responses will be to these comforting thoughts as stimuli and not only to the sad event. Hence suffering may actually be greatly reduced.

"On the Value of Advice" is most specifically concerned with the ways in which precepts can affect conduct. Some of Seneca's statements suggest that he thinks of precepts as having the effect of what a behaviorist would call discriminative stimuli for rule-governed behavior. For example, once the greed for wealth has been overcome, a person needs precepts to learn how to treat money (sec. 23). There is a further suggestion of a stimulus function in the following: "Advice is not teaching; it merely engages the attention and rouses us, and concentrates the memory, and keeps it from losing its grip. . . . Advice is, in fact, a sort of exhortation. The mind often tries not to notice even that which lies before our eyes; we must therefore force upon it the knowledge of things that are perfectly well known" (sec. 25).[5] Thus the condensed form of maxims gives them a force enabling them to have "a sort of shock" effect even though their truth is "unaccompanied by reason" (sec. 43–4). Advice also includes scolding and praising (sec. 39), which are easily explained as aversive stimulation or positive reinforcement. But "the counsel which assists suggestion by reason – which adds the motive for doing a given thing and the reward which awaits one who carries out and obeys such precepts – is more effective and settles deeper in the heart" (sec. 44). Here again the force of reason seems to be in its pointing out the connections between purpose, behavior, and reinforcement, a function entirely consistent with Skinner's ideas of how instructions can operate as discriminative stimuli.

Seneca also emphasizes that when virtue has been learned it must be practiced in order to strengthen the learning (sec. 45–7). In "More About Virtue" he affirms the importance of habit for virtue in describing a person whose actions are always good. He is "not only sound in his judgment but trained by habit to such an extent that he not only can act rightly, but cannot help acting rightly. We have formed the conception that in such a man perfect virtue exists" (sec. 10).[6] In this passage it is evident that Seneca, like Aristotle, associates sound judgment with knowing what to do, and habit with a prepotent tendency to do it.

Plutarch's moral psychology is generally quite Aristotelian. He writes in his essay "Can Virtue be Taught?" that indeed it can, and he briefly indicates the process: ". . . tutors by the habits they inculcate train the child's character to take a first step, as it were, on the path of virtue. So the Spartan, when he was asked what he effected by his teaching, said, 'I make honourable things pleasant to children'" (439F). Here we have the familiar proto-behaviorist pattern of making an action pleasant so it will become habitual, but Plutarch's essays on the correction of particular vices go beyond what Plato and Aristotle had written to explain the behavioral process through which bad habits may be replaced by virtues. The explanation makes clear the functions of reason and habit in this process. In essays on the busybody, on talkativeness, and on excessive compliancy, Plutarch says that reason contributes to overcoming these vices by enabling a person to learn the bad consequences of the vice and the good consequences of the virtue, along with the precepts defining the means that are to guide virtuous action ("Talkativeness" 510D–E; "Busybody" 520C–D; "Compliancy" 528C–30E, 532D). Reason's function is thus, in behaviorist terms, to provide the rules for rule-governed behavior, and especially to explain the contingencies of reinforcement in such a way that we will find it reinforcing to think we should change. But Plutarch says that such persuasion is not enough to change more than our thinking: if our other behavior is to change, too, we must be habituated. In "Concerning Talkativeness" he writes that "it is impossible to check the babbler by gripping the reins, as it were; his disease must be mastered by habituation" (511E; cf. 514E, 515; "Busybody" 520D; "Compliancy" 530E–1A).

In his essays on the busybody and on compliancy Plutarch proposes a process of habituation in which one is first to abstain from manifestations of the vice that are easy to give up, and then gradually to abstain from the stronger behavior of the vice ("Busybody" 520D–E, 521A, E–F;

"Compliancy" 530E–2A). This process is quite similar to techniques used in behavior modification as described by Skinner and others. In "On Compliancy" Plutarch says that instances in which "we practise firmness at the cost of but slight dissatisfaction, condition us to meet more difficult occasions" (531A; cf. 531B, D).

In writing of the busybody's vice of curiosity, he indicates how to overcome the force of habit of a vice and its immediate rewards to be able to act for the sake of the more remote rewards of future virtue: "you will obtain great benefit from forcibly turning aside your curiosity and curtailing it and training it to obey reason." And he continues by urging that we "should avoid and guard against such sights and sounds as master and attract us . . ." (521E–F). Here it is not that reason's logic has an inherent capacity to alter behavior, but that we can force ourselves to act for our betterment, and through this habituate ourselves to obey reason's rules. The central understanding of self-control in all this is close to that in Skinner's chapter on self-control in *Science and Human Behavior*, where techniques of self-control include suppression of undesirable behavior by "repeating proverbs which warn of the wages of sin" (236), avoiding tempting stimuli, and using the principle of prepotency by forcefully engaging in competing behavior which has reinforcing outcomes (230–40).

In the Christian tradition of the later Middle Ages we find the proto-behaviorist view in Thomas Aquinas, who writes extensively in the *Summa Theologica* on habits as the basis of moral virtues as well as vices (see also Fuchs for William of Ockham on habits). Aquinas draws systematically on Aristotle, chiefly the *Nicomachean Ethics*, for his discussion of habit and moral virtue, and he reconciles this with Augustine and Pauline Christianity by saying that although moral virtue acquired through our own actions is enough for us to live according to human reason, in order to avoid *all* mortal sin and to be saved we need God's grace to infuse the theological virtues of faith, hope, and charity which perfect us (I–II.63.2; cf. 62.1, 63.4, 109.8). Following both the classical philosophers and the Augustinian tradition, Aquinas asserts the familiar notion that by nature we seek the good, but the good as we apprehend it (I–II.1.6–7). Although our natural love of self should move us to love God and to seek the rewards of eternal happiness, the pleasures of sin may become the good we seek instead for the sake of self.

Aquinas uses "habit" to refer broadly to characteristics which dispose us toward functioning well or ill and are hence subject to reason and will rather than being innately or naturally determined in their operation (I–II.49.1, 50.3). A moral habit is a disposition which is difficult to change (I–II.49.1–2), formed by repeated acts of a like kind (I–II.50.1, 51.3, 52.3, 63.2). Whether we act on the basis of a habit or not depends on our will and reason (I.83.1, I–II.49.3, 50.1, 50.3, 52.3). Aquinas thinks reason is necessary to the formation, existence, and exercise of habits, and we need to understand the sense in which he means this. As part of his argument to prove that there can be habits in the appetites – namely the habits of temperance and fortitude – he compares humans with animals (I–II.50.3). It is true that human appetites are irrational, he says, and therefore cannot use reason to exercise their own habits. But in this irrational part of our nature we are like the animals, which can be habituated to obey reason in the form of human commands. This obedience to an entirely external voice of reason is sufficient for Aquinas to say that animals meet the criterion that reason is necessary to the formation and exercise of habits. And it is in this sense that reason is necessary for human temperance and fortitude. As animals can be conditioned to obey human commands, the irrational appetites of a person can be conditioned to be guided by the voice of reason. Reason is required to enable a person to vary the operations of faculties and appetites according to rules that guide them toward an end. This is all congruent with the idea of rule-governed behavior in Skinner's theory, as I have argued in discussing Aristotle.

However, Aquinas says that "habits of moral virtue are caused in the appetitive powers, according as they are moved by the reason" (I–II.51.2), and we must analyze further the kind of causality he claims for reason in relation to habits and in relation to human behavior generally. Reason's causal function in the formation of habits seems to be in asserting the rule to be obeyed and informing us whether it is being obeyed or not so we can repeatedly correct our behavior until it has just the right shape and is readily performed because it is habitual. Reason has no power to compel obedience, since many acts are needed in habit-formation before "the active principle which is reason" can "entirely overcome the appetitive power . . ." (I–II.51.3). Moreover, he repeatedly asserts the principle from Aristotle's *Politics*, book 1, that whereas the soul rules the movements of the body absolutely, reason only controls the passions and appetites "by a politic power: because the sensitive appetite has something of its own, by virtue whereof it can resist the commands of reason" (quoting *Summa* I.81.3ad2; cf. I–II.9.2ad3, 17.7, 58.2).

Therefore, in addition to reason needing to learn the virtue of prudence, there must "be some virtues in the irascible and concupiscible powers, by which these powers are well disposed to act" (I–II.56.4ad3; cf. I–II.58.2). This means that once a habit is formed, the ability of reason to guide prudently is a dependent variable in relation to conditioning of appetites by habit: "it is requisite for prudence, which is right reason about things to be done, that man be well disposed with regard to the ends: and this depends on the rectitude of his appetite. Wherefore, for prudence there is need of a moral virtue, which rectifies the appetite" (I–II.57.4; cf. 57.5, 58.2–3).

Aquinas repeats Aristotle's definition of the truly virtuous act as requiring both an appetitive inclination to the act, caused by habituation of the appetite to the reasonable principle of the mean for the rewards of the soul *and* the prudent choice of means to the end by reason (I–II.57.5, 58.4–5). "But it is evident that inclination to an action belongs properly to the appetitive power, whose function it is to move all the powers to their acts . . ." (I–II.58.1). Also, a person can be habituated to do good without having learned prudence, but this virtue will not be perfect because it is not well governed by reason (I–II.65.1; cf. II–II.141.1ad2). Aquinas even follows Aristotle in saying that the habit of virtue is seen in what we do when we have no time to reason (II–II.123.9; cf. I–II.109.8 and *Nicomachean* 1117a).

Reason's function in prudence is thus chiefly to guide or "regulate" behavior that has its impetus from appetite. The workings of the various parts of prudence are described as systematic operations which have a rule-governing function (II–II.49.1–8). Indeed, reason itself is described by Aquinas in terms analogous to Skinner's terms for covert operations leading to the construction of rules: reason studies ends and means and issues a conclusion as to what ought to be done (e.g. I–II.58.5). Aquinas says reason proceeds systematically from first principles: "to reason is to advance from one thing understood to another," and to understand is to "apprehend intelligible truth" (I.79.8). Human reason approaches "understanding of truth by arguing, with a certain amount of reasoning and movement," although without the aid of God it is unable to reach full understanding (I.79.4). The intellect works through reason's processes of "composition and division" by "differentiating and comparing" (I.85.5–5ad1). Reason's function thus "is to distinguish things which in reality are united, and to unite together, after a fashion, things that are distinct, by comparing one with another" (I–II.27.2ad2). Reason also is limited in its function by the total dependence of intellect on the senses, imagination, and memory (I.84.6–8, I–II.33.3ad3).[7] Moreover, reason itself is subject to a need for good habits; without frequent exercise of good intellectual habits in judging things aright, "strange fancies" arise which can render a person unable to judge well or "even wholly disposed to the contrary" (I–II.53.3).

Aquinas asserts the doctrine that the will is free because reason can overcome habits and passions (I.83.1ad5), but he emphasizes factors limiting the freedom of both will and reason in his account of the causes of human behavior. The will necessarily seeks happiness (I.82.1–2) and is moved to action by what is *perceived* to be good or bad, pursuing what is seen as good and avoiding the bad (I–II.8.1). First among the causes of the will's movement in any particular case is the object of its willing (I–II.9.4). Although reason's task is to render a judgment of whether this object is good in order to direct the will (I–II.9.1), appetites and passions can cause us to think something desirable which we would not ordinarily desire. Here Aquinas's analysis is similar to a behaviorist account of how emotions affect behavior: "Now it is evident that according to a passion of the sensitive appetite man is changed to a certain disposition. Wherefore according as man is affected by a passion, something seems to him fitting, which does not seem so when he is not so affected: thus that seems good to a man when angered, which does not seem good when he is calm. And in this way, the sensitive appetite moves the will, on the part of the object" (I–II.9.2; cf. I–II.58.5). The sensitive appetite, in turn, is "naturally moved" not only by reason "but also by the imagination and sense" (I.81.3ad2; cf. I–II.75.2). And we have seen that reason itself ultimately depends upon imagination and sense.

The senses and imagination can arouse the sensitive appetite to a desire or passion which moves the will so powerfully that reason has no chance to judge or its voice is disregarded (I–II.74.7ad4, II–II.175.2ad2). Absorption in a pleasure or passion can be so strong (prepotent, Skinner would say) that there is no thought against it (I–II.33.3, 37.1ad2, 77.1, II–II.53.6). Passions such as envy and anger draw reason away into evil, while lust destroys "the judgment of reason entirely" (II–II.53.6ad1; cf. I–II.46, II–II.158).

As good acts form moral habits, so sinful acts diminish the inclination to virtue (I–II.85.2). Repeated acts of sin undo habits of moral virtue and create habits of vice in which a person becomes more and more disposed to sin (I–II.75.4, 88.3). The causal process is that the object which appeals to the senses "moves the sensitive appetite, and the sensitive appetite inclines the reason and will" toward the object (I–II.85.1ad4; cf. 77.1–2). Hence as we sin, we come to think that the ends we pursue are the good, and we lose sight of the good of God and of moral virtue (I–II.78.2). In consenting to sin, a person's mind becomes "the servant or slave of the evil deed" (I–II.74.7ad2, quoting Augustine, *On the Trinity* bk 12, ch. 12). In the intemperate person, "the will is inclined to sin . . . of its own choice, which proceeds from a habit acquired through custom," that is through repeated acts which form a "disposition difficult to remove." The intemperate man "rejoices in having sinned, because the sinful act has become connatural to him by reason of his habit" (II–II.156.3). Habitual action thus becomes pleasurable (see also I–II.32.2ad3, 78.3ad1) and a strong habit can govern a person totally. Aquinas quotes Augustine's *Confessions*, book 8, chapter 5, on this point: "Lust served became a custom, and custom not resisted became necessity" (II–II.142.2).

Among the Renaissance neo-Platonists, Pico della Mirandola is mostly noted today for proposing in his oration *On the Dignity of Man* that humans have complete freedom of choice to make themselves brutes or heavenly creatures, yet Paul J. W. Miller says it is a mistake to think of

Pico as a "philosopher of absolute freedom" (xiv), for his view is based on traditional ideas about human nature:

> God has granted to man every kind of seed. They grow as man culti-vates them. This notion is as old as Aristotle, who maintained that the virtues are innate in man potentially, but need to be actualized through habituation. The context of Pico's affirmation of man's freedom shows that he is thinking above all of moral freedom, the ability to give oneself the character or set of moral habits that one chooses.   (xv–xvi)

Pico's work inspired Juan Luis Vives's *A Fable About Man*, which asserts in apparently absolute terms that humans can become and act as any kind of creature simply by willing to do so. Elsewhere, however, Vives writes that habit-formation is important in shaping human character and think-ing. In *De Anima et Vita* he writes of the power of habit: "The soul is drawn along by custom in established ways, which are called propen-sities; thus anything which has been confirmed by long habit acquires almost the strength of nature . . ." (304). Vives adds here that "Plato says that it matters not a little how we were shaped and what habits we formed in childhood," and in his book on education he emphasizes the power of habit to shape character in childhood before intellectual insight has developed:

> Above all, boys must be accustomed to delight in good things and to love them, and to be grieved at evil things and to detest them; yet their ideas (of good and evil) should be suited to their mental grasp, for they cannot at once apprehend the highest and the absolute. The fact is that habit is most pleasant, and opinions received by us as children follow us very far on the road of our lives, and so much the more if they have been fixed and confirmed in the earliest age by conduct.
>
> (64; bk 2, ch. 2)

In *The Book of the Courtier*, Baldassare Castiglione also emphasizes the proto-behaviorist view that habituation to virtue precedes the use of rea-son in teaching virtue to children. The courtier is to teach virtue to his young prince, and the question is asked whether the courtier should "begin first of use . . . that unawares to him may make him to accustom himself to well-doing," or whether first the courtier should explain "with reason the property of good and ill, and in making him to perceive, before he take the matter in hand, which is the good way and to be followed, and which the ill, and to be shunned: finally whether into that mind of his, the virtues ought to be driven and grounded with reason and understanding first, or with custom." The answer is that the appetitive part of the soul is active in a child before reason develops, and it is the appetites which are "made perfect" in virtue by habituation:

> Therefore ought there to be a ground made first with custom, which may govern the appetites not yet apt to conceive reason; and with that good use lead them to goodness: afterward settle them with understanding, the which although she be last to show her light, yet doth she the more perfectly make the virtues to be enjoyed of whoso hath his mind well instructed with manners.... (320–1; bk 4)

Similarly, Sir Philip Sidney's *Arcadia* tells how "a habit of commanding was naturalized" in the heroes Pyrocles and Musidorus when they were children. Warlike images were used "to make even their sports profitable," and the "delight of tales" of "worthy princes" was used "to move them to do nobly." Their "stronger judgments" later "converted" this to "knowledge" which could "teach them how to do nobly" (189–90; bk 2, ch. 7, sec. 1). Sidney's argument in *A Defense of Poesy* is also based on the psychology of habits. Literature teaches virtue better than history or the precepts of moral philosophy because the poet can transform such historical figures as Alexander the Great into perfectly virtuous models, and can do better than history does to show that virtue is rewarded and vice punished (20–3). Poetry teaches the love of virtue by delighting, or rather, it *moves* to virtue more than it teaches – Aristotle says that in virtue not knowing but doing must be the end. When poetry moves us to virtue, this motivates us to study moral philosophy, which "shows you the way" and "informs you of the particularities" of the virtuous life, but is rather uninteresting and reveals the difficulties of virtue as well as its pleasant end (23). This is the proto-behaviorist view that although reason and precepts guide virtue, we are moved to virtue by models for imitation that are honored and rewarded. As Lewis Soens says, the poet "habituates" his readers, "accustoms them to experience, love, and enact virtue" (xxiii).

Sir Francis Bacon asserts the importance of habit for education in several of his works. In the essay "Of Custom and Education," he writes that "custom is most perfect when it beginneth in young years: this we call education; which is, in effect, but an early custom." The force of custom by itself is great, he says, and then he refers to sources of reinforcements that strengthen habits: "the force of custom copulate and conjoined and collegiate is far greater. For there example teacheth, company comforteth, emulation quickeneth, glory raiseth: so as in such places the force of custom is in his exaltation" (471–2). In *The Advancement of Learning* (438–43; bk 2) and the essay "Of Nature in Men" he explains how habit functions in instruction and in the formation of virtues and vices. For example, in "Of Nature in Men" he asserts the familiar principle that "doctrine and discourse maketh nature less importune; but custom only doth alter and subdue nature" (469). In the essay "Of Custom and Education," Bacon cites Machiavelli for the view that "there is no trusting to the force of nature nor to the bravery of words, except it be corroborate by custom." He then generalizes that "the predominancy of custom is every where visible; insomuch as a man would wonder to hear men profess, protest, engage, give great words, and then do just as they have done before; as if they were dead images, and engines moved only by the wheels of custom" (470–1).

This passage asserts the helplessness of reason, purposes, and precepts which lack the support of conditioning, but Bacon's greatest assault on optimistic ideas about the exercise of reason is in his *New Organon*. Here he argues for new empirical methods of study and thought to aid human reason and the senses to discover the truths of nature. He says that the traditional principles and methods of syllogistic reasoning are false but are accepted as true because people have been habituated to them in school; habit, along with the tendency of people to defend whatever opinion they hold, makes it difficult to overcome received ideas (esp. bk 1, "Author's Preface" and sec. 31–54, 90; bk 2, sec. 32). The "understanding itself" has been "tinged and infected, and at length perverted and distorted, by daily and habitual impressions" of the traditional errors of thought. Hence the valid scientific information which is already available should be used to begin to withdraw "the understanding from the things to which it is accustomed" and to prepare it "for the reception of the dry and pure light of true ideas" (bk 2, sec. 32).

Bacon's concern with bad intellectual habits is of course an extension – albeit a crucial one – of the traditional proto-behaviorist notion that people with habits of vice will think in ways that support their actions. We find the traditional form of this notion in many sixteenth-century literary works. An especially revealing example is *Euphues: The Anatomy of Wyt*, in which John Lyly most deliciously anatomizes the wit of the hero in a way that shows how intelligence, self-love, and habit work together to produce the most extreme self-deception. Euphues is a very intelligent and charming young man, and Lyly says that as each thing in nature has its flaw, the flaw of the very intelligent is to think too much of their own good wits and so to disdain the counsels of wiser men (184–5). In their pride they are "obstinate in their own opinions, impatient of labour, apt to conceive wrong, credulous to believe the worst, ready to shake off their old acquaintance without cause, and to condemn them without colour . . ." (196). Euphues has abandoned himself to a life in which he uses his wits only for frivolous pleasures, and the book begins with a dialogue between Euphues and Eubulus, an older man and a wise counsellor, who tries to tell Euphues that he should have had a better upbringing. In reply,

Euphues's wits marshal a host of clever but specious arguments to the effect that nurture cannot alter what nature has given (187–94). If there is any doubt which side in this debate should be believed, Lyly dispels this later when he includes a translation of the strongly proto-behaviorist *On Education*, adding material of his own to augment the argument of this work, which was then attributed to Plutarch (260–86).

The great joke about Euphues and his fine wits which Lyly anatomizes is that lacking a virtuous character formed in youth, he always uses his wits to justify and plan whatever his whim – or passion – leads him to, whether it be friendship, love, philosophy, or religion. Lyly shows that when such men fall into a life of vice, not only does their wit direct them to do evil, but also "it forgeth them some feat excuse to cloak their vanity" (195). The book moves from one episode to another in which Euphues and others like him deceive themselves. Perhaps the most amusing sequence is the first major one, in which Euphues becomes enthusiastically but rashly engrossed in what he thinks is an ideal friendship with a young man named Philautus ("self-love") and then meets Philautus's beloved, Lucilla. Euphues and Lucilla immediately fall in love, or think they do, and the reader is treated to the most excruciating sophistries as Euphues's wits invent arguments to justify betraying Philautus. He even manages to shift the blame for his falling in love to his friend (196–211). Lucilla soon falls in love with a new man, and then both Euphues and Philautus need a cure for their love-longing. Euphues is full of clever ideas, among them one based on Ovid's suggestion that if a man will behave as if he were no longer in love, this will cure him because his pretense will become a reality through habituation (*Euphues* 255; Ovid, *Remedies for Love* 497–504).

Even if we only pretend an emotion or an attitude in our actions, such is the power of the act and of habit that we may become what we pretend. This points to the Elizabethan psychology of acting, which I have discussed in the first chapter, and to the very limits of the idea that we become what we do. We may well expect to become what we do in earnest, but may not be prepared to be affected by what we "only" pretend. In the *Arcadia*, Sidney presents many examples of the psychology by which we become what we do. In the most striking case, the beautiful and androgynous Pyrocles disguises himself as a woman, the Amazon Zelmane, in order to gain access to the lovely lady Philoclea. Shortly after he dons the disguise, Pyrocles meets his friend Musidorus, who warns him: "And see how extremely every way you endanger your mind; for to take this womanish habit (without you frame your behavior accordingly) is wholly vain: your behavior can never come kindly [i.e. naturally] from you, but as the mind is proportioned unto it" (77; bk 1, ch. 12, sec. 5). Hence if Pyrocles is to play the role of a woman successfully, he must become womanish, and Musidorus warns his friend that he will also become womanish because one becomes like whatever he loves (78). Musidorus condemns women, and concludes by demanding that Pyrocles give up loving Philoclea or lose his friendship (82; sec. 7).

Pyrocles has responded with defenses of women and of his own manhood in pursuing love, but at this ultimatum he is crushed, for his love for his friend is very deep, yet he cannot give up his love of Philoclea. Sidney then gives us a most droll description of how Pyrocles, dressed in woman's clothes, weeps and swoons at Musidorus's feet. Musidorus is touched to the heart by this – he kisses his friend's weeping eyes and says that if he hurt him it was only because of his deep love for him. And so the scene continues in a way that reminds us at every turn of a lover's quarrel, with Musidorus playing the man to Pyrocles's woman. Thus Pyrocles's response to Musidorus's statement of his love is a tearful look which seems to say "And is it possible that Musidorus should threaten to leave me?" This strikes Musidorus dumb with emotion, and so "they rested, with their eyes placed one upon another, in such sort, as might well paint out the true passion of unkindness to be never aright, but betwixt them that most dearly love." Then after a time Musidorus embraces Pyrocles and chides him smilingly, saying he needs the government of "us wise and perfect men," since he is "unperfect" – a woman. And so Musidorus commands Pyrocles to command him to do whatever he can to assist in his love – much like the courtly lover offering to do what his lady commands (83; sec. 7).

In this episode Sidney plays with the relationship between the psychology of love and of friendship, but it is clear that he also plays with gender stereotypes as roles and with the idea that people somehow become what they pretend.[8] As this study has argued, the psychology of habits was central to the understanding that many writers brought to their portrayal or analysis of the way we are affected by our upbringing, behavior, experience, and roles. Fictions such as Lyly's and Sidney's are important in the tradition of works exploring these phenomena, a tradition that in English Renaissance literature came to fruition especially in the plays of Shakespeare.

To conclude this appendix, here is a list of passages in writers after Aristotle that employ or depend on the psychology of habits and have not been cited above or in Chapter 1. The items are in alphabetical order by author, and abbreviated titles are supplied when the bibliography has more than one title for an author:

Ascham, Roger, 26, 31, 42–9, 64, 89; bk 1.
Augustine, St, *Acts or Disputation* 121–2; sec. 22. *Confessions* 116–25; bk 8, ch. 5–11. *Morals* 322; ch. 5; 323; ch. 6; 345; ch. 30; 350; ch. 31.
Bright, Timothy, 78; ch. 14.

Burton, Robert, 328–31; pt 2, sec. 2, mem. 6, subs. 1–2.

Calvin, [Jean], bk 2, ch. 2, sec. 23; bk 3, ch. 20, sec. 46.

Canons, 2:156; 14th Session, ch. 8.

Cardano, Giralamo, 18r–18v.

Castiglione, Baldassare, 304; bk 4.

Charron, Pierre, 264, 268–9; bk 2, ch. 3; 352; bk 3, ch. 1; 461, 464–5, ch. 14.

Davies, John, 1:36–8.

Della Casa, Giovanni, 96–100.

Donne, John, 25–6; pt 1, distinction 1, sec. 1; 201; pt 3, distinction 5, sec. 4.

Dyke, Daniel, 192, 197; ch. 15.

Elyot, Sir Thomas, *Castel* 17r; bk 2, ch. 3; 63r; bk 3, ch. 2. *Education*, esp. A4v–B2r; ch. 2. *Governor* 15–16; bk 1, ch. 4; 17; ch. 5; 19; ch. 6; 26–7; ch. 9; 30; ch. 10; 46–7; ch. 13.

Epictetus, 69; bk 1, ch. 27; 107–8; bk 2, ch. 9; 138–41; bk 2, ch. 18.

Erasmus, Desiderius, *De Pueris* 184; sec. 4; 197–9; sec. 17–18; 203–14; sec. 22–30. *Education* 144–5, 149–50; ch. 1; 184–5; ch. 1. *Enchiridion* 61; ch. 4; 71; ch. 6; 181; ch. 33; 197–8; ch. 39. *Freedom* 51; pt. 1.

Ford, John, 5.2.75–9, 130–3.

Greville, Fulke, "Treatie" 170–1; st. 67–71; 184; st. 123.

Guazzo, Stephano, 1:20, 22, 44, 49, 79, 142; 2:16–17, 44, 70–1, 76, 79.

Hooker, Richard, bk 1, ch. 6, sec. 5; ch. 7, sec. 6; ch. 8, sec. 11; ch. 10, sec. 1–6; bk 5, ch. 71, sec. 2; ch. 75, sec. 4; ch. 77, sec. 14.

Huarte, Juan, 13; ch. 2; 256; ch. 14.

John of Salisbury, 172; bk 3.

Jonson, Ben, ll. 1093–9.

La Primaudaye, Pierre de, 20; bk 1, ch. 4; 26; ch. 5; 29; ch. 6; 36; ch. 8; 71–3; ch. 16; 106; ch. 24; 129; ch. 29; 218–19; ch. 49; 227; ch. 51; 263, 265; ch. 59; 461–2; bk 2, ch. 42.

Luther, Martin, 8.

Machiavelli, Niccolo, *Discourses* 243; bk 1, ch. 18; 452–3; bk 3, ch. 9; 525; bk 3, ch. 46.

More, Sir Thomas, *Dialogue* 324; bk 3, ch. 3. *Utopia* 71, 79, 84–90; bk 2.

Mulcaster, Richard, 22; ch. 4; 27–9, 31; ch. 5; 277–80; ch. 43.

Ovid, *Art of Love* bk 1, 608–12.

Palingenius, Marcellus, 76–8; bk 5; 184; bk 10.

Perkins, William, 13–15; bk 1, ch. 2, sec. 2; 39; ch. 2, sec. 10; 43; ch. 2, sec. 11; 71; ch. 5, sec. 5; 519; bk 3, ch. 3, sec. 2.

Philibert de Vienne, 6–7, 11–12, 26–7.

Plutarch, "Education" 3A–B. "On Moral Virtue" 443B–D, 444A–C. "On the Delays" 551E–F, 562B.

Puttenham, George, 154; bk 3, ch. 2; 289–92; ch. 24; 310–13; ch. 25.

Notes

Notes for Chapter 1: Introduction

1. For the debate about representation with reference to Shakespeare see Altman; Belsey, *Subject*; Harry Berger, Jr; Bloom ix–xiv, 1–5; Braunmuller; Edward Burns; Cartelli, esp. 9–37; Cartwright, esp. 1–42; Lloyd Davis; Dollimore 61–82 and *passim*; Evans 102–219; Faas; Felperin; Frattaroli; Freedman; Friedman; Frye; Goldberg 1–13, 68–100; Gurr, *Playgoing*, esp. 105–69, and *Shakespearean* 95–103; Haley, esp. 32–36; Joan Lord Hall, esp. 1–8; Hampton 205–36; Iser, "Representation"; Robert S. Knapp; Richard Levin 11–22; Mann; Mullaney, esp. 96–103, 112–13, 132; Nuttall; Paglia 194–229; Paris, *Character*; Patterson; States, *Hamlet*; Styan, "In Search"; Vickers, *Appropriating*, esp. 129–44; Weimann, "Mimesis," "Representation," "Bifold Authority," esp. 409–10, and "Shakespeare (De)Canonized"; Susan Wells; Wilshire 22–3.
    Cf. Harry Berger's defense of reading as a mode of representation of character with Buzacott 1–13, 88–91, 137; Cole, *Acting as Reading*; Desmet; Goldman, "*Hamlet*"; Marvin Rosenberg, *Masks of Hamlet* ix–xv.
2. Eden and Nuttall have especially thorough discussions of the importance of the mimetic dimension for our responses as critics, readers, and audience. Cf. Hernadi 39, 40, 47, 136–7; Arthur Kirsch, esp. 1–20, on the importance of affective responses. See Bloom ix–xiii on Shakespeare's importance for the construction of self and character in our culture.
3. Freedman's Lacanian analysis of the theatrical situation is complex and far-reaching. Also see, for example, Evans, esp. 102–218; Weimann, "Mimesis," "Bifold Authority," esp. 409–10 and "Representation"; Susan Wells. For recent discussions of how non-representational elements such as our awareness that we are watching an actor perform may facilitate audience involvement with representation, see esp. Cartwright, esp. 1–39; Grainger 17–22; Styan, "In Search." Cf. Parry.
4. See esp. Eden; Edward Burns. Cf. Altman; Hampton; Arthur Kirsch, esp. 1–20. See Richard Levin 11–22 for evidence that actors' performances were responded to much as if the behavior portrayed were actual and not fictional. The main dispute among the Elizabethans concerned the Puritan charge that these representations and the theatrical process are morally corrupting rather than beneficial for the audience (see, for example, Heywood's *Apology* and Green's *Refutation*).
    Recent studies of Shakespeare's use of rhetoric and poetic meter argue that the arts of language were used to create the sense of natural speech, heightened for expressive effect. See Hardison, esp. 236–41, 254–7; Vickers, *In Defence*, esp. 1–5, 64–7, 296–7, 314; George T. Wright 229–63.
5. See Eden's analysis of Aristotle's *Poetics* and the tradition it influenced. Eden shows the importance of pity and other empathic emotions in Renaissance views of tragedy. Cf. Edward Burns.
6. See Cicero, *de Oratore* 137; bk 2, ch. 47; Quintilian, bk 6, ch. 2, sec. 26–8. These writers are echoed in Elizabethan discourse on rhetoric. See, for example, the

quotations from Thomas Wilson's *Arte of Rhetorique* and Henry Peacham's *The Garden of Eloquence* in Miriam Joseph, 386–9.

7.   See Quintilian, bk 6, ch. 2, sec. 29–36; Bertram Joseph, *Acting Shakespeare* 2–3, 19, 22–3, 40, 194, *Elizabethan Acting* 71, 80, 84–5; Roach 23–57. In *Character: Acting and Being on the Pre-Modern Stage*, Edward Burns does not develop the ideas about the *psychology* of acting and character that I bring out here. See also note 18 and Chapter 4, note 1.

8.   See, for example, the many quotations from Elizabethan writers collected by Bertram Joseph, *Elizabethan Acting* 1–5, and again see Richard Levin 11–22.

9.   In the scholarly debate on Elizabethan acting, until the ascendance of post-structuralist theory the majority view was that actors were expected to assimilate themselves to the characters they play. For this view, see esp. Bertram Joseph, *Acting Shakespeare* 2–3, 15–18, 23, 60, 80–93 and *Elizabethan Acting* 1–24; Roach 23–57. Also see Donawerth 171; Downer 629; Faas 42–3; Harbage 96; Marker 91–2, 99; Marvin Rosenberg, "Elizabethan Actors" 103–4; Seltzer 15; Skura, esp. 49–52. John Russell Brown says that the actor *might* identify in this way ("On the Acting" 49). For the view that Elizabethan actors were not expected to feel the emotions of the characters they play, see, for example, Peter Holland 53–5; Jones-Davies; Styan, *Drama* 141–8. Cf. also Bethell 87; Bevington 68, 87–91; Edward Burns 9–13, 120–6; Buzacott 67–71, 105–7, 130–1, 137; Mann ch. 1 and 201–2; Worthen, *Idea* 16–21 and "Deeper" 454–5 on this question.

10. Cf. Puttenham 151, 153–4 and 155 (bk 3, ch. 2) on the use of heightened figurative language and the force of eloquence. On *enargeia* and the power of the image see Eden; Tuve 29–31; Vickers, *In Defence* 321–2.

11. T. W. Baldwin 2:204–5 suggests that Shakespeare drew on the passage in Quintilian quoted below in composing Hamlet's lines about the player being moved.

12. For discussions of ideas about role-playing, about representation of character, and about the psychology of acting in relation to characterization that are relevant to Shakespeare and that have not been cited or have not been cited for all of these topics that they discuss, see Abel; Allman; Baker; Barish; Barroll; Beckerman; Berry; Bevington; Bock 155–72; Bradbrook, "Shakespeare and the Use"; Burckhardt; Elizabeth Burns; Calderwood, *Shakespearean Metadrama*; Dawson; Driscoll; Eagleton, *Shakespeare*; Edwards; Elam; Frye; Goldman, *Acting and Action*, *Actor's Freedom*, and *Shakespeare and the Energies*; Granville-Barker 1:25–7; Greenblatt, "Circulation" and *Renaissance*; Grene; Joan Lord Hall; Hart; Hernadi 136–73; Hornby 67–87; Kernan, *Playwright*; Lanham; Lyman and Scott; Mack, "Engagement"; Mehl; Proser; Rabkin, *Shakespeare and the Common* 192–237; Rackin, "Shakespeare's Boy Cleopatra" and *Stages*; Righter; Harold Rosenberg; Siemon; Soellner; Ure, "Character" and "Shakespeare"; Van Laan; Vickers, "Shakespeare's Hypocrites"; Wilshire; Winny; Worthen, *Idea*. See also notes in Chapters 4–7 for references regarding the psychology of role-playing in the specific plays I discuss: *Ham.*, the three plays of the Henriad, *AYL*, and *WT*.

13. See esp. *Science and Human Behavior*, *Contingencies of Reinforcement*, and *Verbal Behavior*. Noland (102) argues that psychological criticism should employ all contemporary psychological theories. Cf. John V. Knapp. Dougan uses principles of reinforcement to argue for a behaviorist reading of *The Taming of the Shrew*. Shupe applies the behaviorist ideas of Bem (see the latter's *Beliefs*) in explaining Lady Anne's acceptance of Richard of

Gloucester's proposal of marriage in *R3* (34–5). Natoli and Rusch's bibliography of psychological studies of literature, 1969–1982, has no behaviorist entries for Shakespeare, and only a very few for all studies of literature. The cognitivist literature of the study of role-playing and self-presentation by social psychologists can easily be enfolded into a behaviorist interpretation. (See Chapter 3.)

Some behaviorist and cognitive psychologists are working toward a synthesis of their paradigms: see Moerk; Robert G. Burton. Also see the essays in *The Restoration of Dialogue*, ed. Ronald B. Miller and in *Reflections on B. F. Skinner and Psychology*, ed. Kennon A. Lattal. For refutation of the view that radical behaviorism is discredited with positivism, also see O'Donohue and Smith.

14. Notable exceptions among students of Shakespeare are Curry and Shenk, who provide systematic discussions of Elizabethan psychology giving due attention to the function of habits. See also the exposition of the psychology of habits in Hankins's discussion of Hamlet, 210–13. Other scholars using ideas related to this psychology in discussing Elizabethan society or Elizabethan drama are Berry 58–61, 97; Desmet 3–8, 18–21; Dollimore 11, 16–19, 169–76; Goldman, *Acting and Action* 6–16; Joan Lord Hall 46–7; Kastan 120–1; Siemon 108–14. Also see scholars listed in note 5 of Chapter 4 on *Hamlet*. Dollimore shows that for Montaigne and Bacon social custom is the basis for ideology. In his survey of medieval and Renaissance psychology, however, Dollimore does not refer to the importance of the concept of habit in writers earlier than Montaigne (158–69; "custom" as well as "habit" was used in Elizabethan English for what I call "habit"). Nor does Dollimore discuss the way terms for custom are used by Montaigne and Bacon to refer not only to social custom but also to the habitual behavior and belief of individual subjects, which may oppose social customs. Dollimore does not explain the psychology of habits.

The psychology of habits has not been discussed in studies of Elizabethan acting, but Roach shows the importance of this psychology in eighteenth-century works on acting.

For discussions of the psychology of habits in Aristotle by historians of psychology, see Brett 146–8; Esper 179–201; Robinson 84–93. Cf. Rachlin. Gerald Strauss has an extended discussion of the importance of this psychology in his account of education in the German Reformation, *Luther's House*, esp. 39–84. See also his summary article, "Capturing Hearts." Bencivenga discusses the psychology of habits in his study of Montaigne's ideas about the subject: see note 24 below. Among modern thinkers, William James uses the concept of habit, and John Dewey repeatedly echoes Aristotle's psychology. See Charles Camic and John D. Baldwin on the concept of habit in nineteenth- and early twentieth-century sociological theory. In contemporary sociological thinking, "habitus" is used by Bourdieu as a term for the internalized product of cultural training that causes a person to generate practices conforming to the norms of the culture.

15. For the questions about essentialism and the subject see Aers; Belsey, *Subject*; Bloom ix–xiv, 1–5; Lloyd Davis; Dollimore 9–19, 153–81, 249–71; Evans 116–17, 126–40, 155–7, 168–84, 209–17; Foucault 303–87; Freedman; Frye; Goldberg, esp. 3–4, 8–10, 68–100; Arthur Kirsch, esp. 127–44; Paglia; Marvin Rosenberg, *Masks of Hamlet* ix–xv. For the questions about a self or inner psyche see also Bencivenga; Harry Berger, Jr; Bock; Edward Burns, esp. 139–55;

Natalie Zemon Davis; Ferry; Gallagher; Greenblatt, "Psychoanalysis"; Greene, "Flexibility"; Haley; Hyde; Levine; Macrone; Maus; Mayer and Amos; Proctor; Quint; Rothwell; William O. Scott; Shuger, esp. 69–119; Soellner Chapters 1 and 2; Weinstein and Bell; Wilks.

16. See Draper 49, 53, 67–8, 77–9, 106; Reed 69–71; Babb 16–17, 23–9.

17. See Bright 30–1; ch. 6; 81–8; ch. 15; 92–103; ch. 16–7; 129–30; ch. 22; 242–9; ch. 37; 257–65; ch. 39. Robert Burton, too, writes of melancholy in relation to habituation: see, for example, 246; pt. 1, sec. 3, mem. 1, subs. 4.

18. Cf. Michael Scott's discussion of this passage in relation to the idea that the actor may "become" the character he plays (5–29).

Edward Burns also discusses this Induction, but does not refer to this part of it. Nor does his discussion develop the points about the psychology of habit that the Induction alludes to in the parts of it that he quotes (121–2). Thus he does not consider the implications of one actor urging another who is to play a tyrant to "frame your exterior shape / To haughty form of elate majesty" and "grow big in thought." Nor does he analyze the lines saying that everyone can "be proud" and "strut," that this "rank custom is grown popular" (the Induction, lines 7–19). Burns does not discuss what these lines may imply about the connection of outer behavior and inner thought, feeling, and being, nor does he comment on the use of "custom" here, a term that in this context probably plays on the relation between its meanings as "habit" and as socially conventional behavior. A little later Burns says that "all" the actors in the Induction "strive to find fitting action, fitting epithets, and to 'dispose my speech to the habit of my part' " (quoting line 54), but Burns does not comment on the use of "habit" here. Instead he emphasizes that an actor's doubling of parts or a character's change in life situation and hence role can be seen as multiplicity or discontinuity of character, and he asks regarding "the problem of interiority, of asocial selves – what is the 'action' of the philosopher, the exile, the man without 'the stamp' of his immediate society?" (122–3).

19. Some passages in the *Nicomachean Ethics* refer to innate virtue, but these are generally believed to be derived from the earlier *Eudemian Ethics*. Here are Aristotle's ideas that are basically the same as Plato's: virtues and vices are formed by habit, through repeated actions (*Nicomachean* 1103a–b). From childhood we must be habituated to find pleasure in virtue, pain in vice – to love virtue for its nobility and despise vice for its baseness (1104b–05a; cf. 1172a; bk 10, sec. 1). Children should hear tales singing the praises of noble virtue, be praised for acting nobly, and so come to take pleasure in acting virtuously because they love the noble (*Politics* 1339a–40b). If we are not habituated to virtue, we become habituated to seek easy pleasures and to avoid pain (*Nicomachean* 1104b; cf. 1150a). Once a person is habituated to vice, "it is no longer possible for him not to be what he is" (1114a; cf. 1150b, 1114b–15a). The analyses of Aristotle's psychology of behavior by Brett (134–49), Esper (179–81, 196–7), and Shute (57–83) are basically consistent with my behaviorist view. As indicated earlier, Robinson specifically mentions the similarity of Aristotle's psychology to Skinner's (84, 91, 93).

20. Aristotle does not in these passages specifically say that the self-indulgent person is *habituated* to seeking pleasure, but habituation is his idea of the process by which vices as well as virtues are formed, as we have seen. The self-indulgent person simply indulges his appetites, and so perhaps Aristotle sometimes thinks of this as a natural state rather than as an acquired one. See *Nicomachean* 1119b for this view and for a reference to habituation: "the

active gratification of appetite will increase the appetite with which we were born. . . ."

21. W. D. Ross says (145) that for Aristotle the "one faculty that sets us in movement" is desire, which includes wish as well as appetite. See also Brett 146, Shute 60–78.

22. See Gerald Strauss, *Luther's House*, and Perkins 71 (bk 1, ch. 5, sec. 5).

23. See Mayer and Amos and also Weinstein and Bell for evidence of interiority in medieval religious practices as well.

24. Bencivenga's more complete analysis of Montaigne's ideas about the subject discusses the importance of habit for Montaigne, but I believe Bencivenga constructs more of a binary opposition between habit and the exercise of thought than Montaigne does (40–3). I think that in Montaigne, as in the pre-modern tradition in general, the point is more that habit controls thought than that it deadens thought or by-passes reason's control in a "system of automatic responses" (41–2). Indeed, on these pages Bencivenga quotes Montaigne on how "*good* minds" (my emphasis) easily make "whatever they like seem true" (41) and our rationalizations *dignify* habitual behavior (43).

25. See esp. *passim* in "Of Custome," "Of the Caniballes," "Of Sumptuarie Lawes," and "Of Ancient Customes"; also see "Apologie," esp. 2: 296–9, "Of a Monstrous" 2: 430, "Of Phisiognomy" 3: 296, and "Of Experience" 3: 340–1.

26. On the importance of an individual's habits, see "That the Taste" 1: 287, "How a Man" 2: 415–6, "Of Repenting" 3: 30–1, and "Of Experience" 3: 340. On self-love, see esp. *passim* "Apologie," "Of Presumption," and "Of Vanitie"; also see "Upon Some Verses" 3: 67–8, 85. "Of Repenting" is somewhat exceptional in asserting that each of us has an inner form from nature which, although it is a "swaying" form, resists habits and passions it tends to oppose. But Montaigne's specific example is that when he speaks from the heart his words come to him in Latin, which he acquired before learning French. He says on this basis that "The Latin tongue is to me in a manner natural," but of course he *learned* Latin: behavior that was habituated in him at an impressionable and emotional stage of development feels natural to him (30).

27. On the effects of environment, see "Apologie" 2: 292. For the other factors mentioned, see "Of Readie" 1: 51, "How We Weepe" 1: 250, "Of the Inconstancie" 2: 11–12, "Apologie" 2: 277–80, "Of Repenting" 3: 23, and "Of the Art" 3: 172.

Notes for Chapter 2: The Behaviorism of B. F. Skinner

1. In this chapter, I will cite Skinner's texts only when I quote or when I want the reader to see what Skinner specifically says. The main text I draw on is *Science and Human Behavior*, but very important also are *Verbal Behavior*, *Contingencies of Reinforcement*, and *About Behaviorism*.

2. See Libet for experiments studying the temporal relation between willing to make a physical movement and the onset of the actual movement. Gopnik, a cognitive-developmental psychologist, argues that our sense that we have direct knowledge of our intentions is an illusion caused by our common-sense interpretation of how our cognitive processes relate to our actions. For more on how our conscious cognitions relate to the cognitions controlling our

behavior, see Bargh, esp. 237–40; Pittman, esp. 286–93. Cf. the discussions of intentions and causality by philosophers: see, for example, Searle; Strawson.

While it seems clear to all psychologists that intentions, beliefs, and attitudes should at least correlate with other behavior, it has not been easy to prove substantial correlations. On the weakness of the correlation except under limited circumstances, esp. see William J. McGuire 251–3; also see Kleinke, "Two Models"; Snyder, "When Believing," esp. 128. For various other views of the relation between intentions, attitudes, or beliefs and other behavior, cf. Ajzen with Chaiken and Stangor; see Abelson 721–2; Bandura; Blass; Eagly and Chaiken; Forsyth and Nye; Koestner, Bernieri, and Zuckerman; Schlenker and Weigold. See Fazio for a proposed model for the processes governing the relation between attitudes and behavior. See Olson and Zanna; Tesser and Shaffer for reviews of studies of this relationship. See Zettle for a behaviorist response to cognitivist claims. Also cf. the items cited in Chapter 3, note 16.

Cf. the research on "attributions" of causes of behavior to ourselves and others, research which shows how much we tend to err in such judgments: see Gilovich 76–87; Harvey and Weary; Kleinke, *Self-Perception* 191–214; Kunda; McClure; Pyszczynski and Greenberg; Michael Ross and Fletcher.

See also the literature on "self-deception." I use "self-deceived" simply to mean deceived and not deceived by others, so that a person's thinking errs through processes such as rationalization. Cf. other definitions and discussions of self-deception in Bok 59–72; Haight; Quattrone and Tversky; Rorty; Sartre, *Being* 112–15. See Taylor and Brown on the positive relation between some degree of self-deception and mental health.

3. Later Skinner used "person" instead of "self" in such contexts ("The Originating Self"), but it might not be clear if I refer to persons within a person. For ideas about the multiplicity of our selves, see esp. James 1: 294; Mead 142–4; Anselm L. Strauss 152–3; Sullivan, "Self as Concept" 184. Also see Brown and Smart, esp. 373–4; Ewing. Psychologists find it difficult to show very much consistency in individuals' behavior in different situations. See Bem and Allen and also the failure to replicate their finding of consistency by Chaplin and Goldberg. Also see discussions of cross-situational consistency in Doherty and Schlenker; Eagly and Chaiken; McBroom and Reed; Lee D. Ross and Nisbett; Snyder, *Public Appearances*; Snyder and Ickes 883–907; Stryker and Statham 357–9. Cf. the items cited in note 2 on whether people behave in a way consistent with their attitudes.

For the view that the self-concept more or less automatically regulates behavior, see, for example, Stone 194. Cf. Backman 234–7; Bruner 130; Fazio, Effrein, and Falender; Stryker and Statham 324–7.

For the view that we are born with a "biologically-based inner nature" that is the basis for a "true self" which we should develop, see esp. Maslow 3, 24ff., Rogers 107–24, and Allport. Cf. Laing, *Self and Others* 152. Contrast Santayana's view of what constitutes the true self, esp. 133–4. See Young-Eisendrath and Hall for ideas about the true self in Jungian and some other contemporary theories. See Gergen "Theory" for a review of the development of theories of the self. Cf. Alan O. Ross on many of these matters.

4. These systems of responses are Skinner's counterparts of the Freudian id and superego: *Science* 284–8.

5. Skinner, *Science* 293–4. Skinner says here that he is in "essential agreement" with Freud's interpretation of dreams.

6. See Aronfreed's detailed account of the formation of conscience as the socialization of internalized control of behavior.

Notes for Chapter 3: Character Formation and the Psychology of Role-playing and Acting

1. See, for example, Goffman, *Presentation* 16. For a definition of "role" in technical behaviorist terminology, see Ullman and Krasner 99. For a phenomenologist's perspective, see Wilshire. For a variety of other perspectives on role-theory, including some in which the relationship to role-playing in the theater is considered, see Brim; Buss and Briggs; Harré 189–231; Mixon, "Theory of Actors"; Sarbin and Allen, "Role-Theory"; Victor Turner, *From Ritual* 102–23; T. R. Young.

    Terms designating identity, in the basic sociological sense I will use, place persons in relation to social categories such as family, occupation, gender, and ethnic group. Cf. the various uses of "identity" in DeLevita; Driscoll 9–26; Erikson, *Identity: Youth*; Laing, *Self and Others* 86–8; Gregory P. Stone, "Appearance" 188–9; Stryker and Statham 345–7; Wilshire. Weigart provides a history of the use of "identity" in social psychology.

2. Stryker and Statham discuss a renewed concern for the "creative possibilities" in role-playing (359–67).

3. Cf. Goffman, *Presentation* 6, 30–3. Goffman cites Sartre: see Sartre's *Being* 103.

4. Stryker and Statham note that in symbolic interactionist social psychology the cognitive aspects of self and roles have been studied more fully than the emotional aspects (355).

5. See esp. Money, *Love* 5–11 and "Sin." Cf. Maccoby and Jacklin 363; Parsons, Preface xiii; Stoller 313–14. See Jacklin for a review of research in this area.

    Many experts believe that biological factors cause aggressive behavior to be more likely for males: see Money, *Love* 29–31; Bee 24; Maccoby and Jacklin 360; Parsons, "Psychosexual" 26. See Jacklin for a review. Cf. Archer and Lloyd, 124–59. A behaviorist explanation would be that biological factors such as hormones cause males to have a greater susceptibility to reinforcement for aggression (cf. Money, *Love* 5–6). But in a behaviorist view, most specific occasions for aggression are learned, and learning also accounts for much of the individual variation in aggressive behavior among males.

6. See Stoller 313–14. The work of John Money and Anke A. Erhardt with children having defective and ambiguous genitals led them to conclude that such children, with the help of surgery and hormone injections, can be raised to think of themselves as persons of the gender discordant with their "chromosomal sex, prenatal hormonal sex, and even postnatal hormonal sex and secondary sexual body morphology" (*Man and Woman* 234). Money reports that in most cases of androgenital syndrome hermaphroditism, even sexual preference can be manipulated through surgery, hormonal treatment, and the social learning of gender identity (*Love* 28).

7. See Adler, Kless, and Adler; John Archer; John Archer and Lloyd 250–80; Aronfreed 44 ff.; Bee 27–35; Cahill; Kohlberg 431–2; Maccoby and Jacklin 277–348; Petersen 36–67; West and Zimmerman. See Jacklin; Maccoby "Gender" and "The Role" for reviews. Cf. Chodorow, esp. 89, 113–14, 136–7, 173–7, 263–9; also see Gardiner's response to Chodorow. See Morawski for the question of how psychologists have assumed that the study of gender especially entails the study of differences, and so may have "confected" differences (200). Cf. Hare-Mustin and Maracek on this question.

8. Piaget, esp. 132–3, 149, 162–3, 166–7; cf. Erikson, *Childhood* 212, 216ff; Peller; McCall and Simmons 208–13. For discussions of creativity and other healthy

Notes to pp. 41–7

functions of play, see esp. Bretherton; Erikson, *Childhood* 222; Peller 123–4; Singer and Singer; Sutton-Smith, "The Role of Play" 254–8; Herron and Sutton-Smith, "Introduction to 'Theoretical' " 310; Tower; Victor Turner, *Anthropology* 167–70; Winnicott 56, 62–7. On Lev Vygotsky's theory of play see Bugrimenko and Smirnova. For discussions focused on play as performance, see Furth and Kane; Magee; Marjanovic-Shane; Sutton-Smith, "Introduction." See Alvarez for a comparison of theories of play put forward by psychoanalysts and by researchers in child development. Cf. Nardo 1–11 on theories of play.

9.   Cf. Goffman, *Encounters* 37–81, and among later authors, Athey and Darley; Brockner; Buss and Briggs; Donahue, Robins, Roberts, and John; Fenigstein; Anne J. Wells, esp. 164–79; Zelen.

10.   Skinner points out that generally rule-governed behavior is anxious and intuitive behavior is more pleasurable (*Contingencies* 169–70).

11.   Becker has a cogent discussion of this: esp. see 101, 139. Cf. Berger and Luckmann.

12.   See esp. Becker 66–71, 99; Goffman, *Encounters* 80–1; Anselm L. Strauss 40; Stryker and Statham 323–57; Ralph H. Turner 1–18. There is evidence that role-playing an assumed identity, even one that is opposed to one's true identity, tends to cause a "role-person merger" (Girodo 304–5). Cf. Frank and Gilovich; Williams, McCandless, Hobb, and Williams.

13.   Cf. Evreinoff's discussion of how we become what we pretend to be, with quotes from Nietzsche and Max Burckhardt (49–51).

14.   See George A. Kelly 1: 379–417. Moreno has been another important innovator in this kind of work. See his "Introduction" for a summary of theory and techniques in "psychodrama." Eric Bentley discusses the relation of theater to psychodrama in "Theater and Therapy" 131–52. Cf. Anselm L. Strauss's discussion of how a person not in need of therapy can experiment with new selves by trying them out in social life, 97. See Lueger's survey of the use of imagery, imagination, and role-playing in various therapeutic paradigms. Kipper provides an overview of role-playing therapies and a discussion of the way people become absorbed in roles they play. Williams, Pettibone, and Thomas describe strategies for self-change that fit a behaviorist paradigm very well – see esp. 175. For behavior modification in general, see Schwitzgebel and Kolb; Sulzer-Azaroff and Mayer.

15.   Cf. Aronson; Bem 54–61. Bem, a radical behaviorist, argues that this shows we base our interpretation of our own behavior partly on what we observe ourselves saying and doing, much as if we were interpreting the behavior of another person. Thus in the experiment described here, the persons paid the small amount might primarily observe that they had said the task was interesting and so infer that therefore they thought it was interesting, since the amount of money they received was too insignificant to consider seriously as a motivator. The experiment included measures to make sure that the subjects had not seen the "point" of the experiment and had not consciously reasoned that the task must have been interesting because they would not have lied for only one dollar.

16.   How attitudes change in cognitive dissonance experiments and counter-attitudinal role-playing continues to be an important area of study in social psychology. The more recent discussions tend to take the view that a purely cognitivist explanation is inadequate, that motivational factors such as self-esteem or an aversive sense of having produced an unwanted result are important causes of the attitude changes. For extensive reviews of the litera-

ture, see Cooper and Fazio; Eagly and Chaiken; Tesser and Shaffer; Thibodeau and Aronson. See Cooper and Aronson 290–6 on applications of these procedures in psychotherapy. Kleinke uses language designed for the non-specialist to summarize many studies (*Self-Perception* 78–127). See Aronson and the commentaries by others published with his essay regarding ideas for a synthesis of theories developed to explain these phenomena.

For discussions of cognitive dissonance as an aversive arousal state, or of reinforcement or self-esteem as factors in causing attitude change, see also Cushman; Fazio and Cooper; Lott and Lott 128; McGuire; Schlenker; Steele and Liu.

For discussions of how individuals differ in their tendency to change attitudes, see Jones, Brenner, and Knight; Schlenker 218–20; Schlenker and Trudeau; Snyder, "Self-Monitoring" 97–8; Tice. See Gibson for a discussion of attitude change in men trained to be torturers.

17. Cf. Brecht. See Carlson; States, "Actor's"; esp. for my concerns, Hernadi 136–73; see Kelsey for discussions of the ways an actor can relate to the character he or she plays. See Kochnev for a discussion of actors experiencing emotions appropriate to the character even in plays written and produced in what Kochnev calls "conventional-metaphorical" theater as contrasted with "psychological" theater.

18. *Sartre on Theater* 162–5, 170, 170–4; Weissman, esp. 11–12, 227–8. See Goldman on this Freudian view, *Actor's Freedom* 122.

19. See Cole, *Theatrical* 40; Kirby xiii, 5; Belo 150–1, 158–61; Schechner 128–33.

20. Coe and Sarbin; Spanos and Coe. The general view of these writers is that hypnotized persons perform a role, fulfilling their expectations for the hypnotic experience by complying with the hypnotist's suggestions in a way that causes them to believe that they see things that are not there, etc., while actually they have access to perceptions that could refute their belief.

For the relation between absorption, hypnosis, imaginative involvement, fantasy proneness, and a variety of other behavior, see also Crawford and Gruzelier, esp. 265; Glisky, Tataryn, Tobias, Kihlstrom, and McConkey; Ernest Hilgard; Josephine Hilgard; Johnstone; Lynn and Rhue; McConkey; Nadon, Laurence, and Perry; Pekala, Wenger, and Levine; Roche and McConkey; Shor; Tellegen and Atkinson; Wilson and Barber.

Some research suggests that hypnotizability is only found to correlate with a tendency to absorption in various activities when absorption is measured in the same session as the hypnotizability, so that the context induces subjects to say that they tend to become absorbed (Irving Kirsch and Council; Spanos, Arango, and deGroot). But my reading of the scholarship suggests that this research is faulty (see Nadon, Kihlstrom, Hoyt, and Register; Shames and Bowers). Especially when behavioral measures of absorption as well as hypnotizability are used – as opposed to mere self-report measures of absorption on a standard questionnaire – the relationship between absorption and hypnotizability seems clear (see, for example, Shames and Bowers). In any case, there seems to be some consensus that hypnotized persons are in an absorbed state as I have described it.

For the idea that hypnosis can help actors, see Fowler. For hypnotic or nearly hypnotic absorption in role-playing therapy, see, for example, Johnson, esp. 293–8; Shean. For evidence that playing the role of hypnotic subject increases hypnotizability, see Gorassini, Sowerby, Creighton, and Fry. For discussions of suggestibility in hypnosis and in many related phenomena, including role-playing, see the essays in the volume edited by Schumaker. For the importance of suggestibility in hypnosis, esp. see Irving Kirsch and Council. Additional evidence that late-twentieth-century actors experience emotions of characters is provided by Bates.

21.   See esp. *Verbal* 154–6 and *Science* 56, 169, 275. Cf. Leventhal and Mosbach 367.

22.   See esp. *Creating* 139–40; cf. *Building* 109. See Freed 35–6 for a discussion of how work on subtext may bring actors into contact with the unconscious purposes of the characters they play.

23.   Cf. Freed 69; McGaw 60; Skinner, *Contingencies* 151; Stanislavski, *Actor* 185–6, 190–3. Goldman discusses the importance of the "stress of encounter" for bringing a sense of self or selves to fruition (*Shakespeare and the Energies* 10–11).

24.   "Grammar" 36–7; see also Wiles 34–5. There are behaviorist analyses of Stanislavski's methods by Schulman, Simonov, and Sturm. Schulman discusses the use of conditioned emotional responses to create real emotions, and the use of operant conditioning to shape more realistic and creative behavior. Simonov is chiefly concerned with the communication of emotion ("Grammar" and *Science*). Sturm's summary analysis mentions several causes of fusion with a character, describing them as resulting in acting with "the appearance of naturalness and truth" in which the actor's emotions are "empathically appropriate" to the character (89–90). Konečni 220–2 describes the neurophysiological and cognitive processes that result in the Stanislavskian actor experiencing emotions that are "presumably highly similar to those that occur in real life" (222). See Sonia Moore for a discussion of many Soviet studies of the neurophysiology of the relation between emotions and behavior in the Stanislavski system (esp. vii, 9, 12–13, 17–21, 40–3, 68–73, 91–2).
       The idea that Stanislavski's techniques are mostly behaviorist has been questioned by Carnicke and others on the basis of new translations of his works in the post-Soviet era, but the evidence in Carnicke's essay suggests to me that the summary of Stanislavski's techniques I give here is accurate. The one passage from his writings in the new translation by Jean Benedetti that I have seen published alongside the corresponding passage in the heretofore standard English translation by Elizabeth Hapgood is, if anything, more clearly behaviorist than Hapgood's (see Stanislavsky, "From *The Actor*"). The new translation repeatedly emphasizes the stimulus function of the "magic if" itself, whereas Hapgood refers to the "if" as producing an "inner stimulus" that moves the actor. Hapgood emphasizes the statements in which Stanislavski says "if" works without forcing a response, and includes, in her greatly condensed translation, few of the many phrases in which the new translation shows that Stanislavski speaks of "if" as the initiator of action, as "a stimulating force," as "provoking instantaneous, instinctive actions" which seem "to happen unawares." Hapgood's emphasis on the actor's sense of acting freely is close to Skinner's radical behaviorism; Stanislavski's dual emphasis on this idea and on the idea that "if" is a stimulus that directly provokes action places him somewhere between "stimulus–response psychology" and Skinner with respect to the relation between stimuli and human responses. See Chapter 2.

25.   See esp. *Actor* 122, 126–42, 266–79, 288–95; cf. *Creating* 85–106, 148–50, 240–9.

26.   Blunt 287; Kjerbühl-Petersen 169; James 2: 462–3; cf. Skinner, *Verbal* 410. For
      experimental work showing that enacting the expression of an emotion can
      generate the emotion, see Laird; Leventhal and Mosbach 358; Petty and
      Cacioppo 88–9; Rhodewalt and Comer 43; Strack, Martin, and Stepper. For
      reviews of this phenomenon, see Ekman, and see Ekman and O'Sullivan,
      esp. 188–91. See Zillmann for an analysis of some of the emotional processes
      I have discussed and cf. Sturm's analysis of Stanislavski's method, 89–91.
27.   Stern and Lewis have shown that Stanislavskian "method" actors generate
      greater galvanic skin responses than non-method actors when asked to
      imagine emotional situations. A striking kind of physical effect is reported
      by Orne. In an experiment, subjects who could not be hypnotized but who
      simulated hypnosis were startled and even frightened to discover that when
      the hypnotist told them they could not bend their arm, they actually were
      unable to do so (542).

Notes for Chapter 4: Hamlet

1.   For the view that Hamlet is psychologically incoherent, see Barker 39–40,
      Belsey, *Subject* 41–2, and Weimann, "Mimesis," and for an important earlier
      essay that has contributed to this view, cf. Booth. Ferry sees Hamlet as
      having an inwardness we can recognize as like our own (2–3), but she is not
      specifically concerned with the cultural materialist concepts of the subject:
      see my discussion of these concepts in Chapter 1, 5–22 and my notes there.
      Ferry argues that the tradition before Shakespeare provides very little sense
      of the sort of inward life we find in Hamlet. For powerful defenses of the
      view that Hamlet's character has a certain identity within its great variability,
      see Frye; Marvin Rosenberg, *The Masks of Hamlet*, esp. ix–xv. Cf. Friedman;
      Morin; see Cruttwell for an earlier essay with this view, esp. 121–8.
          On Hamlet as a subject, cf. also Edward Burns 139–58; Eagleton, *William
      Shakespeare* 70–3; William O. Scott; States, *Hamlet*; Wilks 100–24; Luke Wilson.
      Wilks's use of Renaissance ideas of conscience, reason, and passion to analyze
      Hamlet's moral struggle converges with my analysis on a number of points.
          I am not persuaded that the variability of Hamlet can in part be attributed
      to revisions in the second quarto edition making him a *different character*
      from the Hamlet of the first folio edition (see David Ward and also Werstine
      on this possibility). Thus I use the conflated text of *Hamlet* ed. by Jenkins,
      not least because I want to discuss the Hamlet of our cultural and critical
      tradition.
          In his book on much the same topic as mine, *Character: Acting and Being
      on the Pre-Modern Stage*, Edward Burns defends the (near) "absence of psy-
      chology" from his "discourse of character" by analyzing Hamlet's response
      to Horatio's questions about the Danish custom of drinking (155–8). In Burns's
      reading, Hamlet locates all the "forces and effects" of the subject "outside
      it," and thus "The subject position, the 'I' from which a Shakespeare 'char-
      acter' speaks is . . . separate from, anterior to his or her 'character' (in the
      sense of the word known to Shakespeare) . . ." (157–8). This may justify, as
      Burns says, not analyzing Shakespeare's characters in terms of a post-romantic
      notion of the subject which "would locate the reality of" psychological forces
      such as humoral temperament, reason, and habit "within the individual

subjectivity" (158). His logic, however, leads not to a dismissal of *psychology* but to an analysis based on *pre-modern* psychology and its formulations of the sort of divided subjectivity Hamlet describes. In pre-modern discourse we typically find humoral temperament and reason within individual subjectivity, and we certainly find habit within both individual subjectivity and character, with character as habit a crucial source of subjectivity *and* its expression.

Thus Burns employs an inadequate analysis of pre-modern psychology, and he also errs in treating Hamlet's speech as a representative explanation of that psychology. Perhaps most importantly, Burns tends to take Hamlet's discourse as Shakespeare's. This is a general tendency in his analyses, deriving from his tight focus on character construction as a rhetorical practice. Rather than tracing the psychological tradition in relation to character, acting, and being, Burns comes to Shakespeare by way of Theophrastian character description, ancient biographical writing, the *Psychomachia* of Prudentius, and the Tudor allegorical drama. Thus Burns tends to write of Hamlet as *constructing* a subject position or an interiority in his metaphors and his grammar (147, 153; cf. 154, 157–8). Burns argues that Hamlet's use of the infinitive in "To be or not to be," and also his use of "we" in this soliloquy, show that the speech is an "almost subjectless utterance." Only the "we" suggests "a subject position," and it "evades any sense of a *particular* subject, any urgent individualism, or special subjectivity" (154). But Hamlet's grammar is not used by him or Shakespeare to construct a subject position in Burns's sense; Hamlet's grammar is an *expression of* his subjectivity as constructed by Shakespeare in the rhetorical mode of mimesis. Thus Hamlet as speaker expresses his thoughts and feelings about his dilemma, so that the use of the infinitive and "we" conveys Hamlet's *characteristic* tendency as a subject to think and hence express himself in a generalizing and philosophical manner. The speech also conveys Hamlet's characteristic concern for nobility, and much more – see my analysis in this chapter.

2.   For the defense of reading as a mode of character construction and the relation of reading to acting, also see Buzacott 1–13, 88–91, 137; Cole, *Acting as Reading*; Desmet; Goldman, *"Hamlet"*; Marvin Rosenberg, *Masks of Hamlet* ix–xv.

3.   A. C. Bradley held that "the psychological point of view is not equivalent to the tragic . . . ," but that to comprehend Hamlet's tragedy it is necessary to understand how and why he thinks and feels as he does (101–2). See again note 2 in Chapter 1.

4.   It is impossible to cite all those who have discussed Hamlet's character, but for discussions that at least implicitly consider the psychology of role-playing in relation to Hamlet which have not been cited earlier in this chapter regarding this psychology, see esp. Abel 41–58; Allman 211–54; Battenhouse 252–62; Calderwood, *To Be*, esp. 18–50, and "Hamlet's Readiness"; Calhoun; Cartwright 89–137; Charney, *Hamlet's* 15–34, *Style* 267–95; Danson 22–49; Draper 95, 103–5; Eagleton, *Shakespeare* 39–65; Ellrodt 41–8; Garber, *Coming of Age* 198–205; Goldman, *Shakespeare and the Energies* 79–93, *Actor's Freedom* 146–57 and *Acting and Action* 17–45; Gorfain, "Toward"; Gottschalk; Granville-Barker 1: 245–50; Greene, "Postures"; Joan Lord Hall 34–48; Hedrick; Peter Holland; Lanham 129–43; Harry Levin, esp. 111–26; Mack, "Engagement" 286–87 and "World"; Mann, esp. 44–53; Nardo 15–34; Paris, "Hamlet"; Rabey; Righter 142–7; Harold Rosenberg 68–102; Marvin Rosenberg, *Masks of Hamlet*, esp. 167–85; Siemon 108, 116; Soellner 135–8, 172–94; Ure, "Character"

21–8; Van Laan 171–80; Walcutt, esp. 20–32; Weimann, "Mimesis"; David Young 9–44.

5. A number of critics since Bradley have made more than passing mention of the psychology of habits in their interpretations of *Hamlet* and Hamlet: see Battenhouse 255–9; Calderwood, "Hamlet's Readiness"; Hankins 210–13; McDonald 342–8; Shenk 139–64; Siemon 108, 116; Skulsky 25–6, 44–5; Stirling 72; Walcutt 23–32; Whitaker 271–3. Cf. Parker, who alludes indirectly to the psychology of habits, 108–9.

For Coleridge's thesis on Hamlet and habit, see 158; cf. 175. That habit could have its full traditional meaning for Coleridge is seen in a comment that Claudius does not have the "guilt of habit" because his conscience still speaks (170). Cf. Hazlitt's statement that Shakespeare "has kept up the distinction . . . between the understandings and the moral habits of men" (237).

6. John Keble quotes the Puritan Thomas Cartwright as opposed to wearing mourning clothes because he believed that all outward expressions of mourning provoke a deepening of grief (1:491n). And this was not only the Puritans' idea, for we saw in Chapter 1 that Montaigne believed outward expressions of grief, even insincere ones, induce the feeling. Montaigne's favorite, Plutarch, says in his "Consolation to His Wife" that mourning clothes and other outward displays of sorrow, such as shearing one's hair, make the mind "dispirited, cramped, shut in, deaf to all soothing influences, and a prey to vain terrors" (609F–10A).

7. Here I agree with Nardo's view that to be in "deadly earnest" is opposed to being playful, but I disagree with her view that Hamlet is playful: see Nardo 10–11, 15–34.

As the reader will see, my analysis also finds no basis in the text for the actor to make us aware that he is "playing" Hamlet in any way that would detach him from the character. Hamlet's self-absorption is unusually intense and should be strongly communicated by the actor to the audience. Hamlet comments on the drama and himself in theatrical terms, but the nature of his comments can always be plausibly construed as expressing his own perspective. This is not to say that we should not infer further metatheatrical commentaries from the text, but these are authorial irony.

8. Now of course if Hamlet were an actual person, it might not be realistic to think of him as so absorbed in his antic disposition when he thinks of his foes that he tends not to think of what to do for revenge. However, we are analyzing the text of *Hamlet*, in which nearly all that exists of this character after he says he will put on an antic disposition until the news of the actors is his playing that role.

9. For these writers it does not matter that a reason to delay may be self-deceiving or even evil so long as it diverts one until more thought is possible. Thus Montaigne writes of how he diverted a young man from revenge by spurring his ambition to seek honor in rising above revenge in a noble forgiveness, and he says he once diverted himself from revenge with a love affair ("Of Diverting" 3:56–7). Bacon says that in anger the best way to make oneself delay is to think that the time for revenge has not yet come ("Of Anger" 511). Seneca writes that one may tell a person to delay revenge in order to take a heavier revenge later, apparently with the understanding that when the anger has passed, the heavier revenge will not be sought ("On Anger" bk 3, ch. 39, sec. 3). There is a variation on the theme of this kind of thinking in Sidney's *Arcadia* when Pyrocles is about to commit suicide and

a voice, possibly that of "his good angel," urges him first to seek *revenge*, in order to divert him from his suicidal purpose (483; bk 3, ch. 22, sec. 7).

10.   On most important questions, my reading agrees with that of Jenkins in the Arden ed., 484–93.

11.   Robert Burton writes of how a friend should keep a melancholy person busy, and, if all else fails, resort to threats and even whipping: 331–3; pt. 2, sec. 2, mem. 6, subs. 2.

12.   See Walley on *Lucrece*, esp. 483–4, and in the plays see passages such as *Tro.* 2.2.164–74.

13.   Hamlet speaks here to other characters, so we cannot assume he says what he feels. However, he generally speaks what he feels to Horatio. Further, the text does not suggest he has any other thoughts, but it does indicate considerable absorption in the narrow line of thought his speech conveys.

Notes for Chapter 5: Prince Hal – King Henry V

1.   On the issues relating to Hal taken up in this chapter, including especially discussions of him as an actor or role-player, see Allman 53–123; Barton, "King Disguised"; Bradbrook, "King Henry IV"; Burckhardt 144–205; Calderwood, *Metadrama in . . . Henriad*, esp. 51–87, 139–42, 150–61, 170–3; Peter B. Erickson, "The Fault" and *Patriarchal* 39–65; Goldman, *Shakespeare and the Energies* 45–73; Greenblatt, "Invisible Bullets"; Kahn 70–80; Kernan, "Henriad" 245–6, 265–75, *Playwright* 82–4; Kris; Lanham 190–200, 203–9; Leggatt, *Shakespeare's Political* 88–138; Mack, "Engagement" 291–4; Ornstein 125–202; Palmer 180–249; Paris, *Character* 71–109; Rabkin, *Shakespeare and the Problem* 33–62; Rackin, *Stages* 71–85; Richmond 145–9, 156–8, 170–200; Seltzer; Tillyard 300–20, 344–52; Traversi, *Approach* 208–25, 234–7, 244–7, 253–76 and *Shakespeare: From Richard II* 1–11, 49–198; J. Dover Wilson, *Fortunes* 22, 36–81, 114–28; Winny 131–51, 172–97, 202–4, 208–14.

2.   When I refer to a character as thinking, etc., I mean the text implies this: see the second through the fourth paragraphs of Chapter 4.

3.   See Ornstein 136–7 for an especially cogent argument that the soliloquy expresses Hal's thinking. Ornstein's main points are that Shakespeare's audience was so familiar with Hal's legend that they would have needed no reminder that he would reform, that the soliloquy cannot be a mere statement that he will reform when it tells us so much more, replacing the prodigal Hal of popular legend with a Prince the audience might not like nearly so much. Thus, Ornstein observes that it is "preferable to interpret the soliloquy as soliloquy rather than to turn Shakespeare into a blunderer who did not realize the chilling effect of Hal's contemptuous lines about his comrades and who failed to see how Hal's diction and metaphors associate his calculated redemption with the crassness of commodity and sharp business practices" (137).

4.   Bacon writes of the defensive use of gibes at others: "Whosoever hath any thing fixed in his person that doth induce contempt, hath also a perpetual spur in himself to rescue and deliver himself from scorn. Therefore all deformed persons are extreme bold. First, as in their own defence, as being exposed to scorn; but in process of time by a general habit. Also it stirreth in them industry, and especially of this kind, to watch and observe the weakness of others, that they may have somewhat to repay" ("Of Deformity" 480). Some

writers of Shakespeare's time and earlier discuss how a person may deceive himself about his gibing. Thus Guazzo writes of "mockers and flouters, who without any comely grace, deride every man, and more easily persuade themselves that they are pleasant and merry conceited fellows, than perceive themselves to be ignorant and undiscreet fools" (1: 72). La Primaudaye urges his readers to avoid "scoffing, which (as Theophrastus saith) is nothing else but a close and coloured reproof of some fault, which by little and little inureth him that mocketh, to backbite another openly and untruly" (190–1; bk 1, ch. 43).

5. Gamble suggests that Hal is controlled by his father's ideas and manipulations in the deathbed scene and in this scene.

Notes for Chapter 6: *As You Like It*

1. When I refer to what characters see and think, etc., I mean this is what the text implies: see the second through the fourth paragraphs of Chapter 4.
    For discussion of the psychology and role-playing of Rosalind, see Barber 3–10, 222–39; Beckman; Belsey, "Disrupting," esp. 180–5; Bloom 1–5; Bono; John Russell Brown, *Shakespeare's Dramatic* 72–103; Dreher 119–23; Dusinberre 231–71; Greenblatt, "Fiction"; Howard, esp. 434–5; Iser, "Dramatization"; Katherine E. Kelly 88–90; Kimbrough 108–14; Lifson; Marcus; Paglia 199–212; Rackin, "Androgyny"; Shaw and Stevenson; Stanton; Traub 117–30; John Powell Ward 38–56.
2. See Murray; cf. John Russell Brown, *Shakespeare's Dramatic* 101–3; Kuhn.
3. Compare the use of "if" in the episode of the duel between "Cesario" and Sir Andrew in *Twelfth Night* 3.4.274, 300, 310, 319, 321, 325, 329–30.
4. For the issues discussed here, especially see discussions by Steve Brown, by Evans 145–71, by Forker in "Sexuality," by Garber, *Vested* 72–7, by Heise, by Jardine 9–36, by Bruce R. Smith 146–55, and by Traub 117–30, 138–44. On the relation between Rosalind and the boy actor, also see discussions by Parry and by Soule. Cf. Kott on these issues, too. Some critics argue that Rosalind evokes responses to the fact that "she" is played by a boy so much that she tends to get lost as a character. As I have argued from the beginning, I think this greatly underestimates the power of mimesis on the Elizabethan stage, and in this chapter I try to show how things Rosalind says and does that others have seen as anti-mimetic should be seen as expressing her character.
5. Rosalind incorporates Touchstone's view into her own in a way analogous to Lear's absorption of the Fool's perspective that allows the Fool to disappear in Act 3.
6. We may think we should attribute the skilled role-taking of a character entirely to the dramatist, who creates and therefore of course knows the thoughts and feelings of all the characters. But the dramatist does not create all characters so they understand what others think and feel: the ability to take the role of the other is an important feature in the individuation of characters.
7. My thinking about Rosalind has been especially stimulated by the discussion of Barber 233–9.
8. This discussion of what might come after the play's events is based on what the text invites us to imagine. My readers are not being asked to think that the characters exist apart from what is asserted or implied in the text.

Notes for Chapter 7: Absorbed Action: "Sure this robe of mine does change my disposition"

1. Compare the discussion of Perdita in Dusinberre 238–9; Eagleton, *Shakespeare* 142–51; Egan 68–9; Farrell 56; Forker, *Fancy's* 122–3; Garber, *Dream* 138, 178–9; Goldman, *Shakespeare and the Energies* 130–2; Joan Lord Hall 22; Hubert 122–4; Righter 177–9; Van Laan 232–4.
2. When I refer to what a character thinks, I mean that this is what the text implies: see the second through the fourth paragraphs of Chapter 4.

Notes for Appendix: The Psychology of Habits

1. Cf. *Nicomachean* bk 3, ch. 3, "Deliberation," with *Science and Human Behavior*, ch. 16.
2. W. D. Ross says that for Aristotle the "one faculty that sets us in movement" is desire, which includes wish as well as appetite (145). See also Brett 146; Shute 60–78. The ideas in this passage from *On the Soul* are also in *Movement of Animals* 700b10–2a1.
3. Cf. "To Marcia" ch. 7, sec. 4, on the dependence of a person's feelings about "poverty, grief, and ambition" on habit.
4. Indeed, in "On Our Blindness" sec. 5, he will not despair of the possibility that philosophy might be able to reach the soul even of a hardened sinner.
5. Even Seneca's least "proto-behaviorist" formulations of the operation of precepts treat the precepts themselves as stimuli in relation to innate tendencies to virtue: "On the Value" sec. 29.
6. For more on the importance of practice see, for example, "On the Part" sec. 46; habit is again associated with virtue as well as vice in "On Tranquility" ch. 1, sec. 3; ch. 10, sec. 1.
7. There is also a view of reason consistent with a basic point of behaviorist psychology in Aquinas's approving quotation of Aristotle's principle that "the intellect understands itself in the same way as it understands other things" – by observing its own acts, not by grasping its essence (I.87. 1, citing *On the Soul* 3.4).
8. Cf. Jordan's discussion of this episode in relation to Renaissance ideas about androgyny, 223–9, and Bruce R. Smith's discussion of the episode in relation to homosexual desire, 139–43.

Works Cited

Abel, Lionel, *Metatheatre: A New View of Dramatic Form* (New York: Hill, 1963).

Abelson, Robert, "Psychological Status of the Script Concept," *American Psychologist*, 36 (1981): 715–29.

Adler, Patricia A., Kless, Steven J., and Adler, Peter, "Socialization to Gender Roles: Popularity among Elementary School Boys and Girls," *Sociology of Education*, 65 (1992): 169–87.

Aers, David, "A Whisper in the Ear of Early Modernists; or, Reflections on Literary Critics Writing the 'History of the Subject,'" *Culture and History 1350–1600: Essays on English Communities, Identities and Writing*, ed. David Aers (Detroit: Wayne State University Press, 1992) pp. 177–202.

Ajzen, Icek, "Attitudes, Traits, and Actions: Dispositional Prediction of Behavior in Personality and Social Psychology," *Advances in Experimental Social Psychology*, 20 (1987): 1–63.

Allman, Eileen Jorge, *Player-King and Adversary: Two Faces of Play in Shakespeare* (Baton Rouge: Louisiana State University Press, 1980).

Allport, Gordon, *Becoming: Basic Considerations for a Psychology of Personality* (New Haven: Yale University Press, 1955).

Altman, Joel B, "'Vile Participation': The Amplification of Violence in the Theater of *Henry V*," *Shakespeare Quarterly*, 42 (1991): 1–32.

Alvarez, Anne, "Beyond the Unpleasure Principle: Some Preconditions of Thinking Through Play," *Journal of Child Psychotherapy*, 14.2 (1988): 1–13.

Anscombe, G. E. M., "Thought and Action in Aristotle: What is 'Practical Truth'?," *New Essays on Plato and Aristotle*, ed. Renford Bambrough (New York: Humanities; London: Routledge, 1965) pp. 143–58. Rpt. in *Aristotle's Ethics: Issues and Interpretations*, ed. James J. Walsh and Henry L. Shapiro (Belmont, CA: Wadsworth, 1967) pp. 56–69.

Aquinas, St Thomas, *Summa Theologica*, trans. Fathers of the English Dominican Province, 3 vols (New York: Benziger, 1947–1948).

Archer, John, "Childhood Gender Roles: Social Context and Organisation," *Childhood Social Development: Contemporary Perspectives*, ed. Harry McGurk (Hove: Erlbaum, 1992) pp. 31–61.

Archer, John and Lloyd, Barbara, *Sex and Gender*, rev. ed. (Cambridge: Cambridge University Press, 1985).

Archer, William, *Masks or Faces? The Paradox of Acting*, by Denis Diderot, and *Masks or Faces?* by William Archer (New York: Hill, 1957) pp. 75–226.

Aristotle, *Eudemian Ethics*, trans. J. Solomon, rev. Jonathan Barnes, *The Complete Works of Aristotle*, ed. Barnes, rev. Oxford trans, vol. 2, Bollingen Series 71, pt 2 (Princeton: Princeton University Press, 1984) pp. 1922–81, 2 vols.

Aristotle, *Movement of Animals*, trans. A. S. L. Farquharson, *The Complete Works of Aristotle*, ed. Jonathan Barnes. rev. Oxford trans, vol. 1. Bollingen Series 71, pt 2 (Princeton: Princeton University Press, 1984) pp. 1087–96, 2 vols.

Aristotle, *Nicomachean Ethics*, trans. Martin Ostwald, The Library of Liberal Arts (Indianapolis: Bobbs, 1962).

Aristotle, *On the Soul*, trans. J. A. Smith, rev. Jonathan Barnes, *The Complete Works of Aristotle*, ed. Barnes, rev. Oxford trans, vol. 1, Bollingen Series 71, pt 2 (Princeton: Princeton University Press, 1984) pp. 641–92, 2 vols.

Aristotle, *Politics*, trans. Benjamin Jowett, rev. Jonathan Barnes, *The Complete Works of Aristotle*, ed. Barnes, rev. Oxford trans, vol. 2, Bollingen Series 71, pt 2 (Princeton: Princeton University Press, 1984) pp. 1986–2129, 2 vols.

Aristotle, *Rhetoric*, trans. W. Rhys Roberts, rev. Jonathan Barnes, *The Complete Works of Aristotle*, ed. Barnes, rev. Oxford trans, vol. 2, Bollingen Series 71, pt 2 (Princeton: Princeton University Press, 1984) pp. 2152–269, 2 vols.

Aronfreed, Justin, *Conduct and Conscience: The Socialization of Internalized Control over Behavior* (New York: Academic, 1968).

Aronson, Elliot, "The Return of the Repressed: Dissonance Theory Makes a Comeback," *Psychological Inquiry*, 3 (1992): 303–11.

Ascham, Roger, *The Scholemaster*, ed. Edward Arber, 1920 (English reprints; n.p.: Folcroft, 1976).

Athey, Michael and Darley, John, "Social Roles as Interaction Competencies," *Personality, Roles, and Social Behavior*, ed. William Ickes and Eric S. Knowles (Springer Series in Social Psychology; New York: Springer, 1982) pp. 55–83.

Augustin[e], St, "Acts or Disputations against Fortunatus, the Manichaean," trans. Albert H. Newman, *A Select Library of the Nicene and Post-Nicene Fathers of The Christian Church*, first series, ed. Philip Schaff, vol. 4 (Grand Rapids, MI: Eerdmans, 1956) pp. 113–24, 14 vols.

Augustin[e], St, *The Confessions*, trans. J. G. Pilkington, *Basic Writings of Saint Augustine*, ed. Whitney J. Oates, vol. 1 (New York: Random, 1948) pp. 3–256, 2 vols.

Augustin[e], St, *The Morals of the Catholic Church*, trans. R. Stothert, *Basic Writings of Saint Augustine*, ed. Whitney J. Oates, vol. 1 (New York: Random, 1948) pp. 319–57, 2 vols.

Augustin[e], St, "Our Lord's Sermon on the Mount, According to Matthew," trans. William Findlay, rev. and ed. David S. Schaff, *A Select Library of the Nicene and Post-Nicene Fathers of the Christian Church*, first series, ed. Phillip Schaff, vol. 6 (Grand Rapids, MI: Eerdmans, 1956) pp. 1–63, 14 vols.

Babb, Lawrence, *The Elizabethan Malady: A Study of Melancholia in English Literature from 1580 to 1642* (East Lansing: Michigan State University Press, 1951).

Backman, Carl W., "Toward an Interdisciplinary Social Psychology," *Advances in Experimental Social Psychology*, 16 (1983): 219–61.

Bacon, Francis, *The Advancement of Learning. The Works of Francis Bacon*, ed. James Spedding, Robert Leslie Ellis, and Douglas Denon Heath, 1857–74, vol. 3 (New York: Garrett, 1968) pp. 261–491, 14 vols.

Bacon, Francis, *The Essays or Counsels, Civil and Moral. The Works of Francis Bacon*, ed. James Spedding, Robert Leslie Ellis, and Douglas Denon Heath, 1857–74, vol. 6 (New York: Garrett, 1968) pp. 377–517, 14 vols.

Bacon, Francis, *The New Organon. The Works of Francis Bacon*, ed. James Spedding, Robert Leslie Ellis, and Douglas Denon Heath, 1857–74, vol. 4 (New York: Garrett, 1968) pp. 39–248, 14 vols.

Bacon, Francis, "Of Anger," *Essays* 510–12.

Bacon, Francis, "Of Custom and Education," *Essays* 470–2.

Bacon, Francis, "Of Deformity," *Essays*, 480–1.

Bacon, Francis, "Of Honour and Reputation," *Essays*, 505–6.

Bacon, Francis, "Of Nature in Men," *Essays*, 469–70.

Baker, Susan, "Personating Persons: Rethinking Shakespearean Disguises," *Shakespeare Quarterly*, 43 (1992): 303–16.

Baldwin, John D., "Habit, Emotion, and Self-Conscious Action," *Sociological Perspectives*, 31.1 (1988): 35–57.

Baldwin, T. W., *William Shakspere's Small Latine and Lesse Greeke*, vol. 2 (Urbana: University of Illinois Press, 1944) 2 vols.

Bandura, Albert, "Human Agency in Social Cognitive Theory," *American Psychologist*, 44 (1989): 1175–84.

Barber, C. L., *Shakespeare's Festive Comedy: A Study of Dramatic Form and its Relation to Social Custom* (New York: World, 1959).

Bargh, John A., "Does Subliminarity Matter to Social Psychology? Awareness of the Stimulus Versus Awareness of Its Influence," *Perception Without Awareness: Cognitive, Clinical, and Social Perspectives*, ed. Robert F. Bornstein and Thane S. Pittman (New York: Guilford, 1992) pp. 236–55.

Barish, Jonas, *The Antitheatrical Prejudice* (Berkeley: University of California Press, 1981).

Barker, Francis, *The Tremulous Private Body: Essays on Subjection* (London: Methuen, 1984).

Barroll, J. Leeds, *Artificial Persons: The Formation of Character in the Tragedies of Shakespeare* (Columbia: University of South Carolina Press, 1974).

Barton, Anne, "The King Disguised: Shakespeare's *Henry V* and the Comical History," *The Triple Bond: Plays, Mainly Shakespearean, in Performance*, ed. Joseph G. Price (University Park: Pennsylvania State University Press, 1975) pp. 92–117.

Bates, Brian, "Performance and Possession: The Actor and Our Inner Demons," *Psychology and Performing Arts*, ed. Glenn D. Wilson (Amsterdam: Swets and Zeitlinger, 1991) pp. 11–18.

Battenhouse, Roy [W.], *Shakespearean Tragedy: Its Art and Its Christian Premises* (Bloomington: Indiana University Press, 1969).

Becker, Ernest, *The Birth and Death of Meaning: An Interdisciplinary Perspective on the Problem of Man*, 2nd ed. (New York: Free; London: Collier Macmillan, 1971).

Beckerman, Bernard, *Shakespeare and "The Purpose of Playing,"* The Andrew W. Mellon Lectures (New Orleans: Graduate School of Tulane, 1983).

Beckman, Margaret Boerner, "The Figure of Rosalind in *As You Like It*," *Shakespeare Quarterly*, 29 (1978): 44–51.

Bee, Helen L., "Sex Differences," *Social Issues in Developmental Psychology*, ed. Bee, 2nd ed. (New York: Harper, 1978) pp. 3–38.

Belo, Jane, "Trance Experience in Bali," *Ritual, Play, and Performance: Readings in the Social Sciences/Theatre*, ed. Richard Schechner and Mary Schuman (New York: Seabury, 1976) pp. 150–61.

Belsey, Catherine, "Disrupting Sexual Difference: Meaning and Gender in the Comedies," *Alternative Shakespeares*, ed. John Drakakis (London: Methuen, 1985) pp. 166–90.

Belsey, Catherine, *The Subject of Tragedy: Identity and Difference in Renaissance Drama* (London: Methuen, 1985).

Bem, Daryl J., *Beliefs, Attitudes, and Human Affairs* (Basic Concepts in Psychology Series, Belmont, CA: Brooks/Cole, 1970).

Bem, Daryl J. and Allen, Andrea, "On Predicting Some of the People Some of the Time: The Search for Cross-Situational Consistencies in Behavior," *Psychological Review*, 81 (1974): 506–20.

Bencivenga, Ermanno, *The Discipline of Subjectivity: An Essay on Montaigne* (Princeton: Princeton University Press, 1990).

Bentley, Eric, "Theater and Therapy," *New American Review*, 8 (1970): 131–52.

Berger, Harry, Jr, *Imaginary Audition: Shakespeare on Stage and Page* (Berkeley: University of California Press, 1989).

Berger, Peter L. and Luckmann, Thomas, *The Social Construction of Reality: A*

Treatise in the Sociology of Knowledge, 1966 (Garden City, NY: Anchor-Doubleday, 1967).

Berry, Edward, *Shakespeare's Comic Rites* (Cambridge: Cambridge University Press, 1984).

Bethell, S. L., *Shakespeare and the Popular Dramatic Tradition* (New York: Staples, 1944).

Bevington, David, *Action is Eloquence: Shakespeare's Language of Gesture* (Cambridge: Harvard University Press, 1984).

Blass, Thomas, "Understanding Behavior in the Milgram Obedience Experiment: The Role of Personality, Situations, and Their Interactions," *Journal of Personality and Social Psychology*, 60 (1991): 398–413.

Bloom, Harold, "The Analysis of Character" and Introduction, *Rosalind*, ed. H. Bloom (Major Literary Characters, New York: Chelsea, 1992) pp. ix–xiv, 1–5.

Blunt, Jerry, *The Composite Art of Acting* (New York: Macmillan, 1966).

Bock, Philip K., *Shakespeare and Elizabethan Culture: An Anthropological View* (New York: Schocken, 1984).

Bok, Sissela, *Secrets: On the Ethics of Concealment and Revelation* (New York: Pantheon-Random, 1982).

Bono, Barbara J., "Mixed Gender, Mixed Genre in Shakespeare's *As You Like It*," *Renaissance Genres: Essays on Theory, History, and Interpretation*, ed. Barbara Kiefer Lewalski (Harvard English Studies 14, Cambridge: Harvard University Press, 1986) pp. 189–212.

Booth, Stephen, "On the Value of *Hamlet*," *Reinterpretations of Elizabethan Drama*, ed. Norman Rabkin (Selected Papers from the English Institute, New York: Columbia University Press, 1969) pp. 137–76.

Bourdieu, Pierre and Passeron, Jean-Claude, *Reproduction: In Education, Society and Culture*, trans. Richard Nice (Sage Studies in Social and Educational Change 5, London: Sage, 1977).

Bradbrook, M[uriel] C., "King Henry IV," *The Artist and Society in Shakespeare's England: The Collected Papers of Muriel Bradbrook*, vol. 1 (Sussex: Harvester; Totowa, NJ: Barnes, 1982) pp. 121–32.

Bradbrook, M[uriel] C., "Shakespeare and the Use of Disguise in Elizabethan Drama," *Essays in Criticism*, 2 (1952): 159–68.

Bradley, A. C., *Shakespearean Tragedy: Lectures on* Hamlet, Othello, King Lear, Macbeth, 2nd ed. (1905; New York: St Martin's; London: Macmillan, 1966).

Braunmuller, A. R., "The Arts of the Dramatist," *The Cambridge Companion to English Renaissance Drama*, ed. A. R. Braunmuller and Michael Hattaway (Cambridge: Cambridge University Press, 1990) pp. 53–90.

Brecht, Bertolt, *Brecht on Theatre: The Development of an Aesthetic*, ed. and trans. John Willett (New York: Hill, 1957).

Breer, Paul E. and Locke, Edwin A., *Task Experience as a Source of Attitudes* (The Dorsey Series in Anthropology and Sociology, Homewood, IL: Dorsey, 1965).

Bretherton, Inge, "Pretense: The Form and Function of Make-Believe Play," *Developmental Review*, 9 (1989): 383–401.

Brett, George Sidney, *A History of Psychology: Ancient and Patristic* (London: George Allen, 1912, vol. 1 of *A History of Psychology*, 3 vols, 1912–21).

Bright, Timothy, *A Treatise of Melancholie* (London, 1586) Facsimile Text Society 50 (New York: Columbia University Press, 1940).

Brim, Orville G., Jr, "Personality Development as Role-Learning," *Personality Development in Children*, ed. Ira Iscoe and Harold W. Stevenson (Austin: University of Texas Press, 1960) pp. 127–59.

Brockner, Joel, "Self-Esteem, Self-Consciousness, and Task Performance: Replications, Extensions, and Possible Explanations," *Journal of Personality and Social Psychology*, 37 (1979): 447–61.

Brook, Peter, *The Empty Space* (New York: Atheneum, 1969).

Brown, John Russell, "On the Acting of Shakespeare's Plays," *Quarterly Journal of Speech*, 34 (1953): 477–84. Rpt. in *The Seventeenth Century Stage: A Collection of Critical Essays*, ed. Gerald Eades Bentley (Chicago: University of Chicago Press, 1968) pp. 41–54.

Brown, John Russell, *Shakespeare's Dramatic Style* (London: Heinemann, 1970).

Brown, Jonathon D. and Smart, S. April, "The Self and Social Conduct: Linking Self-Representations to Prosocial Behavior." *Journal of Personality and Social Psychology*, 60 (1991): 368–75.

Brown, Steve, "The Boyhood of Shakespeare's Heroines: Notes on Gender Ambiguity in the Sixteenth Century," *Studies in English Literature*, 30 (1990): 243–63.

Bruner, Jerome, *Actual Minds, Possible Worlds* (Cambridge: Harvard University Press, 1986).

Bugrimenko, Elena A. and Smirnova, Elena O., "Paradoxes of Children's Play in Vygotsky's Theory," *Emerging Visions of the Aesthetic Process: Psychology, Semiology, and Philosophy*, ed. Gerald C. Cupchik and János László (Cambridge: Cambridge University Press, 1992) pp. 286–99.

Burckhardt, Sigurd, *Shakespearean Meanings* (Princeton: Princeton University Press, 1968).

Burns, Edward, *Character: Acting and Being on the Pre-Modern Stage* (New York: St Martin's, 1990).

Burns, Elizabeth, *Theatricality: A Study of Convention in the Theatre and in Social Life* (New York: Harper, 1972).

Burton, Robert, *The Anatomy of Melancholy* (New York, 1847).

Burton, Robert G., "Reduction, Elimination, and Strategic Interdependence," *Natural and Artificial Minds*, ed. Robert G. Burton (Scientific Studies in Natural and Artificial Intelligence, Albany: State University of New York Press, 1993) pp. 231–43.

Buss, Arnold H. and Briggs, Stephen R., "Drama and the Self in Social Interaction," *Journal of Personality and Social Psychology*, 47 (1984): 1310–24.

Buzacott, Martin, *The Death of the Actor: Shakespeare on Page and Stage* (London: Routledge, 1991).

Cahill, Spencer E., "Fashioning Males and Females: Appearance Management and the Social Reproduction of Gender," *Symbolic Interaction*, 12 (1989): 281–98.

Calderwood, James L., "Hamlet's Readiness," *Shakespeare Quarterly*, 35 (1984): 267–73.

Calderwood, James L., *Metadrama in Shakespeare's Henriad: Richard II to Henry V* (Berkeley: University of California Press, 1979).

Calderwood, James L., *Shakespearean Metadrama: The Argument of the Play in* Titus Andronicus, Love's Labor's Lost, Romeo and Juliet, A Midsummer Night's Dream, *and* Richard II (Minneapolis: University of Minnesota Press, 1971).

Calderwood, James L., *To Be and Not to Be: Negation and Metadrama in* Hamlet (New York: Columbia University Press, 1983).

Calhoun, Jean S., "*Hamlet* and the Circumference of Action," *Renaissance News*, 15 (1962): 281–98.

Calvin, [Jean], *Institutes of the Christian Religion*, trans. Ford Lewis Battles, ed. John T. McNeill, 2 vols (The Library of Christian Classics 20, 21, Philadelphia: Westminster, 1960).

Camic, Charles, "The Matter of Habit," *American Journal of Sociology*, 91 (1986): 1039–87.

The Canons and Dogmatic Decrees of the Council of Trent. The Creeds of Christendom: With a History and Critical Notes, ed. Philip Schaff, 4th ed., vol. 2 (New York: Harper, 1919) pp. 77–206, 3 vols.

Cardano, Giralamo, *Cardanus Comforte*, trans. Thomas Bedingfield (London, 1576) (The English Experience 82, New York: Da Capo; Amsterdam: Theatrum, 1969).

Carlson, Marvin, "Theatrical Performance: Illustration, Translation, Fulfillment, or Supplement?," *Theatre Journal*, 37 (1985): 5–11.

Carnicke, Sharon Marie, "Stanislavsky: Uncensored and Unabridged," *The Drama Review*, 37 (1993): 22–37.

Cartelli, Thomas, *Marlowe, Shakespeare, and the Economy of Theatrical Experience* (Philadelphia: University of Pennsylvania Press, 1991).

Cartwright, Kent, *Shakespearean Tragedy and Its Double: The Rhythms of Audience Response* (University Park: Pennsylvania State University Press, 1991).

Castiglione, Baldassare, *The Book of the Courtier*, trans. Sir Thomas Hoby (1561) The Tudor Translations 23 (New York: AMS, 1967).

Chaiken, Shelly and Stangor, Charles, "Attitudes and Attitude Change," *Annual Review of Psychology*, 38 (1987): 575–630.

Chaplin, William F. and Goldberg, Lewis R., "A Failure to Replicate the Bem and Allen Study of Individual Differences in Cross-Situational Consistency," *Journal of Personality and Social Psychology*, 47 (1985): 1074–90.

Charney, Maurice, *Hamlet's Fictions* (New York: Routledge, 1988).

Charney, Maurice, *Style in* Hamlet (Princeton: Princeton University Press, 1969).

Charron, Pierre, *Of Wisdome*, trans. Samson Lennard (London, n.d.) (The English Experience 315, New York: Da Capo; Amsterdam: Theatrum, 1971).

Chodorow, Nancy, *The Reproduction of Mothering: Psychoanalysis and the Sociology of Gender* (Berkeley: University of California Press, 1978).

Cicero, [Marcus Tullius], *De Officiis / On Duties*, trans. Harry G. Edinger, (The Library of Liberal Arts, Indianapolis: Bobbs, 1974).

Cicero, [Marcus Tullius], *De Oratore (The Orator)*, trans. John S. Watson (Carbondale, IL: Southern Illinois University Press, 1970).

Clodius, C. A. H., *Ueber Shakespeare's Philosophie besonders im* Hamlet, 1820, excerpted in *A New Variorum Edition of Shakespeare:* Hamlet, ed. Horace Howard Furness (1877), vol. 2 (New York: Dover, 1963) p. 280, 2 vols.

Coe, William C. and Sarbin, Theodore R., "Role Theory: Hypnosis from a Dramaturgical and Narrational Perspective," *Theories of Hypnosis: Current Models and Perspectives*, ed. Steven Jay Lynn and Judith W. Rhue (Guilford Clinical and Experimental Hypnosis Series, New York: Guilford, 1991) pp. 303–23.

Cole, David, *Acting as Reading: The Place of the Reading Process in the Actor's Work* (Ann Arbor: University of Michigan Press, 1992).

Cole, David, *The Theatrical Event, A Mythos, a Vocabulary, a Perspective* (Middletown, CT: Wesleyan University Press, 1975).

Coleridge, Hartley, *Essays and Marginalia*, 1851, excerpted in *A New Variorum Edition of Shakespeare:* Hamlet, ed. Horace Howard Furness (1877), vol. 2 (New York: Dover, 1963) pp. 197–9, 2 vols.

Coleridge, Samuel Taylor, *Coleridge on Shakespeare*, ed. Terence Hawkes (1959) (Harmondsworth: Penguin, 1969).

Cooper, Joel and Aronson, Joshua M., "Attitudes and Consistency Theories: Implications for Mental Health," *The Social Psychology of Mental Health: Basic Mechanisms and Applications*, ed. Diane N. Ruble, Philip R. Costanzo, and Mary Ellen Oliveri (New York: Guilford, 1992) pp. 279–300.

Cooper, Joel and Fazio, Russell H., "A New Look at Dissonance Theory," *Advances in Experimental Social Psychology*, 17 (1984): 229–66.

Cornford, Francis, trans. and ed., *The Republic of Plato* (New York: Oxford University Press, 1945).

Crawford, Helen J. and Gruzelier, John H., "A Midstream View of the Neuropsychophysiology of Hypnosis: Recent Research and Future Directions," *Contemporary Hypnosis Research*, ed. Erika Fromm and Michael R. Nash (New York: Guilford, 1992) pp. 227–66.

Cruttwell, Patrick, "The Morality of Hamlet – 'Sweet Prince' or 'Arrant Knave'?," *Hamlet*, ed. John Russell Brown and Bernard Harris (Stratford-upon-Avon Studies 5, London: Arnold, 1963), pp. 110–28.

Curry, Walter Clyde, "Macbeth's Changing Character," *Journal of English and Germanic Philology*, 35 (1935): 311–38.

Cushman, Philip, "The Self Besieged: Recruitment–Indoctrination Processes in Restrictive Groups," *Journal for the Theory of Social Behaviour* 16 (1986): 1–32.

Danson, Lawrence, *Tragic Alphabet: Shakespeare's Drama of Language* (New Haven: Yale University Press, 1974).

Davies, John, "Microcosmos," *The Complete Works of John Davies of Hereford*, ed. Alexander B. Grosart (1878), vol. 1 (New York: AMS, 1967) pp. 23–88, 2 vols.

Davis, Lloyd, *Guise and Disguise: Rhetoric and Characterization in the English Renaissance* (Toronto: University of Toronto Press, 1993).

Davis, Natalie Zemon, "Boundaries and the Sense of Self in Sixteenth-Century France," *Reconstructing Individualism: Autonomy, Individuality, and the Self in Western Thought*, ed. Thomas C. Heller, Morton Sosna, and David E. Wellbery (Stanford: Stanford University Press, 1986) pp. 53–63.

Dawson, Anthony B., "The Impasse over the Stage," *English Literary Renaissance*, 21 (1991): 309–27.

DeLevita, David J., *The Concept of Identity*, trans. Ian Finlay (The Hague: Mouton; New York: Basic, 1965).

Della Casa, Iohn, *A Treatise of the Maners and Behaviours*, trans. Robert Peterson (1576) (The English Experience 120, Amsterdam: Theatrum; New York: Da Capo, 1969).

Demos, Raphael, *The Philosophy of Plato* (1939) (New York: Octagon, 1966).

Desmet, Christy, *Reading Shakespeare's Characters: Rhetoric, Ethics, and Identity*, ed. Arthur F. Kinney (Massachusetts Studies in Early Modern Culture, Amherst: University of Massachusetts Press, 1992).

Dewey, John, *Human Nature and Conduct: An Introduction to Social Psychology* (New York: Holt, 1922).

Diderot, Denis, *The Paradox of Acting. The Paradox of Acting*, by Denis Diderot and *Masks or Faces?*, by William Archer (New York: Hill, 1957) pp. 11–71.

Doherty, Kevin and Schlenker, Barry R., "Self-Consciousness and Strategic Self-Presentation," *Journal of Personality*, 59 (1991): 1–18.

Dollimore, Jonathon, *Radical Tragedy: Religion, Ideology and Power in the Drama of Shakespeare and His Contemporaries*, 2nd ed. (Durham: Duke University Press, 1993).

Donahue, Eileen M., Robins, Richard W., Roberts, Brent W., and John, Oliver P., "The Divided Self: Concurrent and Longitudinal Effects of Psychological Adjustment and Social Roles on Self-Concept Differentiation," *Journal of Personality and Social Psychology*, 64 (1993): 834–46.

Donawerth, Jane L., "Shakespeare and Acting Theory in the English Renaissance," *Shakespeare and the Arts: A Collection of Essays from the Ohio Shakespeare Conference (5th) 1981: Wright State University*, ed. Cecile Williamson Carey and Henry S. Limouze (Washington: University Press of America, 1982) pp. 165–78.

Donne, John., *Biathanatos* (London, 1644) (The Literature of Death and Dying, New York: Arno, 1977).

Dougan, James D., "Reinforcement in the Sixteenth Century: Was the Bard a Behaviorist?," *The Behavior Analyst*, 10.2 (1987): 189–96.

Downer, Alan S., "Prolegomenon to a Study of Elizabethan Acting," *Maske und Kothurn*, 10 (1964): 625–36.

Draper, John W., *The Humors and Shakespeare's Characters* (Durham: Duke University Press, 1945).

Dreher, Diane Elizabeth, *Domination and Defiance: Fathers and Daughters in Shakespeare* (Lexington: University Press of Kentucky, 1986).

Driscoll, James P. *Identity in Shakespearean Drama* (Lewisburg, PA: Bucknell University Press, 1983).

Dusinberre, Juliet, *Shakespeare and the Nature of Women* (New York: Barnes; London: Macmillan, 1975).

Dyke, Daniel, *The Mystery of Selfe-Deceiving: or, A Discourse and Discovery of the Deceitfulnesse of Mans Heart* (London, 1633).

Eagleton, Terence, *Shakespeare and Society: Critical Studies in Shakespearean Drama* (New York: Schocken, 1967).

Eagleton, Terry, *William Shakespeare* (Oxford: Blackwell, 1986).

Eagly, Alice H. and Chaiken, Shelly, *The Psychology of Attitudes* (Fort Worth: Harcourt, 1993).

Eden, Kathy, *Poetic and Legal Fiction in the Aristotelian Tradition* (Princeton: Princeton University Press, 1986).

Edinger, Harry G., Introduction, *De Officiis / On Duties*, by Cicero (The Library of Liberal Arts, Indianapolis: Bobbs, 1974) pp. ix–xxix.

Edwards, Philip, "Person and Office in Shakespeare's Plays," *Proceedings of the British Academy*, 56 (1970): 93–109.

Egan, Robert, *Drama Within Drama: Shakespeare's Sense of His Art in* King Lear, The Winter's Tale, *and* The Tempest (New York: Columbia University Press, 1975).

Ekman, Paul, "Facial Expressions of Emotion: an Old Controversy and New Findings," *Processing the Facial Image*, ed. V. Bruce, A. Cowey, A. W. Ellis, and D. I. Perrett (Oxford: Clarendon, 1992) pp. 63–9.

Ekman, Paul and O'Sullivan, Maureen, "Facial Expression: Methods, Means, and Moues," *Fundamentals of Nonverbal Behavior*, ed. Robert S. Feldman and Bernard Rimé (Studies in Emotion and Social Interaction, Cambridge: Cambridge University Press; Paris: Maison des Sciences de l'Homme, 1991) pp. 163–99.

Elam, Keir, *Shakespeare's Universe of Discourse: Language-Games in the Comedies* (Cambridge: Cambridge University Press, 1984).

Ellis, M. J., *Why People Play* (Englewood Cliffs, NJ: Prentice, 1973).

Ellrodt, Robert, "Self-Consciousness in Montaigne and Shakespeare," *Shakespeare Survey*, 28 (1975): 37–50.

Elyot, Sir Thomas, *The Book Named the Governor*, ed. S. E. Lehmberg (London: Dent; New York: Dutton, 1962).

Elyot, Sir Thomas, *The Castel of Helth* (1541) (New York: Scholars' Facsimiles and Reprints, n.d.).

Elyot, Sir Thomas, trans. *The Education or Bringing up of Children*, by Plutarch (The English Experience 184, New York: Da Capo; Amsterdam: Theatrum, 1969).

Epictetus, *Epictetus: Discourses and Enchiridion*, trans. Thomas W. Higginson (New York: Black, 1944).

Erasmus, Desiderius, *De Pueris . . . Instituendis* (1529). *Desiderius Erasmus Concerning the Aim and Method of Education*, trans. William Harrison Woodward (Cambridge: Cambridge University Press, 1904).

Erasmus, Desiderius, *The Education of a Christian Prince*, trans. Lester K. Born (Records of Civilization: Sources and Studies 27, New York: Columbia University Press, 1936).

Erasmus, Desiderius, *The Enchiridion of Erasmus*, trans. and ed. Raymond Himelick (Bloomington: Indiana University Press, 1963).

Erasmus, Desiderius, *On the Freedom of the Will. Luther and Erasmus: Free Will and Salvation*, trans. and ed. E. Gordon Rupp and A. N. Marlow (The Library of Christian Classics 17, Philadelphia: Westminster; London: SCM, 1969) pp. 35–97.

Erickson, Peter B., "'The Fault / My Father Made': The Anxious Pursuit of Heroic Fame in Shakespeare's *Henry V*," *Modern Language Studies*, 10.1 (1979–80): 10–25.

Erickson, Peter B., *Patriarchal Structures in Shakespeare's Drama* (Berkeley: University of California Press, 1985).

Erikson, Erik H., *Childhood and Society*, 2nd ed. (New York: Norton, 1963).

Erikson, Erik H., *Identity: Youth and Crisis* (New York: Norton, 1968).

Esper, Erwin A., *A History of Psychology* (Philadelphia: Saunders, 1964).

Evans, Malcolm, *Signifying Nothing: Truth's True Contents in Shakespeare's Text* (Athens: University of Georgia Press, 1986).

Evreinoff, Nicolas, *The Theatre in Life*, ed. and trans. Alex I. Nazaroff (New York: Brentano's, 1927).

Ewing, Katherine P., "The Illusion of Wholeness: Culture, Self, and the Experience of Inconsistency," *Ethos*, 18 (1990): 251–78.

Faas, Ekbert, *Shakespeare's Poetics* (Cambridge: Cambridge University Press, 1986).

Farrell, Kirby, *Shakespeare's Creation: The Language of Magic and Play* (Amherst: University of Massachusetts Press, 1975).

Fazio, Russell H., "Multiple Processes by Which Attitudes Guide Behavior: The MODE Model as an Integrative Framework," *Advances in Experimental Social Psychology*, 23 (1990): 75–109.

Fazio, Russell H. and Cooper, Joel, "Arousal in the Dissonance Process," *Social Psychophysiology: A Sourcebook*, ed. John T. Cacioppo and Richard E. Petty (New York: Guilford, 1983) pp. 122–52.

Fazio, Russell H., Effrein, Edwin A., and Falender, Victoria J., "Self-Perceptions Following Social Interaction," *Journal of Personality and Social Psychology*, 41 (1981): 232–42.

Felperin, Howard, *Shakespearean Representation: Mimesis and Modernity in Elizabethan Tragedy* (Princeton: Princeton University Press, 1977).

Fenigstein, Allan, "Self-Consciousness, Self-Attention, and Social Interaction," *Journal of Personality and Social Psychology*, 37 (1979): 75–86.

Ferry, Anne, *The "Inward" Language: Sonnets of Wyatt, Sidney, Shakespeare, Donne* (Chicago: University of Chicago Press, 1983).

Festinger, Leon and Carlsmith, J. Merrill, "Cognitive Consequences of Forced Compliance," *Journal of Abnormal and Social Psychology*, 58 (1959): 203–10.

Ficino, Marsilio, *Five Questions Concerning the Mind*, trans. Josephine L. Burroughs. *The Renaissance Philosophy of Man*, ed. Ernst Cassirer, Paul O. Kristeller, and John H. Randall, Jr (Chicago: University of Chicago Press, 1948) pp. 193–212.

Flecknoe, Richard, "A Short Discourse of the English Stage," *Critical Essays of the Seventeenth Century*, ed. Joel E. Spingarn (1908), vol. 2 (Bloomington: Indiana University Press, 1957) pp. 91–96, 3 vols.

Ford, John, *Perkin Warbeck*, ed. Donald K. Anderson (Regents Renaissance Drama Series, Lincoln: University of Nebraska Press, 1965).

Forker, Charles, R., *Fancy's Images: Contexts, Settings, and Perspectives in Shakespeare and His Contemporaries* (Carbondale: Southern Illinois University Press, 1990).

Forker, Charles, R., "Sexuality and Eroticism on the Renaissance Stage," *South Central Review*, 7.4 (1990): 1–22.

Forsyth, Donelson R. and Nye, Judith L., "Personal Moral Philosophies and Moral Choice," *Journal of Research in Personality*, 24 (1990): 398–414.

Foucault, Michel, *The Order of Things: An Archaeology of the Human Sciences* (World of Man: A Library of Theory and Research in the Human Sciences, London: Tavistock, 1970).

Fowler, Keith, "Hypnotic Transformation – Three Studies of Theatrical Role-Playing: A Brief Communication," *International Journal of Clinical and Experimental Hypnosis*, 36 (1988): 249–55.

Frank, Mark G. and Gilovich, Thomas, "The Dark Side of Self- and Social Perception: Black Uniforms and Aggression in Professional Sports," *Journal of Personality and Social Psychology*, 54 (1988): 74–85.

Frattaroli, Elio J., "On the Validity of Treating Shakespeare's Characters as if They Were Real People," *Psychoanalysis and Contemporary Thought*, 10 (1987): 407–37.

Freed, Donald, *Freud and Stanislavsky: New Directions in the Performing Arts* (New York: Vantage, 1964).

Freedman, Barbara, *Staging the Gaze: Postmodernism, Psychoanalysis, and Shakespearean Comedy* (Ithaca: Cornell University Press, 1991).

Friedman, Donald, "Bottom, Burbage, and the Birth of Tragedy," *Reconsidering the Renaissance: Papers from the Twenty-First Annual Conference*, ed. Mario A. Di Cesare (Medieval and Renaissance Texts and Studies 93, Binghamton: Medieval and Renaissance Texts and Studies, 1992) pp. 315–26.

Frye, Northrop, "The Stage is All the World," *Northrop Frye: Myth and Metaphor. Selected Essays, 1974–1988*, ed. Robert D. Denham (Charlottesville: University Press of Virginia, 1990) pp. 196–211.

Fuchs, Oswald, *The Psychology of Habit According to William Ockham* (St Bonaventura, NY: Franciscan Institute, 1952).

Furth, H. G. and Kane, S. R., "Children Constructing Society: A New Perspective on Children at Play," *Chilhood Social Development: Contemporary Perspectives*, ed. Harry McGurk (Hove: Erlbaum, 1992) pp. 149–73.

Gallagher, Lowell, *Medusa's Gaze: Casuistry and Conscience in the Renaissance* (Stanford: Stanford University Press, 1991).

Gamble, Giles Y., "The Theme of Confinement in *Henry IV, Part 1*," unpublished essay (1978).

Garber, Marjorie, *Coming of Age in Shakespeare* (London: Methuen, 1981).

Garber, Marjorie, *Dream in Shakespeare: From Metaphor to Metamorphosis* (New Haven: Yale University Press, 1974).

Garber, Marjorie, *Vested Interests: Cross-Dressing and Cultural Anxiety* (New York: Routledge, 1992).

Gardiner, Judith Kegan, "Kohut's Self Psychology as Feminist Theory," *The Book of The Self*, ed. Polly Young-Eisendrath and James A. Hall (New York: New York University Press, 1987) pp. 225–48.

Geertz, Clifford, "Blurred Genres: The Refiguration of Social Thought," *American Scholar*, 49 (1980): 165–79.

Geis, Florence L. and Christie, Richard, "Overview of Experimental Research," *Studies in Machiavellianism*, ed. R. Christie and F. L. Geis (New York: Academic, 1970) pp. 285–313.

Gergen, Kenneth J., *The Concept of Self* (New York: Holt, 1971).

Gergen, Kenneth J., "Theory of the Self: Impasse and Evolution," *Advances in Experimental Social Psychology*, 17 (1984): 49–115.

Gibson, Janice T., "Training People to Inflict Pain: State Terror and Social Learning," *Journal of Humanistic Psychology*, 31.2 (1991): 72–87.

Gilovich, Thomas, *How We Know What Isn't So: The Fallibility of Human Reason in Everyday Life* (New York: Free; Toronto: Maxwell Macmillan, 1991).

Girodo, Michel, "Health and Legal Issues in Undercover Narcotics Investigations: Misrepresented Evidence," *Behavioral Sciences and the Law*, 3 (1985): 299–308.

Glisky, Martha L., Tataryn, Douglas J., Tobias, Betsy A., Kihlstrom, John F., and McConkey, Kevin M., "Absorption, Openness to Experience, and Hypnotizability," *Journal of Personality and Social Psychology*, 60 (1991): 263–72.

Goffman, Erving, *Encounters: Two Studies in the Sociology of Interaction* (Advanced Studies in Sociology 1, Indianapolis: Bobbs, 1961).

Goffman, Erving, *Frame Analysis: An Essay on the Organization of Experience* (New York: Colophon-Harper, 1974).

Goffman, Erving, *The Presentation of Self in Everyday Life* (Garden City, NY: Anchor-Doubleday, 1959).

Goldberg, Jonathan, *Voice Terminal Echo: Postmodernism and English Renaissance Texts* (New York: Methuen, 1986).

Goldman, Michael, *Acting and Action in Shakespearean Tragedy* (Princeton: Princeton University Press, 1985).

Goldman, Michael, *The Actor's Freedom: Toward A Theory of Drama* (New York: Viking; Toronto: Macmillan, 1975).

Goldman, Michael, "*Hamlet*: Entering the Text," *Theatre Journal*, 44 (1992): 449–60.

Goldman, Michael, *Shakespeare and the Energies of Drama* (Princeton: Princeton University Press, 1972).

Gopnik, Alison, "How We Know Our Minds: The Illusion of First-Person Knowledge of Intentionality," *Behavioral and Brain Sciences*, 16 (1993): 1–14.

Gorassini, Donald, Sowerby, David, Creighton, Andrew, and Frye, Gregory, "Hypnotic Suggestibility Enhancement Through Brief Cognitive Skill Training," *Journal of Personality and Social Psychology*, 61 (1991): 289–97.

Gorfain, Phyllis, "Toward a Theory of Play and the Carnivalesque in *Hamlet*," *Hamlet Studies*, 13 (1991): 25–49.

Gottschalk, Paul A., "Hamlet and the Scanning of Revenge," *Shakespeare Quarterly*, 24 (1973): 155–69.

Grainger, Roger, *Drama and Healing: The Roots of Drama Therapy* (London: Kingsley, 1990).

Granville-Barker, Harley, *Prefaces to Shakespeare*, vol. 1 (Princeton: Princeton University Press, 1947) 2 vols.

G[reen], I[ohn], *A Refutation of the Apology for Actors* (1615), *An Apology for Actors* [and] *A Refutation of The Apology for Actors* (New York: Scholars' Facsimiles, 1941).

Greenblatt, Stephen, "The Circulation of Social Energy," *Shakespearean Negotiations: The Circulation of Social Energy in Renaissance England* (The New Historicism: Studies in Cultural Poetics, Berkeley: University of California Press, 1988) pp. 1–20.

Greenblatt, Stephen, "Fiction and Friction," *Reconstructing Individualism: Autonomy, Individuality, and the Self in Western Thought*, ed. Thomas C. Heller, Morton Sosna, and David E. Wellbery (Stanford: Stanford University Press, 1986) pp. 30–52.

Greenblatt, Stephen, "Invisible Bullets: Renaissance Authority and Its Subversion, *Henry IV* and *Henry V*," *Political Shakespeare: New Essays in Cultural Materialism*, ed. Jonathon Dollimore and Alan Sinfield (Ithaca: Cornell University Press, 1985) pp. 18–47.

Greenblatt, Stephen, "Psychoanalysis and Renaissance Culture," *Literary Theory/Renaissance Texts*, ed. Patricia Parker and David Quint (Baltimore: Johns Hopkins University Press, 1986) pp. 210–24.

Greenblatt, Stephen, *Renaissance Self-Fashioning: From More to Shakespeare* (Chicago: University of Chicago Press, 1980).

Greene, Thomas, "The Flexibility of the Self in Renaissance Literature," *The Disciplines of Criticism*, ed. Peter Demetz, Thomas Greene, and Lowry Nelson, Jr (New Haven: Yale University Press, 1968) pp. 241–64.

Greene, Thomas, "The Postures of Hamlet," *Shakespeare Quarterly*, 11 (1960): 357–66.

Grene, David, *The Actor in History: A Study in Shakespearean Stage Poetry* (University Park: Pennsylvania State University Press, 1988).

Greville, Fulke, "An Inquisition upon Fame and Honour," *Poems and Dramas of Fulke Greville*, ed. Geoffrey Bullough, vol. 1 (New York: Oxford University Press, 1945) pp. 192–213, 2 vols.

Greville, Fulke, "A Treatie of Humane Learning," *Poems and Dramas of Fulke Greville*, ed. Geoffrey Bullough, vol. 1 (New York: Oxford University Press, 1945) pp. 154–91, 2 vols.

Guazzo, Steeven, *The Civile Conversation of M. Steeven Guazzo*, trans. George Pettie and Bartholomew Young, ed. Sir Edward Sullivan (New York: Knopf; London: Constable, 1925) 2 vols.

Gurr, Andrew, *Playgoing in Shakespeare's London* (Cambridge: Cambridge University Press, 1987).

Gurr, Andrew, *The Shakespearean Stage, 1574–1642*, 3rd ed. (Cambridge: Cambridge University Press, 1992).

Haight, M. R., *A Study of Self-Deception* (Sussex: Harvester; Atlantic Highlands, NJ: Humanities, 1980).

Haley, David, *Shakespeare's Courtly Mirror: Reflexivity and Prudence in* All's Well That Ends Well (Newark: University of Delaware Press; London: Associated University Presses, 1993).

Hall, Joan Lord, *The Dynamics of Role-Playing in Jacobean Tragedy* (New York: St Martins, 1991).

Hall, Peter, "Mr. Peter Hall on Speaking Shakespeare," London *Times*, 22 December 1958: 5. Rpt. in *Directors on Directing: A Source Book of the Modern Theater*, ed. Toby Cole and Helen Krich Chinoy, rev. ed. (New York: Bobbs, 1963) pp. 423–5.

Hammond, Jacqueline and Edelmann, Robert J., "Double Identity: The Effect of the Acting Process on the Self-Perception of Professional Actors – Two Case Illustrations," *Psychology and Performing Arts*, ed. Glenn D. Wilson (Amsterdam: Swets and Zeitlinger, 1991) pp. 25–44.

Hampton, Timothy, *Writing from History: The Rhetoric of Exemplarity in Renaissance Literature* (Ithaca: Cornell University Press, 1990).

Hankins, John Erskine, *The Character of Hamlet* (1941) (Library of Shakespearean Biography and Criticism. Freeport, NY: Books for Libraries, 1971).

Harbage, Alfred, *Theatre for Shakespeare* (Toronto: University of Toronto Press, 1955).

Hardie, W. F. R., *Aristotle's Ethical Theory* (Oxford: Clarendon, 1968).

Hardison, O. B., Jr, *Prosody and Purpose in the English Renaissance* (Baltimore: Johns Hopkins University Press, 1989).

Hare-Mustin, Rachel T. and Maracek, Jeanne, "The Meaning of Difference: Gender Theory, Postmodernism, and Psychology," *Seldom Seen, Rarely Heard: Women's Place in Psychology*, ed. Janis S. Bohan (Psychology, Gender, and Theory; Boulder, Col.: Westview, 1992) pp. 227–49.

Harré, Rom, *Social Being: A Theory of Social Psychology* (Totowa, NJ: Littlefield, 1980).

Hart, Jonathan, *Theater and World: The Problematics of Shakespeare's History* (Boston: Northeastern University Press, 1992).

Harvey, John H. and Weary, Gifford, "Current Issues in Attribution Theory and Research," *Annual Review of Psychology*, 35 (1984): 427–59.

Hazlitt, William, *Characters of Shakespear's Plays. The Round Table* [and] *Characters of Shakespear's Plays* (London: Dent; New York: Dutton, 1936) pp. 171–361.

Hedrick, Donald K., "'It is No Novelty for a Prince to be a Prince': An Enantiomorphous Hamlet," *Shakespeare Quarterly*, 35 (1984): 62–76.

Heise, Ursula K., "Transvestism and the Stage Controversy in Spain and England, 1580–1680," *Theatre Journal*, 44 (1992): 357–74.

Hernadi, Paul, *Interpreting Events: Tragicomedies of History on the Modern Stage* (Ithaca: Cornell University Press, 1985).

Herron, R. E. and Sutton-Smith, Brian, Introduction to "Comparative Approaches," *Child's Play*, ed. R. E. Herron and B. Sutton-Smith (New York: Wiley, 1971) pp. 185–95.

Herron, R. E. and Sutton-Smith, Brian, Introduction to "Theoretical Overviews," *Child's Play*, ed. R. E. Herron and B. Sutton-Smith (New York: Wiley, 1971) pp. 309–10.

Heywood, Thomas, *An Apology for Actors*. 1612. *An Apology for Actors* [and] *A Refutation of the Apology for Actors* (New York: Scholars' Facsimiles, 1941).

Hilgard, Ernest R., "Dissociation and Theories of Hypnosis," *Contemporary Hypnosis Research*, ed. Erika Fromm and Michael R. Nash (New York: Guilford, 1992) pp. 69–101.

Hilgard, Josephine R., "Imaginative and Sensory-Affective Involvements: In Everyday Life and Hypnosis," *Hypnosis: Developments in Research and New Perspectives*, ed. Erika Fromm and Ronald E. Shor, new and rev. 2nd ed. (New York: Aldine, 1979) pp. 483–517.

Holland, Peter, "*Hamlet* and the Art of Acting," *Drama and the Actor*, ed. James Redmond (Themes in Drama 6. Cambridge: Cambridge University Press, 1984) pp. 39–61.

Holt, Robert R., "Forcible Indoctrination and Personality Change," *Personality Change*, ed. Philip Worchel and Don Byrne (New York: Wiley, 1964) pp. 289–318.

Hooker, Richard, *Of the Laws of Ecclesiastical Polity*, 4 vols to date, vol. 1, ed. Georges Edelen; vol. 2, ed. W. Speed Hill (The Folger Library Edition of the Works of Richard Hooker, Cambridge: Belknap–Harvard University Press, 1977–).

Hornby, Richard, *Drama, Metadrama, and Perception* (Lewisburg, PA: Bucknell University Press; London: Associated University Presses, 1986).

Howard, Jean E., "Crossdressing, the Theatre, and Gender Struggle in Early Modern England," *Shakespeare Quarterly*, 39 (1988): 418–40.

Hoy, Cyrus, ed., *Hamlet*, by William Shakespeare (Norton Critical Edition, New York: Norton, 1963).

Huarte, Juan, *The Examination of Mens Wits*, trans. Richard Carew (1594) (Gainesville, FL: Scholars' Facsimiles, 1959).

Hubert, Judd D., *Metatheater: The Example of Shakespeare* (Lincoln: University of Nebraska Press, 1991).

Hudson, Liam, "The Traffic in Selves," *Times Literary Supplement*, 24 January 1975: 77–8.

Hyde, Thomas, "Identity and Acting in Elizabethan Tragedy," *Renaissance Drama*, 15 (1984): 93–114.

Iser, Wolfgang, *The Act of Reading: A Theory of Aesthetic Response* (Baltimore: Johns Hopkins University Press, 1980).

Iser, Wolfgang, "The Dramatization of Double Meaning in Shakespeare's *As You Like It*," *Theatre Journal*, 35 (1983): 307–32.

Iser, Wolfgang, "Representation: A Performative Act," *The Aims of Representation:*

Subject/Text/History, ed. Murray Krieger (Irvine Studies in the Humanities, New York: Columbia University Press, 1987) pp. 217–32.

Jacklin, Carol Nagy, "Female and Male: Issues of Gender," *American Psychologist*, 44 (1989): 127–33.

James, William, *The Principles of Psychology* (New York, 1890) 2 vols.

Janis, Irving L., "Stages in the Decision-Making Process," *Theories of Cognitive Consistency: A Sourcebook*, ed. Robert P. Abelson, Elliot Aronson, William J. McGuire, Theodore M. Newcomb, Milton J. Rosenberg, and Percy H. Tannenbaum (Chicago: Rand, 1968) pp. 577–88.

Jardine, Lisa, *Still Harping on Daughters: Women and Drama in the Age of Shakespeare* (Brighton: Harvester; Totowa, NJ: Barnes, 1983).

Jenkins, Harold, "Longer Notes," *Hamlet*, by William Shakespeare (London: Methuen, 1982) pp. 421–571.

Joachim, H. H., *Aristotle: The Nicomachean Ethics*, ed. D. A. Rees (Oxford: Clarendon, 1951).

John of Salisbury, *Frivolities of Courtiers . . . a Translation of . . . Selections from . . . Policraticus . . .*, trans. Joseph B. Pike (Minneapolis: University of Minnesota Press; London: Milford, Oxford University Press, 1938).

Johnson, David Read, "The Theory and Technique of Transformations in Drama Therapy," *The Arts in Psychotherapy*, 18 (1991): 285–300.

Johnstone, Keith, Interview. "Acting: Possession, Trance, Hypnosis and Related States," with Zina Barnieh, *Discussions in Developmental Drama*, 4 (1973): 3–8.

Jones, Edward E., Brenner, Kenneth J., and Knight, John G., "When Failure Elevates Self-Esteem," *Personality and Social Psychology Bulletin*, 16 (1990): 200–9.

Jones-Davies, M. T., "'The Players . . . Will Tell All,' or the Actor's Role in Renaissance Drama," *Shakespeare, Man of the Theater*, ed. Kenneth Muir, Jay L. Halio, and D. J. Palmer (Newark: University of Delaware Press; London: Associated University Presses, 1983) pp. 76–85.

Jonson, Ben, *Timber: Or Discoveries. Ben Jonson*, ed. C. H. Herford, Percy Simpson, and Evelyn Simpson, vol. 8 (Oxford: Clarendon, 1947) pp. 561–649, 11 vols, 1925–52.

Jordan, Constance, *Renaissance Feminism: Literary Texts and Political Models* (Ithaca: Cornell University Press, 1990).

Joseph, Bertram L., *Acting Shakespeare*, 2nd ed. (New York: Theatre Arts, 1969).

Joseph, Bertram L., *Elizabethan Acting*, 2nd ed. (Oxford: Clarendon, 1964).

Joseph, Miriam, *Shakespeare's Use of the Arts of Language* (New York: Hafner, 1966).

Kahn, Coppélia, *Man's Estate: Masculine Identity in Shakespeare* (Berkeley: University of California Press, 1981).

Kastan, David Scott, "'His Semblable is His Mirror': *Hamlet* and the Imitation of Revenge," *Shakespeare Studies*, 19 (1987): 111–24.

Keble, John, ed., *The Works of Richard Hooker*, 2 vols (New York, 1849).

Kelly, George A., *The Psychology of Personal Constructs*, vol. 1 (New York: Norton, 1955), 2 vols.

Kelly, Katherine E., "The Queen's Two Bodies: Shakespeare's Boy Actress in Breeches," *Theatre Journal*, 42.1 (1990): 81–93.

Kelsey, R. Bruce, "The Actor's Representation: Gesture, Play, and Language," *Philosophy and Literature*, 8 (1984): 67–74.

Kernan, Alvin B., "The Henriad: Shakespeare's Major History Plays," *Modern Shakespearean Criticism: Essays on Style, Dramaturgy, and the Major Plays*, ed. Alvin B. Kernan (New York: Harcourt, 1970) pp. 245–75.

Kernan, Alvin B., *The Playwright as Magician: Shakespeare's Image of the Poet in the English Public Theater* (New Haven: Yale University Press, 1979).

Kimbrough, Robert, *Shakespeare and the Art of Humankindness: The Essay Toward Androgyny* (Atlantic Highlands, NJ: Humanities Press International, 1990).

Kipper, David A., *Psychotherapy Through Clinical Role Playing* (New York: Brunner / Mazel, 1986).

Kirby, E. T., *Ur-Drama: The Origins of Theatre* (New York: New York University Press, 1975).

Kirsch, Arthur, *The Passions of Shakespeare's Tragic Heroes* (Charlottesville: University Press of Virginia, 1990).

Kirsch, Irving and Council, James R., "Situational and Personality Correlates of Hypnotic Responsiveness," *Contemporary Hypnosis Research*, ed. Erika Fromm and Michael R. Nash (New York: Guilford, 1992) pp. 267–91.

Kjerbühl-Petersen, Lorenz, *Psychology of Acting*, trans. Sarah T. Barrows (Boston: Expression, 1935).

Kleinke, Chris L., *Self-Perception: The Psychology of Personal Awareness* (Books in Psychology, San Francisco: Freeman, 1978).

Kleinke, Chris L., "Two Models for Conceptualizing the Attitude–Behavior Relationship," *Human Relations*, 37 (1984): 333–50.

Knapp, John V., "Introduction: Self-Preservation and Self-Transformation: Interdisciplinary Approaches to Literary Character," *Literary Character*, ed. John V. Knapp (Lanham, MD: University Press of America, 1993) pp. 1–16.

Knapp, Robert S., *Shakespeare – The Theater and the Book* (Princeton: Princeton University Press, 1989).

Kochnev, V. I., "The Stage Emotional Experience: Attempt at the Solution to the Problem," *Soviet Journal of Psychology*, 11 (1990): 56–69.

Koestner, Richard, Bernieri, Frank, and Zuckerman, Miron, "Self-Regulation and Consistency Between Attitudes, Traits and Behaviors," *Personality and Social Psychology Bulletin*, 18 (1992) pp. 52–9.

Kohlberg, Lawrence, "Stage and Sequence: The Cognitive-Developmental Approach to Socialization," *Handbook of Socialization Theory and Research*, ed. David A. Goslin (Rand McNally Sociology Series, Chicago: Rand, 1969) pp. 347–480.

Konečni, Vladimir J., "Psychological Aspects of the Expression of Anger and Violence on the Stage," *Comparative Drama*, 25 (1991): 215–41.

Kott, Jan, "The Gender of Rosalind," *New Theatre Quarterly*, 7 (1991): 113–25.

Kris, Ernst, "Prince Hal's Conflict," *Psychoanalytic Quarterly*, 17 (1948): 487–506.

Kuhn, Maura Slattery, "Much Virtue in *If*," *Shakespeare Quarterly*, 28 (1977): 40–50.

Kunda, Ziva, "The Case for Motivated Reasoning," *Psychological Bulletin*, 108 (1990): 480–98.

Laing, R. D., *The Divided Self: An Existential Study in Sanity and Madness* (1960) (Harmondsworth: Penguin, 1965).

Laing, R. D., *Self and Others* (1969) (Harmondsworth: Penguin, 1971).

Laird, James D., "The Real Role of Facial Response in the Experience of Emotion: A Reply to Tourangeau and Ellsworth, and Others," *Journal of Personality and Social Psychology*, 47 (1984): 909–17.

Lanham, Richard, *The Motives of Eloquence: Literary Rhetoric in the Renaissance* (New Haven: Yale University Press, 1976).

La Primaudaye, Pierre de, *The French Academie*, [trans. T. B.] (London, 1618).

Lattal, Kennon A. ed., *Reflections on B. F. Skinner and Psychology*, Special Issue, *American Psychologist*, 47 (1992): 1269–533.

Leggatt, Alexander, *Shakespeare's Political Drama: The History Plays and the Roman Plays* (London: Routledge, 1988).

Leventhal, Howard and Mosbach, Peter A., "The Perceptual-Motor Theory of

Emotion," *Social Psychophysiology: A Sourcebook*, ed. John T. Cacioppo and Richard E. Petty (New York: Guilford, 1983) pp. 353–88.

Levin, Harry, *The Question of Hamlet* (New York: Oxford University Press, 1959).

Levin, Richard, "The Relation of External Evidence to the Allegorical and Thematic Interpretation of Shakespeare," *Shakespeare Studies*, 13 (1980): 1–29.

Levine, Laura, "Men in Women's Clothing: Anti-Theatricality and Effeminization from 1579 to 1642," *Criticism*, 28 (1986): 121–43.

Libet, Benjamin, "Unconscious Cerebral Initiative and the Role of Conscious Will in Voluntary Action," *The Behavioral and Brain Sciences*, 8 (1985): 529–66.

Lieberman, Seymour, "The Effects of Changes in Roles on the Attitudes of Role Occupants," *Human Relations*, 9 (1956): 385–402.

Lifson, Martha Ronk, "Learning by Talking: Conversation in 'As You Like It,'" *Shakespeare Survey*, 40 (1987): 91–105.

Lifton, Robert Jay, *Thought Reform and the Psychology of Totalism: A Study of 'Brainwashing' in China* (New York: Norton, 1961).

Lindzey, Gardner and Aronson, Elliot, ed., *The Handbook of Social Psychology*, 3rd ed, 2 vols (New York: Random, 1985).

Lott, Bernice and Lott, Albert J., "Learning Theory in Contemporary Social Psychology," *The Handbook of Social Psychology*, ed. G. Lindzey and E. Aronson, 3rd ed., vol. 1 (New York: Random, 1985) pp. 109–35, 2 vols.

Lueger, Robert J., "Imagery Techniques in Cognitive Behavior Therapy," *Anthology of Imagery Techniques*, ed. Anees A. Sheikh (Milwaukee: American Imagery Institute, 1986) pp. 61–83.

Luther, Martin, *Martin Luther: Selections from His Writings*, ed. John Dillenberger (Garden City, NY: Doubleday, 1961).

Lyly, John, *Euphues: The Anatomy of Wyt. The Complete Works of John Lyly*, ed. R. Warwick Bond, vol. 1 (Oxford: Clarendon, 1902) pp. 179–326, 3 vols.

Lyman, Stanford M. and Scott, Marvin B., *The Drama of Social Reality* (New York: Oxford University Press, 1975).

Lynn, Steven Jay and Rhue, Judith W., "Fantasy Proneness: Hypnosis, Developmental Antecedents, and Psychopathology," *American Psychologist*, 43 (1988): 35–44.

Lynn, Steven Jay and Sivec, Harry, "The Hypnotizable Subject as Creative Problem-Solving Agent," *Contemporary Hypnosis Research*, ed. Erika Fromm and Michael R. Nash (New York: Guilford, 1992) pp. 292–333.

Maccoby, Eleanor E., "Gender and Relationships: A Developmental Account," *American Psychologist*, 45 (1990): 513–20.

Maccoby, Eleanor E., "The Role of Gender Identity and Gender Constancy in Sex-Differentiated Development," *New Directions for Child Development*, 47 (1990): 5–20.

Maccoby, Eleanor Emmons and Jacklin, Carol Nagy, *The Psychology of Sex Differences* (Stanford: Stanford University Press, 1974).

Machiavelli, Niccolo, *Discourses on the First Decade of Titus Livius. Machiavelli: The Chief Works and Others*, trans. Allan Gilbert, vol. 1 (Durham, NC: Duke University Press, 1965) pp. 188–529, 2 vols.

Machiavelli, Niccolo, *The Prince. Machiavelli: The Chief Works and Others*, trans. Allan Gilbert, vol. 1 (Durham, NC: Duke University Press, 1965) pp. 10–96, 2 vols.

Mack, Maynard, "Engagement and Detachment in Shakespeare's Plays," *Essays on Shakespeare and Elizabethan Drama in Honor of Hardin Craig*, ed. Richard Hosley. (Columbia: University of Missouri Press, 1962) pp. 275–96.

Mack, Maynard, "The World of *Hamlet*," *Yale Review*, 41 (1952): 502–23.

Macpherson, James, "Appendix," *Studies in Machiavellianism*, ed. Richard Christie and Florence L. Geis (New York: Academic, 1970) pp. 388–99.

Macrone, Michael, "The Theatrical Self in Renaissance England," *Qui Parle: Journal of Literary Studies*, 3 (1989): 72–102.

Magee, Mary Ann, "Social Play as Performance," *Play & Culture*, 2 (1989): 193–6.

Mann, David, *The Elizabethan Player: Contemporary Stage Representation* (London: Routledge, 1991).

Marcus, Leah H., "Shakespeare's Comic Heroines, Elizabeth I, and the Political Uses of Androgyny," *Women in the Middle Ages and the Renaissance: Literary and Historical Perspectives*, ed. Mary Beth Rose (Syracuse: Syracuse University Press, 1986) pp. 135–53.

Marjanovic-Shane, Ana, "'You are a Pig': For Real or Just Pretend? Different Orientations in Play and Metaphor," *Play & Culture*, 2 (1989): 225–34.

Marker, Lise-Lone, "Nature and Decorum in the Theory of Elizabethan Acting," *The Elizabethan Theatre*, 2, ed. David Galloway (Toronto: Macmillan, 1970) pp. 87–107.

Marowitz, Charles, *The Act of Being: Towards a Theory of Acting* (New York: Taplinger, 1978).

Marshall, Cynthia, "Wrestling as Play and Game in *As You Like It*," *Studies in English Literature*, 33 (1993): 264–87.

Marston, John, *Antonio and Mellida, the First Part*, ed. G. K. Hunter (Regents Renaissance Drama Series, Lincoln: University of Nebraska Press, 1965).

Maslow, Abraham, *Toward a Psychology of Being*, 2nd ed. (Princeton: Van Nostrand, 1968).

Maus, Katharine Eisaman, "Proof and Consequences: Inwardness and its Exposure in the English Renaissance," *Representations*, 34 (1991): 29–52.

Mayer, Thomas F. and Amos, Thomas L., "History by Stages: Cognitive Structuralism and the Early Middle Ages," *Annals of Scholarship*, 4.3 (1987): 29–56.

McBroom, William H. and Reed, Fred W., "Toward a Reconceptualization of Attitude–Behavior Consistency," *Social Psychology Quarterly*, 55 (1992): 205–16.

McCall, George J. and Simmons, Jerry L., *Identities and Interactions*, rev. ed. (New York: Free, 1978).

McClure, John, *Explanations, Accounts, and Illusions: A Critical Analysis*, ed. P. Richard Eiser and Klaus R. Scherer (European Monographs in Social Psychology, Cambridge: Cambridge University Press; Paris: Editions de la Maison des Sciences de l'Homme, 1991).

McConkey, Kevin M., "The Construction and Resolution of Experience and Behavior in Hypnosis," *Theories of Hypnosis: Current Models and Perspectives*, ed. Steven J. Lynn and Judith W. Rhue (Guilford Clinical and Experimental Hypnosis Series, New York: Guilford, 1991) pp. 542–63.

McDonald, Charles O., "*Decorum*, *Ethos*, and *Pathos* in the Heroes of Elizabethan Tragedy, with Particular Reference to *Hamlet*," *Journal of English and Germanic Philology*, 61 (1962): 330–48.

McGaw, Charles, *Acting is Believing: A Basic Method*, ed. Gary Blake, 4th ed. (New York: Holt, 1980).

McGuire, William J., "Attitudes and Attitude Change," *The Handbook of Social Psychology*, ed. G. Lindzey and E. Aronson, 3rd ed., vol. 2 (New York: Random, 1985) pp. 233–346, 2 vols.

Mead, George Herbert, *Mind, Self, and Society* (Chicago: University of Chicago Press, 1934).

Mehl, Dieter, "Forms and Functions of the Play within a Play," *Renaissance Drama*, 8 (1965): 41–61.

Miller, Paul J. W., Introduction, *On the Dignity of Man, On Being and the One, Heptaplus*, by Giovanni Pico della Mirandola (The Library of Liberal Arts, Indianapolis: Bobbs, 1965) pp. vii–xxvii.

Miller, Ronald B., ed., *The Restoration of Dialogue: Readings in the Philosophy of Clinical Psychology* (Washington, DC: American Psychological Association, 1992).

Mixon, Don, "A Theory of Actors," *Journal for the Theory of Social Behaviour*, 13 (1983): 97–110.

Moerk, Ernst L., "The Clash of Giants Over Terminological Differences," *Behavior and Social Issues*, 2 (1992): 1–26.

Money, John, *Love and Love-Sickness: The Science of Gender Difference, and Pair-Bonding* (Baltimore: Johns Hopkins University Press, 1980).

Money, John, "Sin, Sickness, or Status? Homosexual Gender Identity and Psychoneuroendocrinology," *Annual Progress in Child Psychiatry and Child Development 1988*, ed. Stella Chess, Alexander Thomas, and Margaret E. Hertzig (New York: Brunner/Mazel, 1989) pp. 41–76.

Money, John and Erhardt, Anke A., *Man and Woman, Boy and Girl: The Differentiation and Dimorphism of Gender Identity from Conception to Maturity* (Baltimore: Johns Hopkins University Press, 1972).

Montaigne, [Michel de], *The Essayes of Michael Lord of Montaigne*, trans. John Florio, 3 vols (London: Dent; New York: Dutton, n.d.).

Montaigne, [Michel de], "An Apologie of Raymond Sebond," 2: 125–326.

Montaigne, [Michel de], "How a Man Should Not Counterfeit to Be Sick," 2: 414–16.

Montaigne, [Michel de], "How One Ought to Governe His Will," 3: 253–77.

Montaigne, [Michel de], "How We Weepe and Laugh at One Selfe-Same Thing," 1: 247–50.

Montaigne, [Michel de], "Of Ancient Customes," 1: 336–41.

Montaigne, [Michel de], "Of the Art of Conferring," 3: 156–83.

Montaigne, [Michel de], "Of the Caniballes," 1: 215–29.

Montaigne, [Michel de], "Of Cato the Younger," 1: 243–7.

Montaigne, [Michel de], "Of Crueltie," 2: 108–25.

Montaigne, [Michel de], "Of Custome, and How a Received Law Should Not Easily Be Changed," 1: 105–23.

Montaigne, [Michel de], "Of Diverting and Diversions," 3: 51–62.

Montaigne, [Michel de], "Of Exercise or Practice," 2: 49–61.

Montaigne, [Michel de], "Of Experience," 3: 322–86.

Montaigne, [Michel de], "Of the Force of Imagination," 1: 92–104.

Montaigne, [Michel de], "Of the Inconstancie of Our Actions," 2: 7–15.

Montaigne, [Michel de], "Of the Institution and Education of Children; to the Ladie Diana of Foix, Countesse of Gurson," 1: 148–90.

Montaigne, [Michel de], "Of the Lame or Crippel," 3: 277–89.

Montaigne, [Michel de], "Of the Liberty of Conscience," 2: 395–9.

Montaigne, [Michel de], "Of a Monstrous Child," 2: 439–40.

Montaigne, [Michel de], "Of Pedantisme," 1: 134–48.

Montaigne, [Michel de], "Of Phisiognomy," 3: 289–322.

Montaigne, [Michel de], "Of Presumption," 2: 355–90.

Montaigne, [Michel de], "Of Readie or Slow Speech," 1: 49–52.

Montaigne, [Michel de], "Of Repenting," 3: 23–37.

Montaigne, [Michel de], "Of Solitarinesse," 1: 250–63.

Montaigne, [Michel de], "Of Sumptuarie Lawes, or Lawes for Moderating of Expences," 1: 305–7.

Montaigne, [Michel de], "Of Three Commerces or Societies," 3: 37–50.

Montaigne, [Michel de], "Of Vanitie," 3: 183–253.

Montaigne, [Michel de], "That the Taste of Goods or Evils Doth Greatly Depend on the Opinion We Have of Them," 1: 269–91.

Montaigne, [Michel de], "Upon Some Verses of Virgil," 3: 62–128.

Montgomery, Robert L. and Haemmerlie, Frances M., "Self-Perception Theory and the Reduction of Heterosocial Anxiety," *Journal of Social and Clinical Psychology*, 4 (1986): 503–12.

Moore, Sonia, *The Stanislavski System: The Professional Training of an Actor*, 2nd rev. ed. (New York: Penguin, 1984).

Morawski, J. G., "The Measurement of Masculinity and Femininity: Engendering Categorical Realities," *Seldom Seen, Rarely Heard: Women's Place in Psychology*, ed. Janis S. Bohan (Psychology, Gender, and Theory, Boulder: Westview, 1992) pp. 199–225.

More, [Sir Thomas], *A Dialogue of Comfort Against Tribulation*. *More's Utopia and A Dialogue of Comfort*, trans. Ralph Robinson, ed. John Warrington, rev. ed. (London: Dent; New York: Dutton, 1951) pp. 143–423.

More, [Sir Thomas], *Utopia*. *More's Utopia and A Dialogue of Comfort*, trans. Ralph Robinson, ed. John Warrington, rev. ed. (London: Dent; New York: Dutton, 1951) pp. 13–142.

Moreno, J[acob] L., Introduction. *Psychodrama*, 1, 3rd ed. (Beacon, NY: Beacon, 1964) pp. i–xxii.

Morin, Gertrude, "Depression and Negative Thinking: A Cognitive Approach to *Hamlet*," *Mosaic*, 25 (1992): 1–12.

Mulcaster, Richard, *Positions*, ed. Robert Hebert Quick (London, 1888).

Mullaney, Steven, *The Place of the Stage: License, Play, and Power in Renaissance England* (Chicago: University of Chicago Press, 1988).

Murray, Peter B., "'Much Virtue in If' in Shakespeare's Comedies," *Library Chronicle*, 32 (1966): 31–9.

Nadon, Robert, Kihlstrom, John F., Hoyt, Irene P. and Register, Patricia A., "Absorption and Hypnotizability: Context Effects Reexamined," *Journal of Personality and Social Psychology*, 60 (1991): 144–53.

Nadon, Robert, Laurence, Jean-Roch, and Perry, Campbell, "Multiple Predictors of Hypnotic Susceptibility," *Journal of Personality and Social Psychology*, 53 (1987): 948–60.

Nardo, Anna K., *The Ludic Self in Seventeenth Century English Literature* (Albany: State University of New York Press, 1991).

Natoli, Joseph and Rusch, Frederick L., comp., *Psychocriticism: An Annotated Bibliography* (Bibliographies and Indexes in World Literature 1, Westport, CT: Greenwood, 1984).

Noland, Richard W., "The Future of Psychological Criticism," *Hartford Studies in Literature*, 5 (1973): 88–105.

Nuttall, A. D., *A New Mimesis: Shakespeare and the Representation of Reality* (London: Methuen, 1983).

O'Donohue, William and Smith, Laurence D., "Philosophical and Psychological Epistemologies in Behaviorism and Behavior Therapy," *Behavior Therapy*, 23 (1992): 173–94.

Olson, James M. and Zanna, Mark P., "Attitudes and Attitude Change," *Annual Review of Psychology*, 44 (1993): 117–54.

Onions, C. T., *A Shakespeare Glossary*, 2nd ed. (Oxford: Clarendon, 1958).

Orne, Martin T., "On the Simulating Subject as a Quasi-Control Group in Hypnosis Research: What, Why, and How," *Hypnosis: Developments in Research and New Perspectives*, ed. Erika Fromm and Ronald E. Shor, 2nd ed. (New York: Aldine, 1979) pp. 519–65.

Ornstein, Robert, *A Kingdom for a Stage: The Achievement of Shakespeare's History Plays* (Cambridge: Harvard University Press, 1972).

Ostwald, Martin, ed. and trans. *Nicomachean Ethics*, by Aristotle (The Library of Liberal Arts. Indianapolis: Bobbs, 1962).

Ovid, *The Loves, The Art of Beauty, The Remedies for Love and the Art of Love*, trans. Rolfe Humphries (Bloomington: Indiana University Press, 1957).

Paglia, Camille, *Sexual Personae: Art and Decadence from Nefertiti to Emily Dickinson* (London: Yale University Press, 1990).

Palingenius, Marcellus, *The Zodiake of Life*, trans. Barnabe Googe (New York: Scholars' Facsimiles, 1947).

Palmer, John, *Political Characters of Shakespeare* (London, Macmillan, 1945).

Paris, Bernard J., *Character as a Subversive Force in Shakespeare: The History and Roman Plays* (Rutherford, NJ: Fairleigh Dickinson University Press; London: Associated University Presses, 1991).

Paris, Bernard J., "Hamlet and His Problems: A Horneyan Analysis," *Centennial Review*, 21 (1977): 36–66.

Parker, M. D. H., *The Slave of Life: A Study of Shakespeare and the Idea of Justice* (London: Chatto, 1955).

Parry, P. H., "The Boyhood of Shakespeare's Heroines," *Shakespeare Survey*, 42 (1990): 99–109.

Parsons, Jacquelynne E., Preface, *The Psychobiology of Sex Differences and Sex Roles*, ed. J. E. Parsons (Washington, DC: Hemisphere; New York: McGraw, 1980) pp. xiii–xv.

Parsons, Jacquelynne E., "Psychosexual Neutrality: Is Anatomy Destiny?," *The Psychobiology of Sex Differences and Sex Roles*, ed. J. E. Parsons (Washington, DC: Hemisphere; New York: McGraw, 1980) pp. 3–29.

Patterson, Annabel, "'The Very Age and Body of the Time His Form and Pressure,'" *Shakespeare and Deconstruction*, ed. G. Douglas Atkins and David M. Bergeron (American University Studies, Series IV: English Language and Literature 57, New York: Lang, 1988) pp. 47–68.

Pekala, Ronald J., Wenger, Cathrine F. and Levine, Ralph L., "Individual Differences in Phenomenological Experience: States of Consciousness as a Function of Absorption," *Journal of Personality and Social Psychology*, 48 (1985): 125–32.

Peller, Lili E., "Models of Children's Play," *Child's Play*, ed. R. E. Herron and Brian Sutton-Smith (New York: Wiley, 1971) pp. 110–25.

Perkins, William, *The Whole Treatise of the Cases of Conscience* (Cambridge, 1606) (The English Experience 482, Amsterdam: Theatrum; New York: Da Capo, 1972).

Petersen, Anne C., "Biopsychosocial Processes in the Development of Sex-Related Differences," *The Psychology of Sex Differences and Sex Roles*, ed. Jacquelynne E. Parsons (Washington: Hemisphere; New York: McGraw, 1980) pp. 31–56.

Petty, Richard E. and Cacioppo, John T., "The Role of Bodily Responses in Attitude Measurement and Change," *Social Psychophysiology: A Sourcebook*, ed. J. T. Cacioppo and R. E. Petty (New York: Guilford, 1983) pp. 51–101.

Philibert de Vienne, *The Philosopher of the Court*, trans. George North (London, 1575).

Piaget, Jean, *Play, Dreams and Imitation in Childhood*, trans. C. Gattegno and F. M. Hodgson (New York: Norton, 1962).

Pico della Mirandola, [Giovanni], "Oration on the Dignity of Man," trans. Charles Glenn Wallis, *On the Dignity of Man, On Being and the One, Heptaplus* (The Library of Liberal Arts, Indianapolis: Bobbs, 1965) pp. 3–34.

Pittman, Thane S., "Perception without Awareness in the Stream of Behavior: Processes that Produce and Limit Nonconscious Biasing Effects," *Perception without Awareness: Cognitive, Clinical, and Social Perspectives*, ed. Robert F. Bornstein and T. S. Pittman (New York: Guilford, 1992) pp. 277–96.

Plato, *The Dialogues of Plato*, trans. B. Jowett, 2 vols (New York: Random, 1937).

Plato, *Gorgias*, 1: 505–87.

Plato, *The Laws*, 2: 407–703.

Plato, *Phaedo*, 1: 441–501.

Plato, *Protagoras*, 1: 81–130.

Plato, *The Republic*, 1: 591–879.

Plutarch, "Can Virtue be Taught?" *Plutarch's Moralia*, vol. 6, trans. W. C. Hembold (The Loeb Classical Library, Cambridge: Harvard University Press; London: Heinemann, 1939) pp. 5–13, 15 vols, 1927–69.

Plutarch, *Cicero*. *Plutarch's Lives*, vol. 7, trans. Bernadotte Perrin (The Loeb Classical Library, Cambridge: Harvard University Press; London: Heinemann, 1919) pp. 83–209, 11 vols, 1914–26.

Plutarch, "Concerning Talkativeness," *Plutarch's Moralia*, vol. 6, trans W. C. Hembold (The Loeb Classical Library, Cambridge: Harvard University Press; London: Heininemann, 1939) pp. 397–467, 15 vols, 1927–69.

Plutarch, "Consolation to His Wife," *Plutarch's Moralia*, vol. 7, trans. Phillip H. DeLacy and Benedict Einarson (The Loeb Classical Library, Cambridge: Harvard University Press; London: Heinemann, 1959) pp. 581–605, 15 vols, 1927–69.

Plutarch, "The Education of Children," *Plutarch's Moralia*, vol. 1, trans. Frank Cole Babbitt (The Loeb Classical Library, Cambridge: Harvard University Press; London: Heinemann, 1927) pp. 5–69, 15 vols, 1927–69.

Plutarch, "Of Curiosity," *Plutarch's "Moralia": Twenty Essays*, trans. Philemon Holland (London: Dent; New York: Dutton, n.d.).

Plutarch, "On Being a Busybody," *Plutarch's Moralia*, vol. 6, trans. W. C. Hembold (The Loeb Classical Library, Cambridge: Harvard University Press; London: Heinemann, 1939) pp. 473–517, 15 vols, 1927–69.

Plutarch, "On Compliancy," *Plutarch's Moralia*, vol. 7, trans. Phillip H. DeLacy and Benedict Einarson (The Loeb Classical Library, Cambridge: Harvard University Press; London: Heinemann, 1959) pp. 47–89, 15 vols, 1927–69.

Plutarch, "On the Control of Anger," *Plutarch's Moralia*, vol. 6, trans. W. C. Hembold (The Loeb Classical Library, Cambridge: Harvard University Press; London: Heinemann, 1939) pp. 93–159, 15 vols, 1927–69.

Plutarch, "On the Delays of the Divine Vengeance," *Plutarch's Moralia*, vol. 7, trans. Phillip H. DeLacy and Benedict Einarson (The Loeb Classical Library, Cambridge: Harvard University Press; London: Heinemann, 1959) pp. 181–299, 15 vols, 1927–69.

Plutarch, "On Moral Virtue," *Plutarch's Moralia*, vol. 6, trans. W. C. Hembold (The Loeb Classical Library, Cambridge: Harvard University Press; London: Heinemann, 1939) pp. 19–87, 15 vols, 1927–69.

Proctor, Robert E., "The *Studia Humanitatis*: Contemporary Scholarship and Renaissance Ideals," *Renaissance Quarterly*, 43 (1990): 813–18.

Proser, Matthew, *The Heroic Image in Five Shakespearean Tragedies* (Princeton: Princeton University Press, 1965).

Puttenham, George, *The Arte of English Poesie* (1906) (Kent, OH: Kent State University Press, 1970).

Pyszczynski, Tom and Greenberg, Jeff, "Toward an Integration of Cognitive and Motivational Perspectives on Social Inference: A Biased Hypothesis-Testing Model," *Advances in Experimental Social Psychology*, 20 (1987): 297–340.

Quattrone, George A. and Tversky, Adam, "Causal versus Diagnostic Contingencies: On Self-Deception and on the Voter's Illusion," *Journal of Personality and Social Psychology*, 46 (1984): 237–48.

Quint, David, Introduction, *Literary Theory/Renaissance Texts*, ed. Patricia Parker and David Quint (Baltimore: Johns Hopkins University Press, 1986) pp. 1–19.

Quintilian, *Institutio Oratoria*, trans. H. E. Butler, 4 vols (The Loeb Classical Library, Cambridge: Harvard University Press; London: Heinemann, 1921–22).

Rabey, David Ian, "Play, Satire, Self-Definition, and Individuation in *Hamlet*," *Hamlet Studies*, 5 (1983): 6–26.

Rabkin, Norman, *Shakespeare and the Common Understanding* (New York: Free; London: Collier, 1967).

Rabkin, Norman, *Shakespeare and the Problem of Meaning* (Chicago: University of Chicago Press, 1981).

Rachlin, Howard, "Teleological Behaviorism," *American Psychologist*, 47 (1992): 1371–82.

Rackin, Phyllis, "Androgyny, Mimesis, and the Marriage of the Boy Heroine on the English Renaissance Stage," *PMLA*, 102 (1987): 29–41.

Rackin, Phyllis, "Shakespeare's Boy Cleopatra, the Decorum of Nature, and the Golden World of Poetry," *PMLA*, 87 (1972): 201–12.

Rackin, Phyllis, *Stages of History: Shakespeare's English Chronicles* (Ithaca: Cornell University Press, 1990).

Rainolds, John, *Th'overthrow of Stage Playes* (London, 1599).

Raleigh, Sir Walter, *The History of the World*, ed. C. A. Patrides (Philadelphia: Temple University Press, 1971).

Reed, Robert Rentoul, Jr, *Bedlam on the Jacobean Stage* (Cambridge: Harvard University Press, 1952).

Rhodewalt, Frederick and Comer, Ronald, "Induced-Compliance Attitude Change: Once More with Feeling," *Journal of Experimental Social Psychology*, 15 (1979): 35–47.

Richmond, Hugh M., *Shakespeare's Political Plays* (New York: Random, 1967).

Righter, Anne, *Shakespeare and the Idea of the Play* (1962) (Harmondsworth: Penguin, 1967).

Roach, Joseph R., *The Player's Passion: Studies in the Science of Acting* (Newark: University of Delaware Press; London: Associated University Presses, 1985).

Robinson, Daniel N., *An Intellectual History of Psychology* (New York: Macmillan, 1981).

Roche, Suzanne M. and McConkey, Kevin M., "Absorption: Nature, Assessment, and Correlates," *Journal of Personality and Social Psychology*, 59 (1990): 91–101.

Rogers, Carl R., *On Becoming a Person: A Therapist's View of Psychotherapy* (Boston: Houghton, 1961).

Romei, Annibale, *The Courtiers Academie*, trans. I. K. (London, 1598) (The English Experience 129, New York: Da Capo; Amsterdam: Theatrum, 1969).

Rorty, Amélie Oksenberg, "Self-Deception, Akrasia, and Irrationality," *Social Science Information*, 19 (1980): 905–22.

Rosenberg, Harold, *Act and the Actor: Making the Self* (New York: NAL and World, 1970).

Rosenberg, Marvin, "Elizabethan Actors: Men or Marionettes?," *The Seventeenth-Century Stage: A Collection of Critical Essays*, ed. Gerald Eades Bentley (Chicago: University of Chicago Press, 1968) pp. 94–109.

Rosenberg, Marvin, *The Masks of Hamlet* (Newark: University of Delaware Press; London: Associated University Presses, 1992).

Ross, Alan O., *The Sense of Self: Research and Theory* (New York: Springer, 1992).

Ross, Lee D. and Nisbett, Richard E., *The Person and the Situation: Perspectives of Social Psychology* (New York: McGraw, 1991).

Ross, Michael and Fletcher, Garth J. O., "Attribution and Social Perception," *The Handbook of Social Psychology*, ed. G. Lindzey and E. Aronson, 3rd ed., vol. 2 (New York: Random, 1985) pp. 73–122, 2 vols.

Ross, W. D., *Aristotle*, 5th ed. (London: Methuen, 1949).

Rothwell, Kenneth S., "Hamlet's 'Glass of Fashion': Power, Self, and the Reformation," *Technologies of the Self: A Seminar with Michel Foucault*, ed. Luther H. Martin (Amherst: University of Massachusetts Press, 1988) pp. 80–98.

Santayana, George, *Soliloquys in England and Later Soliloquys* (1922) (Ann Arbor: Ann Arbor Paperbacks–University of Michigan Press, 1967).

Sarbin, Theodore R. and Allen, Vernon L., "Role Enactment, Audience Feedback, and Attitude Change," *The Reinforcement of Social Behavior*, ed. Elliott McGinnies and C. B. Ferster (Boston: Houghton, 1971) pp. 395–400.

Sarbin, Theodore R. and Allen, Vernon L., "Role-Theory," *The Handbook of Social Psychology*, ed. Gardner Lindzey and Elliot Aronson, 2nd ed., vol. 1 (Reading, MA: Addison, 1968) pp. 488–567, 5 vols, 1968–9.

Sartre, Jean-Paul, *Being and Nothingness: A Phenomenological Essay on Ontology*, trans. Hazel E. Barnes (New York: Washington Square, 1966).

Sartre, Jean-Paul, *Sartre on Theater*, trans. Frank Jellinek, comp. Michel Contat and Michel Rybalka (New York: Pantheon, 1976).

Schachter, Stanley and Singer, Jerome E., "Cognitive, Social, and Physiological Determinants of Emotional State," *Psychological Review*, 69 (1962): 379–99.

Schechner, Richard, *Essays on Performance Theory 1970–1976* (New York: Drama Books Specialists, 1977).

Schlenker, Barry R., "Translating Actions into Attitudes: An Identity–Analytic Approach to the Explanation of Social Conduct," *Advances in Experimental Social Psychology*, 15 (1982): 193–247.

Schlenker, Barry R. and Trudeau, James V., "Impact of Self-Presentations on Private Self-Beliefs: Effects of Prior Self-Beliefs and Misattribution," *Journal of Personality and Social Psychology*, 58 (1990): 22–32.

Schlenker, Barry R. and Weigold, Michael F., "Self-Consciousness and Self-Presentation: Being Autonomous Versus Appearing Autonomous," *Journal of Personality and Social Psychology*, 59 (1990): 820–8.

Schulman, Michael, "Backstage Behaviorism," *Psychology Today* (June 1973): 51–4, 88.

Schumaker, John F., ed., *Human Suggestibility: Advances in Theory, Research, and Application* (New York: Routledge, 1991).

Schwitzgebel, Ralph K. and Kolb, David A., *Changing Human Behavior: Principles of Planned Intervention* (McGraw-Hill Series in Psychology, New York: McGraw, 1974).

Scott, Michael, *John Marston's Plays: Theme, Structure, and Performance* (New York: Barnes, 1978).

Scott, William O., "The Liar Paradox as Self-Mockery: Hamlet's Postmodern Cogito," *Mosaic*, 24 (1991): 13–30.

Searle, John R., "The Intentionality of Intention and Action," *Cognitive Science*, 4 (1980): 47–70.

Seltzer, Daniel, "Prince Hal and Tragic Style," *Shakespeare Survey*, 30 (1977): 13–27.

Seneca, [Lucius Annaeus], *Ad Lucilium Epistulae Morales*, trans. Richard M. Gummere, 3 vols (The Loeb Classical Library, Cambridge: Harvard University Press; London: Heinemann, 1917–25).

Seneca, [Lucius Annaeus], *Moral Essays*, trans. John W. Basore, 3 vols (The Loeb Classical Library, Cambridge: Harvard University Press; London: Heinemann, 1928–35).

Seneca, [Lucius Annaeus], "More About Virtue," *Ad Lucilium*, 3: 381–95.

Seneca, [Lucius Annaeus], "On Anger," *Moral Essays*, 1: 107–355.

Seneca, [Lucius Annaeus], "On the Diseases of the Soul," *Ad Lucilium*, 2: 137–47.

Seneca, [Lucius Annaeus], "On the Natural Fear of Death," *Ad Lucilium* 2: 241–59.

Seneca, [Lucius Annaeus], "On Our Blindness and Its Cure," *Ad Lucilium*, 1: 331–5.

Seneca, [Lucius Annaeus], "On the Part Played by Philosophy in the Progress of Man," *Ad Lucilium*, 2: 395–431.

Seneca, [Lucius Annaeus], "On Reforming Hardened Sinners," *Ad Lucilium*, 3: 281–3.

Seneca, [Lucius Annaeus], "On Tranquility of Mind," *Moral Essays*, 2: 203–85.

Seneca, [Lucius Annaeus], "On the Value of Advice," *Ad Lucilium*, 3: 11–59.

Seneca, [Lucius Annaeus], "To Marcia on Consolation," *Moral Essays*, 2: 3–97.

Shakespeare, William, *As You Like It*, ed. Agnes Latham (London: Methuen, 1975).

Shakespeare, William, *Coriolanus*, ed. Philip Brockbank (London: Methuen, 1976).

Shakespeare, William, *The First Part of King Henry IV*, ed. A. R. Humphreys (1960) (London: Methuen; Cambridge: Harvard University Press, 1961).

Shakespeare, William, *Hamlet*, ed. Harold Jenkins (London: Methuen, 1982).

Shakespeare, William, *King Henry V*, ed. J. H. Walter (London: Methuen; Cambridge: Harvard University Press, 1954).

Shakespeare, William, *King Lear*, ed. Kenneth Muir (1952) (Cambridge: Harvard University Press, 1959).

Shakespeare, William, *King Richard II*, ed. Peter Ure (Cambridge: Harvard University Press, 1956).

Shakespeare, William, *King Richard III*, ed. Anthony Hammond (London: Methuen, 1981).

Shakespeare, William, *Much Ado About Nothing*, ed. A. R. Humphreys (London: Methuen, 1981).

Shakespeare, William, *The Second Part of King Henry IV*, ed. A. R. Humphreys (London: Methuen; Cambridge: Harvard University Press, 1966).

Shakespeare, William, *The Second Part of King Henry VI*, ed. Andrew S. Cairncross (1962) (London: Methuen, 1969).

Shakespeare, William, *Troilus and Cressida*, ed. Kenneth Palmer (London: Methuen, 1982).

Shakespeare, William, *Twelfth Night*, ed. J. M. Lothian and T. W. Craik (London: Methuen, 1975).

Shakespeare, William, *The Winter's Tale*, ed. J. H. P. Pafford (1963) (London: Methuen, 1966).

Shames, Victor A. and Bowers, Patricia G., "Hypnosis and Creativity," *Contemporary Hypnosis Research*, ed. Erika Fromm and Michael R. Nash (New York: Guilford, 1992) pp. 334–63.

Shaw, Fiona and Stevenson, Juliet, "Celia and Rosalind in *As You Like It*," *Players of Shakespeare 2: Further Essays in Shakespearean Performance by Players with the Royal Shakespeare Company*, ed. Russell Jackson and Robert Smallwood (Cambridge: Cambridge University Press, 1988) pp. 55–71.

Shean, Glenn, "Hypnotic Process and PS/P: Similarities and Differences," *Moving Psychotherapy: Theory and Application of Pesso System/Psychomotor Therapy*, ed. Albert Pesso and John Crandell (n.p.: Brookline, 1991) pp. 159–65.

Shenk, Robert, *The Sinner's Progress: A Study of Madness in English Renaissance Drama* (Salzburg Studies in English Literature. Elizabethan and Renaissance Studies 74, Salzburg: Institut für Englische Sprache und Literatur, Universitat Salzburg, 1978).

Shor, Ronald E., "A Phenomenological Method for the Measurement of Variables Important to an Understanding of the Nature of Hypnosis," *Hypnosis: Developments in Research and New Perspectives*, ed. Erika Fromm and Ronald E. Shor, 2nd ed. (New York: Aldine, 1979) pp. 105–35.

Shuger, Debora Kuller, *Habits of Thought in the Renaissance: Religion, Politics, and the Dominant Culture* (Berkeley: University of California Press, 1990).

Shupe, Donald R., "The Wooing of Lady Anne: A Psychological Inquiry," *Shakespeare Quarterly*, 29 (1978): 28–36.

Shute, Clarence, *The Psychology of Aristotle: An Analysis of the Living Being* (1941) (New York: Russell, 1964).

Sidney, Sir Philip, *The Countesse of Pembrokes Arcadia* (Cambridge: Cambridge University Press, 1912); vol. 1 of *The Complete Works of Sir Philip Sidney*, ed. Albert Feuillerat, 4 vols, 1912–26.

Sidney, Sir Philip, *Sir Philip Sidney's Defense of Poesy*, ed. Lewis Soens (Regents Critics Series, Lincoln: University of Nebraska Press, 1970).

Siemon, James Edward, "Disguise in Marston and Shakespeare," *Huntington Library Quarterly*, 38 (1975): 105–23.

Simonov, P. V., "The Grammar of Dramatic Art," *Stanislavski Today: Commentaries on K. S. Stanislavski*, comp., ed., and trans. Sonia Moore (New York: American Center for Stanislavski Theatre Art, 1973) pp. 34–43.

Simonov, P. V., *Science of Human Higher Nervous Activity and Artistic Creation* (Moscow: Nauka, 1985).

Singer, Dorothy G. and Singer, Jerome L., *The House of Make-Believe: Children's Play and the Developing Imagination* (Cambridge: Harvard University Press, 1990).

Skinner, B. F., *About Behaviorism* (New York: Knopf, 1974).

Skinner, B. F., *Beyond Freedom and Dignity* (New York: Knopf, 1971).

Skinner, B. F., *Contingencies of Reinforcement: A Theoretical Analysis* (The Century Psychology Series, New York: Appleton, 1969).

Skinner, B. F., "Creating the Creative Artist," *Cumulative Record: A Selection of Papers*, 3rd ed. (The Century Psychology Series, New York: Appleton, 1972) pp. 333–44.

Skinner, B. F., "Humanism and Behaviorism," *Reflections on Behaviorism and Society* (Englewood Cliffs, NJ: Prentice, 1978) pp. 48–55.

Skinner, B. F., "The Originating Self," *Personality and Psychopathology*, ed. William M. Grove and Dante Cicchetti (Minneapolis: University of Minnesota Press, 1991) pp. 3–9; vol. 2 of *Thinking Clearly About Psychology*, 2 vols.

Skinner, B. F., *Science and Human Behavior* (New York: Free; London: Collier-Macmillan, 1953).

Skinner, B. F., "Selection by Consequences," *Science*, 213 (1981): 501–4.

Skinner, B. F., *Verbal Behavior* (The Century Psychology Series, Englewood Cliffs, NJ: Prentice, 1957).

Skulsky, Harold, *Spirits Finely Touched: The Testing of Value and Integrity in Four Shakespearean Plays* (Athens: University of Georgia Press, 1976).

Skura, Meredith Anne, *Shakespeare the Actor and the Purposes of Playing* (Chicago: University of Chicago Press, 1993).

Smith, Bruce R., *Homosexual Desire in Shakespeare's England: A Cultural Poetics* (Chicago: University of Chicago Press, 1991).

Snyder, Mark, *Public Appearances/Private Realities: The Psychology of Self-Monitoring* (San Francisco: Freeman, 1987).

Snyder, Mark, "Self-Monitoring Processes," *Advances in Social Psychology*, 12 (1979): 85–128.

Snyder, Mark, "When Believing Means Doing: Creating Links between Attitudes and Behavior," *Consistency in Social Behavior: The Ontario Symposium* 2, ed. Mark P. Zanna, E. Tory Higgins, and C. Peter Herman (Hillsdale, NJ: Erlbaum, 1982) pp. 105–30.

Snyder, Mark and Ickes, William, "Personality and Social Behavior," *The Handbook of Social Psychology*, ed. G. Lindzey and E. Aronson, 3rd ed., vol. 2 (New York: Random, 1985) pp. 883–947, 2 vols.

Soellner, Rolf, *Shakespeare's Patterns of Self-Knowledge* (Columbus: Ohio State University Press, 1972).

Soens, Lewis, Introduction, *Sir Philip Sidney's Defense of Poesy*, ed. L. Soens (Regents Critics Series, Lincoln: University of Nebraska Press, 1970) pp. ix–xliii.

Soule, Lesley Anne, "Subverting Rosalind: Cocky Ros in the Forest of Arden," *New Theatre Quarterly*, 7 (1991), 126–36.

Spanos, Nicholas P., Arango, Manuel and deGroot, Hans P., "Context as a Moderator in Relationships Between Attribute Variables and Hypnotizability," *Personality and Social Psychology Bulletin*, 19 (1993): 71–7.

Spanos, Nicholas P. and Coe, William C., "A Social–Psychological Approach to Hypnosis," *Contemporary Hypnosis Research*, ed. Erika Fromm and Michael R. Nash (New York: Guilford, 1992) pp. 102–30.

Stanislavski, Constantin, *An Actor Prepares*, trans. Elizabeth Reynolds Hapgood (New York: Theatre Arts, 1936).

Stanislavski, Constantin, *Building a Character*, trans. Elizabeth Reynolds Hapgood (New York: Theatre Arts, 1949).

Stanislavski, Constantin, *Creating a Role*, trans. Elizabeth Reynolds Hapgood, ed. Hermine I. Popper (New York: Theatre Arts, 1961).

Stanislavsky, Konstantin, "From *The Actor: Work on Oneself*," trans. Jean Benedetti, Introduction by Sharon Marie Carnicke, *The Drama Review*, 37 (1993): 38–42.

Stanton, Kay, "The Disguises of Shakespeare's *As You Like It*," *Iowa State Journal of Research*, 59 (1985): 295–305.

States, Bert O., "The Actor's Presence: Three Phenomenal Modes," *Theatre Journal*, 35 (1983): 359–75.

States, Bert O., *Hamlet and the Concept of Character* (Baltimore: Johns Hopkins University Press, 1992).

Steele, C. M. and Liu, T. J., "Dissonance Processes as Self-Affirmation," *Journal of Personality and Social Psychology*, 45 (1983): 5–19.

Stern, Robert M. and Lewis, Nancy L., "Ability of Actors to Control Their GSRs and Express Emotions," *Psychophysiology*, 4 (1968): 294–9.

Stires, Lloyd K. and McCombe, Randy P., "The Effects of Changes in Roles on the Attitudes of Role Occupants: A Conceptual Replication," *Contemporary Social Psychology*, 14 (1990): 11–14.

Stirling, Brents, *Unity in Shakespearean Tragedy: The Interplay of Theme and Character* (1956) (New York: Gordian, 1966).

Stoller, Robert, *Splitting: A Case of Female Masculinity* (New York: Quadrangle, 1973).

Stone, Gregory P., "Appearance and the Self: A Slightly Revised Version," *Social Psychology Through Symbolic Interaction*, ed. G. P. Stone and Harvey A. Farberman, 2nd ed. (New York: Wiley, 1981) pp. 187–202.

Strack, Fritz, Martin, Leonard L., and Stepper, Sabine, "Inhibiting and Facilitating Conditions of the Human Smile: A Nonobtrusive Test of the Facial Feedback Hypothesis," *Journal of Personality and Social Psychology*, 54 (1988): 768–77.

Strauss, Anselm L., *Mirrors and Masks: The Search for Identity* (Glencoe, IL: Free, 1959).

Strauss, Gerald, "Capturing Hearts and Minds in the German Reformation," *History Today*, 31 (1981): 21–5.

Strauss, Gerald, *Luther's House of Learning: Indoctrination of the Young in the German Reformation* (Baltimore: Johns Hopkins University Press, 1978).

Strawson, Galen, *Freedom and Belief* (Oxford: Clarendon, 1986).

Stryker, Sheldon and Statham, Anne, "Symbolic Interaction and Role Theory," *The*

Handbook of Social Psychology, ed. G. Lindzey and E. Aronson, 3rd ed., vol. 1 (New York: Random, 1985) pp. 311–78, 2 vols.

Sturm, Israel Eli, "Implications of Role-Playing Methodology for Clinical Procedure," *Behavior Therapy*, 2 (1971): 88–96.

Styan, J. L., *Drama, Stage, and Audience* (Cambridge: Cambridge University Press, 1975).

Styan, J. L., "In Search of the Real Shakespeare; or, Shakespeare's Shows and Shadows," *New Issues in the Reconstruction of Shakespeare's Theatre*, ed. Franklin J. Hildy (Artists and Issues in the Theatre 1, New York: Lang, 1990) pp. 185–205.

Sullivan, Harry Stack, *The Interpersonal Theory of Psychiatry*, ed. Helen Swick Perry and Mary Ladd Gawel (New York: Norton, 1953).

Sullivan, Harry Stack, "Self as Concept and Illusion," *Social Psychology Through Symbolic Interaction*, ed. Gregory P. Stone and Harvey A. Farberman, 2nd ed. (New York: Wiley, 1981) pp. 179–85.

Sulzer-Azaroff, Beth and Mayer, G. Roy, ed., *Behavior Analysis for Lasting Change* (Fort Worth: Holt, 1991).

Sutton-Smith, Brian, "Introduction to Play as Performance, Rhetoric, and Metaphor," *Play & Culture*, 2, (1989): 189–92.

Sutton-Smith, Brian, "The Role of Play in Cognitive Development," *Child's Play*, ed. R. E. Herron and B. Sutton-Smith (New York: Wiley, 1971) pp. 252–60.

Taylor, Shelley E. and Brown, Jonathon D., "Illusion and Well-Being: A Social Psychological Perspective on Mental Health," *Psychological Bulletin*, 103 (1988): 193–210.

Tellegen, Auke and Atkinson, Gilbert, "Openness to Absorbing and Self-Altering Experiences ('Absorption'), a Trait Related to Hypnotic Susceptibility," *Journal of Abnormal Psychology*, 83 (1974): 268–77.

Terence, *The Brothers. The Comedies of Terence*, trans. Henry T. Riley (New York, 1896) pp. 200–53.

Tesser, Abraham and Shaffer, David R., "Attitudes and Attitude Change," *Annual Review of Psychology*, 41 (1990): 479–523.

Thibodeau, Ruth and Aronson, Elliot, "Taking a Closer Look: Reasserting the Role of the Self-Concept in Dissonance Theory," *Personality and Social Psychology Bulletin*, 18 (1992): 591–602.

Tice, Dianne M., "Self-Concept Change and Self-Presentation: The Looking-Glass Self is Also a Magnifying Glass," *Journal of Personality and Social Psychology*, 63 (1992): 435–51.

Tillyard, E. M. W., *Shakespeare's History Plays* (1944) (New York: Collier, 1962).

Tower, Roni Beth, "Imagery: Its Role in Development," *Imagery: Current Theory, Research, and Application*, ed. Anees A. Sheikh (New York: Wiley, 1983) pp. 222–51.

Traub, Valerie, *Desire and Anxiety: Circulations of Sexuality in Shakespearean Drama* (Gender, Culture, Difference, London: Routledge, 1992).

Traversi, D[erek] A., *An Approach to Shakespeare*, 3rd ed., vol. 1 (Garden City, NY: Anchor-Doubleday, 1969) 2 vols.

Traversi, D[erek] A., *Shakespeare: From Richard II to Henry V* (Stanford: Stanford University Press, 1957).

Turner, Ralph H., "The Role and the Person," *American Journal of Sociology*, 84 (1978): 1–23.

Turner, Victor, *The Anthropology of Performance* (New York: PAJ, 1986).

Turner, Victor, *From Ritual to Theatre: The Human Seriousness of Play* (Performance Studies Series 1, New York: Performing Arts, 1982).

Tuve, Rosemond, *Elizabethan and Metaphysical Imagery: Renaissance Poetic and Twentieth-Century Critics* (Chicago: University of Chicago Press, 1947).

Ullman, Leonard P. and Krasner, Leonard, *A Psychological Approach to Abnormal Behavior*, 2nd ed. (Englewood Cliffs, NJ: Prentice, 1975).

Ure, Peter, "Character and Role from Richard III to Hamlet," *Hamlet*, ed. John Russell Brown and Bernard Harris (Stratford-upon-Avon Studies 5, London: Arnold, 1963) pp. 9–28.

Ure, Peter, "Shakespeare and the Inward Self of the Tragic Hero," *Elizabethan and Jacobean Drama: Critical Essays by Peter Ure*, ed. J. C. Maxwell (Liverpool English Texts and Studies, Liverpool: Liverpool University Press, 1974) pp. 1–21.

Van Laan, Thomas F., *Role-playing in Shakespeare* (Toronto: University of Toronto Press, 1978).

Vickers, Brian, *Appropriating Shakespeare: Contemporary Critical Quarrels* (New Haven: Yale University Press, 1993).

Vickers, Brian, *In Defence of Rhetoric* (Oxford: Clarendon, 1988).

Vickers, Brian, "Shakespeare's Hypocrites," *Daedalus*, 108 (1979): 45–83.

Vives, Juan Luis, *De Anima et Vita*, excerpt trans. Solomon Diamond, *The Roots of Psychology: A Sourcebook in the History of Ideas*, ed. S. Diamond (New York: Basic, 1974) pp. 303–4.

Vives, Juan Luis, *A Fable About Man*, trans. Nancy Lenkeith, *The Renaissance Philosophy of Man*, ed. Ernst Cassirer, Paul O. Kristeller, and John H. Randall, Jr (Chicago: University of Chicago Press, 1948) pp. 387–93.

Vives, Juan Luis, *On Education: A Translation of the De Trandendis Disciplinis of Juan Luis Vives*, trans. Foster Watson (Cambridge: Cambridge University Press, 1913).

Vives, Juan Luis, *Vives' Introduction to Wisdom: A Renaissance Textbook*, trans. Richard Morison (1540), ed. Marian Leona Tobriner (Classics in Education 35, New York: Teachers College, 1968).

Walcutt, Charles C., "*Hamlet* – The Plot's the Thing," *Michigan Quarterly Review*, 5 (1966): 15–32.

Walley, Harold R., "*The Rape of Lucrece* and Shakespearean Tragedy," *PMLA*, 76 (1961): 480–7.

Ward, David, "The King and *Hamlet*," *Shakespeare Quarterly*, 43 (1992): 280–302.

Ward, John Powell, *As You Like It* (Twayne's New Critical Introductions to Shakespeare, no. 15, New York: Twayne, 1992).

Weigart, Andrew J., "Identity: Its Emergence Within Sociological Psychology," *Symbolic Interaction*, 6 (1983): 183–206.

Weimann, Robert, "Bifold Authority in Shakespeare's Theatre," *Shakespeare Quarterly*, 39 (1988): 401–17.

Weimann, Robert, "Mimesis in *Hamlet*," *Shakespeare and the Question of Theory*, ed. Patricia Parker and Geoffrey Hartman (London: Methuen, 1985) pp. 275–91.

Weimann, Robert, "Representation and Performance: The Uses of Authority in Shakespeare's Theater," *PMLA*, 107 (1992): 497–510.

Weimann, Robert, "Shakespeare (De)Canonized: Conflicting Uses of 'Authority' and 'Representation,'" *New Literary History*, 20 (1988): 65–81.

Weinstein, Donald and Bell, Rudolph M., *Saints and Society: The Two Worlds of Western Christendom, 1000–1700* (Chicago: University of Chicago Press, 1982).

Weissman, Philip, *Creativity in the Theater: A Psychoanalytic Study* (New York: Basic, 1965).

Wells, Anne J., "Variations in Self-Esteem in Daily Life: Methodological and Developmental Issues," *Self-Perspectives Across the Life-Span*, ed. Richard P. Lipka and

Thomas M. Brinthaupt (SUNY Series, Studying the Self, Albany: State University of New York Press, 1992) pp. 151–85.

Wells, Susan, *The Dialectics of Representation* (Baltimore: Johns Hopkins University Press, 1985).

Werstine, Paul, "The Textual Mystery of *Hamlet*," *Shakespeare Quarterly*, 39 (1988): 1–26.

West, Candace and Zimmerman, Don H., "Doing Gender," *Seldom Seen, Rarely Heard: Women's Place in Psychology*, ed. Janis S. Bohan (Psychology, Gender, and Theory, Boulder: Westview, 1992) pp. 379–403.

Whitaker, Virgil K., *Shakespeare's Use of Learning: An Inquiry into the Growth of His Mind and Art* (San Marino, CA: Huntington, 1953).

Wiles, Timothy J., *The Theater Event: Modern Theories of Performance* (Chicago: University of Chicago Press, 1980).

Wilks, John S., *The Idea of Conscience in Renaissance Tragedy* (London: Routledge, 1990).

Williams, Robert H., McCandless, Peter H., Hobb, Dennis A. and Williams, Sharon A., "Changing Attitudes with 'Identification Theory,'" *Simulation and Games*, 17 (1986): 25–43.

Williams, Robert L., Pettibone, Timothy J. and Thomas, Sandra P., "Naturalistic Application of Self-Change Practices," *Journal of Research in Personality*, 25 (1991): 167–76.

Wilshire, Bruce, *Role Playing and Identity: The Limits of Theatre as Metaphor* (Studies in Phenomenology and Existential Philosophy, Bloomington: Indiana University Press, 1982).

Wilson, J. Dover, *The Fortunes of Falstaff* (Cambridge: Cambridge University Press; New York: Macmillan, 1944).

Wilson, Luke, "*Hamlet*, Hales v. Petit, and the Hysteresis of Action," *ELH*, 60 (1993): 17–55.

Wilson, Sheryl C. and Barber, Theodore X., "The Fantasy-Prone Personality: Implications for Understanding Imagery, Hypnosis, and Parapsychological Phenomena," *Imagery: Current Theory, Research, and Application*, ed. Anees A. Sheikh (New York: Wiley, 1983) pp. 340–90.

Wilson, Thomas, *The Arte of Rhetorique* (1553) (Gainesville, FL: Scholars' Facsimiles, 1962).

Winnicott, D. W., *Playing and Reality* (New York: Basic, 1971).

Winny, James, *The Player King: A Theme of Shakespeare's Histories* (London: Chatto, 1968).

Worthen, William B., "Deeper Meanings and Theatrical Technique: The Rhetoric of Performance Criticism," *Shakespeare Quarterly*, 40 (1989): 441–55.

Worthen, William B., *The Idea of the Actor: Drama and the Ethics of Performance* (Princeton: Princeton University Press, 1984).

Wright, George T., *Shakespeare's Metrical Art* (Berkeley: University of California Press, 1988).

Wright, Thomas, *The Passions of the Minde in Generall* (1604) (Urbana: University of Illinois Press, 1971).

Young, David, *The Action to the Word: Structure and Style in Shakespearean Tragedy* (New Haven: Yale University Press, 1990).

Young, T. R., *The Drama of Social Life: Essays in Post-Modern Social Psychology* (New Brunswick, NJ: Transaction Publishers, 1990).

Young-Eisendrath, Polly and Hall, James A., ed., *The Book of the Self: Person, Pretext, and Process* (New York: New York University Press, 1987).

Zelen, Seymour L., "Balance and Reversal of Actor–Observer Perspectives: An

Attributional Model of Pathology," *Journal of Social and Clinical Psychology*, 5 (1987): 435–51.

Zettle, Robert D., "Rule-Governed Behavior: A Radical Behavioral Answer to the Cognitive Challenge," *The Psychological Record*, 40 (1990): 41–9.

Zillman, Dolf, "Transfer of Excitation in Emotional Behavior," *Social Psychophysiology: A Sourcebook*, ed. John T. Cacioppo and Richard E. Petty (New York: Guilford, 1983) pp. 215–40.

Index of Names

Index of Subjects

Cross references to main entries are capitalized, to sub-entries not capitalized.
Cross references within a single main entry are indicated by "above" or "below."

Absorption, *see under* Acting and
role-playing; *see also As You Like It*,
Hamlet, Perdita, Prince Hal–Henry
V, Rosalind
Acting and role-playing, psychology of,
absorption in an activity, in self, or in
a social role, 8–10, 38–44 *passim*,
47, 50–6 *passim*, 207n19–20;
see also As You Like It, Hamlet,
Perdita, Prince Hal–Henry V;
see also assimilation, *below*
acting, modern psychology of, 48–56,
207–9n17–27
assimilation or fusion of actor with
character, 2–4, 8–10, 39, 43,
48–56, 199n7–9, 207n19–20,
208n22–3; *see also* absorption, *above*
"backstage" behavior, 39, 113–14
and behaviorism, 4–5, 42, 51–2, 54,
55, 200n13, 206n10, 208n21,23–4
and behavior modification, 18, 44–5,
187–8
and cognitive dissonance reduction,
counter-attitudinal role-playing,
46–7, 98, 206n15–16
and counter-attitudinal role-playing,
46–7, 206n16
detachment from role or self, 4, 38–42
passim, 45, 47–50 *passim; see also*
Awareness
emotions in, 2–4, 8–11, 19–22, 38–56
passim, 195–8, 199n2–6, 200n7–9,
202n16–17, 203n26–7, 205n4,
206n16, 207n17, 208n21–2,
209n26–7
and gender identity, 40–1, 205n5–7;
see also gender roles *under*
Rosalind
and hypnosis, 50–1, 207n20, 209n27
and play, 41, 205n8
Renaissance (and Ancient), 2–4, 8–10,
19–20, 195–6; *see also* Renaissance
(and Ancient) psychology, *separate
entry*

and Renaissance (and Ancient) theory
of oratory, 2–4, 199n6, 200n7,11
role (social), defined, 38, 205n1
role-playing, and character and
attitude formation and change,
modern psychology of, 38–47,
205–6n1–16; *see also* Behaviorism
role-taking, defined, 39–40
and self, 38–50 *passim*, 52, 55, 208n3;
see also Behaviorism, Subject
and Shakespeare's characters, general,
1–5, 9–10, 40, 199n1,4, 200n7,9,12
B. F. Skinner on, 51–2, 54, 55,
208n21,23–4
and Constantin Stanislavski, 48–50,
52–5, 208–9n22–7
Agency and self-control in behaviorism,
23–7, 29, 32–3, 34, 35–7, 203n2,
204n3,6
As You Like It, 4, 22, 146–72; *see also*
Rosalind
absorbed action in, 146, 153–4
acting and role-playing, psychology
of, 146–9, 152–63 *passim*,
166–9 *passim*, 171–2; *see also*
Rosalind; *see also* Acting and
role-playing
androgyny and Orlando, 172
behaviorist analysis of, 151, 152, 162,
166; *see also* Rosalind; method
for behaviorist analysis, 5, 22,
23–37, 57–9; *see also* Acting and
role-playing
detachment, 153, 154, 163, 166, 167,
171, 172; *see also* Rosalind
"if" and pretense in, 146–8, 166–7,
171–2; *see also* Rosalind
pity vs. envy, 150–2
"role-stealing," 150–2
role-taking, 149–56 *passim; see also*
Rosalind; *see also* 39–40
Attitudes, behavior, and self, 33–7,
38–47 *passim*, 204n2–6, 205n3,
206n9–13

251

Rosalind – *continued*
  behaviorist analysis of, 157, 159, 164,
    165, 168, 170, 171; method for
    behaviorist analysis, 5, 22,
    23–37, 57–9; *see also* Acting and
    role-playing
  boy actor and, 148–9, 157, 172, 213n1,4;
    see also as Ganymede, *below*
  detachment and engagement, 146, 149,
    156, 159, 162, 164–8 *passim*, 170,
    213n1,5–6; *see also* detachment
    under Acting and role-playing
  as Ganymede, 147–9, 157–72, 213n1,4;
    see also boy actor, *above*
  and gender roles, 156–61 *passim*,
    165, 170, 172, 213n1,4; *see also*
    androgyny, *above, and* gender
    identity *under* Acting and
    role-playing
  "if" and pretense, 146–8, 160, 166–7,
    168, 171, 172, 213n1–3
  and Renaissance (and Ancient)
    psychology, 160
  role-taking, 150, 156, 159, 165, 169–72
    passim, 213n6; *see also* 39–40
  self-awareness, *see* detachment, *above*
  self-realization, 159, 160–1, 162, 165,
    168–9, 170–1, 213n1
  see also As You Like It
Rule-governed behavior, explained, 13,
    26, 38, 40–3 *passim*, 206n10

Self in behaviorism, 33–5, 204n3–6
Self-absorption, *see* absorption *under*
  Acting and role-playing
Self-control, *see* Agency
Subject, the person as,
  in behaviorism, 4–6, 23–37,
    203–4n2–6
  in modern psychology of acting,
    character and attitude
    formation and change, and
    role-playing, 38–56,
    205–9n1–27
  in Renaissance (and Ancient)
    psychology, 5–22, 179–98, 200n6,
    201–3n14–27, 214n1–7 for
    Appendix

Troilus and Cressida, 212n12
Twelfth Night, 7, 213n3

Will, choice, 9–13, 15–18 *passim*,
    179–84, 188–92, 193, 194,
    196–8
The Winter's Tale, 22, 173–8, 214 notes
  for Ch. 7
  absorbed action in, 173–8, 214n1 for
    Ch. 7; *see also* absoption *under*
    Acting and role-playing
  boy actor, 177–8, 214n1 for Ch. 7
  see also Acting and role-playing
  see also Perdita